中国履行《禁止化学武器公约》报告（2023）

国家履行《禁止化学武器公约》工作办公室/编

人民邮电出版社
北京

《中国履行〈禁止化学武器公约〉报告（2023）》
编委会

编辑撰稿（按姓氏笔画排序）

丁天佐	丁莹莹	马力利	马勇良	王　飞	王　旭
王　冰	王　钰	王　雅	王收强	王思官	王晓玥
王海军	王聪敏	尤澈冰	方　波	尹　玲	邓　雪
卢锦容	田　娟	田晓慧	白　娜	白布刚	成贞辉
朱小庆	刘　龙	刘　伟	刘　伯	刘　昭	刘元东
刘代联	刘宇轩	刘红宁	刘竞争	刘基伟	汤　旺
汤文侃	汤铭留	许永西	许永利	孙文杰	孙秀敏
苏　凯	苏健梅	李　飞	李　茜	李　峰	李　爽
李　强	李　鹏	李　蕾	李　鑫	李龙飞	李亚娇
李迎春	李海峰	李雪玲	李维强	李超伟	杨开伦
杨浩祥	励　斌	时　钟	吴　凡	吴东文	邱模松
何力行	何国强	余陈荣	邹钟嘉	沈忠平	宋召勤
宋晓明	张　莉	张　倩	张　雪	张　颖	张　翠
张芬林	张英伟	张建伟	陆　寅	陈万明	陈忠明
陈显光	陈俊妃	陈道勇	武俊凤	林　清	罗　明
罗天进	岳双艳	金　康	周　珊	周昌平	郑　杰
郑　威	郑　婕	郑丽琼	郑晚亮	单学店	赵　帅
赵亚茹	赵建华	钟志军	侯胜明	姜　丽	姚念深
班　慧	袁波明	殷立科	高志雷	郭生俊	郭逸纯
唐　旭	陶宏伟	黄明辉	常永武	寇世平	彭　忠
葛振平	董　猛	韩　星	韩中星	韩浩维	覃玉红
童晓炜	曾　涛	曾向军	游建荣	谢建波	谢秋云
樊小娟	樊东方	颜志伟	戴兰林		

目录

特稿

综合篇

地方篇

企业篇

支撑篇

附　录

Contents

Special Reports

General Reports

Local Efforts

Enterprise Efforts

Support Efforts

Appendixes

China 特稿

中国履行《禁止化学武器公约》报告（2023）

工业和信息化部部长主持召开《禁止化学武器公约》履约工作部际联席会议[①]

2023年4月4日，《禁止化学武器公约》（以下简称“《公约》”）履约工作部际联席会议（以下简称“履约工作部际联席会议”）第五次全体会议在北京召开。总召集人、工业和信息化部部长主持会议并讲话。副总召集人、工业和信息化部副部长徐晓兰，副总召集人、中央军委国际军事合作办公室副主任宋延超，联席会议成员国家移民管理局副局长刘海涛、中国国家铁路集团有限公司副总经理李文新等出席会议。

会议指出，在以习近平同志为核心的党中央坚强领导下，履约工作部际联席会议各成员单位密切配合，扎实履行国家宣布、接受国际视察、出口防扩散等《公约》义务，大力推动日本遗弃在华化学武器（以下简称“日遗化武”）销毁，积极参与国际履约事务，全面完成履约各项任务，有力维护国家安全发展利益和负责任大国形象。各级政府及相关部门切实履职，统筹做好禁化武履约监管和服务企业工作，加强履约普法宣传，推动企业不断增强依法经营、依法履约意识。

会议强调，要深入学习贯彻习近平新时代中国特色社会主义思想，全面落实党的二十大精神，牢固树立总体国家安全观，统筹国内国际两个大局，统筹发展和安全，全面做好履约各项工作，为维护世界和平和国家安全发展作出更大贡献。要提高政治站位，高质量做好国家宣布和接受国际视察准备工作，严格实施监控化学品行政许可，切实加强审批事项事中事后监管，敦促日方加快日遗化武销毁处置。要坚持系统观念，加强对国际禁化武领域重大问题前瞻性研究，提出更多中国倡议和中国方案。要加强

---

① 本文来源于工业和信息化部网站，现有文字调整。

队伍建设，重视国际型人才发掘培养，更好地发挥联席会议制度作用，强化部省联动机制，优化提升履约工作体系和效能，集智聚力服务履约事业。

履约工作部际联席会议联络员、工业和信息化部有关司局负责同志列席会议。

Minister of Industry and Information Technology Presided over the Inter-ministerial Joint Meeting on the Implementation of the *Chemical Weapons Convention*[①]

On April 4th, 2023, the Fifth Plenary Session of the Inter-ministerial Joint Meeting on the Implementation of the *Chemical Weapons Convention* (hereinafter referred to as "the *Convention*" and "inter-ministerial joint meeting") was held in Beijing. The General Convener and Minister of Industry and Information Technology presided over the meeting and delivered a speech. Xu Xiaolan, the Deputy General Convener and Vice Minister of Industry and Information Technology, Song Yanchao, the Deputy General Convener and Deputy Director of the Office for International Military Cooperation of the Central Military Commission, as well as other members of the joint meeting, including Liu Haitao, Deputy Commissioner of the National Immigration Administration, and Li Wenxin, Vice General Manager of the China State Railway Group Co. Ltd., attended the meeting.

The meeting pointed out that under the strong leadership of the Communist Party of China (hereinafter referred to as "CPC") Central Committee with Xi Jinping at its core, the member units of the inter-ministerial joint meeting closely collaborated to fulfill obligations under the *Convention*, including submission of national declarations, acceptance of international inspections, and export non-proliferation, push forward the destruction process of chemical weapons

① Source: Ministry of Industry and Information Technology website, with slight modifications.

abandoned by Japan in China (hereinafter referred to as "Japanese ACWs"), actively participate in international affairs, and fully complete various tasks related to the *Convention* implementation, thereby effectively safeguarding the national security and development interests and maintaining the image of a major responsible country. Local governments at all levels and relevant departments effectively performed their duties, coordinated the supervision of and the service for enterprises, strengthened the publicity of the implementation of the *Convention*, and promoted enterprises to continuously enhance the awareness of operating in accordance with the *Convention* and domestic law.

The meeting emphasized the importance of thoroughly studying and implementing Xi Jinping Thought on Socialism with Chinese Characteristics for a New Era, fully realizing the guiding principles of the 20th National Congress of the CPC, firmly upholding the holistic approach to national security, giving full consideration to both domestic and international imperatives, ensuring both development and security, comprehensively implementing the *Convention*, and making greater contributions to maintaining world peace and national security and development. We should enhance political stance, ensure high-quality of national declarations and preparation for acceptance of international inspections, strictly implement administrative licensing for controlled chemicals, effectively strengthen supervision during and after granting the licenses, and urge Japan to accelerate the destruction of Japanese ACWs. We should adhere to a systemic perspective, strengthen forward-looking research on internationally significant issues regarding the *Convention* implementation, and contribute more China' s solutions and wisdom. It is necessary to strengthen team building, attach importance to the discovery and cultivation of international talents, better utilize the joint meeting system, strengthen the interactive mechanism between ministries and provinces, optimize the *Convention* implementation working system and improve its efficiency, and gather wisdom and efforts to support the *Convention* implementation.

Liaison officers of the inter-ministerial joint meeting and officials from relevant departments and bureaus of the Ministry of Industry and Information Technology attended the meeting.

外交部副部长孙卫东考察调研哈尔巴岭 敦促日方全面加快日遗化武处理进程[①]

2023 年 10 月 13 日，外交部副部长孙卫东赴吉林省延边朝鲜族自治州敦化市考察调研哈尔巴岭日遗化武处理作业现场。

哈尔巴岭是国内已发现的最大日遗化武埋藏点。孙卫东详细了解了日遗化武挖掘回收、鉴别包装、运输看管、销毁处理等作业流程，检查安全管理工作，并慰问中方现场作业人员，听取日方团队介绍作业情况。

外交部副部长孙卫东（右二）会见日方作业团队

在会见日方作业团队负责人时，孙卫东严肃指出，日遗化武是日本军国主义在侵华战争期间犯下的严重罪行之一。中国政府坚持人民至上、生命至上，强烈要求日方切实履约尽责，全方位加大投入，全链条加快工作，

① 本文来源于外交部网站，现有文字调整。

在确保人员和环境安全的前提下，早日彻底清除日遗化武毒害，还中国人民一片净土。日方表示高度重视中方关切，将按照日中双方商定的计划，安全、高效开展作业，全力尽早完成哈尔巴岭日遗化武销毁工作。

Vice Foreign Minister Sun Weidong Inspected Haerbaling and Urged Japan to Accelerate the Process of Disposing Chemical Weapons Abandoned by Japan in China in an All–round Way①

On October 13th, 2023, Vice Foreign Minister Sun Weidong went to Dunhua City, Yanbian Korean Autonomous Prefecture, Jilin Province, to inspect the site of disposing Japanese ACWs in Haerbaling.

Haerbaling is the largest identified burial site of Japanese ACWs in China. Sun Weidong learned in detail the disposal process such as excavation and recovery, identification and package, transportation and custody, and destruction of Japanese ACWs, inspected safety management, visited China's personnel for on-site disposal, and got briefed by Japan's team on the situation of disposal.

Vice Foreign Minister Sun Weidong (second from the right) met with the Japanese disposal team

① Source: Ministry of Foreign Affairs website, with slight modifications.

When meeting with the responsible person of Japan's disposal team, Sun Weidong solemnly pointed out that Japanese ACWs are one of the severe crimes committed by Japan's militarists during the war of aggression against China. The Chinese government adheres to putting people and their lives front and center, and strongly asks Japan to earnestly shoulder the responsibility and carry out the duty, increase the input across the board, accelerate the work throughout the whole chain, and eliminate the poisonous harm of Japanese ACWs in a complete and thorough manner at an early date on the premise of ensuring personnel's safety and environmental security, so as to return to the Chinese people a clean land. The Japanese side expressed that it takes China's concerns seriously, and it will follow the plan agreed by Japan and China, carry out the disposal in a safe and efficient manner, and make an all-out effort to destroy Japanese ACWs in Haerbaling.

China 综合篇

中国履行《禁止化学武器公约》报告（2023）

一、政府对履约工作的组织领导

中国政府一贯支持《公约》的目标和宗旨，高度重视禁化武履约工作，建立了完备的履约法律法规体系和多层次的履约工作机制，在工业和信息化部设立国家履约主管机构国家履行《禁止化学武器公约》工作办公室（以下简称“国家禁化武办”），在各省（自治区、直辖市）政府设立省级履约主管机构，分级负责组织协调全国和辖区的履约工作。国务院批准建立了以工业和信息化部为总召集人单位，外交部、中央军委国际军事合作办公室为副总召集人单位，公安部等 14 个相关部门为成员单位的履约工作部际联席会议制度，部署协调解决履约重大事项。各部门、单位及各级履约主管部门坚持以习近平新时代中国特色社会主义思想为指导，深入贯彻落实总体国家安全观，严格履行《公约》规定的各项义务。

2023 年，相关领导高度重视履约工作，认真听取履约工作汇报，参加履约相关活动，给予工作指导，协调解决问题。工业和信息化部党组将禁化武履约工作列入重要议事日程，部党组书记、部长亲自主持党组会议，指导国家禁化武办做好履约工作，并以总召集人身份主持召开履约工作部际联席会议第五次全体会议，对各级履约主管部门全面完成履约各项任务表示充分肯定，对进一步做好禁化武履约工作提出工作要求。外交部副部长孙卫东赴吉林省敦化市哈尔巴岭作业现场考察调研，详细了解日遗化武挖掘回收与销毁作业流程，检查安全管理工作，慰问中方现场作业人员，并敦促日方切实履约尽责，全方位加大投入，早日安全彻底地清除日遗化武毒害。原中央纪委驻工业和信息化部纪检组组长、国家履行《禁止化学武器公约》专家委员会（以下简称“专家委”）高级顾问金书波，工业和信息化部原副部长、十三届全国政协经济委员会副主任、专家委高级顾问刘利华出席国家禁化武办组织的履约调研、国际视察演练、履约人才培养等活动，在提升履约能力、强化依法监管、加强人才队伍建设等方面给予工作指导。

工业和信息化部切实履行主管部门职责，认真做好全国禁化武履约的组织协调工作，将禁化武履约工作纳入部年度重点工作计划，列入重点任务和目标责任制清单。持续完善监控化学品法规体系建设，聚焦反映集中、涉及面广的低浓度三乙醇胺进出口问题，联合商务部、海关总署印发《关于优化低浓度三乙醇胺混合物进出口监管措施的通知》（工信厅联安全函〔2023〕394号），对部分三乙醇胺含量较低的消费类产品免于办理监控化学品进出口审批手续以及两用物项和技术进出口许可，进一步提升监控化学品进出口管理效能，促进低浓度监控化学品贸易便利化。国家禁化武办认真落实各项工作要求，切实做好工业履约及监控化学品管理工作。年初印发《2023年履行〈禁止化学武器公约〉工作要点》（禁化武办发〔2023〕40号），部署全年履约工作，构筑全国履约一盘棋的工作格局。严格履行《公约》义务，全年扎实做好年度宣布、接受国际视察、进出口管制和防扩散相关工作，为国际社会树立履约典范，展现中国负责任大国形象。积极参与履约国际规则制定，向《公约》第五次审议大会（以下简称“五审会”）提交《中华人民共和国关于工业核查问题的立场文件》，成功推动附表2B04视察机制改革中国方案被禁止化学武器组织（以下简称“禁化武组织”）采纳，为减轻全球工业界履约负担作出重要贡献。加强监控化学品监督管理，依法实施监控化学品行政许可，开展监控化学品执法检查，形成常态化监督检查工作机制。加大对省级工业和信息化主管部门的行政执法监督力度，组织监控化学品生产特别许可督查，落实国务院深化“证照分离”改革的有关要求。强化履约激励约束机制，完善年度先进表扬及重点工作通报制度，调动地方工作积极性。强化履约能力建设，组织国际视察演练，举办全国履约综合培训班，加强履约人才队伍建设，指导地方开展履约培训，指导专家委开展地方服务行，有效提升地方履约主管部门履约监管能力，提升监控化学品企业接受国际视察的能力和水平。加大普法宣传力度，组织“4·29 国际禁止化学武器组织日”宣传活动，编撰出版履约年度报告，编印履约工作简报，及时更新履约专栏信息，扩大履约宣传范围，提高履约宣传精准度，营造良好的社会履约氛围。

外交部认真做好履约国际事务及推动日遗化武销毁等工作。积极参与化学领域全球治理，代表中国政府在联合国安全理事会（以下简称“联合国安理会”）、禁化武组织等多边讨论中多次就妥善解决化学武器热点问题、推进日遗化武销毁、维护《公约》权威性和有效性、促进和平利用国际合作等方面阐述中方立场和主张。全力推动日遗化武销毁，与日方、禁化武组织举行日遗化武问题三方磋商，持续敦促日方早日完成日遗化武销毁；向五审会提交中国关于日遗化武的立场文件，牵头举办日遗化武专题展览，持续推动禁化武组织和国际社会加大对日遗化武销毁的关注和监督，为促进尽快彻底销毁日遗化武、促进《公约》全面有效实施作出了重要贡献。

中央军委国际军事合作办公室认真组织军队履约工作，按时提交第一类监控化学品年度宣布及国家防备化学武器方案，以实际行动践行国际履约承诺。与外交部密切配合，认真做好日遗化武作业现场技术监督、应急处置、安全看管等工作，监督协助日方实施日遗化武挖掘回收及销毁作业，全力协助接待禁化武组织对日遗化武设施的现场视察，为早日实现日遗化武全面销毁作出巨大努力。

公安部、财政部、生态环境部、交通运输部、商务部、国家卫生健康委员会、应急管理部、海关总署、国家市场监督管理总局、国家移民管理局、国家铁路局、中国民用航空局、中国国家铁路集团有限公司等履约工作部际联席会议成员单位，地方政府及各级履约主管部门高度重视禁化武履约工作，各司其职，密切配合，通力合作，在接受国际视察、进出口管制及防扩散、监控化学品管理等方面提供了有力支持，为全面做好履约各项工作作出了重要贡献。

二、向禁止化学武器组织提交国家宣布

根据《公约》第六条及有关条款，中国向禁化武组织提交监控化学品国家宣布。截至 2023 年 12 月 31 日，中国累计向禁化武组织提交国家宣布 54 次。2023 年 3 月，提交 2022 年第一类、第二类、第三类和第四类监控化学品过去活动年度宣布①及国家防备化学武器方案；9 月，提交 2024 年第一类、第二类和第三类监控化学品预计活动年度②宣布。2022 年达到宣布阈值的监控化学品工业设施总数为 1450 个，约占全世界总数的 27.2%。其中，第一类监控化学品宣布设施 1 个，第二类监控化学品宣布设施 60 个，第三类监控化学品宣布设施 159 个，第四类监控化学品宣布设施 1230 个。2013—2022 年过去活动年度宣布设施数量按类别分布如图 1 所示。2022 年过去活动年度宣布设施比例按地区分布如图 2 所示。2022 年过去活动年度宣布设施数量按省份分布如图 3 所示。

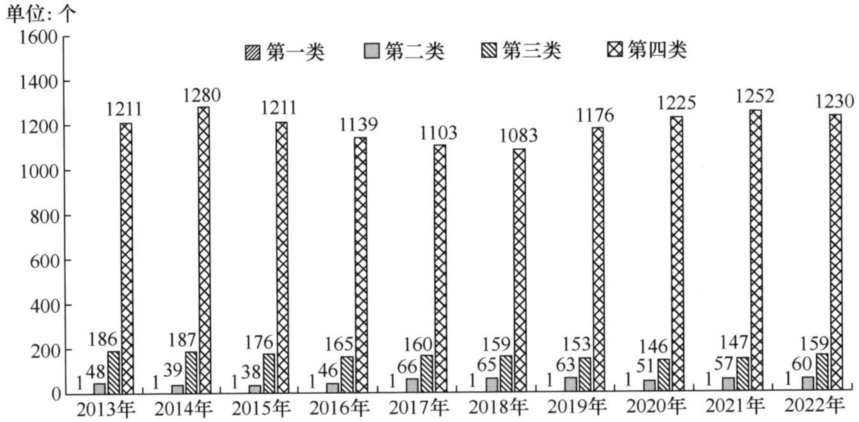

图 1　2013—2022 年过去活动年度宣布设施数量按类别分布

① 过去活动年度宣布的宣布范围为第一类、第二类、第三类和第四类监控化学品设施。
② 预计活动年度宣布的宣布范围为第一类、第二类和第三类监控化学品设施。

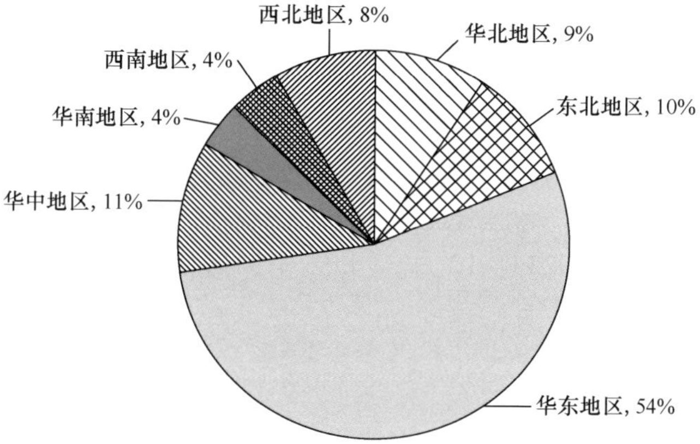

图 2　2022 年过去活动年度宣布设施比例按地区分布

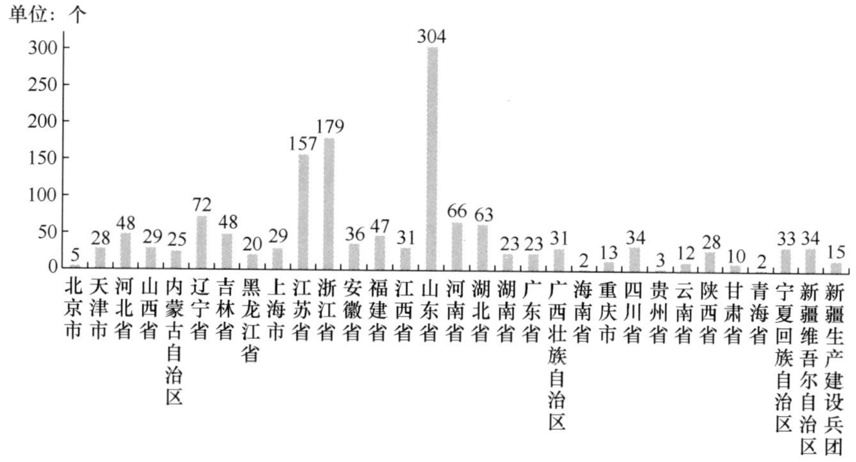

图 3　2022 年过去活动年度宣布设施数量按省份分布

根据《公约》有关遗弃化学武器的规定，中国向禁化武组织提交了日遗化武宣布，主要包括新发现或销毁的日遗化武的分布地点、类型、数量和目前保管状况。2023 年 6 月、9 月、12 月，分别向禁化武组织提交了吉林省珲春市、敦化市哈尔巴岭，黑龙江省哈尔滨市、齐齐哈尔市、伊春市、佳木斯市、宁安市，广东省广州市的日遗化武托管库和天津市蓟州区，山西省太原市、晋城市，内蒙古自治区巴彦淖尔市、黑龙江省鸡西市、江西省九江市、湖北省武汉市的日遗化武临时托管库更新宣布。

三、接受《公约》第六条视察

根据《公约》第六条及有关条款，中国接受禁化武组织现场视察。截至 2023 年 12 月 31 日，中国累计接受《公约》第六条视察 499 次，占全球总数的 11%。其中，累计接受对第一类监控化学品设施视察 24 次，累计接受对第二类、第三类和第四类监控化学品设施视察 475 次。视察结果表明，中国严格履行了《公约》义务。2014—2023 年中国接受《公约》第六条视察数量如图 4 所示。

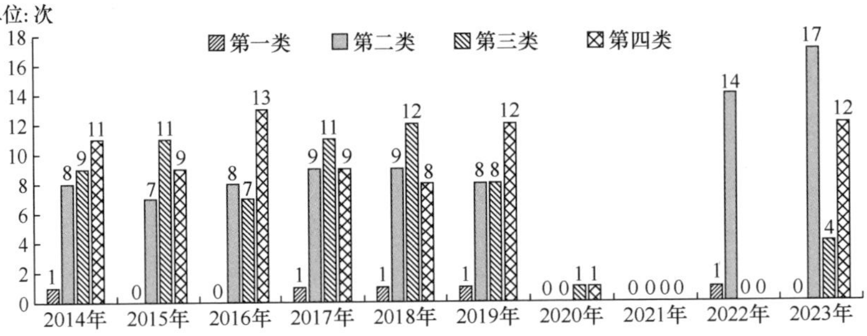

图 4　2014—2023 年中国接受《公约》第六条视察数量

2023 年，中国共接受《公约》第六条视察 33 次。其中，第二类监控化学品生产、加工、消耗设施视察 17 次，第三类监控化学品生产设施 4 次，第四类监控化学品生产设施 12 次。2023 年中国接受《公约》第六条视察分类及数量如图 5 所示。

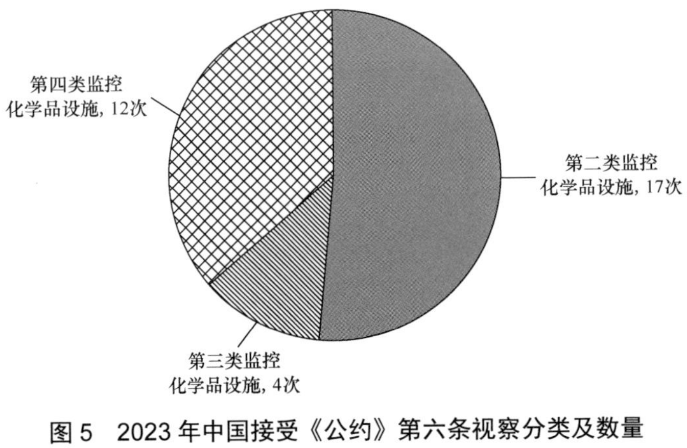

图 5　2023 年中国接受《公约》第六条视察分类及数量

2023 年，中国第二类、第三类、第四类监控化学品被视察设施分布在河北省、内蒙古自治区、辽宁省、上海市、江苏省、浙江省、江西省、山东省、河南省、湖北省、宁夏回族自治区。2023 年中国接受《公约》第六条视察数量按省份分布如图 6 所示。

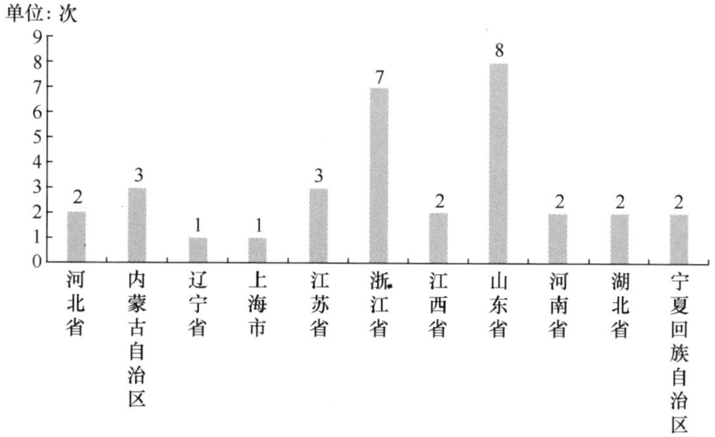

图 6　2023 年中国接受《公约》第六条视察数量按省份分布

四、日本遗弃在华化学武器处理

2023 年 7 月，全球库存化学武器完成销毁。日遗化武已成为实现“无化武世界”最现实的挑战。日遗化武是日本军国主义犯下的严重罪行之一。侵华战争期间，日军在华使用化学武器的地点遍及中国 19 个省（自治区），其中有确切时间、地点和伤亡人数记载的高达 1241 次，共造成 20 多万中国军民伤亡。1945 年战败前夕，侵华日军为掩盖罪行，秘密将大量化学武器就地掩埋或弃于中国江河湖泊之中。日遗化武埋藏数十年，锈蚀严重并出现毒剂泄漏，严重威胁、危害中国人民生命财产安全和当地生态环境安全。据不完全统计，日本投降至今日遗化武已造成中国民众 2000 余人伤亡，并且对土壤、空气和水造成污染，导致有关地区耕地无法使用、居民整体搬迁等问题。

由于日方消极应对，未能履行销毁义务，致使日遗化武销毁计划4次逾期。2023年，中国向五审会递交了《中华人民共和国关于日本遗弃在华化学武器问题的立场文件》，梳理日遗化武销毁法理依据，阐述日遗化武危害严重性和销毁迫切性，敦促日方切实履行政治责任和国际义务，早日安全、干净、彻底销毁日遗化武，呼吁各方保持和加大对日方的监督、核查力度，推动销毁进程取得更大、更快的进展。中国还在五审会会议现场举办日遗化武专题展览，得到禁化武组织总干事、审议大会主席、50余个缔约国常驻代表和官员、禁化武组织技秘处核查司和视察局负责人等100余人关注。此外，中方同日方、禁化武组织技秘处举行日遗化武问题第37轮、第38轮三方磋商，就日遗化武销毁进展、新销毁计划落实、日遗化武现场视察等交换意见，并持续敦促日方全面、完整、准确落实销毁计划。

2023年，中国协助接待禁化武组织对吉林省敦化市哈尔巴岭，山西省太原市，黑龙江省哈尔滨市、佳木斯市、宁安市，江西省九江市，湖北省武汉市7地的日遗化武设施进行12次现场视察，累计协助安排禁化武组织对日遗化武设施和作业视察156次。中方积极为日方作业提供必要的协助和便利，保障处理日遗化武作业需要，监督协助日方实施吉林省敦化市哈尔巴岭和黑龙江省哈尔滨市的日遗化武销毁作业，共销毁日遗化武22261枚（件），销毁量是2022年的3.8倍。监督协助日方开展吉林省珲春市、敦化市哈尔巴岭和黑龙江省佳木斯市、尚志市、牡丹江市、伊春市日遗化武挖掘回收作业，共挖掘回收日遗化武17714枚（件），挖掘回收量是2022年的2.3倍。监督协助日方开展吉林省辽源市详细调查作业，吉林省敦化市、天津市、山西省太原市日遗化武现场调查作业以及黑龙江省哈尔滨市、湖北省武汉市日遗化武鉴别包装作业。

2023年，受日方委托，中方协助进行了黑龙江省鸡西市、佳木斯市、齐齐哈尔市至哈尔滨市，广东省清远市、江西省九江市至湖北省武汉市，内蒙古自治区巴彦淖尔市、山西省晋城市至太原市的5699枚（件）日遗化武运输作业。同时开展了湖北省武汉市销毁设施建设工作。此外，根据各地新发现日遗化武情况，中方在内蒙古自治区巴彦淖尔市，吉林省通化市，湖南省长沙市、衡阳市、岳阳市，云南省大理白族自治州，甘肃省兰州市等地实施了内部调查作业，确认并回收日遗化武10枚（件）。

五、监控化学品进出口管制与防扩散

中国严格执行《公约》有关规定，对监控化学品进出口采用国际通行的许可证管理、清单控制、最终用途证明等制度和标准，实行指定公司经营制度和生产源头管控措施，坚持严格管理，防范扩散风险。

国家禁化武办严格按照《中华人民共和国监控化学品管理条例》（以下简称“《条例》”）和《〈中华人民共和国监控化学品管理条例〉实施细则》（以下简称“《细则》”）规定，开展监控化学品进出口审批工作，2023年共批准进出口申请874项，实现出口防扩散零责任事件。加强与商务部、海关总署等单位联动，强化《监控化学品进出口核准单》与《两用物项和技术进出口许可证》管理衔接，为含低浓度三乙醇胺混合物的进出口提供便利。指导北京市经济和信息化局查处某公司违规出口监控化学品行政处罚案件，有力维护了法律的严肃性。

各级履约主管部门加强源头管控，持续开展对监控化学品生产、经营、使用企业的进出口管制和防扩散教育，引导企业建立自律机制。

六、监控化学品监督管理

为有效防范扩散风险，确保企业履行《公约》义务，中国严格规范监控化学品监督管理，对监控化学品设施建设、生产等活动实行许可制度。

各级履约主管部门坚持依法行政，依据《条例》《细则》等相关法律法规，严格实施监控化学品生产设施建设审批制度。2023年，审查批准建设监控化学品生产设施176项。其中，第二类监控化学品生产设施13项，第三类监控化学品生产设施30项，含磷、硫、氟的第四类监控化学品生产设施133项。

2023年，国家禁化武办严格落实《国务院关于深化“证照分离”改革进一步激发市场主体发展活力的通知》（国发〔2021〕7号）（以下简称“《通知》”）要求，对黑龙江省、福建省、湖北省、广西壮族自治区、四川省、甘肃省实施监控化学品生产特别许可情况进行督查，规范监控化学品行政执法行为。省级履约主管部门依据《通知》，严格执行监控化学品生产特别许可考核标准，全年共颁发监控化学品生产特别许可证147个。

2023年，国家禁化武办根据《国务院办公厅关于推广随机抽查规范事中事后监管的通知》（国办发〔2015〕58号），加强监控化学品事中事后监管，对辽宁省、甘肃省4家企业开展监控化学品执法检查。各地结合本地实际对辖区内企业进行检查，发现问题迅速整改，有效推动企业改进禁化武履约工作。

七、履约宣传

2023年，国家禁化武办继续扩大履约宣传教育，出版发行《中国履行〈禁止化学武器公约〉报告（2019—2021）》，组织编撰《中国履行〈禁止化学武器公约〉报告（2022）》，编印12期《履行〈禁止化学武器公约〉工作简报》，并在工业和信息化部网站禁化武履约工作专栏更新信息，为地方禁化武办、监控化学品企业等搭建交流学习的平台，全面展示国家履约成果和各地履约动态。

以“4·29 国际禁止化学武器组织日”为履约宣传重要节点，国家禁化武办精心组织全国各级履约主管部门、监控化学品企业、行业协会、高校和科研院所，围绕《公约》宗旨目标，以“携手共创一个永无化学武器的世界”和“化学领域成就完全用于造福人类”为主题开展多种形式的履约宣传活动，面向全社会征集第 8 个“国际禁止化学武器组织日”主题宣传海报，组织开展禁化武履约普法知识竞赛，与省级履约主管部门联合制作“地方禁化武履约工作巡礼”在线展览，进一步提高全社会对履约工作的认知度。宣传活动在线参与总人次超过 11 万，其中，参与在线履约普法知识竞赛达 94716 人次，主题海报评选投票达 15813 人次。

全国各级履约主管部门积极响应，充分利用地方报刊、机关电子屏以及门户网站、微信等媒体平台，在监控化学品企业厂区、政府集中办公区等重点区域，通过开辟宣传专栏、发布短视频、悬挂横幅、张贴海报、发放宣传品、播放宣传片以及举办专题研讨会、履约宣传普法主题知识竞赛等形式开展宣传活动，扩大宣传面和影响力。

八、履约培训

2023 年，国家禁化武办继续加强对禁化武履约工作人员的业务培训和岗位培训，在银川市举办全国禁化武履约综合培训班，来自各省、自治区、直辖市及新疆生产建设兵团履约主管部门共 105 人参加培训。本次培训创新思路，依据学员履约工作基础水平设置初训班和复训班，针对性地设计培训课程，内容包括履约基础知识和国内履约法律法规、依法行政、第二类监控化学品监管、人才队伍建设等。培训班学员普遍反映，此次培训内容丰富、模式新颖、实操性强，非常及时、非常“解渴”，达到了预期效果。

天津市、河北省、山西省、内蒙古自治区、辽宁省、吉林省、黑龙江省、上海市、江苏省、浙江省、安徽省、福建省、江西省、山东省、河南省、湖北省、湖南省、广东省、广西壮族自治区、四川省、贵州省、陕西省、宁夏回族自治区及新疆生产建设兵团履约主管部门积极开展本地区履约培训工作，培训内容涉及监控化学品数据宣布、接受国际视察、行政许可、执法检查等履约业务，有效提高了地方履约能力和水平。

九、《公约》在港澳台的适用

中国政府高度重视《公约》在香港特别行政区、澳门特别行政区和台湾地区的适用问题。

中央政府遵循“一国两制”原则和《中华人民共和国香港特别行政区基本法》，在与香港特别行政区政府充分协商后，确定了《公约》在香港特别行政区适用的模式。香港特别行政区于2003年通过《化学武器（公约）条例》，于2004年起开始实施。《化学武器（公约）条例》赋予香港特别行政区海关全面的执法权力，违反《化学武器（公约）条例》规定属于刑事犯罪，最高刑罚为终身监禁。香港特别行政区政府对履约相关化学品实行完备的许可证和呈报制度。香港特别行政区目前没有应向禁化武组织宣布的化学品设施，只有少量涉及监控化学品的进口贸易活动，主要用于本地科研或工业。按《公约》规定，2023年3月，香港特别行政区通过中央政府，向禁化武组织提交了2022年过去活动年度宣布。

中央政府与澳门特别行政区政府已就《公约》在澳门特别行政区的适用问题举行数轮磋商，澳门特别行政区履约立法等筹备工作正在有序进行。

台湾是中国领土不可分割的一部分，必须在一个中国前提下履行《公约》义务。中国政府一直积极、务实地寻求妥善解决《公约》在台湾地区适用问题的途径。

十、深入参与化学领域全球治理

《公约》是全球安全治理体系的重要支柱，对维护国际和平与安全、促进化学科技和平利用发挥重要作用。作为联合国安理会常任理事国、《公约》原始缔约国和第二大会费国，中国政府积极参与联合国为主的多边体系下的防扩散合作，一贯主张全面禁止和彻底销毁包括化学武器在内的所有大规模杀伤性武器，坚决反对化学武器及其技术的扩散。

当今世界变乱交织、动荡不安，国际社会面临前所未有的挑战。习近平主席提出全球安全倡议，倡导坚持共同、综合、合作、可持续的安全观，推动国际社会秉持团结精神和共赢思维，携手完善安全治理、解决安全难题、消弭安全赤字，实现世界持久和平与发展。中国政府将以此为指引，践行真正的多边主义，深入参与《公约》履约和审议进程，坚定维护《公约》的宗旨和目标。

中国一贯坚决反对任何国家、任何组织、任何个人在任何情况下研发或使用化学武器，始终秉持客观公正立场，致力于推动通过政治外交手段解决化武热点问题。中国政府主张《公约》是处理化武热点问题的准绳和依据，按照《公约》规定处理相关问题是唯一正确途径。2023 年 2 月，中国发布《关于政治解决乌克兰危机的中国立场》，明确反对研发、使用生化武器。中国呼吁缔约国总结经验教训坚持对话协商，共同探索化武热点问题解决之道。

十一、国际合作

中国政府高度重视履约国际合作，努力促进《公约》和平利用国际合作与援助的实施，积极参与国际履约重要会议和重要事务，务实推进多双边交流，积极呼应广大发展中国家要求加强《公约》国际合作领域的合理主张，为履行《公约》、维护世界和平发挥了重要作用。

2023年，中国政府组团参加禁化武组织五审会，第28届缔约国大会，第102次、第103次、第104次执理会，第21届亚洲国家履约主管部门会议，第25届国家履约主管部门会议、工业磋商等重要国际会议，在履行《公约》、维护《公约》权威和有效性、日遗化武销毁、民用工业视察等问题上阐明我国立场和主张。中国与巴基斯坦等14国共同向五审会提交《关于在〈禁止化学武器公约〉框架下促进和平利用国际合作的立场文件》，积极倡导化学和平利用，呼吁加强化工领域国际合作，保护广大发展中国家和平利用权利。中国向禁化武组织推荐2家国内企业承担禁化武组织在华化工研修项目，为促进化学化工科学技术发展与和平利用提供交流平台。截至2023年，中国连续4年向禁化武组织输送优秀人才，为国际履约工作提供宝贵人力资源。近年来，中国年均缴纳禁化武组织会费超过1000万欧元，为禁化武组织提供强有力的支持，彰显大国担当。

2023年，中国军事科学院军事医学研究院毒物分析实验室、防化研究院化学分析实验室参加了禁化武组织第8次生物医学样品分析国际联试，防化研究院化学分析实验室参加禁化武组织第54次环境样品分析国际联试，均取得优异成绩。

I. Governmental Organisation and Guidance of *Convention* Implementation Work

The Chinese government has consistently upheld the purposes and objects of the *Convention,* attached great importance to the implementation of the *Convention*, and established a complete legislation and regulation system and a multilevel working mechanism for the implementation affairs. The National Chemical Weapons Convention Implementation Office (hereinafter referred to as the "National CWC Implementation Office") has been established under the Ministry of Industry and Information Technology as the national authority for the *Convention* implementation. All provinces, autonomous regions and municipalities directly under the Central Government have set up provincial competent departments for organising and coordinating the work relating to the *Convention* implementation at provincial level. The State Council has approved the establishment of an inter-ministerial joint meeting system for the *Convention* implementation work, with the Ministry of Industry and Information Technology as the general convener unit, the Ministry of Foreign Affairs and Office for International Military Cooperation of the Central Military Commission as the deputy general convener unit, and the Ministry of Public Security as well as 13 other relevant departments as member units, to arrange and coordinate the work and deal with the affairs about the *Convention* implementation. All departments and competent authorities at all levels adhere to the guidance of Xi Jinping Thought on Socialism with Chinese Characteristics for a New Era, thoroughly implement the holistic approach to national security, and strictly fulfill all the obligations stipulated in the *Convention*.

The relevant leaders attached great importance to the implementation of the *Convention*. In 2023, they carefully listened to reports on the *Convention* implementation work, participated in the relevant activities, gave guidance and approaches to the relevant work. The leading Party members group of the Ministry of Industry and Information Technology has included the implementation of the *Convention* as a significant agenda. The Party Secretary and Minister guided the National CWC Implementation Office in advancing the *Convention* implementation work in the leading Party members group meetings. As the General Convener, he presided over the Fifth Plenary Session of the inter-ministerial joint meeting, fully affirming the comprehensive completion of various tasks of the *Convention* implementation by the competent authorities at all levels and outlining requirements for further improvements in the related work. Vice Foreign Minister Sun Weidong inspected the Haerbaling Japanese ACWs operations site in Dunhua City, Jilin Province, learned in detail the disposal process, including excavation, recovery, and destruction of Japanese ACWs, inspected safety management, visited China's personnel for on-site disposal, and urged Japan to earnestly shoulder the responsibility and carry out the duty, increase the efforts in all aspects, and eliminate the poisonous harm of Japanese ACWs in a complete and thorough manner at an early date. Jin Shubo, former leader of the Discipline Inspection Team of the Central Commission for Discipline Inspection in the Ministry of Industry and Information Technology and senior advisor to the National Committee of Experts on *Chemical Weapons Convention* Implementation (hereinafter referred to as the "Expert Committee"), and Liu Lihua, former Vice Minister of the Ministry of Industry and Information Technology, Deputy Director of the Economic Committee of the 13th National Committee of the Chinese People's Political Consultative Conference, and senior advisor to the Expert Committee, participated in activities organized by the National CWC Implementation Office, including the research on the *Convention* implementation work, inspection exercises, and the training of talents, providing guidance on improving the domestic working capability, strengthening legal regulation, and cultivating an effective talent team for the *Convention* implementation.

The Ministry of Industry and Information Technology effectively fulfilled the responsibilities as the competent authority and earnestly made efforts in organising and coordinating the national implementation of the *Convention*, incorporating the implementation of the *Convention* into annual key work plan along with the list of key tasks and objectives. It continued to refine the regulation system for controlled chemicals. To solve the issue regarding the imports and exports of low-concentration triethanolamine, it issued, in collaboration with the Ministry of Commerce and the General Administration of Customs, the *Notice on Optimizing the Import and Export Supervision Measures for Low-Concentration Triethanolamine Mixtures* to exempt certain consumer products with low concentrations of triethanolamine from import and export approval for controlled chemicals and import and export license for dual-use items and technologies, thereby further improving the efficiency of the management of the import and export of controlled chemicals, and promoting the facilitation of trade in low-concentration controlled chemicals. The National CWC Implementation Office conscientiously implements various work requirements and earnestly makes efforts in the *Convention* implementation in industrial sector and controlled chemicals management. At the beginning of the year, it issued the *Key Points of Work for Implementing the Chemical Weapons Convention in 2023* to arrange the domestic work of the *Convention* implementation throughout the year. It has strictly implemented the obligations of the *Convention*, ensuring thorough completion of annual declarations, acceptance of international inspections, import and export control, and non-proliferation efforts throughout the year, establishing a model in the *Convention* implementation in the international community and showcasing China's image as a responsible major country. It has actively participated in the formulation of international rules for the *Convention* implementation, submitting the *Position Paper of the People's Republic of China on Industry Verification* to the Fifth Review Conference of the *Convention* (hereinafter referred to as the "Fifth Review Conference"), and promoting the adoption of China's proposal on the reform of the Schedule 2B04 verification mechanism by the Organisation for the Prohibition of Chemical Weapons (hereinafter referred to as the "OPCW"), which makes significant contributions to alleviating the burden on the global industrial sector. To strengthen the supervision and regulation of controlled chemicals, it has implemented administrative licenses for controlled chemicals in accordance with the law, carried out law enforcement inspections of controlled chemicals, and formed a normalized supervision and inspection work mechanism. It has enhanced administrative law enforcement supervision of provincial competent authorities in industry and information technology, organized inspections on special licenses for the production of controlled chemicals, and implemented the relevant requirements of the State Council on deepening the reform of "separating permits from business licenses". It has strengthened the incentive and constraint mechanism, annually commending units and persons that have made significant contributions to the *Convention* implementation work, and reporting the outcome of the key work, to arouse the enthusiasm of local competent authorities. To strengthen capacity building, it has organized an exercise on accepting international inspections, held national comprehensive training courses, enhanced the cultivation of talent, guided local competent authorities to organise training programs, instructed the Expert Committee to provide on-site guidance to enterprises. These efforts have effectively improved the regulation capabilities of local competent authorities, and enhanced the ability of relevant enterprises to accept international inspections. To increase the awareness of the *Convention* implementation, it has organised publicity activities for the "4•29 OPCW Day" , compiled and published annual report on China's efforts to implement the *Convention*, as well as monthly news reports on the *Convention* implementation, timely updated relevant information on the official website, which have widely and pertinently publicize the concept of the *Convention* implementation , and fostered a positive social atmosphere for the related work.

The Ministry of Foreign Affairs has actively engaged in international affairs related to the *Convention* implementation and efforts to expedite the destruction of Japanese ACWs. It has actively participated in global governance in chemical field, and has on behalf of the Chinese Government, repeatedly elaborated on China's position and propositions on the proper resolution of hotspot issues related to chemical weapons, the promotion of the destruction of Japanese ACWs, the safeguarding of the authority and effectiveness of the *Convention*, and the promotion of international cooperation on peaceful uses at multilateral meetings held by the United Nations Security Council (hereinafter referred to as the "UN Security Council") and the OPCW. It has made every effort to promote the destruction of Japanese ACWs, conducted trilateral consultations with Japan and the OPCW on issues concerning Japanese ACWs continuously urged Japan to complete the destruction of Japanese ACWs at an early date, submitted China's Position Paper on Japanese ACWs to the Fifth Review Conference, held a special exhibition on Japanese ACWs, and continued to promote the OPCW and the international community to increase attention and supervision on the destruction of Japanese ACWs, thereby making significant contributions to accelerating the thorough destruction of Japanese ACWs and ensuring the comprehensive and effective implementation of the *Convention*.

The Office for International Military Cooperation of the Central Military Commission has conscientiously organised the military's work on the *Convention* implementation. It submitted the annual declaration for Schedule I chemicals and the National Protective Program on time, fulfilling international commitments with concrete actions. In close coordination with the Ministry of Foreign Affairs, it has diligently carried out technical supervision, emergency handling, and safety oversight at the operational sites of Japanese ACWs, supervised and assisted Japan's team in implementing excavation, recovery, and destruction operations for Japanese ACWs, and fully assisted in hosting OPCW's on-site inspections of facilities for Japanese ACWs, making tremendous efforts to achieve the complete destruction of Japanese ACWs as soon as possible.

The Ministry of Public Security, the Ministry of Finance, the Ministry of Ecology and Environment, the Ministry of Transport, the Ministry of Commerce, the National Health Commission, the Ministry of Emergency Management, the General Administration of Customs, the State Administration for Market Regulation, the National Immigration Administration, the National Railway Administration, the Civil Aviation Administration of China, the China State Railway Group Co. Ltd. and other member units of the inter-ministerial joint meeting, along with local governments and competent authorities at all levels, have attached great importance to the implementation of the *Convention*. They have been performing their respective duties and cooperating closely to provide strong support in the acceptance of international inspections, import and export control, non-proliferation, and the management of controlled chemicals, thereby making significant contributions to the comprehensive implementation of the *Convention*.

II. Submission of the National Declarations to Organisation for the Prohibition of Chemical Weapons

In accordance with Article VI and the relevant provisions of the *Convention,*

China submitted the annual national declarations on Scheduled chemicals to the OPCW on time. As of December 31st, 2023, China has submitted a total of 54 national declarations to the OPCW. In March 2023, China submitted the annual declaration on past activities of Schedule I, Schedule II, Schedule III chemicals, and Unscheduled Discrete Organic Chemicals (hereinafter referred to as the "DOC") and National Protective Program for 2022; and in September 2023, China submitted the annual declaration on anticipated activities of Schedule I, Schedule II, and Schedule III chemicals for 2024. In 2022, the total number of declarable industrial facilities was 1450, accounting for approximately 27.2% of the global total. Among them, there is 1 Schedule I facility, 60 Schedule II facilities, 159 Schedule III facilities, and 1230 other chemical production facilities (hereinafter referred to as the "OCPF"). The distribution of declared facilities by schedule in the annual declarations on past activities from 2013 to 2022 is shown in Fig.1. The distribution of the proportion of declared facilities by region in the annual declarations on past activities in 2022 is shown in Fig.2. The distribution of declared facilities by province in the annual declarations on past activities in 2022 is shown in Fig.3.

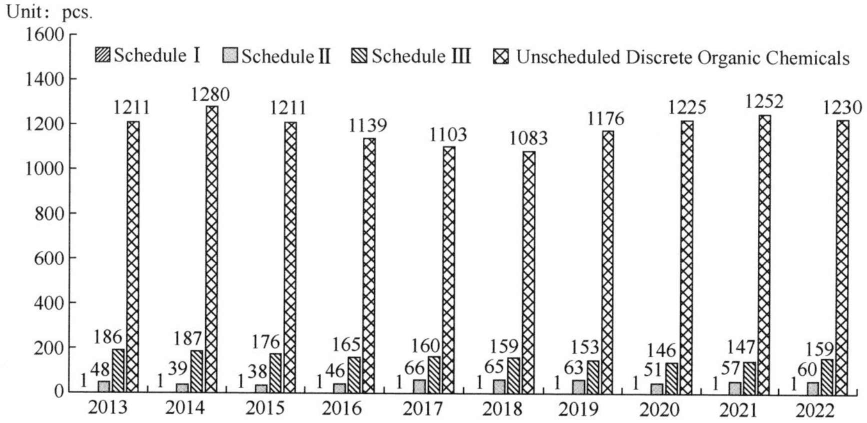

Fig. 1 The Distribution of Declared Facilities by Schedule in the Annual Declarations on Past Activities from 2013 to 2022

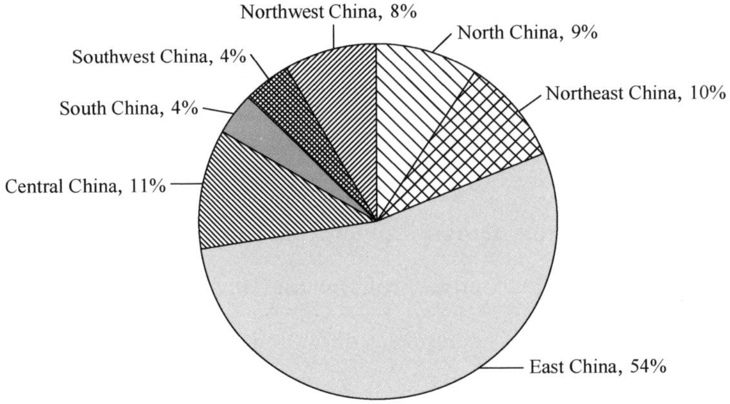

Fig. 2 The Distribution of the Proportion of Declared Facilities by Region in the Annual Declarations on Past Activities in 2022

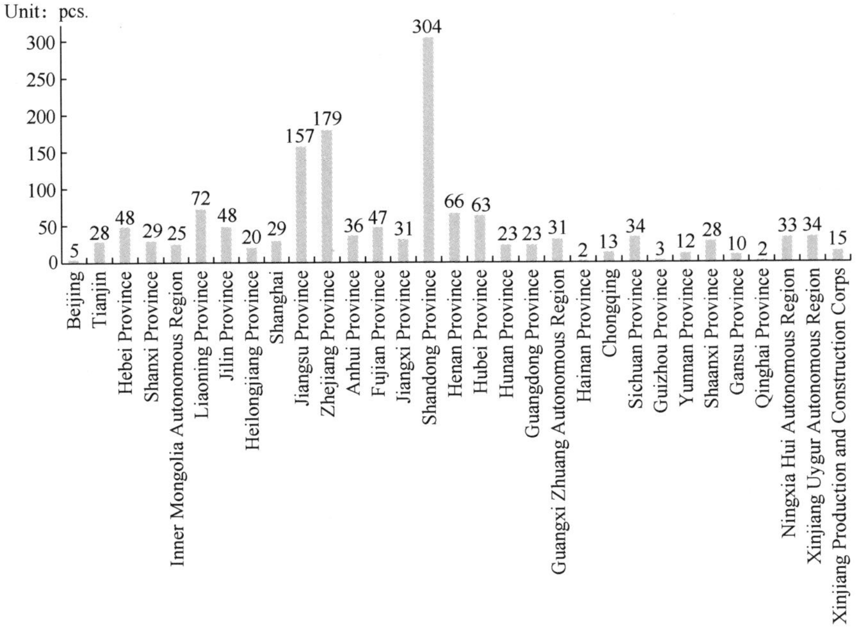

Fig. 3 The Distribution of Declared Facilities by Province in the Annual Declarations on Past Activities in 2022

In accordance with the provisions of the *Convention* on abandoned chemical weapons, China submitted to the OPCW the declaration of Japanese

ACWs, mainly including the distribution locations, types, quantities, and current storage conditions of newly discovered or destroyed Japanese ACWs. In June, September, and December 2023, China submitted updated declarations to the OPCW of the trust warehouses of Japanese ACWs in Hunchun City and Haerbaling in Dunhua City of Jilin Province, Harbin City, Qiqihar City, Yichun City, Jiamusi City, and Ning' an City of Heilongjiang Province, and Guangzhou City of Guangdong Province, as well as the temporary trust warehouses of the Japanese ACWs in Jizhou District of Tianjin City, Taiyuan City and Jincheng City of Shanxi Province, Bayannur City of Inner Mongolia Autonomous Region, Jixi City of Heilongjiang Province, Jiujiang City of Jiangxi Province, and Wuhan City of Hubei Province.

III. Receiving Inspections under Article VI of the *Convention*

In accordance with Article VI of the *Convention* and related provisions, China accepted on-site inspections by the OPCW. As of December 31st, 2023, China had received 499 inspections under Article VI of the *Convention*, accounting for 11% of the global total, including 24 Schedule I inspections and 475 inspections for Schedule II facilities, Schedule III facilities and OCPF. All the inspection results show that China has strictly fulfilled its obligations under the *Convention*. The number of inspections received by China under Article VI of the *Convention* from 2014 to 2023 is shown in Fig.4.

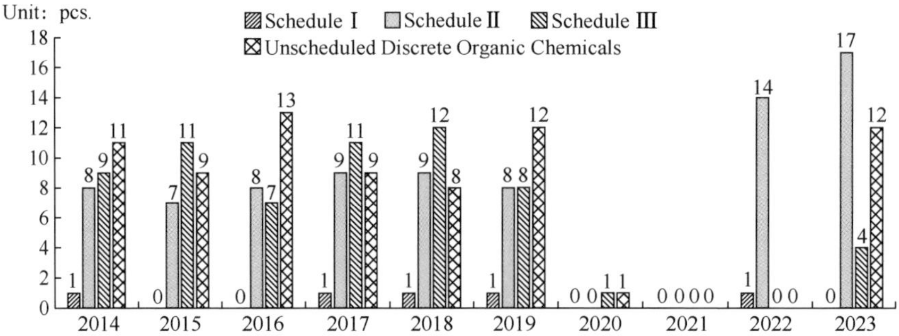

Fig. 4 Number of Inspections Received by China under Article VI of the *Convention* from 2014 to 2023

In 2023, China received a total of 33 on-site inspections under Article VI of the *Convention*, including 17 Schedule II inspections, 4 Schedule III inspections, and 12 OCPF inspections. The number of inspections received by China under Article VI of the *Convention* in 2023 by category is shown in Fig.5.

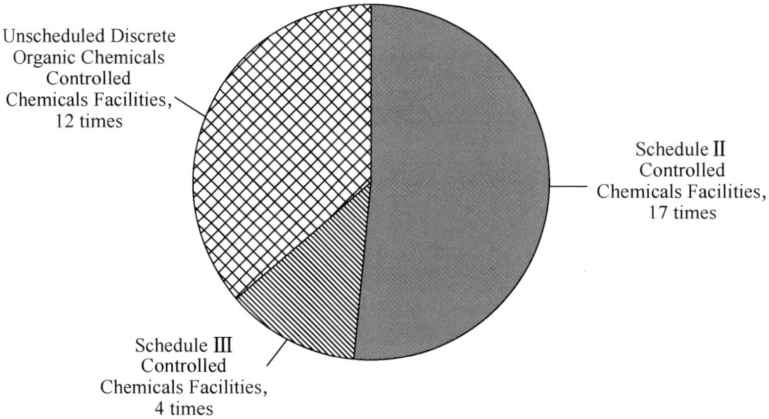

Fig. 5 Number of Inspections Received by China under Article VI of the *Convention* in 2023 by Category

The facilities in Hebei Province, Inner Mongolia Autonomous Region, Liaoning Province, Shanghai Municipality, Jiangsu Province, Zhejiang Province, Jiangxi Province, Shandong Province, Henan Province, Hubei Province, and Ningxia Autonomous Region received inspections in 2023. The number of inspections received by China under Article VI of the *Convention* in 2023 by province is shown in Fig.6.

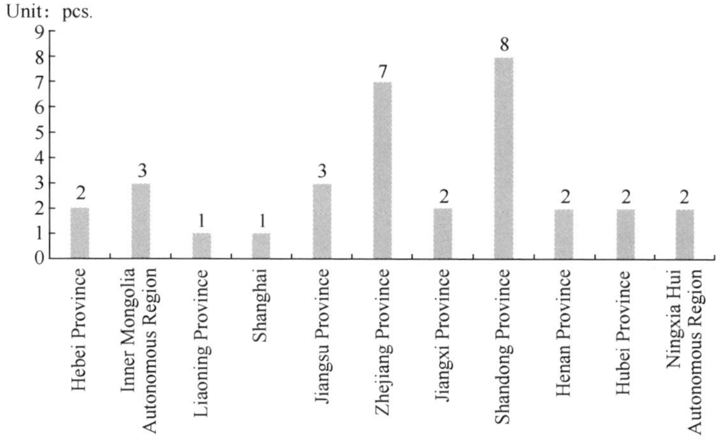

Fig. 6 Number of Inspections Received by China under Article VI of the *Convention* in 2023 by Province

IV. Disposal of Chemical Weapons Abandoned by Japan in China

In July 2023, all declared chemical weapons stockpiles were completely destroyed. Japanese ACWs have become the most realistic challenge to achieving a "world free of chemical weapons" . Japanese ACWs are one of the severe crimes committed by Japan's militarists. During the war of aggression against China, the Japanese army used chemical weapons across 19 provinces (including autonomous regions) in China, of which 1,241 incidents were recorded with accurate time, location, and number of casualties, causing more than 200,000 Chinese military and civilian casualties. On the eve of their defeat in 1945, the Japanese invaders secretly buried large quantities of chemical weapons on the spot or abandoned them in rivers and lakes in China to cover up their crimes. Having been buried for decades, these Japanese ACWs have corroded severely and leaked toxic agents, posing a severe threat to the safety of Chinese people's lives and property as well as the local ecological environment. According to incomplete statistics, since Japan's surrender, the Japanese ACWs have caused over 2,000 Chinese civilian casualties and polluted soil, air, and water, causing farmland to become unusable and forcing local residents to relocate.

Due to Japan's passive response and failure to fulfill its obligations to destruct the ACWs, the destruction plans for Japanese ACWs have been overdue 4 times. In 2023, China submitted the *Position Paper of the People's Republic of China on the Chemical Weapons Abandoned by Japan in China* to the Fifth Review Conference, outlining the legal basis for the destruction of Japanese ACWs, explaining the serious harm caused by Japanese ACWs and the urgency of their destruction, urging Japan to earnestly fulfill its political responsibilities and international obligations to ensure the safe, clean, and complete destruction of the Japanese ACWs at an early date, and calling upon all relevant parties to maintain and intensify their supervision and verification on the Japanese side to promote greater and faster progress in the destruction process. China also hosted a special exhibition on Japanese ACWs at the site of the Fifth Review Conference, which attracted over 100 attenders, including the Director-General of the OPCW, the Chairperson of the Fifth Review Conference, the permanent representatives and officials from over 50 States Parties, and heads of the Verification Division and Inspectorate Division of the OPCW Technical Secretariat. Additionally, China conducted the 37th and 38th rounds of trilateral consultations with Japan and the OPCW Technical Secretariat, exchanging views on the progress of destruction, implementation of new destruction plans, and on-site inspections of Japanese ACWs, and continued to urge Japan to implement the destruction plans in a comprehensive, complete and accurate manner.

In 2023, China facilitated 12 on-site inspections of Japanese ACWs facilities by the OPCW in 7 locations, including Haerbaling in Dunhua City of Jilin Province, Taiyuan City of Shanxi Province, Harbin City, Jiamusi City, and Ning'an City of Heilongjiang Province, Jiujiang City of Jiangxi Province, and Wuhan City of Hubei Province. Cumulatively, China has arranged 156 on-site inspections by the OPCW of Japanese ACWs facilities and operations. China has actively provided necessary assistance and facilitation for Japan's operations to meet the needs for the disposal of Japanese ACWs, and supervised and assisted Japan in the destruction of Japanese ACWs in Haerbaling in Dunhua City of Jilin Province and Harbin City of Heilongjiang Province, with a total of 22,261 pieces of Japanese ACWs destroyed, which was 3.8 times that of the destruction volume of 2022. China has supervised and assisted in the excavation and recovery operations of Japanese ACWs in Hunchun City and Haerbaling in Dunhua City of Jilin Province, Jiamusi City, Shangzhi City, Mudanjiang City, and Yichun City of Heilongjiang Province, with a total of 17,714 pieces of Japanese ACWs excavated and recovered, which was 2.3 times the excavation and recovery volume of 2022. China has supervised and assisted in the detailed investigation operations in Liaoyuan City of Jilin Province, the on-site investigation operations of Japanese ACWs in Dunhua City of Jilin Province, Tianjin Municipality, and Taiyuan City of Shanxi Province, as well as the identification and packaging operations of Japanese ACWs in Harbin City of Heilongjiang Province and Wuhan City of Hubei Province.

In 2023, at Japan's request, China facilitated the transportation of 5,699 pieces of Japanese ACWs from Jixi City, Jiamusi City, and Qiqihar City to Harbin City of Heilongjiang Province; from Qingyuan City of Guangdong

Province, Jiujiang City of Jiangxi Province to Wuhan City of Hubei Province; and from Bayannur City of Inner Mongolia Autonomous Region and Jincheng City to Taiyuan City of Shanxi Province. China also carried out construction work for destruction facilities in Wuhan City, Hubei Province. Additionally, based on newly discovered Japanese ACWs, China conducted internal investigations in Bayannur City of Inner Mongolia Autonomous Region, Tonghua City of Jilin Province, Changsha City, Hengyang City, and Yueyang City of Hunan Province, Dali Bai Autonomous Prefecture of Yunnan Province, and Lanzhou City of Gansu Province, identifying and recovering 10 pieces of Japanese ACWs.

V. Import and Export Control and Non-proliferation of Controlled Chemicals

China has strictly implemented the relevant provisions of the *Convention,* adopted internationally accepted systems and standards for the management of import and export of controlled chemicals, including license management, control by list and end-use certification, designated certain companies for the import and export business and taken production source control measures, so as to strictly regulate the import and export of controlled chemicals, and prevent the proliferation risk.

The National CWC Implementation Office strictly follows the provisions of the *Regulations of the People's Republic of China on the Administration of Controlled Chemicals* (hereinafter referred to as "*Regulations*") and the *Rules of Implementation for the Regulations* (hereinafter referred to as "*Rules*") to carry out the review and approval of the import and export of controlled chemicals. In

2023, it approved a total of 874 import and export applications. No proliferation incident has occurred. In coordination with the Ministry of Commerce and the General Administration of Customs, it has improved the integration of the *Approval Certificate for the Import and Export of Controlled Chemicals* and the *Import and Export Licenses for Dual-use Items and Technologies*, and facilitated the import and export of low-concentration triethanolamine mixtures. It has provided guidance to the Beijing Municipal Bureau of Economy and Information Technology to investigate and administratively penalize a company for illegal export of controlled chemicals, effectively upholding the authority of the law.

The competent authorities at all levels strengthened source control and continuously carried out education activities about import and export control and non-proliferation for enterprises producing, using, and operating controlled chemicals, guiding the enterprises to establish a self-discipline mechanism.

VI. Supervision and Regulation of Controlled Chemicals

To effectively prevent the risk of proliferation and ensure that enterprises fulfill their obligations under the *Convention*, China strictly supervises and regulates controlled chemicals and implements a licensing system for relevant activities such as the facility construction and production of controlled chemicals.

Competent authorities at all levels adhere to law-based administration, and strictly implement the approval system for the construction of production facilities of controlled chemicals in accordance with the *Regulations*, the *Rules* and other laws and regulations. In 2023, 176 production facilities of controlled chemicals were approved. Among them, there were 13 production facilities of

Schedule II chemicals, 30 production facilities of Schedule III chemicals and 133 production facilities of DOC containing phosphorus, sulfur and fluorine.

In 2023, the National CWC Implementation Office strictly implemented the requirements of the *Notice of the State Council on Deepening the Reform of Separating Permits from Business Licenses and Further Increasing the Development Vitality of Market Participants* (hereinafter referred to as "*Notice*"), and conducted inspections for the review of licenses for the production of controlled chemicals in Heilongjiang Province, Fujian Province, Hubei Province, Guangxi Zhuang Autonomous Region, Sichuan Province, and Gansu Province, and standardized the administrative law enforcement. Provincial competent authorities, based on the *Notice*, strictly followed the assessment standards for granting licenses for the production of controlled chemicals and issued a total of 147 licenses for the production of controlled chemicals throughout the year.

In 2023, the National CWC Implementation Offce strengthened the supervision during and after granting the licenses of controlled chemicals in accordance with domestic regulations, and conducted law enforcement inspections on 4 enterprises in Liaoning Province and Gansu Province. Local competent authorities carried out inspections on relevant enterprises within their jurisdictions. Problems identified during the inspections were promptly rectified. These efforts have effectively promoted enterprises to improve their awareness and abilities of the implementation of the *Convention*.

VII. Outreach of the Implementation of the *Convention*

In 2023, the National CWC Implementation Office continued to expand publicity and education on the implementation of the *Convention*.

It published and distributed the *Report on China's Efforts to Implement the Chemical Weapons Convention (2019—2021)*, organised the compilation of the *Report on China's Efforts to Implement the Chemical Weapons Convention (2022)*, and compiled and printed 12 issues of monthly news reports on the *Convention* implementation. It also updated information on the column about the implementation of the *Convention* on the official website of the Ministry of Industry and Information Technology, establishing a platform for experience sharing and exchange among local competent authorities and enterprises, and comprehensively showcasing China's national achievements and local practices in implementation of the *Convention*.

Taking the "4•29 OPCW Day" as an important opportunity for the publicity, the National CWC Implementation Office organised competent authorities at all levels, controlled chemicals enterprises, industry associations, universities, and research institutes to carry out various forms of publicity activities focusing on the purposes and objectives of the *Convention* and themed at "Joining Hands to Create a World Free of Chemical Weapons" and "Ensuring Achievements in the Chemical Field Only Used for the Benefit of Humanity" . During the activities in 2023, the National CWC Implementation Office encouraged people from all walks of life to design themed posters for the 8th "OPCW Day" , organised an online quiz on the implementation of the *Convention*, and collaborated with provincial competent authorities to hold an online exhibition about local efforts to implement the *Convention*, further enhancing public awareness of the implementation of the *Convention*. The publicity activities have gained over 110,000 online participants, including 94,716 participants in the online quiz and 15,813 participants in the voting activity for the themed poster.

Competent authorities at all levels across the country responded positively, fully leveraging local newspapers, electronic displays, official websites, WeChat, and other media platforms for publicity, and conducted various activities in key areas such as plants of controlled chemicals enterprises and government office areas through setting publicity columns, playing videos, hanging banners, posting posters, distributing publicity materials, holding special seminars and organising quizzes, aiming to expand the reach and impact of the publicity.

VIII. Training on the Implementation of the *Convention*

In 2023, the National CWC Implementation Office continued to strengthen staff training on the implementation of the *Convention*. It organised a nationwide comprehensive training program in Yinchuan City, which was attended by 105 trainees from the competent authorities of provinces, autonomous regions, municipalities directly under the Central Government, and Xinjiang Production and Construction Corps. This training program was organised in an innovative way, providing tailored courses at beginner level and advanced level respectively based on the participants' knowledge and working experience about the *Convention* implementation. The curriculum included basics of the *Convention*, China's domestic laws and regulations on the *Convention* implementation, law-based administration, Schedule II chemicals regulation, and team building. The training program won wide praise for its rich content, novel form, and practical guidance. Participants considered it so timely and highly beneficial that it perfectly met their expectations.

The competent authorities in Tianjin Municipality, Hebei Province, Shanxi Province, Inner Mongolia Autonomous Region, Liaoning Province, Jilin Province, Heilongjiang Province, Shanghai Municipality, Jiangsu Province, Zhejiang Province, Anhui Province, Fujian Province, Jiangxi Province,

Shandong Province, Henan Province, Hubei Province, Hunan Province, Guangdong Province, Guangxi Zhuang Autonomous Region, Sichuan Province, Guizhou Province, Shaanxi Province, and Ningxia Hui Autonomous Region, as well as Xinjiang Production and Construction Corps actively carried out local training programs, covering topics including data declaration, acceptance of international inspections, administrative licensing, law enforcement inspections, etc., which effectively improved the local working capacity for the *Convention* implementation.

IX. Application of the *Convention* in Hong Kong, Macao and Taiwan

The Chinese Government attaches great importance to the application of the *Convention* in the Hong Kong Special Administrative Region, Macao Special Administrative Region and Taiwan Region.

In accordance with the principle of "one country, two systems" and the *Basic Law of the Hong Kong Special Administrative Region of the People's Republic of China*, the Central Government determined the mode of application of the *Convention* in the Hong Kong Special Administrative Region after full consultation with the Government of the Hong Kong Special Administrative Region. The Hong Kong Special Administrative region passed the *Chemical Weapons (Convention) Ordinance* in 2003, and began to implement it in 2004. *The Chemical Weapons (Convention) Ordinance* empowers the Customs and Excise Department of the Hong Kong Special Administrative Region to fully enforce the law. Violation of the provisions of the *Chemical Weapons (Convention) Ordinance* is defined as a criminal offense, and the maximum penalty is life imprisonment. The Government of the Hong Kong Special Administrative Region implemented a complete licensing and reporting system for chemicals under supervision of the *Convention*. The Hong Kong Special Administrative Region currently does not have chemical facilities that should be declared to the OPCW, and there are only a few import trade activities involving controlled chemicals, which are mainly used for local scientific research or industry. According to the provisions of the *Convention,* in March 2023, the Hong Kong Special Administrative Region submitted its annual declaration on past activities in 2022 to the OPCW through the Central Government.

The Central Government and the Government of the Macao Special Administrative Region have held several rounds of consultation on the application of the *Convention* in the Macao Special Administrative Region. Such preparatory work as legislation for the implementation of the *Convention* in the Macao Special Administrative Region is being carried out in an orderly manner.

Taiwan is an inalienable part of Chinese territory and it must fulfill its obligations under the *Convention* on the premise of the one-China principle. The Chinese government has been actively and pragmatically seeking ways to properly resolve the issue of the application of the *Convention* in Taiwan Region.

X. In-depth Participation in Global Governance in the Chemical Field

The *Convention* is a key pillar of the global security governance system, playing a significant role in maintaining international peace and security and promoting the peaceful use of chemical technology. As a permanent member of the United Nations Security Council, an original State Party to the *Convention*, and the second largest contributor to the OPCW, China actively participates in non-proliferation international cooperation within the UN-led multilateral framework. It consistently advocates the comprehensive prohibition and complete destruction of all weapons of mass destruction, including chemical weapons, and firmly opposes the proliferation of chemical weapons and the relevant technologies.

In today's world, turmoil and instability are intertwined, and the international community is facing unprecedented challenges. President Xi Jinping proposed the Global Security Initiative, advocating a vision of common, comprehensive, cooperative, and sustainable security, and encouraging the international community to uphold a spirit of solidarity and a win-win mindset and work together to enhance security governance, address security challenges, eliminate security deficits, and achieve lasting peace and development globally. Guided by this Initiative, the Chinese government genuinely practices multilateralism, deeply engages in the implementation and review of the *Convention*, and firmly upholds the purpose and objectives of the *Convention*.

China firmly opposes the research and development or use of chemical weapons by any country, organisation, or individual under any circumstances, consistently maintains an objective and fair stance, and is committed to promoting the resolution of the hotspot issues related to chemical weapons through political and diplomatic means. The Chinese government advocates that the *Convention* serves as the guideline and basis for addressing hotspot issues related to chemical weapons, and handling such issues in accordance with the *Convention* is the only correct approach. In February 2023, China released *China's Position on the Political Settlement of the Ukraine Crisis*, clearly opposing the development and use of biochemical weapons. China urges the States Parties to the *Convention* to summarize the experiences and lessons from past events, and jointly explore solutions to issues related to chemical weapons through dialogues and consultations.

XI. International Cooperation

The Chinese government has attached great importance to international cooperation of the *Convention* implementation. It has promoted the international cooperation and assistance on peaceful uses of chemicals, actively engaged in major international conferences and affairs, pragmatically promoted multilateral and bilateral communications, and actively responded to the reasonable demands of developing countries to strengthen the international cooperation regarding the *Convention* implementation. With these efforts, China has played an important role in implementing the *Convention* and safeguarding world peace.

In 2023, the Chinese delegations attended international conferences on the *Convention* implementation, including the Fifth Review Conference, the 28th Conference of the States Parties, the 102nd, 103rd, and 104th sessions of the Executive Council, the 21st Regional Meeting of National Authorities of States Parties in Asia, the 25th Annual Meeting of National Authorities, and multiple industry consultations, and clarified China's position on the implementation of the *Convention*, safeguarding the authority and effectiveness of the *Convention*, destruction of Japanese ACWs, and OPCW inspections of civil industries. China, together with 13 countries, jointly submitted the *Position Paper on Promoting International Cooperation on Peaceful Uses Under the Framework of the Chemical Weapons Convention* to the Fifth Review Conference, actively advocating the peaceful uses of chemicals, calling for strengthening international cooperation in the chemical industry, and safeguarding developing countries' rights to peaceful uses. China recommended two Chinese enterprises to the OPCW to undertake the OPCW's chemical research and training programs in China, providing a platform for exchanges that promote the development and peaceful uses of chemical science and technology. As of 2023, China has recommended talent to the OPCW for 4 consecutive years, contributing valuable human resources to international efforts on the *Convention* implementation. In recent years, China has paid the annual contribution of an average of over 10 million euros to the OPCW, providing robust support to the OPCW and demonstrating its role of a responsible major country.

In 2023, the Toxicological Analysis Laboratory of the Military Medical Research Institute of the China Academy of Military Sciences and the Analytical Chemical Laboratory of the Institute of Chemical Defense participated in the 8th OPCW International Joint Proficiency Test for Biomedical Samples, and the Analytical Chemical Laboratory of the Institute of Chemical Defense participated in the 54th OPCW International Joint Proficiency Test for Environmental Samples, and achieved excellent results.

China

地方篇

中国履行《禁止化学武器公约》报告（2023）

北京市

组织协调

2023 年，北京市禁化武办组织监控化学品企业学习《公约》《宣布手册》《条例》《细则》《全国监控化学品统计调查制度》等履约法律法规和相关文件，要求监控化学品企业全面准确掌握宣布工作的要求，熟练使用数据宣布系统，认真核对宣布数据，确保准确无误，按时上报。同时，进一步加强监控化学品行政许可审批和日常监管工作，夯实履约基础，做好履约宣传、培训工作，为履约创造良好的环境。

数据宣布与接受视察

2023 年，在我国向禁化武组织提交的 2022 年过去活动年度宣布中，北京市有宣布设施 4 个。2024 年预计活动年度宣布中，北京市没有宣布设施。

2023 年，禁化武组织没有对北京市监控化学品企业进行现场视察。

监督管理

2023 年，北京市禁化武办审批第二类监控化学品使用许可申请 1 项，完成监控化学品进口审批最终用途审查 28 项，指导 66 家监控化学品企业落实《条例》《细则》有关的要求。

宣传

2023 年，北京市禁化武办积极开展禁化武履约宣传工作，下发《关于做好2023年禁化武履约宣传作品征集活动组织工作的通知》，组织企业及社会公众积极参与征集活动，共征集主题海报6张，经过筛选报送国家禁化武办3张。同时，通过办公楼宇张贴海报等方式，以及利用门户网站、内部办公软件、微信等线上渠道大力宣传，进一步强化履约责任感和使命感。

专项工作

2023年，北京市禁化武办对3家监控化学品企业开展专项监督检查，主要检查企业遵守监控化学品相关法律法规情况、落实《接受禁止化学武器组织现场视察工作规范（试行）》情况、有无违规经营监控化学品情况、相关管理制度建立情况、台账流向信息等。指导中国石化集团北京燕山石油化工有限公司完善《接受禁化武组织现场视察工作预案》，提升数据宣布、接受国际视察等方面的能力。

2023年，北京市经济和信息化局收到国家禁化武办转来的关于1家企业涉嫌违规出口监控化学品的举报后，迅速启动调查处理工作。在北京市经济和信息化局领导的精准指导和局法制部门的全力配合下，北京市禁化武办依法依规开展查处工作，扎实推进询问、协查、现场调查等程序，确保违规主体和违规事实清楚，行政处罚依据充分。按照《条例》第二十三条的规定，北京市经济和信息化局于2023年2月24日对该企业作出没收违法所得共计人民币26332624.53元的行政处罚决定。截至2023年12月31日，该行政处罚正处于行政诉讼二审阶段，尚未正式生效。

（**撰稿**　赵帅　刘昭）

天津市

组织协调

2023 年，天津市工业和信息化局认真落实国家禁化武办工作部署，结合天津市监控化学品监管工作实际，认真做好监控化学品数据宣布、行政许可和宣传培训等基础工作。同时，进一步完善天津市接受国际视察工作机制，督促企业完善接受国际视察预案，强化履约意识，提高天津市接受国际视察的能力。在监控化学品行业管理方面，通过明确责任边界，完善工作制度，强化部门联动，规范行政执法行为，切实提升监控化学品行政管理的效率，加大履约全流程监管力度，夯实各项工作的基础。

数据宣布与接受视察

2023 年，在我国向禁化武组织提交的 2022 年过去活动年度宣布中，天津市有宣布设施 28 个。2024 年预计活动年度宣布中，天津市有宣布设施 2 个。

2023 年，禁化武组织没有对天津市监控化学品企业进行现场视察。

监督管理

2023 年，天津市工业和信息化局累计出动执法人员 86 人次，对 38 家监控化学品企业进行现场检查，深入企业开展数据核查、生产特别许可证书和车间设备设施检查，严格按照《条例》《细则》规定，切实做好日常监督管理工作，坚决查处违法行为，督促企业落实监控化学品全生命周期管控措施。对 1 家未经生产特别许可，而违法生产监控化学品的企业开展执法检查，经现场对建设监控化学品生产设施的批复和相关资料的调查取证后，下达《责令改正通知书》，要求企业限期内完成整改。

天津市工业和信息化局进一步深化“证照分离”改革要求，优化审批服务方式，实现由“最多跑一次”向“零跑动”的延伸。持续完善《监控化学品行政许可服务指南》，最大限度地方便企业办事，降低企业办事的成本，激发监控化学品领域市场活力。2023年，共办理监控化学品相关行政许可21项，其中审核上报监控化学品生产设施建设审批申请3项，组织监控化学品生产设施竣工验收2项，审批监控化学品生产特别许可申请7项、第二类监控化学品使用许可申请4项，完成监控化学品进口审批最终用途审查5项。

宣传

2023年，为广泛宣传禁化武履约工作的重要意义和中国履约的丰硕成果，天津市工业和信息化局组织各区履约主管部门和监控化学品重点企业的履约负责同志共计50余人开展“4·29国际禁止化学武器组织日”宣传活动，播放《禁化武履约课堂——禁化武组织国际视察情景模拟》宣传视频，宣讲禁化武履约工作重点内容、国际视察流程、监控化学品行政许可有关工作和监控化学品相关法律法规等，加深企业对国际视察流程和监控化学品管理的了解和认识，提升企业的履约能力。

为进一步提升宣传的时效性和针对性，天津市工业和信息化局结合日常检查开展以案释法和精准普法36次，推动法治宣传与法治实践的有机结合，有效地提升企业的法治意识和法治素养。

培训

2023年，天津市工业和信息化局组织重点辖区工业和信息化主管部门及多家监控化学品重点企业，参加中国监控化学品协会举办的禁化武履约能力培训班。同时，结合“4·29国际禁止化学武器组织日”，天津市工业和信息化局向各区工业和信息化主管部门及监控化学品企业发放《监控化学品行政执法法律法规汇编》，宣讲监控化学品法律法规条款、禁化武履约工作重点及接受国际视察工作流程等，帮助各区主管部门和企业加深对监控化学品法律法规的理解，进一步提升企业主体履约意识和履约能力，为接受国际视察打下坚实基础。

专项工作

2023 年，天津市工业和信息化局对 12 家监控化学品企业开展“双随机、一公开”执法检查，重点检查企业生产特别许可证书、车间新（改、扩）建情况、生产工艺变更情况等，督促企业扎实做好监控化学品各项基础管理工作，充分做好迎接国际视察准备。对照接受国际视察工作要求，对 3 家监控化学品企业开展专项执法检查，严格按照《监控化学品管理抽查事项表》中 45 项内容开展逐项检查，对企业存在接受国际视察预案不完善、监控化学品统计数据不清晰等问题现场进行指导修改，督促企业练好应战基本功，有效帮助企业提高履约管理水平和接受国际视察能力。

（撰稿　郭生俊　邓雪）

河北省

组织协调

2023 年，河北省禁化武办认真贯彻落实国家禁化武办工作部署，组织各市、县（区）主管部门及监控化学品企业，认真履行《公约》义务，严格执行《条例》《细则》规定，圆满完成全年履约工作任务。

数据宣布与接受视察

2023 年，在我国向禁化武组织提交的 2022 年过去活动年度宣布中，河北省有宣布设施 48 个。2024 年预计活动年度宣布中，河北省有宣布设施 13 个。

2023 年，禁化武组织先后对石家庄化工有限公司宏润分公司和河北威远生物化工有限公司的第二类监控化学品生产、消耗设施进行现场视察。2 家企业均顺利通过了现场视察。

监督管理

河北省禁化武办认真贯彻《条例》《细则》，严格按照监控化学品行政许可要求，认真做好监控化学品生产设施建设、竣工验收、生产特别许可等各项行政许可审核审批工作。2023 年，审核上报监控化学品生产设施建设审批申请 7 项，组织监控化学品生产设施建设竣工验收 4 项，审批监控化学品生产特别许可申请 4 项并上报工业和信息化部备案。

宣传

河北省高度重视禁化武履约宣传，并在“4·29 国际禁止化学武器组织日”期间开展集中宣传活动，利用机关电子屏、门户网站、微信公众号、工作群等渠道推送履约宣传海报和宣传手册，扩大履约宣传面和影响力。各市禁化武履约主管部门、监控化学品企业通过张贴海报、悬挂条幅、摆放展板、专题培训、观看视频等方式进行宣传，普及履约知识，提高公众对履约工作的认知度，营造良好的社会履约氛围。

培训

2023 年 10 月 8 日，河北省禁化武办在石家庄市举办了全省禁化武履约培训班，各市工业和信息化局、重点县（区）和监控化学品企业履约工作负责同志、履约技术专家共计 170 余人参加培训。培训班介绍了《公约》《条例》《细则》等法律法规，详细讲解了监控化学品管理有关内容、标准和要求，重点对接受国际视察注意事项、被视察企业资料准备及常见问题等方面进行详细介绍。通过此次培训，全省履约工作者对禁化武履约工作有了更为深刻的理解和认识，责任担当和履约能力得到了进一步提高，监控化学品企业自觉履约、守法经营的意识得到了增强，培训达到了预期效果。

专项工作

认真落实监控化学品“双随机、一公开”执法检查专项工作，全年对4家监控化学品企业开展了执法检查，通过听取视察前情况介绍、核对相关数据、查看生产现场等方式重点对企业履约基础工作、接受视察资料准备情况、贯彻《条例》《细则》等方面进行检查，对企业存在的不足和短板及时进行指导和督促整改，不断夯实企业履约的基础。

（**撰稿** 刘伯 董猛）

山西省

组织协调

2023年，在国家禁化武办和山西省政府的正确领导下，山西省禁化武办结合山西履约的实际情况，突出重点，认真抓好各项任务落实，开创履约工作新局面。进一步加强对年度数据宣布工作的组织指导和审核把关，查漏补缺，不断提高宣布工作的质量，按时保质完成了2022年过去活动年度宣布和2024年预计活动年度宣布。

数据宣布与接受视察

2023年，在我国向禁化武组织提交的2022年过去活动年度宣布中，山西省有宣布设施29个。2024年预计活动年度宣布中，山西省有宣布设施1个。

2023年，禁化武组织没有对山西省监控化学品企业进行现场视察。

监督管理

山西省禁化武办严格依据《条例》《细则》和国家产业政策的要求，转变重审批轻监管、以审批代管理的倾向，进一步做好监控化学品许可审批和监管工作。2023年，审核上报监控化学品生产设施建设审批申请1项，审批监控化学品生产特别许可申请3项，组织2家永久停产的第四类监控化学品企业按照规定办理宣布退出手续。

宣传

按照国家禁化武办的统一部署，山西省禁化武办组织开展了“4·29国际禁止化学武器组织日”主题宣传活动。一是在全省范围内积极组织各市、履约企业和高校参与由国家禁化武办举办的履约宣传海报征集和在线禁化武履约普法知识竞赛等活动，全省参与知识竞赛超过1.7万人次，约占全国总人次的20%，二是组织履约宣传进企业、进园区、进学校，印制《监控化学品管理常用法律法规汇编》并向省内履约单位发放。通过开展一系列宣传活动，企业的履约意识得到进一步增强，社会公众对履约工作的认知度得到进一步提高，禁化武履约工作的影响力得到进一步扩大。

培训

2023年6月13日，山西省禁化武办在太原市举办了2023年全省禁化武履约工作培训班，全省履约队伍的130多名同志参加培训。此次培训对增强参训学员的履约意识、提升履约队伍的专业能力起到有效作用，为进一步加强监控化学品管理、应对国际视察等各项工作奠定了坚实的基础。

专项工作

2023 年，山西省禁化武办利用化工园区调研和入企服务等契机，多次深入园区和企业，进一步掌握监控化学品使用和生产情况，及时研究和协调解决履约相关问题和困难。对 3 家监控化学品企业开展“双随机、一公开”执法检查，查找企业履约工作的短板，指导企业进行针对性的整改，及时发现和化解履约风险与隐患，帮助企业做好接受国际视察的各项准备工作。

（**撰稿** 寇世平 樊小娟）

内蒙古自治区

组织协调

内蒙古自治区禁化武办依托《禁止化学武器公约》履约工作厅际联席会议（以下简称“履约工作厅际联席会议”）制度，在内蒙古自治区人民政府领导下，研究履约重大问题，协调处理履约重要事项，组织接受禁化武组织现场视察，做好监控化学品管理各项工作。2023 年，组织召开由履约工作厅际联席会议成员单位、呼伦贝尔市、阿拉善盟政府及有关部门、企业负责人等参加的专题会议，研究部署接受禁化武组织现场视察工作，提前派员带领专家赴企业进行现场指导，邀请国家履约专家委专家进行线上指导，并开展视察演练活动，为顺利通过国际视察夯实工作基础。

数据宣布与接受视察

2023 年，在我国向禁化武组织提交的 2022 年过去活动年度宣布中，内蒙古自治区有宣布设施 25 个。2024 年预计活动年度宣布中，内蒙古自治区有宣布设施 7 个。

2023年，禁化武组织先后对齐鲁制药（内蒙古）有限公司呼伦贝尔分公司的第二类监控化学品消耗设施，内蒙古浩普科技有限公司及内蒙古灵圣作物科技有限公司的第二类监控化学品生产、消耗设施进行现场视察。3家企业均顺利通过了现场视察。

监督管理

2023年，内蒙古自治区禁化武办审核上报监控化学品生产设施建设审批申请22项，组织监控化学品生产设施竣工验收10项，审批监控化学品生产特别许可申请3项并报工业和信息化部备案。制定了2023年度内蒙古自治区《监控化学品专项监督检查工作计划》，对区内21家监控化学品生产企业开展了专项监督检查，及时向各盟（市）工业和信息化局反馈检查发现的问题及整改要求，要求企业一个月内完成整改，上报整改报告，督促企业进一步规范和完善履约基础管理工作，不断提升接受禁化武组织现场视察的能力。

宣传

开展了丰富多彩的“4·29国际禁止化学武器组织日”宣传普法活动。一是组织履约普法知识竞赛，组织各盟（市）及全区监控化学品生产企业积极参加由国家禁化武办举办的在线禁化武履约普法知识竞赛，实现了普法知识纵向全覆盖。二是张贴履约宣传材料，内蒙古自治区党政办公区、各盟（市）工业和信息化局、监控化学品生产企业通过张贴履约宣传海报、拉横幅、立展架等多种形式进行宣传。三是制作履约宣传手册，制作300份“4·29国际禁止化学武器组织日”宣传手册，分送区履约工作厅际联席会议成员单位、各盟（市）工业和信息化局及监控化学品生产企业，同时将宣传手册刊登在自治区政府门户网站“4·29国际禁止化学武器组织日”专栏。宣传手册介绍了化学武器的定义、化学武器的危害、中国履约成果及内蒙古自治区2022年履约工作。四是开展现场宣讲活动，自治区履行《公约》工作领导小组办公室全体成员在自治区党政机关大楼现场宣讲了“4·29 国际禁止化学武器组织日”的有关情况，向各机关工作人员介绍《公约》相关内容，进一步提高党政机关的履约责任感和使命感。

培训

内蒙古自治区禁化武办组织禁化武组织离任视察员、禁化武履约专家对监控化学品生产企业集中、履约基础薄弱的呼伦贝尔市、阿拉善盟、乌海市和通辽市分别开展了禁化武履约专题业务培训和一对一指导工作，帮助企业提高履约能力和水平。

专项工作

为提高应对禁化武组织现场视察的能力，内蒙古自治区禁化武办组织禁化武履约专家赴乌海市和阿拉善盟，对 6 家第四类监控化学品生产企业开展禁化武组织现场视察演练活动，逐页指导企业修改完善《视察前情况介绍》，抽查生产原始记录、统计台账、统计报表等相关材料，开展现场巡视，指导企业做好数据资料及现场准备工作。演练活动强化了各级履约主管部门和企业的履约意识，提升了企业履约的能力，尤其是接受国际视察的能力，帮助企业扎实做好履约的各项基础工作，为做好年度宣布工作和顺利通过禁化武组织现场视察夯实工作基础。

（撰稿　姜丽）

辽宁省

组织协调

2023 年，辽宁省禁化武办认真履行履约职能，做好各项履约管理工作。

4月，贯彻落实国家禁化武办《2023年履行〈禁止化学武器公约〉工作要点》有关工作要求，部署2023年禁化武履约重点工作。9月，召开全省禁化武履约工作会，传达国家禁化武办有关要求和省政府主要领导批示，印发《关于进一步加强禁化武履约工作的通知》。

数据宣布与接受视察

2023年，在我国向禁化武组织提交的2022年过去活动年度宣布中，辽宁省有宣布设施72个。2024年预计活动年度宣布中，辽宁省有宣布设施15个。

2023年，禁化武组织对营口营新化工科技有限公司的第三类监控化学品生产设施进行现场视察。企业顺利通过了现场视察。

监督管理

按照《条例》《细则》要求，认真开展行政许可工作，审核审批监控化学品各类行政许可20项，其中审核上报监控化学品生产设施建设审批申请5项，组织监控化学品生产设施竣工验收5项，审批监控化学品生产特别许可申请7项、监控化学品使用许可申请1项，完成监控化学品进口审批最终用途审查2项。10月，对1家违规生产第三类监控化学品的企业进行行政处罚，对2家监控化学品企业开展行政执法检查，组织各市开展监控化学品企业全覆盖排查检查工作。11月，指导抚顺市禁化武办对1家监控化学品企业开展行政执法检查。

宣传

2023年4月29日是《公约》生效26周年纪念日、第8个国际禁止化学武器组织日，辽宁省禁化武办在辽宁省工业和信息化厅网站首页发布了题为“2023年4月29日——中国履行《禁止化学武器公约》26周年”的宣传报道，并组织各市禁化武办通过门户网站、微信、微博等渠道进行宣传。此外，抚顺、阜新、营口等市工业和信息化局组织相关处室人员开展座谈宣传。

培训

2023 年 6 月，委派 1 名鞍山市工业和信息化局相关工作负责人，赴韩国参加禁化武组织亚洲地区化学防护援助初级培训班（一期）。7 月，辽宁省工业和信息化厅在沈阳市召开全省禁化武履约培训班，各市禁化武办、履约专家及监控化学品企业共 80 余人参加培训。培训邀请了履约专家讲解接受国际视察工作注意事项、数据宣布系统和监控化学品行政许可工作流程，传达了国家禁化武办的工作要求，并部署下一步重点工作。通过本次培训，各地禁化武办和监控化学品企业的履约意识得到有效增强，全省履约队伍的专业能力得到有效提升，为进一步做好监控化学品管理及接受国际视察等工作提供了保障。9 月，参加国家禁化武办全国禁化武履约综合培训班。10 月，委派 1 名鞍山市工业和信息化局相关工作负责人，赴马来西亚参加禁化武组织亚洲地区化学防护援助初级培训班（二期）。组织企业参加 2023 年监控化学品企业履约及高质量发展大会。11 月，参加国家禁化武办接受禁化武组织现场视察座谈会。

专项工作

加强履约支撑体系建设，建立完善辽宁省禁化武履约工作专家库，为宣布、视察和监控化学品管理等工作提供技术支持，进一步提高监控化学品管理工作的科学性和精准性，促进全省禁化武履约能力不断提升。

（撰稿　邹钟嘉　丁天佐）

吉林省

组织协调

2023 年 12 月 6 日，吉林省禁化武办组织召开了全省禁化武履约年度工作会议，会议总结了全省 2023 年履约工作取得的成效和存在的问题，安排部署了 2024 年履约重点工作。

数据宣布与接受视察

2023 年，在我国向禁化武组织提交的 2022 年过去活动年度宣布中，吉林省有宣布设施 48 个。2024 年预计活动年度宣布中，吉林省有宣布设施 7 个。

2023 年，禁化武组织没有对吉林省监控化学品企业进行现场视察。

监督管理

2023 年，吉林省禁化武办进一步加强监控化学品生产设施建设和生产活动管理，在指导企业办理监控化学品行政许可的基础上开展专项排查整治工作。审核上报监控化学品生产设施建设审批申请 2 项，审批监控化学品经营许可申请 1 项。结合近两年禁化武组织现场视察情况，组织对省内部分监控化学品企业开展巡查指导工作。对 2022 年达到视察阈值的第二类、第三类监控化学品企业实行全覆盖检查，对第四类监控化学品生产企业进行抽查检查。按照接受国际视察工作的要求，从资料准备、宣布数据、工艺流程等方面指导企业查漏补缺，增强企业履约主体的责任意识，提高企业履约的能力和水平。

宣传

组织开展“4·29国际禁止化学武器组织日”宣传活动，利用政府机关和化工园区公共电子屏幕，以及门户网站、微信群等平台，发布宣传海报、普及履约知识、讲解监控化学品管理工作，广泛开展履约宣传。

培训

2023年5月16日，组织开展禁化武履约工作专题培训，并通过培训效果测试，择优选拔一批省级履约专家。10月10日—11日，在吉林市吉化北方联腾化工有限公司开展了2023年度吉林省接受禁化武组织现场视察演练，各地区工业和信息化局禁化武履约工作分管领导、具体负责人员及省内第二类、第三类监控化学品企业参加了演练。通过本次演练，进一步提高各市（州）对禁化武履约工作的重视程度，监控化学品企业履约主体的责任意识也得到加强。12月6日—7日，在敦化市召开全省监控化学品企业宣布培训会议，邀请国家履约专家委专家现场授课，指导企业认真申报过去活动年度宣布数据，并按照履约新要求做好视察的各项准备工作。

（撰稿　马力利　韩星）

黑龙江省

组织协调

2023年，黑龙江省禁化武办按照国家禁化武办统一部署，认真抓好履约各项任务落实，结合黑龙江省的实际情况印发了《2023年履行〈禁止化学武器公约〉工作要点》，要求各地严格审核行政许可申请，加大事中事后的监管力度，督促企业打好履约工作的基础，高标准做好年度宣布工作，积极开展履约宣传。

数据宣布与接受视察

2023 年，在我国向禁化武组织提交的 2022 年过去活动年度宣布中，黑龙江省有宣布设施 20 个。2024 年预计活动年度宣布中，黑龙江省有宣布设施 5 个。

2023 年，禁化武组织没有对黑龙江省监控化学品企业进行现场视察。

监督管理

2023 年，黑龙江省禁化武办贯彻落实省政府统一部署，将监控化学品行政许可事项全部入驻黑龙江政务服务网，严格按照《公约》《条例》《细则》等有关规定开展行政执法活动。黑龙江省禁化武办印发《关于监控化学品企业申报行政许可工作流程的通知》，对行政许可名称、申报工作流程和实施规范进行详细说明，并提供办理行政许可的工作流程图。全年审核上报监控化学品生产设施建设审批申请 5 项，组织监控化学品生产设施竣工验收 2 项，审批监控化学品生产特别许可申请（含届满延续）4 项，完成监控化学品进口审批最终用途审查 1 项。

宣传

2023 年是《公约》开放签署 30 周年，4 月 29 日是第 8 个国际禁止化学武器组织日，黑龙江省禁化武办抓住契机，组织全省各级履约主管部门和监控化学品企业在门户网站、微信公众号等渠道，办公大楼、生产厂区等地，通过电子屏、知识展板、条幅和视频等多种形式开展广泛宣传，营造良好的履约宣传氛围，进一步提升全社会对禁化武履约工作在维护世界和平和国家安全方面的重要性的认识，增加社会各界对《公约》的关注度，全面提高监控化学品生产企业的履约意识和工作水平。

培训

3 月，黑龙江省禁化武办组织专家到 3 个地市对监控化学品企业进行专项培训指导，帮助企业提高履约能力。12 月 25 日，组织召开了 2023 年过去活动年度宣布培训，有关地市禁化武办工作负责同志和监控化学品企业履约负责人共计 50 余人参加培训。通过本次培训，企业宣布数据报送质量和各地禁化武办审核质量均有较大提升。

专项工作

按照国家禁化武办的要求，黑龙江省禁化武办对 2022 年 5 月 1 日—2023 年 5 月 31 日的监控化学品生产特别许可审批和备案情况开展自查，均符合有关要求。

（**撰稿** 陈显光 张英伟）

上海市

组织协调

2023 年，上海市禁化武办认真贯彻国家禁化武办的任务部署，组织协调履约成员单位，扎实推进各项履约工作。继续深化行政审批改革，不断优化行政审批流程，加强完善监控化学品管理平台建设，提高行政许可办理效率，提升企业服务的满意度。严格依法规范行政许可，严谨审查许可材料，严肃对待现场验收，提高行政许可和审查质量，切实发挥源头管控作用。督促企业认真填写禁化武数据申报与宣布系统，按照要求及时、准确提交宣布数据。开展监控化学品专项监督检查工作，督促企业完善接受国际视察预案，扎实做好各项准备工作，增强企业的履约意识，提高企业的履约能力。

数据宣布与接受视察

2023年，在我国向禁化武组织提交的2022年过去活动年度宣布中，上海市有宣布设施29个。2024年预计活动年度宣布中，上海市有宣布设施9个。

2023年，禁化武组织对上海金力泰化工股份有限公司的第二类监控化学品消耗设施进行现场视察。企业顺利通过了现场视察。

监督管理

依法加强对监控化学品设施建设、生产、经营、使用活动的管理，及时组织专家对相关企业提交的许可申请进行审查。2023年，组织监控化学品生产设施竣工验收2项，审批监控化学品生产特别许可申请1项、经营许可证申请1项、使用许可证申请5项，完成监控化学品进口审批最终用途审查60项，并根据合同检查企业销售、使用等原始记录台账，切实把好防扩散关口。

宣传

认真贯彻依法办事的行政理念，深入广泛开展监控化学品领域的普法教育宣传工作。在“4·29国际禁止化学武器组织日”期间，以电子屏滚动播放、电子海报、微信公众号等多种渠道和形式，在上海市政府集中办公点进行普法宣传。此外，通过上海市经济和信息化委员会官方网站向社会广泛宣传《公约》履约知识和上海市履约工作情况，进一步增强企业的履约责任感和自觉性。

培训

组织开展2023年履约工作专题培训，邀请上海市禁化武专家，从禁化武组织、法律法规、工作实践、操作程序、审查标准等方面进行解读，要求企业认真学习，细化落实责任。印制《监控化学品管理常用法律法规汇编》并向企业发放，夯实履约的工作基础，提高企业履约的工作能力。

专项工作

深入开展监控化学品专项监督检查工作。对企业的《视察前情况介绍》、物料平衡计算、生产原始记录、原料产品购买及出入库记录、产品销售台账、生产能力评估及产量统计台账等方面加强检查，共完成 2 家企业的专项检查。针对专项检查暴露出的问题，要求企业及时整改，持续完善，不断提高履约的工作能力。推荐上海赛科石油化工有限责任公司为禁化武组织化工研修班实习企业。

（**撰稿** 陆寅　刘元东）

江苏省

组织协调

江苏省根据国家禁化武办 2023 年履约工作要求和江苏省履约工作的实际情况，系统谋划，在认真做好年度数据宣布、接受国际视察、行政许可和宣传培训等常规工作的基础上，组织开展监控化学品专项排查整治、编制《视察前情况介绍》范本等系列活动，完善化工园区履约管理机制，推动成立江苏省监控化学品工作促进会，省、市、县（区）政府主管部门不断加强规范管理，广大企业积极主动履约的意识和能力大幅提高。

数据宣布与接受视察

2023 年，在我国向禁化武组织提交的 2022 年过去活动年度宣布中，江苏省有宣布设施157个。2024年预计活动年度宣布中，江苏省有宣布设施40个。

2023年，禁化武组织先后对扬州晨化新材料股份有限公司的第二类监控化学品生产设施，淮安华源化工有限公司的第三类监控化学品生产设施和利民化学有限责任公司的第四类监控化学品生产设施进行现场视察。3家企业均顺利通过了现场视察。

监督管理

一是进一步规范行政许可。2023年，审核上报监控化学品生产设施建设审批申请13项，组织监控化学品生产设施竣工验收7项，审批监控化学品生产特别许可申请27项、第二类监控化学品使用许可申请10项、第二类监控化学品经营许可申请1项。为提高行政许可事项申请材料的编写质量，江苏省工业和信息化厅组织专家对企业编写的材料进行事前预审，同时加强对许可事项申报材料内容的审核，高质量完成监控化学品行政许可事项受理和转报审批工作。

二是开展事中事后监管。江苏省工业和信息化厅根据行政许可监管工作的要求，强化事中事后监督管理，确保相关监控化学品建设项目、生产特别许可、监控化学品进口过程环节合法合规。

宣传

江苏省工业和信息化厅认真组织“4·29国际禁止化学武器组织日”的宣传活动，推动禁化武履约工作深入车间和班组。发动企业干部职工近1.1万人次参加国家禁化武办举办的在线禁化武履约普法知识竞赛，参赛人次位居全国前列。江苏省内监控化学品企业在厂区宣传栏、电子屏幕播放禁化武履约宣传标语、视频。各设区市分别结合各地的实际情况，在机关办公场所、社区街道、企业和学校开展化学知识、环境污染治理、和平利用化学的演讲或海报展示等活动，进一步扩大履约工作的影响力。

培训

为进一步提高各设区市主管部门的管理水平和企业的履约能力，2023年7月，江苏省禁化武办在南京市举办了全省禁化武履约综合培训班，本次培训以面向主管部门工作人员和企业为主，邀请履约专家授课，通过介绍监控化学品行政许可审查的主要问题，把行政许可要求讲深讲透；通过企业专家现场讲解生产、分析数据采集统计方法、常见问题及解决策略，了解履约工作对企业日常管理的具体要求。各设区市也举办了培训班，交流热烈、精彩纷呈。苏州市组织辖区内市、县主管部门和履约企业赴湖北省开展学习交流，并聘请外省专家开展指导。南通市、扬州市组织本地培训持续巩固履约基础，企业参与度进一步提高。泰州市开展视察演练活动，组织辖区内企业前往省内常熟氟化工园区、南通江山农药化工股份有限公司进行现场学习，取得良好效果。

专项工作

一是开展监控化学品违规项目建设和生产专项排查整治。为切实纠正监控化学品违规建设和生产行为，根据国家禁化武办的统一要求，江苏省工业和信息化厅组织各设区市对所有已建、在建化工项目逐一排查，梳理出未批先建的项目清单，组织3批工作组逐一上门核实，对核实的违规建设和生产行为提出责令改正的要求，经过4个月的排查整治，全省共发现和核实违规建设及生产监控化学品项目97个，全部按照《条例》《细则》有关要求实施整改。按照年度计划持续开展监控化学品“双随机、一公开”执法检查活动，全年对16家企业进行现场检查，发现企业在生产数据统计、宣布数据、《视察前情况介绍》编制修订等方面的问题32项，全部反馈各设区市并督促整改到位，进一步规范全省数据统计方法，宣布数据错误率持续降低，各企业的《视察前情况介绍》文本制作水平向示范文本目标迈进。

二是组织宣布数据申报工作事前预审和事后“回头看”。探索宣布数据事前预审，防止企业漏报车间和化学品，规范填报厂区信息。完成宣布数据工作后，省、市、县分级组织专家对企业的宣布数据进行“回头看”，及时纠正形式审查中不易发现的车间数目不正确、数据链不完整、宣布数据和实际生产数据不一致的问题。

三是组织《视察前情况介绍》范本编制。为全省企业做好接受视察准备工作打好基础，组织40余家磷化工、农药、医药等细分领域企业开展《视察前情况介绍》文本编写，并初步评选出23家企业编写的文本作为示范文本，邀请省内外专家、重点企业代表进行评审，进一步加深专家、企业对《视察前情况介绍》的结构和内容要求的理解，从被动接受视察迈向主动准备接受视察。

四是参与国际履约合作，推荐扬子石化—巴斯夫有限责任公司为禁化武组织化工研修班实习企业。

（撰稿　马勇良　陈忠明）

浙江省

组织协调

为确保履约各项工作顺利开展，浙江省禁化武办年初转发《国家禁化武办关于印发2023年履行〈禁止化学武器公约〉工作要点的通知》，并就浙江省做好禁化武履约工作提出五点要求。一是规范视察预案，积极应对国际视察。随着现场视察次数大幅增长，浙江省禁化武办编制《视察前情况介绍》范本，要求各地制定本地区《接受禁化武组织现场视察工作预案》，督促有关企业编制《视察前情况介绍》，规范管理各类数据资料，加强生产管理，做好接受现场视察的各项准备工作，确保顺利通过国际视察。二是严格依法行政，落实监督管理职责。按照“放管服”改革要求，制定细化行政许可实施规范。开展分类监督检查，对第二类、第三类监控化学品企业全覆盖检查，对第四类监控化学品生产企业实行“双随机、一公开”执法检查。各级经济和信息化部门加强事中事后监管要求，督促和指导企业做好禁化武数据宣布和监控化学品行政许可审查审批工作，防范化解履约的风险和隐患。三是开展普法宣传，树立主动履约理念。要求各地要结合本地的实际情况，创新宣传方式，加强工业履约和化工安全宣传，提高全社会对履行《公约》重要性的认识。开展形式多样的培训活动，深入宣传贯彻《条例》《细则》，促进企业树立社会责任意识、安全安保意识和履约主体意识，营造主动履约的良好社会氛围。四是加强组织保障，健全履约管理体系。要求各地加强履约工作领导，根据《细则》的有关要求，抓好履约工作体系和队伍建设，为做好履约工作提供组织保障。五是充实专家队伍，构建履约支撑平台。浙江省禁化武办不断优化充实履约专家队伍，完善相关工作机制，加强国际组织职员后备人才选拔培养和推送工作，组织化工相关专业技术人员参与履约培训，着力构建稳固的履约技术支撑平台。各地充分发挥履约专家队伍的作用，帮助企业提高技术能力和管理水平，夯实履约工作的基础。

数据宣布与接受视察

2023 年，在我国向禁化武组织提交的 2022 年过去活动年度宣布中，浙江省有宣布设施 179 个。2024 年预计活动年度宣布中，浙江省有宣布设施 20 个。

2023 年，禁化武组织先后对浙江科达新型建材有限公司、浙江万盛股份有限公司的第二类监控化学品加工设施，浙江沙星科技股份有限公司的第四类监控化学品生产设施，永农生物科学有限公司的第二类监控化学品消耗设施，以及浙江医药股份有限公司昌海生物分公司、台州达辰药业有限公司、浙江华海药业股份有限公司临海川南分公司的第四类监控化学品生产设施进行现场视察。7 家企业均顺利通过了现场视察。

监督管理

为深化“放管服”改革优化营商环境，根据《浙江省全面实行行政许可事项清单管理工作实施方案》的要求，细化完善第二类、第三类和含磷、硫、氟的第四类监控化学品的生产设施建设审核、竣工验收、生产特别许可，第二类监控化学品经营许可，第一类、第二类监控化学品使用许可，变质或者过期失效监控化学品处理方案审批 6 项行政许可实施规范，编制新版办事指南，严格依照清单实施行政许可，形成全省统筹、分级负责、事项统一、权责清晰的监控化学品行政许可事项清单体系。认真贯彻执行《条例》《细则》的有关要求，依法加强对监控化学品设施建设、生产、使用、进口等活动的事中事后监管，全年审核上报监控化学品生产设施建设审批申请 66 项，组织监控化学品生产设施竣工验收 5 项，审批监控化学品生产特别许可申请 63 项、监控化学品使用许可申请 5 项，完成监控化学品进口审批最终用途审查 24 项。

根据《中华人民共和国行政处罚法》《国务院办公厅关于进一步规范行政裁量权基准制定和管理工作的意见》和《关于行政裁量权基准制定和管理的工作指引的通知》的规定和要求，对未经批准，新建、扩建或改建用于生产监控化学品设施的违法行为，违法生产监控化学品的行为，违法使用监控化学品的行为，违法经营监控化学品的行为，违法隐瞒、拒报有关监控化学品的资料、数据的行为，拒绝履行接受国际视察义务的行为，未按规定保存、移交有关监控化学品的生产、使用记录的违法行为 7 项行政处罚事项，统一表述规则，细化违法行为表现形式，合理设置裁量阶次，清晰行政处罚依据，细化明确裁量标准和适用条件，制定了新版本《浙江省监控化学品行政处罚裁量基准》。

宣传

结合 2023 年《公约》开放签署 30 周年和第 8 个国际禁止化学武器组

织日，积极部署和组织开展履约主题宣传活动和普法教育。一是征集第 8 个国际禁止化学武器组织日主题宣传海报。支持指导浙江工业大学参与海报征集，选出 7 幅海报报送至国家禁化武办，其中 6 幅海报作品入围线上评选环节。二是积极参与禁化武履约宣传普法知识竞赛。组织动员浙江省履约干部、履约企业和相关高校等 3836 人参加国家禁化武办举办的在线禁化武履约普法知识竞赛。三是多平台多方式开展禁化武履约工作宣传。4 月 29 日，在微信公众号“浙江经信”推送“履行公约，为世界和平担当尽责，为共同发展贡献力量”宣传信息，在微信公众号“浙江工业大学”“宁波经信”“宁波石化协会”相继推送履约新闻内容。在浙江省经济和信息化厅官网首页开设禁化武履约宣传专栏。浙江省、市、县经济和信息化部门联动，在行政中心、高校、履约企业布置展板、张贴宣传海报、滚动播放履约宣传册和宣传视频，加强工业履约宣传，推动企业增强守法履约的主动性，提高社会公众对禁化武履约的认知度，营造良好的履约环境。

培训

为提高企业履约的积极性和主动性，规范企业的履约行为，提升浙江省履约管理的水平，开展分层次、分类型的履约培训工作。一是组织市级禁化武办参加国家禁化武办举办的履约综合培训班，帮助地方履约工作主管部门及时了解国内外履约新形势、新动态，掌握禁化武法律法规，并运用《公约》赋予缔约国的权利，履行《公约》规定的义务，维护好我国负责任的大国形象，同时最大限度地保护企业的利益。二是继续推进禁化武履约培训教材的学习应用。选派专家分赴杭州市、宁波市、温州市、衢州市、台州市 5 地宣讲，合计约 450 人参加培训。三是结合生产特别许可考核和监督检查工作，现场指导企业建立健全生产记录、出入库记录和销售记录等原始记录和台账，规范工艺技术标准和操作规程，指导和督促企业加强生产管理和制度建设，不断提升企业履约的能力。

专项工作

为加强禁化武履约和监控化学品管理工作，推进相关行业高质量发展，守住国家安全底线。2023 年 2 月，国家禁化武办、外交部军控司赴浙江省调研国际视察和工业履约工作。3 月，国家禁化武办、国家履约专家委赴浙江省调研禁化武履约工作，并在杭州市召开国家履行《禁止化学武器公约》专家委员会第二次全体会议，在浙江工业大学莫干山校区召开专家委专题研讨会。调研组充分肯定了浙江省禁化武履约和监控化学品管理工作所取得的成效，并就进一步做好履约工作提出要求。

深入开展监控化学品领域"互联网 + 监管"工作，在浙江省行政执法监管平台持续推进跨层级的监控化学品"双随机、一公开"监管机制。第一季度，公布 2023 年度监控化学品"双随机、一公开"执法检查计划。第二季度，迭代更新监控化学品监管信息，细化抽查任务，完成信用规则设置、检查对象和检查人员抽取、任务分发等工作。第三季度和第四季度，开展省市联合监控化学品"双随机、一公开"执法检查，11 月底完成检查任务。2023 年，随机抽取 9 家监控化学品企业和相关执法检查人员，检查对象涉及杭州市、宁波市、温州市、衢州市、台州市 5 个市辖区的企业，全省 10 个市禁化武办参与执法检查，通过"浙政钉 • 掌上执法"系统录入检查结果，做好结果公示，督查工作做到操作透明、程序规范、公开及时。

做好杭州第 19 届亚运会服务保障工作。亚运会前夕，浙江省禁化武办会同杭州市、宁波市、嘉兴市、绍兴市、金华市、衢州市、台州市 7 个市禁化武办对 29 家的第二类、第三类监控化学品生产、使用企业及监控化学品进口经营企业进行专项监督检查，对存在的问题限期整改，属地经济和信息化局负责整改情况再检查，落实闭环管理，护航杭州亚运会成功举办。

做好现场视察的复盘工作，不断完善《视察前情况介绍》范本，在全省推广应用，指导帮助企业做好接受国际视察及国内现场检查、考核的各项准备工作。

（撰稿　沈忠平　朱小庆）

安徽省

组织协调

2023 年 7 月 12 日，安徽省禁化武办召开安徽省禁化武履约工作会议，有关市、县履约工作主管部门负责人，以及履约企业的设施代表和数据宣布人员参加会议。

数据宣布与接受视察

2023 年，在我国向禁化武组织提交的 2022 年过去活动年度宣布中，安徽省有宣布设施 36 个。2024 年预计活动年度宣布中，安徽省有宣布设施 7 个。

2023 年，禁化武组织没有对安徽省监控化学品企业进行现场视察。

监督管理

2023 年，安徽省禁化武办审核上报监控化学品生产设施建设审批申请 4 项，组织监控化学品生产设施竣工验收 2 项，审批监控化学品生产特别许可申请 3 项。

宣传

积极开展“4 • 29 国际禁止化学武器组织日”宣传活动。在全省各级履约主管部门、履约企业、相关大专院校化工学院开展广泛宣传，征集履约宣传海报和短视频宣传作品。组织各级履约主管部门、履约企业工作人员参加国家禁化武办举办的在线禁化武履约普法知识竞赛，提高从业人员对履约工作重要性的认识。深入履约企业宣讲履约政策，发放禁化武宣传手册，指导企业做好禁化武履约工作。

培训

2023 年 7 月 13 日—14 日，安徽省禁化武办在六安市霍山县举办安徽省禁化武履约工作培训班，有关市、县履约工作主管部门负责人，以及履约企业的设施代表和数据宣布人员 100 余人参加培训。培训班邀请禁化武履约专家解读当前国际国内履约形势，讲解接受禁化武组织现场视察的有关注意事项，履约企业代表作视察前情况介绍演练。此次培训进一步增强了安徽省监控化学品企业履约的意识，切实提高了安徽省监控化学品企业做好数据宣布、接受国际视察等履约工作的能力。

专项工作

全年对 3 家监控化学品企业开展“双随机、一公开”执法检查。

（撰稿　苏凯　唐旭）

福建省

组织协调

为进一步加强监控化学品管理，做好履行《公约》工作，印发了《福建省 2023 年履行〈禁止化学武器公约〉工作要点》，明确年度目标任务，全面夯实履约基础，提高监管效能。

数据宣布与接受视察

2023 年，在我国向禁化武组织提交的 2022 年过去活动年度宣布中，福建省有宣布设施 47 个。2024 年预计活动年度宣布中，福建省有宣布设施 9 个。

2023 年，禁化武组织没有对福建省监控化学品企业进行现场视察。

监督管理

在日常监督管理方面，福建省主要抓好 4 个方面的工作。一是不断完善制度建设。对照国家行政审批目录，更新和完善 10 项涉及监控化学品的行政服务事项，形成相对完善的行政审批机制。二是积极服务企业，指导企业做好行政许可有关事项。全年共审核上报监控化学品生产设施建设审批申请 11 项，组织监控化学品生产设施竣工验收 7 项，审批监控化学品生产特别许可申请 5 项、监控化学品使用许可申请 1 项、监控化学品经营许可申请 1 项，完成监控化学品进口审批最终用途审查 28 项。三是积极做好防扩散工作。加强对监控化学品进口企业——福州特威化工有限公司的管理，督促企业强化进口监控化学品管控，规范监控化学品的经营活动。四是强化日常监督检查，完成对 12 家企业日常监督检查，下发 2 份整改通知书。

宣传

积极开展禁化武相关普法宣传工作。一是认真组织开展线上宣传工作，在福建省内各级工业和信息化部门门户网站、微信公众号发布禁化武有关的普法宣传海报和专题知识，提升线上宣传的覆盖率。二是开展专题宣传活动，组织福州市、龙岩市、南平市等地市工业和信息化部门，围绕“4・29 国际禁止化学武器组织日”，以履约普法知识竞赛、志愿者服务队进社区、企业家微信群平台等方式开展禁化武组织日专题宣传。活动期间，福建全省工业和信息化系统共举办各类线下宣传活动 7 场，发放宣传资料 500 余份，参加禁化武履约普法知识线上答题达 1800 人次，营造了良好的履约宣传氛围。

培训

2023 年 9 月 21 日—22 日，在福建省南平市邵武市举办了全省禁化武履约工作专题培训班，各级工业和信息化部门、重点履约企业近 100 人参加。培训班以“视察演练 + 专题讲座”方式，视察演练按照接受禁化武组织视察流程规范，从《视察前情况介绍》、现场巡视和文件检查 3 个方面，对视察整体流程、视察准备资料、视察过程中可能提出的问题进行全方位演练。专题讲座围绕履约基础知识、当前履约形势分析和履约工作要点等内容进行了细致讲解。通过此次培训，各级工业和信息化部门有关同志和重点企业主管人员熟悉了禁化武组织现场视察流程和模式，提升了履约知识水平，福建省禁化武履约基础管理工作得到进一步规范，为接受禁化武组织现场视察打下了良好的基础。

专项工作

2023 年 4 月—11 月，以“服务、宣传、培训”等线下现场指导为主，开展了为期 8 个月的履约宣贯“敲门行动”，实现服务化工园区 4 家，上门服务重点企业 25 家，通过开展履约宣贯“敲门行动”，进一步延伸对相关企业的服务触角，提升基层的专业技术水平，实现省、市、县三级联动服务圈，有效减轻企业履约的负担，降低履约的风险。通过“双随机、一公开”执法检查方式加强对企业的监督抽查，2023 年共抽查了 3 家企业，指导企业加强监控化学品日常生产、经营等管理工作。

（**撰稿**　罗天进　余陈荣）

江西省

组织协调

2023 年，江西省禁化武办在江西省人民政府和国家禁化武办的坚强领导下，按照江西省工业和信息化厅党组的工作部署，认真做好江西省禁化武履约的各项工作。江西省工业和信息化厅党组高度重视禁化武履约工作，主要领导及分管领导多次强调要抓好监管、培训、接受国际视察等基础性工作，持续提高江西省禁化武履约工作的能力和水平。江西省禁化武办会同全省各级工业和信息化主管部门及监控化学品企业，切实履行《公约》义务，扎实工作，团结奋进，圆满完成了年度禁化武履约的各项工作。

数据宣布与接受视察

2023 年，在我国向禁化武组织提交的 2022 年过去活动年度宣布中，江西省有宣布设施 31 个。2024 年预计活动年度宣布中，江西省有宣布设施 15 个。

2023 年，禁化武组织先后对江西名成科技发展有限公司和江西理文化工有限公司的第二类监控化学品生产、消耗设施进行现场视察。2 家企业均顺利通过了现场视察。

监督管理

2023 年，江西省禁化武办审核上报监控化学品生产设施建设审批申请 8 项，组织监控化学品生产设施竣工验收 8 项，审批监控化学品生产特别许可申请 10 项、监控化学品使用许可申请 1 项。

为进一步提高工作效率，江西省禁化武办将“一网通办”材料审核办结时限调整为 8 个工作日，较以往减少 1 个工作日。针对监控化学品企业申请事项，均按规定组建专家审查组，严格按程序完成各项审查工作。在开展禁化武组织现场视察演练活动时，落实事中事后监督管理的要求，对 1 家企业未严格落实有关行政许可手续问题，江西省禁化武办向其下发了整改通知书，责令企业按照要求整改。

宣传

2023 年，根据国家禁化武办的要求，制定下发了《江西省禁化武办关于开展第 8 个国际禁止化学武器组织日主题宣传海报征集活动的通知》，广泛宣传征集主题海报，并按要求上报国家禁化武办，其中南昌市工业和信息化局、南昌市红谷滩区科技和工业信息化局、江西惠南新材料科技有限公司等上报的海报，受到国家禁化武办的表扬并发放了证书。

此外，江西省禁化武办还通过微信工作群及时转发在线履约普法知识竞赛的有关工作，组织动员各级工业和信息化部门履约工作人员和监控化学品企业积极参与网上答题。按照要求及时向国家禁化武办报送江西省禁化武履约工作信息，其中 5 篇信息被《履行〈禁止化学武器公约〉工作简报》采用。

培训

2023 年 7 月 25 日，江西省禁化武办在南昌市召开了江西省禁化武履约工作培训会议，市、县（区）工业和信息化部门及监控化学品企业共 110 余人参加了培训。培训期间，通报了 2022 年江西省禁化武组织现场视察演练情况，部署了 2023 年视察演练工作，解读了禁化武履约政策，江西名成科技发展有限公司就做好接受视察工作做了经验交流。同时，还邀请了禁化武履约专家就接受视察进行专题讲座。这次培训增强了江西省禁化武履约队伍的履约意识，有效提升业务工作的能力和水平，为做好禁化武履约工作奠定了良好基础。

2023 年 8 月，根据工作需要，江西省禁化武办更新并扩充了江西省禁化武履约专家库的人员力量，目前共有 44 人。9 月 7 日，在南昌市召开了江西省禁化武履约专家培训班，共 30 余名禁化武履约专家参加了培训。培训重点讲解了履约法律法规和政策文件，2 名禁化武履约专家分别就做好接受国际视察、行政许可有关事项现场审查工作进行授课。

专项工作

2023 年 10 月，江西省禁化武办组织开展了禁化武组织现场视察演练活动。活动期间，江西省禁化武办组织省内禁化武履约专家，参照国际视察的相关要求，对 11 家监控化学品企业开展视察演练。禁化武履约专家认真听取企业视察前情况介绍、查阅核对相关资料，并对监控化学品生产、加工、消耗设施等进行现场巡视，仔细核实宣布信息，逐个指出存在的问题，并提出整改建议。为巩固视察演练成果，增强企业履约主体的责任意识，进一步提升禁化武履约的能力和水平，江西省禁化武办将视察演练发现的问题建立清单，印发《关于进一步督促指导监控化学品企业做好履约有关工作的通知》，要求有关设区市工业和信息化局督促指导相关企业抓好问题整改。截至 2023 年 12 月底，视察演练中发现的 71 个问题均已完成整改。

（撰稿　王海军）

山东省

组织协调

2023 年，山东省禁化武办组织各市、县（区）及监控化学品企业，履行《公约》义务，贯彻《条例》规定，按照国家禁化武办的工作部署开展各项履约工作。组织协调省有关部门、市工业和信息化部门及企业接受国际视察。

数据宣布与接受视察

2023 年，在我国向禁化武组织提交的 2022 年过去活动年度宣布中，山东省有宣布设施 304 个。2024 年预计活动年度宣布中，山东省有宣布设施 50 个。

2023 年，禁化武组织先后对山东滨农科技有限公司、聊城氟尔新材料科技有限公司的第二类监控化学品生产、消耗设施，山东国邦药业有限公司、山东普洛得邦医药有限公司的第四类监控化学品生产设施，山东化学股份有限公司、山东海江化工有限公司的第三类监控化学品生产设施，以及潍坊加华化工有限公司、山东海利尔化工有限公司的第四类监控化学品生产设施进行现场视察。8 家企业均顺利通过了现场视察。

监督管理

按照《条例》的要求，及时开展监控化学品日常监管工作，审核上报监控化学品生产设施建设审批申请 35 项，组织监控化学品生产设施竣工验收 24 项，审批监控化学品生产特别许可申请 33 项、监控化学品使用许可申请 8 项，完成监控化学品进口审批最终用途审查 4 项。

对辖区内监控化学品企业的情况进行调查，对设施建设和生产特别许可有缺失的进行整改和补办相关手续，对企业办理各类行政许可事项进行辅导和服务。认真审核监控化学品进出口事项，有效管控各类监控化学品用于和平的目的。

宣传

积极参与国家禁化武举办的在线禁化武履约普法知识竞赛，下发文件，通过微信群、短视频等新媒体手段宣传履约活动。充分调动基层履约机构加强履约宣传，广泛印发宣传册、海报。向应该提交宣布和办理设施建设等行政许可事项的企业，宣传《公约》《条例》《细则》的相关规定，敦促企业办理许可事项。

培训

2023 年 3 月 29 日—31 日，山东省禁化武办在淄博市组织各市县（区）、重点企业以视频会议方式开展山东省重点监控化学品企业接受国际视察准备工作培训，讲解当前国际形势，通报山东省 2022 年以来履约工作情况和履约业务，开展接受国际视察准备工作专题讲座，组织企业设施代表分享经验、展开交流，并就履约工作答疑。

9 月 14 日，山东省禁化武办召开全省禁化武履约工作视频会议，传达国家禁化武办通知通报精神和工作要求，安排部署下一步的重点工作。山东省各市、县工业和信息化部门禁化武履约工作分管负责同志、有关科（处、室）全体人员及监控化学品企业设施代表和数据申报人员共计 700 余人参会。

10 月 13 日，山东省禁化武办在潍坊市召开全省禁化武履约专题培训会议，就履约知识进行培训，其他市工业和信息化部门和监控化学品企业线上参训。

12 月 26 日，山东省禁化武办召开全省禁化武履约工作视频会议，全面总结全年履约工作的情况，部署 2023 年过去活动年度宣布工作，安排下一年的重点工作。

专项工作

按照国家、省级人民政府和各级工业和信息化部门的要求，对全省 25 家监控化学品企业进行“双随机、一公开”执法检查，敦促企业完善日常监管，提高履约工作水平。

（**撰稿**　许永利　田晓慧　王思官）

河南省

组织协调

为了全面推进各项履约工作开展，河南省禁化武办组织各市级禁化武办和监控化学品企业认真落实《条例》《细则》的要求，履行《公约》的义务。一是印发了《2023 年河南省履行〈禁止化学武器公约〉工作要点》，详细布置全年的履约工作任务。二是举办了全省监控化学品工作会，全面提升履约的能力。三是出台了《关于组织开展第 8 个国际禁止化学武器组织日宣传活动的通知》，扩大履约工作的社会影响力。四是完成全省数据宣布工作任务。

数据宣布与接受视察

2023 年，在我国向禁化武组织提交的 2022 年过去活动年度宣布中，河南省有宣布设施 66 个。2024 年预计活动年度宣布中，河南省有宣布设施 12 个。

2023 年，禁化武组织先后对河南九势制药股份有限公司的第二类监控化学品生产、消耗设施和新乡市瑞丰新材料股份有限公司的第四类监控化学品生产设施进行现场视察。2 家企业均顺利通过了现场视察。

监督管理

一是依法依规落实行政许可事项。河南省禁化武办依据《条例》《细则》的规定依法对监控化学品生产设施建设、竣工验收、生产特别许可等事项进行审核和审批。2023 年，审核上报监控化学品生产设施建设审批申请 5 项，审批监控化学品生产特别许可申请 9 项。

二是强化监控化学品进口监管工作。做好对第三类监控化学品三乙醇胺的进口审查工作，严防非法转让。2023 年完成第三类监控化学品进口审批最终用途审查 2 项。

宣传

河南省禁化武办下发了《关于组织开展第 8 个国际禁止化学武器组织日宣传活动的通知》，广泛宣传履约工作的重要意义和丰硕成果，提高全社会对履约工作的认知程度。一是河南省禁化武办于 4 月 29 日通过电子屏宣传主题词和易拉宝展览宣传页等形式在单位大厅进行宣传，向全厅工作人员展示了一年来禁化武工作取得的成果。二是在河南省工业和信息化厅门户网站和微信公众号对外发布宣传了第 8 个国际禁止化学武器组织日的活动，扩大了履约宣传的效果。三是通过中国电信、中国移动和中国联通三大运营商向全省发布了履约公益短信，取得了较好的社会宣传效果。

培训

为了扎实做好全省监控化学品管理工作，河南省禁化武办于 8 月 31 日在郑州市召开了 2023 年全省监控化学品工作会，省辖市履约主管部门分管领导和第二类、第三类、第四类监控化学品重点企业负责人共约 120 人参加了会议。会议结合全省近两年企业接受国际视察的实际经验，详细讲解了《视察前情况介绍》、视察现场准备要点和数据宣布等内容，增强了河南省履约机构和监控化学品企业的履约意识，提升了履约的能力，为下一步规范全省监控化学品管理工作，保障企业顺利通过国际视察打下坚实基础。

专项工作

根据上级要求，2023 年 8 月和 12 月分别对 5 家第三类监控化学品生产企业在遵守《条例》《细则》的情况、履行《公约》数据宣布和接受禁化武组织现场视察准备等情况，采取听取汇报、现场检查、查看资料等形式进行了执法检查，对存在的问题要求企业限期整改，降低了企业履约的风险。

（撰稿　赵建华　韩中星）

湖北省

组织协调

为加强湖北省监控化学品管理，促进监控化学品企业高质量发展，抓好履约各项任务的落实。湖北省禁化武办印发《湖北省禁化武履约2023工作要点》至市、县、区经济和信息化主管部门，促使全省禁化武履约工作进一步规范化和制度化，企业履约守法的意识得到加强。

数据宣布与接受视察

2023年，在我国向禁化武组织提交的2022年过去活动年度宣布中，湖北省有宣布设施63个。2024年预计活动年度宣布中，湖北省有宣布设施15个。

2023年，禁化武组织先后对湖北省襄阳金达成精细化工有限公司的第二类监控化学品生产设施，洪湖市一泰科技有限公司的第二类监控化学品生产、消耗设施进行现场视察。2家企业均顺利通过了现场视察。

监督管理

加强监控化学品的日常监管。一是严格监控化学品行政许可审核和审批，全年共计审核上报监控化学品生产设施建设审批申请13项，组织监控化学品生产设施竣工验收6项，审批监控化学品生产特别许可申请8项、监控化学品使用许可申请1项（法定代表人变更）。二是积极做好防扩散工作，认真做好监控化学品进口审批最终用途的审查工作。三是强化基础管理和制度建设，健全履约保证体系，制定《湖北省经信厅监控化学品企业履约日常监督管理工作方案》及起草情况说明。四是加大执法力度，严肃查处违规行为。湖北省禁化武办依据《条例》的规定，按照国家禁化武办的要求，对第二类、第三类和含磷、硫、氟的第四类监控化学品的设施建设、生产、经营、使用活动开展监督检查，对检查中发现问题的企业，下达整改通知书，限期整改，将其纳入合法的轨道。

扎实做好接受国际视察和视察演练的各项工作。一是指导省内2家监控化学品企业顺利通过禁化武组织现场视察。二是加强同省履约工作领导小组相关部门的协调配合，完善接受国际视察的工作机制。三是深入宜昌、襄阳、荆州等重点市和重点企业，检查企业接受国际视察各项准备工作的情况。四是组织对松滋市璐达科技有限公司和湖北丽源科技股份有限公司开展接受禁化武组织国际视察演练。

服务指导企业严格履约。组织专家赴市、县（区）开展履约技术咨询服务，赴监控化学品企业进行现场指导，依据《条例》《细则》和国家产业政策，加强对沿江监控化学品企业搬迁建设的业务指导。

宣传

以“4・29 国际禁止化学武器组织日”为契机，开展《公约》生效 30 周年纪念活动。翻印发送国家禁化武办制作的“4・29 国际禁止化学武器组织日”宣传画册，组织各市经济和信息化局以及监控化学品企业积极参加国家禁化武办举办的在线禁化武履约普法知识竞赛，进一步增强社会公众的履约意识，提高全社会对履约工作的认知度，扩大了禁化武履约工作的影响，取得了良好的效果。

培训

在湖北省襄阳市举办了 2023 年湖北省禁化武履约业务工作培训班，邀请 5 名省履约专家现场授课，印发《2023 湖北省禁化武履约工作培训教材》。培训教材贴近湖北省禁化武履约工作的实际，专家讲授深入浅出，授课内容富有知识性和指导性，培训深受广大企业的好评。

专项工作

加大专项监督检查力度。2023 年 9 月，接受国家禁化武办监控化学品生产特别许可督查。会同国家履约专家委在湖北省开展地方服务行活动。选派相关市经济和信息化局的同志与专家组成检查组赴荆州市、宜昌市的 7 家监控化学品企业开展专项监督检查，将监督检查中发现新增的 6 家监控化学品企业全部纳入了监管的范围。推动各地区交流学习，整体提升各级履约主管部门和企业履约的能力和水平，进一步夯实企业履约工作的基础。强化安全生产责任意识，从禁化武履约工作的角度对安全工作提出要求，真正把安全工作落到实处。

加强对协会的指导和履约专家队伍的建设。发挥协会在政府和企业间的桥梁纽带作用，做好“两个服务”。充实履约专家和人才库，来自高校、科研院所的24位专家入库，参与湖北省履约工作。组织召开专题会，邀请国家履约专家委委员对《新形势下省级及以下履约主管部门工作机制和方法及协会组织支撑作用研究》的课题进行论证。

（**撰稿** 郑晚亮 戴兰林）

湖南省

组织协调

湖南省工业和信息化厅领导高度重视湖南省禁化武履约和监控化学品管理工作，亲自部署、提前谋划、明确要求，每年主持召开禁化武履约工作培训班，要求不断增强履约意识和责任，认真做好数据宣布、接受视察、行政许可等工作。厅领导亲自谋划部署第8个国际禁止化学武器组织日宣传活动，带头参与线上答题，亲自组织协调相关院校、企业参与系列宣传活动。

数据宣布与接受视察

2023年，在我国向禁化武组织提交的2022年过去活动年度宣布中，湖南省有宣布设施23个。2024年预计活动年度宣布中，湖南省有宣布设施3个。

2023年，禁化武组织没有对湖南省监控化学品企业进行现场视察。

监督管理

一是优化行政审批流程。根据《湖南省加快推进“互联网＋政务服务”工作实施方案》和湖南省人民政府统一部署，湖南省工业和信息化厅对涉及监控化学品的行政审批和初审事项，全部按要求进驻“湘易办”超级服务端，实现了企业群众既可网上办理，又可“掌上办事”，加快推进监控化学品管理政务服务事项改革。二是认真开展行政许可。对申请监控化学品生产设施建设和生产特别许可的企业，严格按照工作流程，认真进行审核，并严格执行考核标准，组织专家现场考核。2023 年，组织监控化学品生产设施竣工验收 1 项，审批监控化学品生产特别许可申请 1 项。三是加强日常监管。严格依据《条例》《细则》对监控化学品设施建设、生产、进口等活动进行全程监管，积极做好防扩散工作，规范监控化学品生产企业的经营活动。四是 2023 年 6 月—7 月，根据国家禁化武办统一部署，湖南省禁化武办对 2022 年 6 月 1 日—2023 年 5 月 31 日期间监控化学品生产特别许可审批和备案情况开展全面自查。

宣传

2023 年 4 月 29 日是第 8 个国际禁止化学武器组织日，湖南省工业和信息化厅高度重视，分管副厅长亲自部署，在厅官网上发布活动宣传通知文件，组织厅属单位、厅内机关干部、省内高校化工学院、石化联合会、协会积极参与国家禁化武办举办的在线禁化武履约普法知识竞赛，各市州积极宣传发动，湖南省内累计参与答题人数 47000 余人，全国排名第一，占比达到 49.6%。制作 2 张宣传海报参与“地方禁化武履约工作巡礼”在线展览，并在厅机关大楼循环播放，集中展示湖南省履约工作精神风貌。探索将履约宣传融入日常工作的新模式和新思路，结合日常考察、调研、检查等工作开展履约普法宣传，提高履约宣传实效。

培训

为贯彻落实国家禁化武办有关文件精神，进一步增强湖南省工业和信息化系统、监控化学品生产企业的履约意识，切实提高湖南省履约能力，2023 年 12 月 13 日，湖南省工业和信息化厅举办了 2023 年湖南省禁化武工作培训班，各市州工业和信息化局分管负责人和有关县（区）工业和信息化局分管负责人、监控化学品生产企业的设施代表和数据宣布代表共 90 余人参加了培训。培训对湖南省内 2023 年禁化武履约工作进行了全面的总结和 2024 年工作进行了部署和安排，并对《公约》《条例》《细则》和《接受禁止化学武器组织现场视察工作规范（试行）》等进行系统学习和交流，切实提高湖南省履约工作能力和水平。

（**撰稿**　殷立科　汤旺）

广东省

组织协调

组织召开广东省履行《禁止化学武器公约》工作联席会议 2023 年全体会议，广东省工业和信息化厅厅长作为联席会议总召集人出席会议并讲话，会议通报了 2022 年广东省禁化武履约工作情况和省内企业接受国际禁化武组织现场视察情况，调整 14 家联席会议成员及联络员名单，健全履约工作体系，完善部门沟通机制，切实做好接受禁化武组织现场视察各项准备工作。

加强履约基础能力建设。结合国家禁化武办的最新要求，指导 23 家监控化学品企业完善《视察前情况介绍》，编制印发《企业〈视察前情况介绍〉编制要素指引》，指导地市工业和信息化主管部门、监控化学品企业积极准备接受禁化武组织现场视察。

数据宣布与接受视察

2023 年，在我国向禁化武组织提交的 2022 年过去活动年度宣布中，广东省有宣布设施 23 个。2024 年预计活动年度宣布中，广东省有宣布设施 11 个。

2023 年，禁化武组织没有对广东省监控化学品企业进行现场视察。

监督管理

对广东省监控化学品企业开展全覆盖监督检查，认真做好监控化学品全流程监管，发现宣布数据遗漏、台账不规范等问题，现场提出整改要求，强调逐级上报整改报告，强化提升地市、县级工业和信息化主管部门监督检查能力。

制定监控化学品设施竣工验收审核和生产特别许可审批工作流程指引，指导 7 家企业完成监控化学品生产特别许可材料的编制工作，审核上报监控化学品生产设施建设审批申请 2 项，组织监控化学品生产设施竣工验收 6 项，审批监控化学品生产特别许可申请 3 项、监控化学品使用许可申请 4 项，完成监控化学品进口审批最终用途审查 9 项。

宣传

采购禁化武履约相关法律法规文件汇编下发给各地市工业和信息化局并组织学习，加大履约普法宣传力度。制作“2022 年广东省禁化武履约工作情况”图文电子展板，参与国家禁化办举办的“地方禁化武履约工作巡礼”在线展览。2023 年 4 月 29 日，通过微信公众号、政务大屏、政务网站工作动态和业务发布等栏目公开宣传第 8 个国际禁止化学武器组织日主题宣传海报，同时向广东省内履约成员单位、各地市工业和信息化局、有关企业发放主题宣传海报。

培训

举办广东省“禁化武履约业务培训专题研修班”，针对履约企业负责人、设施代表和数据申报人等履约相关工作人员进行为期3天的培训，同时在相关企业开展现场教学活动。

（撰稿　李迎春　郑威　张莉）

广西壮族自治区

组织协调

广西壮族自治区履行《禁止化学武器公约》工作领导小组办公室设在广西壮族自治区工业和信息化厅。2023年，按照国家禁化武办工作要求，广西工业和信息化厅强化贯彻落实，严抓履约监管，从年度数据宣布、接受国际视察准备、加强履约监督管理、强化履约宣传培训、优化履约体系建设、发挥专家智库支撑作用等方面部署2023年履约工作，广西壮族自治区全区履约工作进一步规范化、制度化，企业履约守法意识进一步提升。

数据宣布与接受视察

2023年，在我国向禁化武组织提交的2022年过去活动年度宣布中，广西壮族自治区有宣布设施31个。2024年预计活动年度宣布中，广西壮族自治区有宣布设施1个。

2023年，禁化武组织没有对广西壮族自治区监控化学品企业进行现场视察。

监督管理

广西壮族自治区禁化武办继续加强对监控化学品生产设施建设、生产、经营、使用等活动管理。大力推进“减证便民”工作，按照“最多跑一次”的要求，进一步深化“互联网 + 政务服务”，优化行政审批流程，推进审批服务便民化。严格执行《条例》《细则》有关规定，审核上报监控化学品生产设施建设审批申请 2 项，审批监控化学品生产特别许可申请 2 项、第二类监控化学品使用许可申请 1 项。

宣传

创新履约宣传工作思路。以“4•29 国际禁止化学武器组织日”为契机，广西壮族自治区禁化武办精心筹划、认真准备宣传活动，利用海报、电子屏、新媒体等媒介向监控化学品企业、社会大众普及禁化武履约知识，广泛宣传禁化武履约工作的重要意义，取得了较好的效果。广西壮族自治区禁化武办印发《监控化学品管理文件汇编》给各市、县（区）履约主管部门、履约专家和履约重点企业，进一步增强其履约意识，提高其对履约工作的认知度，扩大了履约工作的影响力，取得了良好效果。

培训

2023 年 10 月 18 日—20 日，广西壮族自治区禁化武办在河池市举办了“2023 年全区禁化武履约能力提升培训班”，全区各级履约主管部门有关负责同志、监控化学品企业负责同志等 150 余人参加了培训。本次培训围绕禁化武履约基础知识、当前履约面临机遇与挑战及履约工作要点等方面进行授课，同时开展了禁化武组织国际视察演练。这次培训，进一步提升了广西壮族自治区各级履约主管部门及监控化学品企业的履约能力和工作水平，为接受禁化武组织现场视察打下坚实基础。

2023 年 12 月 11 日—12 日，广西壮族自治区禁化武办在南宁市举办了

“2023 年监控化学品企业《视察前情况介绍》情景模拟演练培训会”。广西壮族自治区各级履约主管部门有关负责同志、重点监控化学品企业负责同志及区内禁化武专家等 60 余人参加了培训会。通过培训，参加培训的人员学习了《视察前情况介绍》及接受国际视察准备等相关知识，切实提升了履约的能力和应对国际视察的水平。

（撰稿　彭忠　陈俊妃）

海南省

组织协调

2023 年，海南省工业和信息化厅印发《关于进一步加强 2023 年履行〈禁止化学武器公约〉工作的通知》，加强对履约工作的组织领导，层层落实责任，确保海南省履约各项工作顺利推进。向海南省履约企业宣贯《公约》《条例》《细则》《接受禁化武组织现场视察工作规范（试行）》《宣布手册》等履约法规和相关文件，夯实履约工作基础，充分做好接受禁化武组织现场视察各项工作准备。

数据宣布与接受视察

2023 年，在我国向禁化武组织提交的 2022 年过去活动年度宣布中，海南省有宣布设施 2 个。2024 年预计活动年度宣布中，海南省有宣布设施 1 个。

2023 年，禁化武组织没有对海南省监控化学品企业进行现场视察。

监督管理

一是制定《海南省监控化学品管理领域行政处罚裁量权基准》。从处罚依据和裁量因素及裁量基准方面，就监控化学品设施违规建设、生产、使用、经营和数据统计等方面进行裁量基准细化。健全行政裁量权基准制度，规范行使行政裁量权。二是督促监控化学品生产企业开展竣工验收。多次赴中海油富岛（海南）化工有限公司海南精细化工项目二期工程（丙烯腈系列装置）项目现场调研，督促企业加强管理，规范生产，尽快完善试生产数据，办理第三类监控化学品竣工验收审核手续。三是组织指导海南省监控化学品企业完成2022年过去活动年度宣布及2024年预计活动年度宣布工作。

宣传

对照国家禁化武办关于“4·29国际禁止化学武器组织日”宣传工作要求，海南省工业和信息化厅提前谋划，组织海南省工业和信息化部门及履约企业深入扎实做好本次系列宣传活动，制作海南省宣传海报并在厅机关大楼张贴，通过厅门户网站、微信公众号转发宣传内容，同时组织履约企业张贴宣传海报。

培训

海南省工业和信息化厅积极参加国家禁化武办举办的全国禁化武履约综合培训班及禁化武组织国际视察演练。深入海南省内监控化学品企业点对点开展学习培训，帮助企业了解国际禁化武履约形势，掌握接受国际视察知识和技能，完善监控化学品管理制度建设，不断夯实履约基础。

（撰稿　谢秋云　侯胜明）

重庆市

组织协调

组织重庆市监控化学品企业，向其普及《公约》《条例》《细则》《关于优化低浓度三乙醇胺混合物进出口监管措施的通知》等履约相关文件。

数据宣布与接受视察

2023年，在我国向禁化武组织提交的2022年过去活动年度宣布中，重庆市有宣布设施13个。2024年预计活动年度宣布中，重庆市有宣布设施6个。

2023年，禁化武组织没有对重庆市监控化学品企业进行现场视察。

监督管理

按照《重庆市人民政府办公厅关于在“渝快办”平台配置政务服务事项并推进数据归集共享和系统对接工作的通知》要求，将监控化学品相关行政审批转移至“渝快办”平台，同步规范了申报指南及申报材料（模板）、审核要点等资料。

组织监控化学品生产设施竣工验收1项，审批监控化学品生产特别许可1项。加强事后监管，对2022年新增的1家第二类监控化学品企业进行回访，调研并核实企业宣布数据、生产工艺、使用台账、三废处理等情况。

宣传

一是加强履约宣传。将《条例》《细则》及低浓度监控化学品进出口相关规定集中在重庆市经济和信息化委员会网站上开展宣贯，组织重庆市化工职业学院师生参与国家禁化武办举办的在线禁化武履约普法知识竞赛。二是抓好工作重点。广泛发动监控化学品企业开展履约宣传，组织监控化学品企业参与履约知识竞赛，指导企业利用宣传栏、工作群等开展履约宣传。

培训

组织履约相关负责同志参加全国禁化武履约综合培训班和接受禁化武组织现场视察座谈会。

专项工作

开展监控化学品企业“双随机、一公开”执法检查。对2家企业开展了现场检查，未发现企业存在违法违规行为，并将检查结果进行了公示。

按照国家禁化武办的要求，对2022年6月1日以来监控化学品生产特别许可审批和备案情况开展了自查，并上报了自查情况。

（撰稿　尹玲　陈万明）

四川省

组织协调

落实国家禁化武办《2023年履行〈禁止化学武器公约〉工作要点》文件精神，结合四川省的实际情况，制定四川省禁化武办《2023年履行〈禁止化学武器公约〉工作要点》。

数据宣布与接受视察

2023年，在我国向禁化武组织提交的2022年过去活动年度宣布中，四川省有宣布设施34个。2024年预计活动年度宣布中，四川省有宣布设施9个。

2023年，禁化武组织没有对四川省监控化学品企业进行现场视察。

监督管理

认真执行《条例》《细则》有关规定，加强对监控化学品设施建设、生产、使用等活动的监督管理。审核上报监控化学品生产设施建设审批申请2项，组织监控化学品生产设施竣工验收1项，审批监控化学品生产特别许可申请4项、第二类监控化学品使用许可4项、第二类监控化学品经营许可2项。

宣传

以第8个国际禁止化学武器组织日为契机，4月29日前后，组织市（州）履约主管部门、化工园区和监控化学品企业，积极参加国家禁化武办举办的在线禁化武履约普法知识竞赛。通过门户网站、电子显示屏、宣传海报等渠道，广泛宣传履行《公约》的重要意义和取得的丰硕成果，提升社会公众对禁化武履约的认知度。

培训

2023年4月，组织8家第二类、第三类监控化学品生产企业和5个重点市履约主管部门，在广安利尔化学有限公司开展禁化武组织国际视察演练。5月，组织四川省市（州）履约主管部门、重点化工园区和监控化学品生产使用经营企业分管负责人和具体经办人约150人，在自贡市举办四川省禁化武履约综合培训班，进一步提升禁化武履约队伍的业务能力和监管水平。

专项工作

对3家监控化学品企业开展“双随机、一公开”执法检查。

（**撰稿**　罗明　刘代联）

贵州省

组织协调

2023年，贵州省禁化武办根据国家禁化武办履约工作要求，在贵州省工业和信息化厅党组的正确领导下，不断强化思想认识、加强工作协调、严格监督检查、凝聚履约共识，严格履行《公约》义务，认真做好数据宣布、行政许可、监督管理和宣传培训等工作，圆满完成禁化武履约各项工作任务。

数据宣布与接受视察

2023 年，在我国向禁化武组织提交的 2022 年过去活动年度宣布中，贵州省有宣布设施 3 个。2024 年预计活动年度宣布中，贵州省没有宣布设施。

2023 年，禁化武组织没有对贵州省监控化学品企业进行现场视察。

监督管理

为进一步规范行政许可，贵州省禁化武办严格按照《条例》《细则》的有关规定，加强对监控化学品生产和建设的管理，加大对生产特别许可工作的督导力度，做好监控化学品设施建设、竣工验收及生产特别许可证办理和换发工作。

2023 年共完成行政许可审核审批 3 项，其中审核上报监控化学品生产设施建设审批申请 2 项，审批监控化学品生产特别许可申请 1 项。

按照《国务院关于深化“证照分离”改革进一步激发市场活力的通知》《工业和信息化部关于深化“证照分离”改革的通告》《行政许可事项实施规范》（监控化学品许可事项）的要求，更新了办事指南。

宣传

贵州省禁化武办按照国家禁化武办《关于组织开展第 8 个国际禁化武组织日宣传活动的通知》要求，提前部署安排，组织动员各市（州）禁化武履约部门、履约企业、学校和化工院所积极参加系列主题宣传活动，积极推动主题海报征集投稿，开展海报评选、在线知识竞赛、电子展板制作等活动。在“4·29 国际禁止化学武器组织日”前后，各宣传活动紧紧围绕《公约》宗旨目标、《条例》《细则》的普法教育、展现我国履约成就的目的，以2023年履约工作要点为重点，充分利用官方网站、电子屏幕、微信工作群等渠道宣传履约工作，在厅官网专题专栏及单位大屏播放宣传视频，在厅人流量较大的位置张贴主题海报，营造浓郁的宣传氛围，取得了良好的宣传效果。

贵州省各市（州）相关企业按部署要求并结合自身工作开展了一系列宣传活动。安顺市工业和信息化局组织全市工业和信息化系统人员、民爆企业及履约企业人员积极参与履约普法主题知识竞赛，进一步通过播放宣传视频、微信群转发学习等方式扩大履约工作影响力。六盘水市工业和信息化局组织机关、企业干部职工积极参与答题，全市共有736人参与答题，并完成6幅主题海报。贵阳市监控化学品企业自行制作宣传海报。一系列宣传活动增强了社会公众的履约意识和对履约工作的理解和支持，以及对世界和平、国家安全重要意义的认识，达到了预期的目的。

培训

一是积极参加国家禁化武办组织的各类培训及会议，组织参加在宁夏回族自治区银川市举办的全国禁化武履约综合培训班和在陕西省西安市召开的接受禁化武组织现场视察座谈会，现场观看了企业接受禁化武组织国际视察演练。二是认真组织开展培训，邀请国家禁化武履约专家库专家以“加强监控化学品的监管监控，切实提升履约履职能力”为主题，围绕监控化学品现状、基础知识、法律法规等内容授课，对贵阳市各市（州）、县（区）工业和信息化部门分管领导及负责人开展培训，并现场答疑解惑。贵州省各市（州）、县（区）工业和信息化部门分管领导及负责人共100余人参加培训。三是为提高应对国际视察能力，熟悉国际视察流程规范要求，强化禁化武履约工作的交流学习，经请示国家禁化武办同意，在江苏省禁化武办大力支持下，经分管厅领导同意，贵州省工业和信息化厅派员赴江苏省扬州市现场参观学习了禁化武组织对江苏省的1家监控化学品企业的现场视察。

专项工作

认真组织开展2023年度“双随机、一公开”执法检查工作。结合国家禁化武办“双随机、一公开”工作有关要求，以及贵州省工业和信息化厅抽查事项清单和2023抽查工作计划，通过省级“双随机、一公开”监管平台，随机抽取执法检查人员和检查对象，10月18日—19日组织专家对2家监控化学品企业开展“双随机、一公开”执法检查，依法依规公示了检查结果，同时以检查为契机，宣传履约法律法规，推动企业增强履约意识，提高履约工作能力。

（**撰稿**　杨开伦　周珊）

云南省

组织协调

2023年，云南省禁化武办在国家禁化武办的领导和帮助下，切实履行《公约》义务，认真贯彻实施《条例》《细则》要求，圆满完成年度履约工作任务。一是及时转发《国家禁化武办关于印发2023年履行〈禁止化学武器公约〉工作要点》，明确履约工作要求，指导云南省履约工作开展。二是印发有关通知指导各地按时完成监控化学品2022年过去活动年度宣布和2024年预计活动年度宣布工作。三是印发《关于督促做好监控化学品企业履行〈禁止化学武器公约〉义务有关工作的通知》，并对属地和企业开展了《公约》《条例》《细则》等法规宣贯。四是经与国家禁化武办沟通，同意长期停产的昆明精奥化工有限公司退出监控化学品监管数据库。

数据宣布与接受视察

2023 年，在我国向禁化武组织提交的 2022 年过去活动年度宣布中，云南省有宣布设施 12 个。2024 年预计活动年度宣布中，云南省有宣布设施 1 个。

2023 年，禁化武组织没有对云南省监控化学品企业进行现场视察。

监督管理

根据云南省政府领导批示，要求请省禁化武办（省工业和信息化厅）牵头，会同云南省履行《禁止化学武器公约》工作厅际联席会议成员单位和有关州、市人民政府吸取教训举一反三，全面起底开展云南省化工企业监控化学品生产履约问题大排查和大排除，细化落实通报各项要求，切实加强监管执法，坚决防止类似情况发生。云南省禁化武办快速反应，在全省范围内开展监控化学品企业大排查和大整治工作，及时掌握监控化学品生产企业情况，并指导新增企业按要求开展年度数据宣布。

宣传

严密组织履约宣传活动，2023 年 4 月 29 日，是第 8 个国际禁止化学武器组织日，结合云南省禁化武履约工作实际和地区特点，云南省各地利用宣传展板、电子屏幕和网络平台，策划开展了群众参与度高、传播效果好的宣传活动，重点推动监控化学品企业、高校、科研院所等单位举办展览、专家讲座等活动，积极组织云南省履约工作者参与线上履约知识竞赛，充分营造浓郁的履约宣传氛围。

专项工作

2023 年 9 月 22 日，云南省工业和信息化厅发布《云南省工业和信息化领域行政处罚裁量权基准适用规则（试行）》，包含了 7 个行政处罚裁量权基准附件，其中《监控化学品管理行政处罚裁量权基准》将《条例》和《细则》中涉及特定违法行为的所有罚则均列入裁量条款，设置了处罚依据、具体情形、裁量标准，科学合理地规范了云南省行政区域内的监控化学品行政裁量权责，为云南省监控化学品行政裁量提供了明确依据，为监控化学品管理者依法行政提供了根本遵循。完成年度“双随机、一公开”抽查检查计划，在云南省宣布的监控化学品生产企业中，分两批次随机抽取了云南先锋化工有限公司、云南大为制氨有限公司等 4 家企业进行了现场检查，对企业履约工作中的薄弱环节和存在的问题给予指导并督促整改。

（撰稿　曾涛　宋召勤）

西藏自治区

无监控化学品相关设施。

陕西省

组织协调

2023 年 11 月 17 日—18 日，陕西省禁化武办协助国家禁化武办在陕西省西安市召开了接受禁化武组织国际视察座谈会，在西安彩晶光电有限公司开展第 12 次禁化武组织国际视察演练，并组织各设区市禁化武办和履约重点企业有关负责人、省内履约专家全程参加，邀请相关部门现场观摩。本次会议和活动有力促进陕西省履约工作再上新台阶。一是增进参训人员对国际视察的了解和认识。参训学员认真聆听讲座，观摩演练活动各环节，以练促学，提高了对禁化武工作的认识，开阔了国际视野，提升了履约能力。二是提高企业应对国际视察的能力。活动从视察前情况介绍、问题答疑、现场查看、数据整理核对等方面全方位进行演练，为企业做好接受视察各项准备工作提供全面参考。三是锻炼了履约队伍接受国际视察的能力。本次活动使陕西省各级履约主管部门和企业深入了解接受国际视察的程序及注意事项，专家队伍也得到了全方位的锻炼和提高。

数据宣布与接受视察

2023 年，在我国向禁化武组织提交的 2022 年过去活动年度宣布中，陕西省有宣布设施 28 个。2024 年预计活动年度宣布中，陕西省有宣布设施 2 个。

2023 年，禁化武组织没有对陕西省监控化学品企业进行现场视察。

监督管理

一是认真组织年度数据宣布工作。严格按照国家禁化武办要求，督促指导各市区履约主管部门和监控化学品生产企业认真开展年度数据宣布工作，按时保质提交 2022 年过去活动年度宣布和 2024 年预计活动年度宣布。二是加强监控化学品监督管理。认真做好对监控化学品企业的监督管理，密切关注省内新增和停产企业，仔细摸排，掌握信息，严格落实监控化学品全生命周期行政许可管控措施，确保企业及时按规定程序申办相关手续。三是做好行政许可工作。2023 年审批第二类监控化学品使用许可申请 1 项、第二类监控化学品经营许可申请 1 项，完成监控化学品进口审批最终用途审查 1 项。

宣传

按照国家禁化武办有关要求，陕西省组织开展了“4 • 29 国际禁止化学武器组织日”宣传活动，在陕西省政府大院举办禁化武履约主题宣传展板展览，其他各级单位也纷纷通过门户网站、电子屏、展板、微信公众号等渠道广泛宣传，进一步提高了社会公众对禁化武履约工作的认知度。

培训

2023 年 10 月，陕西省禁化武办派人员赴山东省现场观摩禁化武组织对山东省两家企业的现场视察，近距离感受和学习接受国际视察相关工作。11 月，参加国家禁化武办举办的全国禁化武履约综合培训班。

专项工作

按照《国家禁化武办关于开展监控化学品生产特别许可督查工作的通知》要求，完成陕西省第二类监控化学品生产特别许可督查自查工作并上报国家禁化武办。

（撰稿　赵亚茹）

甘肃省

组织协调

2023 年 4 月，甘肃省工业和信息化厅开展禁化武履约年度培训，组织各相关市州和企业，认真回顾过去工作情况，找出存在的问题，提出 2023 年的工作思路，为履约工作奠定坚实基础。

数据宣布与接受视察

2023 年，在我国向禁化武组织提交的 2022 年过去活动年度宣布中，甘肃省有宣布设施10个。2024年预计活动年度宣布中，甘肃省有宣布设施6个。

2023年，禁化武组织没有对甘肃省监控化学品企业进行国际视察。

监督管理

一是认真做好数据宣布工作。及时下发通知，明确工作要求，在宣布工作过程中，抓落实，认真审核每家企业的宣布数据。二是认真做好监控化学品生产特别许可证考核换证工作。2023年，审批监控化学品生产特别许可申请8项、第二类监控化学品使用许可申请1项。三是根据《国家禁化武办关于开展监控化学品专项监督检查工作的通知》精神，对甘肃省内相关监控化学品企业下达通知，提出工作要求。在企业自查自纠的基础上，组织专家对5家企业进行专项检查。

宣传

在“国际禁止化学武器组织日”期间，通过发送短信方式，向广大市民宣传《公约》《条例》《细则》，增进社会对履约工作的认识、理解和支持。

（撰稿　刘伟）

青海省

组织协调

2023年以来，青海省深入贯彻落实《条例》《细则》要求，将青海省禁化武履约工作纳入青海省工业和信息化厅2023年度目标考核任务，全面推进监控化学品各项工作。青海省禁化武办积极衔接省级财政预算，保证年度工作经费，重点围绕省内专家培养、国际禁化武组织日宣传、履约企业和地方工业及信息化主管部门负责同志培训等重点任务开展工作，顺利完成年度宣布任务和监控化学品行政许可督查自查等工作。

数据宣布与接受视察

2023 年，在我国向禁化武组织提交的 2022 年过去活动年度宣布中，青海省有宣布设施 2 个。2024 年预计活动年度宣布中，青海省有宣布设施 1 个。

2023 年，禁化武组织没有对青海省监控化学品企业进行现场视察。

监督管理

2023 年，组织监控化学品生产设施竣工验收 1 项，审批监控化学品生产特别许可申请 1 项。4 月，邀请甘肃省化工设计研究院监控化学品行业专家对西部矿业同鑫化工有限责任公司开展专项服务，针对企业接受禁化武组织现场视察材料进行指导。5 月和 6 月，组织专家对西部矿业同鑫化工有限责任公司开展含磷、硫、氟的第四类监控化学品生产设施竣工验收和生产特别许可考核，并依法颁发了生产特别许可证。

按照工作计划安排，青海省禁化武办会同西宁市工业和信息化局对青海制药有限公司和西部矿业同鑫化工有限责任公司开展监控化学品使用、生产情况监督检查，并组织专家开展履约能力提升服务，帮助企业提升履约能力和规范管理水平。

宣传

为广泛宣传禁化武履约工作的重要意义和丰硕成果，提高全社会对禁化武履约工作的认知度，青海省禁化武办制定了《“4·29 国际禁止化学武器组织日”宣传工作方案》，通过衔接青海省通信管理局向全省手机用户推送履约主题宣传短信，营造全社会关心支持履约工作的舆论氛围。在工业和信息化厅机关楼道和电梯内张贴宣传海报，巩固机关工作人员履职意识。组织监控化学品企业开展组织日学习宣传，扩大对《公约》的认知范围，进一步强化相关企业的履约认识。

（撰稿　王飞　陶宏伟）

宁夏回族自治区

组织协调

2023 年，在国家禁化武办、宁夏回族自治区人民政府的部署要求下，宁夏回族自治区履行《禁止化学武器公约》工作领导小组成员单位紧密配合，强化服务、加大监管力度，认真履行《公约》的义务，严格执行《条例》《细则》的要求，紧紧围绕禁化武履约和监控化学品管理工作目标，力促履约工作与产业高质量发展同频同进，不断提高履约能力，夯实履约基础，全面推进各项履约工作落实、落地、落细。

数据宣布与接受视察

2023 年，在我国向禁化武组织提交的 2022 年过去活动年度宣布中，宁夏回族自治区有宣布设施 33 个。2024 年预计活动年度宣布中，宁夏回族自治区有宣布设施 8 个。

2023 年，禁化武组织先后对宁夏格瑞精细化工有限公司和宁夏东吴农化股份有限公司的第四类监控化学品生产设施进行现场视察。2 家企业均顺利通过了现场视察。

监督管理

强化行政许可事项审批监控。根据《国务院关于深化“证照分离”改革进一步激发市场主体发展活力的通知》要求，宁夏回族自治区禁化武办深化“放管服”改革，逐步优化行政许可事项审批流程，强化行政许可事项审批监控。目前，宁夏回族自治区内监控化学品行政许可事项由市、宁夏回族自治区工业和信息化部门逐级审核，并全部实现“网上办”。2023年，审核上报监控化学品生产设施建设审批申请2项，组织监控化学品生产设施竣工验收1项，审批生产特别许可申请3项，并及时向工业和信息化部备案。

严格监控化学品监督管理。一是按照《条例》《细则》的规定，明确监管责任及企业主体责任，加大对监控化学品的监管力度，定期统计监管区内监控化学品企业的生产、加工、消耗数据，并对存在问题的企业进行多次专项业务指导，主动帮助企业加强日常监控化学品监管。二是指导企业完善履约制度建设。协助各相关企业完善禁化武履约工作管理体系，培训企业相关工作人员履约的专项技能，按《公约》《条例》《细则》的要求做好日常生产原始记录、原料产品购买及出入库等台账。组织专家到现场考核，指导企业制定监控化学品管理制度和《接受禁化武组织现场视察工作预案》等，将履约工作融入日常生产工作中。三是对企业进行行政执法专项检查，对发现的问题进行指导纠正，并责令企业限期整改。

完善日常管理。宁夏回族自治区禁化武办加强日常监管和服务，将企业调研和履约工作紧密结合，在调研过程中，宣传履约工作的相关内容，不断增强企业的主体责任和履约意识。在年度宣布工作中，对重点企业的数据进行现场核实和抽查，确保宣布数据准确无误。

宣传

2023年，宁夏回族自治区禁化武办积极开展禁化武履约宣传工作，印发《关于组织开展第8个国际禁止化学武器组织日宣传活动的通知》，组织各市各有关企业积极参与。宁夏回族自治区禁化武办精心挑选素材，撰写宣传文字，制作电子展板1幅。宁夏回族自治区各市工业和信息化局和各企业结合自身工作，在4月29日前后开展了形式多样的宣传工作，扩大了《公约》的公众知晓度，凝聚了履约的共识。

培训

2023 年 3 月 2 日—3 日，在国家禁化武办的部署与大力支持下，宁夏回族自治区开展了为期 2 天的禁化武组织国际视察演练和履约专题培训。宁夏回族自治区各市工业和信息化局的工作人员及区内禁化武专家、监控化学品企业的设施代表、数据统计员共计 80 余人参加培训。组织开展第二类监控化学品生产企业接受禁化武组织国际视察演练，专家针对企业存在的问题进行了现场指导并提出了针对性的整改措施，为相关企业顺利通过禁化武组织的现场视察打下了良好的基础。

9 月 25 日—27 日，国家禁化武办在宁夏回族自治区银川市举办了全国禁化武履约培训班，各省、自治区、直辖市及新疆生产建设兵团履约主管部门 120 余名履约工作人员参加培训。本次培训开展了系统全面的培训辅导，有力地提升了参训学员的业务能力和工作水平。同时为宁夏回族自治区全区各级履约工作人员提供了系统、深入学习监控化学品有关法规、业务知识的机会，进一步搭建了与兄弟省份奋战在禁化武工作一线同志们交流的平台。

专项工作

2023 年，宁夏回族自治区禁化武办对相关企业开展多次专项指导检查工作，提出整改意见，督促企业限期整改，及时帮助企业完善了监控化学品管理制度，化解了履约的风险。协助相邻兄弟省份做好接受禁化武组织视察时在自治区境内的安全保卫工作。在日常工作中，把行业管理工作与禁化武工作融合，用行业管理的手段力促禁化武工作。例如，在审核技改贴息、绿色工厂、数字化车间、专精特新等项目中，严格把关，对未办理监控化学品行政审批手续的项目，一律不予通过，多措并举，形成工作合力。

（**撰稿** 张颖）

新疆维吾尔自治区

组织协调

2023 年，新疆维吾尔自治区禁化武办认真落实国家禁化武办的工作部署，组织协调各地（州、市）相关部门及各监控化学品企业，扎实推进各项履约工作。严格审核年度宣布数据，按时提交活动宣布。认真做好监控化学品行政许可审批工作，夯实履约工作基础。专题部署开展“4·29 国际禁止化学武器组织日”和履约法律法规宣传活动。

数据宣布与接受视察

2023 年，在我国向禁化武组织提交的 2022 年过去活动年度宣布中，新疆维吾尔自治区有宣布设施 34 个。2024 年预计活动年度宣布中，新疆维吾尔自治区有宣布设施 1 个。

2023 年，禁化武组织没有对新疆维吾尔自治区监控化学品企业进行现场视察。

监督管理

严格按照《条例》《细则》规定，依法加强对监控化学品设施建设、生产、经营、使用等活动的管理，进一步规范新疆维吾尔自治区禁化武履约工作。一是切实做好生产特别许可工作，审批监控化学品生产特别许可申请 1 项。二是积极组织自治区相关生产、使用监控化学品企业开展自查，做好禁化武组织视察准备工作以及国家禁化武办抽查的迎检工作。三是加强新疆维吾尔自治区监控化学品企业互联网信息发布管理工作。经排查，截至 2023

年年底，暂未发现有企业违规发布虚假信息。

宣传

积极开展《公约》正式生效26周年和第8个“国际禁止化学武器组织日”纪念宣传活动。安排各地（州、市）工业和信息化部门和各监控化学品生产及使用企业深入学习《条例》等相关法律法规，指导企业依法做好监控化学品日常管理、数据宣布等相关内容。组织各单位和企业多方联动，采用悬挂横幅、张贴海报、举办展览、播放宣传片等方式，开展形式多样、内容丰富的宣传活动，增加社会对履约工作的理解和支持，进一步增强企业的履约意识和守法意识。

培训

组织来自新疆化工设计院有限责任公司、新疆石油和化学工业协会、新疆巨力化学有限公司的3名履约专家和有关工作人员参加国家禁化武办接受禁化武组织现场视察座谈会和西安彩晶光电科技股份有限公司国际视察演练，为强化新疆维吾尔自治区履约专家队伍建设、提高企业接受国际视察能力夯实基础。

（撰稿　吴凡　王雅）

新疆生产建设兵团

组织协调

自2019年12月起，经新疆生产建设兵团分管领导同意，建立了由新疆生产建设兵团工业和信息化局主要负责同志为召集人，新疆生产建设兵团公安局、财政局、生态环境局、交通运输局、商务局、市场监督管理局、外事办公室、应急管理局等部门为成员单位的新疆生产建设兵团履行《禁止化学武器公约》联席会议制度。2023 年，各联席会议成员单位各司其职、分工配合，切实做好新疆生产建设兵团禁化武履约相关工作，全面完成履约各项任务。

为规范工业和信息化领域行政处罚裁量权，强化权力监督制约，促进严格规范公正文明执法，根据《条例》《细则》等相关法律法规和《兵团办公厅印发〈关于规范行政裁量基准的指导意见〉的通知》要求，研究制定了《新疆生产建设兵团监控化学品行政处罚裁量基准》，于 2023 年 8 月 18 日正式印发执行。

数据宣布与接受视察

2023 年，在我国向禁化武组织提交的 2022 年过去活动年度宣布中，新疆生产建设兵团有宣布设施 15 个。2024 年预计活动年度宣布中，新疆生产建设兵团有宣布设施 2 个。

2023 年，禁化武组织没有对新疆生产建设兵团监控化学品企业进行现场视察。

监督管理

依据《条例》《细则》规定，依法加强对监控化学品设施建设、生产、经营、使用等活动的管理，进一步规范新疆生产建设兵团禁化武履约工作。2023 年审核上报监控化学品生产设施建设审批申请 1 项。

宣传

为增强社会履约意识，宣传履约意义，促进履约工作，以第 8 个“国际禁止化学武器组织日”为重点，围绕“携手共创一个永无化学武器的世界”“化学领域成就完全用于造福人类”“4·29 国际禁止化学武器组织日”等主题，组织新疆生产建设兵团各相关师（市）开展线上履约知识竞赛活动、普法讲座、工作巡礼在线展览和“履约促和平 携手向未来”短片宣传等活动。

培训

为贯彻落实国家履约工作要求，提升新疆生产建设兵团工业和信息化系统履约能力，强化相关企业的履约意识，2023 年 7 月 5 日，新疆生产建设兵团工业和信息化局在石河子市组织开展禁化武履约工作培训。新疆生产建设兵团有关师（市）的业务负责人，16 家监控化学品生产、使用企业的业务负责人共计 40 余人参加了此次培训。国家履约专家委委员受邀对参训人员进行了培训，就接受国际视察要点、监控化学品数据宣布、行政许可申请与审批等内容进行了授课，并组织赴新疆上昵生物科技有限公司进行了现场教学，开展国际视察演练，就视察前准备工作、重点设施核查等内容进行重点交流。通过培训，参训人员对国际国内履约形势有了新的认识，深刻理解国家关于监控化学品管理规定，进一步提高监控化学品管理能力。

专项工作

依据《细则》和国家禁化武办有关工作要求，按照《监控化学品“双随机、一公开”抽查实施办法》规定，新疆生产建设兵团工业和信息化局随机抽取了 2 名检查人员、1 名辅助人员组成检查组，从新疆生产建设兵团监控化学品企业名录中随机选取了 4 家企业进行现场检查，并在门户网站公示检查结果。针对检查中发现的问题下发整改通知，要求各师（市）工业和信息化部门履行好监管责任，督导企业在规定期限内完成整改并通过验收。

（**撰稿**　李龙飞）

China 企业篇

中国履行《禁止化学武器公约》报告（2023）

浙江科达新型建材有限公司

企业概况

浙江科达新型建材有限公司成立于1992年，专业生产聚氨酯保温复合板、保温装饰一体化板、防水保温一体化板等系列节能板材，是一家集科研、生产、销售、服务为一体的民营科技型企业。

企业用于生产聚氨酯保温复合板的助剂甲基膦酸二甲酯属于第二类监控化学品。

履约日常工作

加强组织领导，健全履约管理体系。企业于2013年成立了禁化武履约工作领导小组，由公司董事长担任组长，下设禁化武履约工作办公室和数据组、工艺设备组、现场组以及后勤接待组4个工作小组。禁化武履约办公室主要负责日常监控化学品管理、数据审核及年度宣布工作，同时负责外部联络及各工作小组间的沟通协调。4个工作小组按照职责分工，随时做好接受禁化武组织国际视察准备。企业制定了监控化学品全流程管理制度，明确各部门的工作职责和分工，责任落实到人。

加强日常管理，夯实履约基础。日常加强对甲基膦酸二甲酯储存和使用环节的管理，实行独立储存，双人双锁，加装视频监控等管理措施，建立了甲基膦酸二甲酯储存、使用登记表，如实登记领用情况，及时做好日、月、年度统计报表，按时完成年度数据宣布工作。

加强培训宣传，增强履约意识，提高履约能力。企业定期召开内部履约工作会议，宣贯《公约》《条例》《细则》，学习履约知识，让全体职工明确履约责任和义务，帮助增强员工履约意识和主动性，确保高效有序开展履约工作。

加强协调配合，做好视察迎检。接受禁化武组织国际视察期间，企业各部门各司其职、密切配合、主动作为，并在视察前开展全面自查，对发现的问题立行立改，有力保障了现场视察顺利开展。

接受国际视察情况

2023 年 1 月 30 日—2 月 1 日，企业顺利通过了禁化武组织的现场视察。

（撰稿　童晓炜）

襄阳金达成精细化工有限公司

企业概况

襄阳金达成精细化工有限公司成立于 2010 年，是一家专业从事紫外线吸收剂和医药中间体研发、生产的国家级高新技术企业。公司先后通过了质量、环境、职业健康安全和知识产权管理体系认证，获批湖北省知识产权示范建设企业、数字化车间示范建设单位，建立了湖北省精细化学品企校联合创新中心和专家工作站 2 个省级新型研发机构，拥有已授权专利 36 项，其中已授权发明专利 8 项。

企业生产活动涉及第二类监控化学品 N,N- 二乙基 -2- 氯乙胺盐酸盐，含磷、硫、氟的第四类监控化学品丁丙硫脲、光引发剂 908，第四类监控化学品盐酸氨基脲、UV-0、UV-9、UV-531、氯代正辛烷、氯代十二烷。

履约日常工作

按照《条例》《细则》要求，企业设立了监控化学品管理机构，制定了监控化学品统计申报制度、监控化学品储运管理制度等，每年不定期开展履约宣传培训工作，按时完成监控化学品年度宣布工作。

接受国际视察情况

2023 年 2 月 13 日—16 日，企业顺利通过了禁化武组织的现场视察。

（撰稿　张雪）

山东滨农科技有限公司

企业概况

山东滨农科技有限公司成立于 2003 年 10 月，占地面积 646670 平方米，员工 1200 余人，是一家集科、工、贸于一体的高新技术企业，国家农药定点生产厂家，拥有独立的外贸进出口权。企业主要生产、销售农药原药及制剂产品，生产的草铵膦中间体甲基二氯化磷和甲基亚磷酸二乙酯属于第二类监控化学品。厂区公共设施及通信设施配套完善，安全环保消防等各项制度已建立健全并顺利通过审批。

履约日常工作

企业高度重视履约工作，成立了以主要负责人为组长，合成与自控技术部、生产服务部、安全部、行政办公室等部门负责人为组员的履约工作领导小组，统筹协调履约各项工作。

企业制定了《接受禁化武组织现场视察工作预案》，明确了各部门的职责分工。编制了《视察前情况介绍》，并根据每年的生产变化进行更新修改。认真做好数据统计工作，落实专人进行记录、核对、统计上报、分类装订保存，保证数据真实准确。每年按时保质提交年度活动宣布数据。

接受国际视察情况

2023 年 2 月 27 日—3 月 2 日，企业顺利通过了禁化武组织的现场视察。

（撰稿　孙文杰）

聊城氟尔新材料科技有限公司

企业概况

聊城氟尔新材料科技有限公司成立于 2012 年 2 月，占地面积 10 万平方米，现有员工 260 人。企业厂区公共设施及通信设施配套完善，安全环保消防等各项制度已建立健全并顺利通过审批。企业已通过质量管理体系和 CNAS 实验室认证。

企业主要产品及产能为六氟丙烯 17000 吨 / 年、二氟甲烷 20000 吨 / 年、二氟一氯甲烷 80000 吨 / 年、四氟乙烯 40000 吨 / 年、八氟环丁烷 1800 吨 / 年，均为第四类监控化学品。企业在生产六氟丙烯的过程中副产第二类监控化学品八氟异丁烯，八氟异丁烯与甲醇反应转成醚后进行高温焚烧无害化处理。

履约日常工作

企业高度重视禁化武履约工作，成立了由企业法定代表人（总经理）为组长，安全总监及生产经理为副组长，安全科、生产科、技术科、设备科、综合科、质检中心相关负责人为组员的履约工作领导小组，明确各部门的职责和分工。

制定了监控化学品管理制度，明确了生产使用管理、数据统计申报、接受视察等相关要求，细化各项管理措施。制定了《接受禁化武组织现场视察工作预案》，编制了《视察前情况介绍》，保障国际视察工作顺利开展。

加强监控化学品日常管理，指定专业人员进行记录、核对、统计上报、分类装订保存，保证数据真实准确。将监控化学品管理纳入年度培训计划，定期解读《条例》《细则》及监控化学品使用规范标准。积极参加省级、市级禁化武履约培训，不断提升监控化学品管理水平。

接受国际视察情况

2023 年 3 月 14 日—16 日，企业顺利通过了禁化武组织的现场视察。

（撰稿　韩浩维）

河南九势制药股份有限公司

企业概况

河南九势制药股份有限公司（前身是新乡市常乐制药厂原料药分厂，2008 年 6 月更名）始建于 1993 年，占地面积 5.3 万平方米，生产区域面积 1.5 万平方米，拥有职工 114 人，其中专业技术人员 30 人。厂区内水、电、气、冷冻等公用工程配套完善，通信设施健全。企业通过了药品生产质量管理规范（GMP）认证。

企业共有侧链盐车间、扑尔敏车间、固体制剂车间 3 个生产车间。第二类监控化学品 N,N- 二甲基 -2- 氯乙胺在侧链盐车间生产，并作为原料药全部用于生产马来酸氯苯那敏，不对外销售。

履约日常工作

企业成立了由总经理为组长的禁化武履约工作小组，下设数据组、工艺组、设备安全组、环保组、后勤组，各小组分工明确，职责清晰。制定了相对完善的监控化学品管理制度，明确了监控化学品管理要求，指定了设施代表、数据申报员等重要岗位人员，明确了各部门和各岗位的工作职责。

企业制定了严格的数据核对制度，生产记录逐批进行审核，生产、消耗台账由专人负责登记，并要求每月与履约工作相关的部门进行数据核对，并登记签字复核，确保上报数据及时准确、完整无误。

接受国际视察情况

2023 年 3 月 27 日—28 日，企业顺利通过了禁化武组织的现场视察。

（**撰稿**　刘竞争）

新乡市瑞丰新材料股份有限公司

企业概况

新乡市瑞丰新材料股份有限公司（前身为新乡市瑞丰化工有限责任公司，2015 年更名）成立于 1996 年，厂区占地 20 万平方米，现有职工 750 人，厂区水、电、气等公用基础工程完善，办公和通信设施健全。企业已通过质量、环境和职业健康安全管理体系认证。

企业共有 7 个第四类监控化学品生产车间，产品共 13 个系列，分别为：PDF 车间，系列产品 4 个，分别为硫醚型抗氧剂、无灰抗氧剂、酚酯型抗氧剂、烷基苯；ZDDP 车间，系列产品 2 个，分别为二烷基二硫代磷酸锌、磷酸酯；高温抗氧剂车间，系列产品 2 个，分别为二苯胺型抗氧剂、烷基酚；磺酸盐车间，系列产品 1 个为磺酸盐清净剂；酚盐车间，系列产品 1 个为酚盐清净剂；树脂车间，系列产品 1 个为烷基水杨酸锌；DZ 车间，系列产品 2 个，分别为金属减活剂、有机钼摩擦改进剂。

履约日常工作

企业制定了监控化学品管理制度，成立了由公司总经理任组长的禁化武工作领导小组，按照职责分为数据组、工艺组、设备安全组、后勤及安全保卫组和综合组共 5 个小组。生产车间生产数据进行每日统计，并与仓库进行每日核验，确保宣布数据准确无误。

接受国际视察情况

2023 年 3 月 29 日—30 日，企业顺利通过了禁化武组织的现场视察。

（**撰稿**　樊东方）

上海金力泰化工股份有限公司

企业概况

上海金力泰化工股份有限公司成立于 1993 年 12 月，是一家集科研、生产、销售和服务于一体的高性能汽车涂料自主品牌领军企业和上市公司，产品广泛应用于乘用车、商用车、工程机械、工业部件，以及建筑幕墙的防护与装饰。厂区占地面积约 4 万平方米，现有员工 500 余名，厂区内水、电、蒸汽、天然气等公用工程配套完善。企业先后获得“中国汽车涂料名牌奖”“上海质量金奖”“上海市高新技术企业”“上海市科技小巨人企业”“上海市优秀院士专家工作站”等荣誉称号。企业在生产 TD 分散树脂、BH-2 分散树脂产品过程中，消耗第二类监控化学品硫二甘醇，年消耗量约为 48 吨。

履约日常工作

企业高度重视禁化武履约工作，对第二类监控化学品硫二甘醇进行严格的标准化管理，确保符合相关法律法规的要求。企业成立了禁化武履约管理委员会，制定了监控化学品管理体系，确立了日常培训和宣传管理制度。同时，企业不断完善《接受禁化武组织现场视察工作预案》，优化接受视察行政安排，组织国际视察演练，通过日常训练和演习，夯实了禁化武履约基础，提高了禁化武履约的能力。2023 年 4 月至今，企业停止使用硫二甘醇。

接受国际视察情况

2023 年 4 月 10 日—12 日，企业顺利通过了禁化武组织的现场视察。

（撰稿　班慧）

洪湖市一泰科技有限公司

企业概况

洪湖市一泰科技有限公司成立于 2012 年，是一家以甲基二氯膦（第二类监控化学品）为中间体生产农药中间体甲基亚膦酸二乙酯（第二类监控化学品）、甲基亚膦酸单正丁酯（第二类监控化学品）和阻燃剂环膦酸酐（含磷、硫、氟的第四类监控化学品）的高新技术企业，拥有 20000 吨 / 年甲基亚膦酸二乙酯、3000 吨 / 年甲基亚膦酸单正丁酯、500 吨 / 年环膦酸酐的生产能力。

企业通过了质量、环境和职业健康安全管理体系认证，被湖北省评为细分领域隐形冠军企业，多次被评为安全生产十佳企业和安全生产先进单位。

履约日常工作

企业严格遵守《条例》《细则》的有关规定，定期进行数据的整理归档工作，定期核实复核生产销售数据，每周汇总数据，每月进行数据的归档。严格按照规定，通过国家禁化武数据申报系统详细、认真申报当年生产数据及下一年预生产数据，做到数据有据可查、核查无误。积极参加各级禁化武办组织的履约培训班，积极开展履约工作宣传，培养干部职工的履约责任感，提升企业的履约能力。

接受国际视察情况

2023 年 4 月 24 日—26 日，企业顺利通过了禁化武组织的现场视察。

（撰稿　成贞辉）

江西名成科技发展有限公司

企业概况

江西名成科技发展有限公司始建于 2012 年，涉及生产和消耗第二类监控化学品环状磷酸酯 CU、甲基磷酸二甲酯，生产第四类监控化学品 N-羟甲基 -3-（二甲氧膦酰基）丙酰胺。

履约日常工作

企业十分重视禁化武履约工作，成立了公司履约工作领导小组，由公司董事长任组长，下设设施代表、数据申报组、工艺设备组、现场管理组和后勤保障组。各小组分工明确，职责清晰：设施代表负责日常管理工作，制定更新《视察前情况介绍》，核实数据并至少保存 3 年数据台账；数据申报组负责整理、汇总、检查原料入库单、原料领用单、成品入库单、成品出库单、生产操作记录、产品出厂检验原始记录、产品出厂检验报告单、三废处理原始记录、销售发票、台账等；工艺设备组负责工艺操作规程、安全管理规定、设备管理制度、岗位操作法、产品标准的修订和生产能力的标定等有关工作；现场管理组负责车间的生产、技术、质量、设备管理，加强对职工应知应会教育和安全教育；后勤保障组负责统筹落实视察时所需场所及办公用品等工作。企业根据《公约》《条例》《细则》的相关规定，制定了监控化学品统计、申报制度，监控化学品储运制度，产品质量管理制度，安全生产管理制度和接受国际视察预案，并将禁化武履约工作纳入日常重点工作管理。

接受国际视察情况

2023 年 5 月 8 日—10 日，企业顺利通过了禁化武组织的现场视察。

（撰稿　方波）

齐鲁制药（内蒙古）有限公司呼伦贝尔分公司

企业概况

齐鲁制药（内蒙古）有限公司呼伦贝尔分公司成立于 2018 年 11 月，主要从事生物农兽药生产销售，主要产品有阿维菌素、多杀霉素、硫酸安普霉素（PSF）、硫酸新霉素（PSF）及延胡索酸泰妙菌素（PSF），均为第四类监控化学品。其中延胡索酸泰妙菌素的生产过程消耗第二类监控化学品 2- 二乙氨基乙硫醇。阿维菌素、多杀霉素取得《农药生产许可证》，延胡索酸泰妙菌素、硫酸安普霉素、硫酸新霉素通过药品生产质量管理规范（GMP）认证，延胡索酸泰妙菌素、多杀霉素通过美国 FDA 认证，延胡索酸泰妙菌素获得欧盟 CEP 认证。

履约日常工作

企业成立了履约工作委员会，总经理为委员会主任，副总经理为委员会副主任，委员会下设履约工作小组，由各部门负责人任小组长。根据《条例》《细则》，企业制定了内部管理制度，包括监控化学品管理制度、数据申报制度，以及监控化学品的采购、储存、领用、使用管理制度。制定了《接受禁止化学武器组织现场视察工作预案》，明确了设施代表、候补设施代表、数据组、现场组、安保组和后勤组的人员及其职责，定期组织自查，排查履约风险点。按时上报过去活动年度宣布及预计活动年度宣布数据，原始数据、报表等如实按期记录，由质量保证部审核并归档保存。积极参加省、市履约主管部门组织的禁化武履约培训班、视察演练活动，利用“4·29 国际禁止化学武器组织日”重要节点，组织职工学习《公约》《条例》《细则》及参加履约知识竞赛，在办公及生产区域开展履约宣传工作，切实增强职工的履约意识，提高履约能力。

接受国际视察情况

2023 年 5 月 22 日—26 日，企业顺利通过了禁化武组织的现场视察。

（撰稿　李亚娇）

山东国邦药业有限公司

企业概况

山东国邦药业有限公司成立于 2006 年，是国邦医药集团在鲁投资的全资子公司，厂区占地面积 31 万平方米，现有员工 2000 多人，其中技术人员 250 人。企业已通过质量、环境、职业健康安全、能源管理体系、药品生产质量管理规范（GMP）、美国 FDA 及欧盟 EMA 认证。

主要产品及产能：硼酸三甲酯 6568 吨 / 年，N- 乙基哌嗪 1000 吨 / 年，N- 甲基哌嗪 2000 吨 / 年，环丙胺 2000 吨 / 年，环丙甲酰胺 120 吨 / 年，氟苯尼考 2000 吨 / 年，D- 对甲砜基苯丝氨酸乙酯 1500 吨 / 年，环丙氨嗪 500 吨 / 年，对甲砜基苯甲醛 2500 吨 / 年，其中属于含磷、硫、氟的第四类监控化学品是氟苯尼考、D- 对甲砜基苯丝氨酸乙酯、对甲砜基苯甲醛，其他为第四类监控化学品。

履约日常工作

企业高度重视禁化武履约工作，成立了以企业负责人为组长，各有关部门负责人为组员的履约工作领导小组。制定了监控化学品统计申报专项管理制度，由专人负责监控化学品数据统计和申报。

在培训方面，企业积极参加由省、市禁化武办举办的禁化武履约综合培训班，并对参与监控化学品生产、使用的员工开展监控化学品相关知识培训，提升了企业履约管理的能力和水平。

在管理方面，日常管理涉及采购、储运、生产、销售、废弃等多个环节，企业以管理制度为抓手，做细做实各项管理工作。每月组织相关人员进行盘存、核对，做好量化分析和物料平衡，做到全过程精准控制，保证数据真实、准确。重视生产数据保存，完整保存了近三年来监控化学品购买凭证、出入库台账、车间使用台账、原始记录等相关证据链。

接受国际视察情况

2023 年 6 月 12 日—13 日，企业顺利通过了禁化武组织的现场视察。

（**撰稿**　钟志军）

山东普洛得邦医药有限公司

企业概况

山东普洛得邦医药有限公司成立于 2005 年，是一家抗生素类原料药和医药中间体生产和销售企业，占地面积 266668 平方米，共有员工 596 人。主要产品包括环合酯、头孢他啶侧链活性酯、AE 活性酯、T-15AE 活性酯等，属于含磷、硫、氟的第四类监控化学品。

企业已通过质量、环境和职业健康安全管理体系认证。

履约日常工作

企业高度重视禁化武履约工作，成立了由企业法人（总经理）为组长，生产总监及行政总监为副组长，生产部、质检部、仓管部负责人为组员的履约工作领导小组，统筹协调各项履约工作。

公司完善了监控化学品管理制度，明确了各部门的职责和分工，细化各项管理措施，真实、准确、完整、及时宣布年度活动数据。同时，积极参加省、市级禁化武履约培训，进一步提升企业对监控化学品的管理水平。

接受国际视察情况

2023 年 6 月 14 日—15 日，企业顺利通过了禁化武组织的现场视察。

（**撰稿**　单学店）

内蒙古浩普科技有限公司

企业概况

内蒙古浩普科技有限公司成立于2018年6月20日，主要从事精细化学品生产与销售，于2020年10月建成年产10000吨的医药农药中间体甲基亚膦酸二乙酯项目，目前实际年产量为4000吨。

企业生产活动涉及甲基二氯化膦、甲基亚膦酸二乙酯2种第二类监控化学品，其中，中间体甲基二氯化膦全部转化为甲基亚膦酸二乙酯，不存在储存或外售情况。

履约日常工作

企业要求各责任部门将履约工作纳入日常管理，常态化组织召开履约工作专题会议，研究安排履约工作任务，分析企业履约工作现状及存在的问题，及时总结，集思广益，持续改进。每月开展以物料平衡为核心的月度生产工作小结，重点对各原辅料的消耗，产品、副产、釜残产量及收率进行分析，做好日常物料平衡计算，为年度宣布提供真实、全面、准确的数据。重视履约宣传，通过在厂区内张贴宣传标语、班前会宣贯强调工作要求或在微信公众号发布履约相关推文等方式开展履约宣传工作，让履约工作深入每一位员工心中，增强员工自觉履约意识，提高履约能力。

接受国际视察情况

2023年6月26日—30日，企业顺利通过了禁化武组织的现场视察。

（撰稿　张芬林）

内蒙古灵圣作物科技有限公司

企业概况

内蒙古灵圣作物科技有限公司始建于2017年6月，占地面积25万平方米，建筑面积2万平方米，现有职工2078人，其中专业技术人员共有212人，主要从事农药及农药中间体的生产与销售。企业涉及12种监控化学品，生产与消耗甲基二氯化膦、甲基亚膦酸二乙酯2种第二类监控化学品，副产第三类监控化学品亚磷酸三乙酯；生产与消耗第三类监控化学品氰化氢；生产销售第四类监控化学品二乙基硫代磷酰氯、氯吡硫磷、氰化钠、草铵膦、肟硫磷、稻瘟灵、吡唑醚菌酯、嘧菌酯。企业已通过质量、环境、职业健康安全和能源管理体系认证。

履约日常工作

企业禁化武履约管理体系较为完善，由公司总经理全面负责履约管理工作，副总经理担任设施代表，体系数据部负责人负责具体履约管理工作，体系数据部部门成员与车间相关人员组成履约工作小组。

企业建立了较为完善的监控化学品管理制度，包括《监控化学品数据统计申报制度》《监控化学品储存、保管、销售及运输制度》《监控化学品台账、记录及资料准备管理制度》《接受监控化学品监督检查与国际视察管理制度》。

企业严格按照《条例》《细则》的有关规定，做好对监控化学品的管理和相关的办证、换证申请及接受监督检查工作。每月制订培训计划，培训履约知识和技能，并对有关人员进行培训效果考核。履约工作小组各成员严格遵守管理制度要求，每月在规定日期内上交车间原始记录，完成台账统计，并由专人逐一核对数据。每年认真做好数据宣布工作，确保宣布数据真实、准确和全面。

接受国际视察情况

2023 年 7 月 10 日—14 日，企业顺利通过了禁化武组织的现场视察。

（撰稿　武俊凤）

营口营新化工科技有限公司

企业概况

营口营新化工科技有限公司成立于 2017 年 2 月，占地面积 15.5 万平方米，是一家专业的精细化工中间体产品生产商，生产高品质原甲酸三甲酯、原乙酸三甲酯、原甲酸三乙酯、甲酸乙酯等系列产品。

企业涉及生产 10 种监控化学品，其中第三类监控化学品 3 种，氰化氢、氰化钠、氯化氰；第四类监控化学品 7 种，三聚氯氰、原甲酸三甲酯、原甲酸三乙酯、原乙酸三甲酯、1.1- 二甲基正癸胺、2- 羟基戊酸甲酯、肌氨酸钠。

企业已通过质量管理体系认证，2022 年被认定为国家级高新技术企业、辽宁省“专精特新”中小企业。

履约日常工作

企业建立了监控化学品履约工作组织管理架构，明确各部门责任分工，确定各项工作责任人。制定印发了《接受禁化武组织现场视察工作预案》《监控化学品统计、申报、管理制度》等，按照制度要求，认真做好禁化武各项履约工作。

积极参加禁化武履约培训。2023 年 7 月 28 日，企业委派技术部副经理参加辽宁省工业和信息化厅组织的全省禁化武履约工作会议，系统学习了国际视察有关工作注意事项、监控化学品相关许可工作内容。8 月 2 日，企业委派技术总监及技术部副经理参加辽宁省工业和信息化厅组织举办的“全市禁化武履约工作会议”，进一步提高了对履约工作重要性的认识。10 月，公司委派技术部副经理赴四川省成都市参加由中国监控化学品协会举办的禁化武履约工作能力提高培训班，了解学习了履约新形势及任务、履约法律法规及监控化学品管理基础知识等内容。

积极开展禁化武履约宣传。4 月 29 日，企业通过微信公众号发布了禁化武履约宣传文章，向员工及合作伙伴宣传禁化武工作重要性。

接受国际视察情况

2023 年 7 月 23 日—25 日，企业顺利通过了禁化武组织的现场视察。

（撰稿　黄明辉）

山东宏旭化学股份有限公司

企业概况

山东宏旭化学股份有限公司成立于 2014 年，是一家精细化学品生产销售企业，占地面积 92667.13 平方米，现有人员 362 人，主要产品为甲基丙烯酸甲酯。在甲基丙烯酸甲酯上游原料的生产过程中，产生中间体氰化氢为第三类监控化学品。

企业已通过质量、环境、职业健康安全和能源管理体系认证。

履约日常工作

企业高度重视禁化武履约工作，成立了由董事长为组长，生产总监为副组长，生产部、质检部负责人为组员的履约工作领导小组，统筹协调各项履约工作。

完善监控化学品管理制度。制定了监控化学品生产管理、数据统计申报、接受视察等制度，明确各部门的职责和分工，及时、准确地宣布年度活动数据。

加强培训学习。积极参加省级、市级禁化武履约培训，在企业内部宣传讲解第三类监控化学品使用规范标准，确保相关员工了解并落实各项管理规定。

接受国际视察情况

2023 年 7 月 26 日—28 日，企业顺利通过了禁化武组织的现场视察。

（撰稿　刘龙）

石家庄瑞凯化工有限公司宏润分公司

企业概况

石家庄瑞凯化工有限公司宏润分公司始建于 2009 年，公司占地面积 10 万平方米，现有员工 20 人，主要产品有草铵膦、2- 氯-5- 氯甲基噻唑、亚氨基二嗪，属于第四类监控化学品，其中草铵膦中间体甲基亚膦酸二乙酯属于第二类监控化学品。

履约日常工作

企业认真履行《公约》义务，遵守监控化学品管理规定，设立了禁化武履约组织领导机构，建立了健全的监控化学品管理制度，编写了详细的接受国际视察预案，定期举行禁化武履约宣讲，积极参加各级履约主管部门组织的履约培训，按要求做好数据宣布、接受视察准备等工作，依法开展生产经营活动。

企业由于市场等因素于 2021 年 6 月 28 日停产至今。

接受国际视察情况

2023 年 8 月 6 日—9 日，企业顺利通过了禁化武组织的现场视察。

（撰稿　王收强）

河北威远生物化工有限公司

企业概况

河北威远生物化工有限公司隶属（江苏）利民控股集团，是一家集农药原料药及制剂研发、生产和销售于一体的现代化企业，拥有 70 多年农药生产经营史，现有杀虫剂、杀菌剂、除草剂三大系列共 400 多个农药产品品规，主要产品有阿维菌素、甲氨基阿维菌素、草铵膦、嘧菌酯、吡蚜酮、噻虫胺、噻唑膦、呋虫胺和除虫脲。

企业生产活动涉及第二类监控化学品有中间体甲基二氯化膦、中间体甲基亚膦酸二乙酯；第三类监控化学品有中间体氰化氢；第四类监控化学品有噻唑膦原药、草铵膦原药、噻虫胺原药、除虫脲原药、氟铃脲原药、吡蚜酮原药、呋虫胺原药、嘧菌酯原药和甲氨基阿维菌素苯甲酸盐原药等。

企业是国家农药定点生产企业、国家高新技术企业，拥有国家级企业技术中心、博士后科研工作站、CNAS 国家认可实验室，也是中国农药发展与应用协会副会长单位，河北省农药工业协会、河北省农药发展与应用协会会长单位。企业已通过质量、环境和职业健康安全管理体系认证。

履约日常工作

企业认真履行《公约》义务，严格执行《条例》《细则》的规定，成立了监控化学品履约工作小组，企业负责人任组长，安全总监任副组长，各车间主任、工艺员、统计员、仓库管理员等为组员，为公司监控化学品管理提供组织保证，履约工作小组办公室设在安全部。同时，企业不断建立健全监控化学品管理制度，积极参加国家、省、市履约主管部门举办的履约培训班，不断提升履约的能力和水平。充分利用“4·29 国际禁止化学武器组织日”重要节点，积极开展履约宣传活动，提高员工对履约工作的认知度和自觉履约意识。

接受国际视察情况

2023 年 8 月 21 日—23 日，企业顺利通过了禁化武组织的现场视察。

（撰稿　王聪敏）

山东海江化工有限公司

企业概况

山东海江化工有限公司成立于 2012 年，现有职工 588 人，专业技术人员 45 人，厂区占地面积为 41 万平方米。主要产品及产能为丙烯腈 13 万吨 / 年、乙腈 4000 吨 / 年、丙酮氰醇 40828 吨 / 年。其中，在丙烯腈的生产过程中产生的中间体氰化氢，属于第三类监控化学品。

企业已通过质量、环境、职业健康安全和能源管理体系认证，厂区公共设施及通信设施配套完善，安全环保消防等各项制度已建立健全并顺利通过审批。

履约日常工作

企业高度重视禁化武履约工作，成立了由企业主要负责人为组长，安全总监及行政总监为副组长，生产部、质检部、仓管部负责人为组员的履约工作领导小组，统筹协调各项履约工作。

企业制定了监控化学品管理制度，细化了各项管理措施，制定《接受禁化武组织现场视察工作预案》，编制《视察前情况介绍》，并根据每年的生产变化进行更新修改。

企业严格监控化学品管理，做细做实各项管理工作，及时、真实、准确地宣布年度活动数据。

接受国际视察情况

2023 年 8 月 24 日—25 日，企业顺利通过了禁化武组织的现场视察。

（**撰稿**　金康）

宁夏格瑞精细化工有限公司

企业概况

宁夏格瑞精细化工有限公司成立于 2005 年，占地面积约 29 万平方米，现有员工 630 人，主要从事农药及农药中间体等精细化工产品生产。企业生产活动涉及 1 个第三类监控化学品，7 个含磷、硫、氟的第四类监控化学品。

企业管理较为规范，安全环保设施配套齐全，先后通过质量、环境、职业健康安全、能源和知识产权管理体系认证。被认定为国家高新技术企业、国家和自治区绿色工厂、国家专精特新“小巨人”企业，自治区行业领先示范企业，安全标准化二级达标企业。

履约日常工作

企业成立了履约工作领导小组，制定《监控化学品管理制度》《接受禁化武组织现场视察工作预案》，认真做好车间、库房、生产、记录、台账等履约基础管理工作，按时提交年度宣布数据。

接受国际视察情况

2023年9月3日—5日，企业顺利通过了禁化武组织的现场视察。

（撰稿　葛振平）

宁夏东吴农化股份有限公司

企业概况

宁夏东吴农化股份有限公司成立于2012年，占地面积14.5万平方米，现有员工416人，其中专业技术人员47人。企业生产活动涉及6个含磷、硫、氟的第四类监控化学品的生产。

企业已通过质量、环境和职业健康安全管理体系认证。2019年，企业被宁夏回族自治区科学技术厅评为国家高新技术企业；2020年，企业被宁夏回族自治区工业和信息化厅评为智能工厂。

履约日常工作

企业在国家禁化武办及宁夏回族自治区工业和信息化厅的组织领导下，认真落实履约主体责任，严格按照《条例》《细则》规定开展生产经营活动，制定完善监控化学品各项管理制度，并在日常生产管理中宣贯履约的相关知识。

接受国际视察情况

2023 年 9 月 6 日—9 日，企业顺利通过了禁化武组织的现场视察。

（撰稿　常永武）

江西理文化工有限公司

企业概况

江西理文化工有限公司成立于 2011 年，占地面积约 106 万平方米，现有职工 1200 多人，主要生产氯碱化工和氟化工产品。企业生产活动涉及的监控化学品包括：第二类监控化学品生产（八氟异丁烯）、第三类监控化学品生产和经营（氯化亚砜）、第三类监控化学品生产（一氯化硫、二氯化硫）、第四类监控化学品生产和经营（六氟丙烯）、第四类监控化学品生产（二氟一氯甲烷、四氟乙烯）。

企业已获得国家高新技术企业、中国氟化工行业“十四五”规划编制单位、工业和信息化部认定的“国家级绿色工厂”及“江西省尘毒危害治理示范企业”“江西民营企业制造业 100 强”“九江市节水型企业”称号，并获得“九江市市长质量奖”荣誉。

履约日常工作

一直以来，企业高度重视禁化武履约工作，成立了以主要负责人为组长的禁化武履约领导小组。严格履行《条例》《细则》有关规定，制定了严格的内部管理制度，制定完善接受国际视察预案，以明确各部门工作职责，做好接受视察的各项准备工作。积极派人参加各级履约主管部门举办的履约培训班，内部定期对相关岗位员工开展《条例》《细则》和履约知识培训，不断增强员工的履约意识，提高履约的能力。严格监控涉及监控化学品的相关过程，准确记录并保存生产、使用、储存等相关的数据信息。与各级履约主管部门保持良好的沟通，及时关注了解履约政策动态和履约工作新要求，定期开展内部自查，发现问题立行立改，持续提升企业履约的能力和水平。

接受国际视察情况

2023 年 9 月 18 日—21 日，企业顺利通过了禁化武组织的现场视察。

（撰稿　李维强）

潍坊加华化工有限公司

企业概况

潍坊加华化工有限公司成立于 2007 年，占地 5 万平方米，现有员工 120 人。主要产品及产能为巯基乙酸异辛酯 3000 吨 / 年、巯基乙酸甲酯 1000 吨 / 年、巯基乙酸甘油酯 500 吨 / 年、巯基乙酸乙二醇酯 500 吨 / 年、巯基乙酸铵 500 吨 / 年、巯基乙酸钾 500 吨 / 年、巯基乙酸钠 500 吨 / 年、巯基乙酸钙 500 吨 / 年、异丙基黄原酸甲酸乙酯 500 吨 / 年、异丁基黄原酸甲酸乙酯 1000 吨 / 年、乙硫氨酯 5000 吨 / 年、N,N- 二乙基二硫代氨基甲酸丙腈酯 3000 吨 / 年、乙硫氮 800 吨 / 年。企业厂区公共设施及通信设施配套完善，安全环保消防等各项制度已建立健全并顺利通过审批。企业已通过质量、环境和职业健康安全管理体系认证。

履约日常工作

企业高度重视履约工作，成立了以总经理为组长，安全管理部、行政管理部、生产技术部、采购部、销售部等各部门负责人为组员的履约工作领导小组。

企业制定了《接受禁化武组织现场视察工作预案》，明确了各部门的职责和分工。编制了《视察前情况介绍》，并根据每年的生产变化进行更新修改。认真做好数据统计工作，落实专人进行记录、核对、统计上报、分类装订保存，保证数据真实准确。每年按时提交年度活动宣布数据。

接受国际视察情况

2023 年 10 月 9 日—10 日，企业顺利通过了禁化武组织的现场视察。

（撰稿　李超伟）

山东海利尔化工有限公司

企业概况

山东海利尔化工有限公司成立于2007年，厂区占地面积22.4万平方米，拥有员工 800 余人，主要从事农药生产和销售，涉及第四类监控化学品噻虫嗪、噻虫胺和丙硫菌唑。

企业是国家绿色工厂、国家高新技术企业，拥有省级企业技术中心等创新平台，先后通过了质量、环境和职业健康安全管理体系认证。

履约日常工作

企业高度重视禁化武履约工作，成立了以总经理为组长的履约工作领导小组，明确设施代表及数据申报人，制定了监控化学品统计申报专项管理制度，编制了《接受禁化武组织现场视察工作预案》和《视察前情况介绍》等材料，做好接受国际视察工作。

设立技术管理部为企业履约机构，制定了《监控化学品管理制度》，严格管理企业涉及的第四类监控化学品的生产、储存、检测、分析、统计、宣布等环节并做好存档工作，准确提交宣布数据。

在培训方面，企业积极参加省、市禁化武办举办的履约综合培训班，将履约工作学习资料印发至有关部门和人员，组织不定期集中学习，对参与监控化学品生产和使用的员工开展监控化学品相关知识培训与考核，提升企业履约管理的能力和水平。

接受国际视察情况

2023 年 10 月 11 日—12 日，企业顺利通过了禁化武组织的现场视察。

（撰稿　王旭）

扬州晨化新材料股份有限公司

企业概况

扬州晨化新材料股份有限公司成立于 1995 年，于 2017 年 2 月 13 日在深圳证券交易所创业板成功上市。厂区占地面积约 9 万平方米，其中建筑面积约 4.5 万平方米。企业生产活动涉及两种第二类监控化学品，即甲基膦酸二甲酯和乙基膦酸二乙酯；两种含磷、硫、氟的第四类监控化学品，即三（β-氯乙基）磷酸酯和三（β-氯丙基）磷酸酯，其中甲基膦酸二甲酯生产装置分别于2002年、2005年、2010年、2016年和2023年接受了禁化武组织的初始视察和后续视察。

履约日常工作

一是加强组织领导和制度建设。成立了以企业董事长为组长，生产部、安全环保部等相关部门负责人为成员的禁化武履约工作领导小组，形成了企业履约组织领导体系，并明确了各部门的职责和分工。制定完善了监控化学品管理制度，并将禁化武履约工作纳入重点工作管理，严格执行制度规定，确保工作健康有序开展。

二是加强管理与检查。企业按照国家和地方监控化学品法律法规、政策要求，严格落实各项管理措施，定期对监控化学品管理工作开展自查自纠，认真接受各级履约主管部门的监督检查。监控化学品生产经营使用数据采用ERP系统进行管理，确保原始数据的真实性、准确性和可追溯性。定期召开专题会议，校对监控化学品产销存各类台账，如数据存在偏差，立即分析并查明原因，及时落实整改，确保统计数据的准确性。

三是强化履约培训。企业积极开展监控化学品管理专题培训，宣贯禁化武履约基础知识、监控化学品法律法规等，学习掌握数据宣布等各项工作要求，宣传履约工作的重要性，以精益求精的工作态度做好履约工作。积极参加禁化武履约相关培训，并将培训资料及时发放至各相关部门，组织有关人员认真学习，不断提高履约的能力。

接受国际视察情况

2023年10月22日—26日，企业顺利通过了禁化武组织的现场视察。

（**撰稿** 林清）

淮安华源化工有限公司

企业概况

淮安华源化工有限公司始建于2006年，占地面积约2.6万平方米，在册职工65人，主要产品有三氯化磷、三氯氧磷、磷酸酯系列阻燃剂，其中三氯化磷、三氯氧磷属于第三类监控化学品，生产能力分别为1.4万吨/年和1.5万吨/年。企业是危险化学品安全生产二级标准化单位，已通过质量、环境和职业健康安全管理体系认证。

履约日常工作

企业成立了以法人代表为组长的禁化武履约工作领导小组，指定了设施代表、候补设施代表和各专业小组负责人及成员，明确了各小组和小组成员的工作职责和任务。确立生产部为企业禁化武履约工作的管理部门，并设立履约管理专员负责日常管理工作。不断完善监控化学品管理制度，把监控化学品基础工作管理责任落实到车间、班组和具体干部及职工。

企业长期聘请两位专家指导禁化武履约和监控化学品管理工作，对主要人员开展《公约》《条例》《细则》培训，现场指导做好监控化学品管理及日常生产数据统计工作。通过以上措施，企业将禁化武履约工作分工到部门、责任到人，为做好监控化学品日常管理和接受国际视察奠定了良好的基础。

强化日常管理积极做好国际视察应对。企业在禁化武履约工作方面始终坚持高标准、严要求，从人员管理到制度落实，从生产数据到分析汇总，在日常工作中专人专职，协调有序，把应对视察的突击性工作融入日常生产管理中，切实做好遇到视察不慌不忙，从容有序，保证视察顺利通过。

接受国际视察情况

2023 年 11 月 6 日—7 日，企业顺利通过了禁化武组织的现场视察。

（撰稿　李峰）

利民化学有限责任公司

企业概况

利民化学有限责任公司成立于 2019 年 9 月，是利民控股集团的全资子公司，占地面积约35万平方米，建筑面积20万平方米，现有职工超过1200人。企业主要从事农药杀菌剂等产品的生产和销售，涉及第四类监控化学品代森锰锌、霜脲氰、嘧霉胺、丙森锌、威百亩、代森锌、代森铵、三乙膦酸铝、乙膦酸钠、苯醚甲环唑、硝磺草酮、环磺酮和噻虫啉等的生产活动。企业已通过质量、环境和职业健康安全管理体系认证。

履约日常工作

建立履约工作组织架构。企业高度重视履约工作，成立由公司董事长为总负责人，生产、仓储、采购、质检、安全、生产车间等部门为成员的履约工作小组，明确各部门的分工和职责，指定设施代表、候补设施代表和数据统计等重点人员，并将履约工作纳入日常绩效考核。

规范监控化学品管理。企业按照《条例》《细则》要求，建立覆盖生产、储存和销售全过程的监控化学品管理制度，制定《接受禁化武组织现场视察工作预案》，编制《视察前情况介绍》并定期修订和更新，保证各项制度运行有效。在日常管理中，由生产管理部根据质量检测记录、原始生产记录、原料消耗、产品质量的日报表、月报表、年报表的数据收集和保存工作，核对各类报表、原料产品出入库单据、产品库存和产品销售，及时做好物料平衡核算工作。同时，企业按照省、市履约主管部门的要求，准确宣布监控化学品年度活动数据。

积极组织履约宣传培训。企业将禁化武履约工作纳入公司年度培训计划，选派员工多次参加省、市履约主管部门举办的培训班，同时在企业内部组织履约宣传活动和监控化学品管理专项培训，增进企业管理人员和全体员工对履约工作的理解和认识。

接受国际视察情况

2023 年 11 月 8 日—9 日，企业顺利通过了禁化武组织的现场视察。

（撰稿　岳双艳）

浙江万盛股份有限公司

企业概况

浙江万盛股份有限公司始建于 1995 年 5 月，前身是浙江万盛化工有限公司，于 2010 年 11 月更名，是一家专业生产、经营阻燃剂和涂料助剂等功能助剂的民营企业。

企业厂区内建有 9 个生产车间，其中二车间为加工第二类监控化学品环状膦酸酯 CU 的车间，一、三、四、五、八车间为第四类监控化学品的生产车间。此外，还有 3 个废水处理车间、1 个机修车间及 1 个在建生产车间。

履约日常工作

在工作机制方面，企业成立了禁化武履约工作领导小组，由企业法人代表担任组长，总经理担任副组长和设施代表，下设数据组、工艺设备组、现场组和后勤接待组共 4 个小组，分别由财务部经理、生产技术副总、生产副总和 2 行政部经理担任小组组长。

在管理制度方面，企业制定了监控化学品相关管理制度及《接受禁化武组织现场视察工作预案》，每年不定期组织相关部门进行履约培训。

在数据统计申报方面，根据企业的管理情况，每日由生产车间及仓库确认原料的发放和储存以及产品的产、销、存数据。每月 15 日前，生产车间完成上个月的生产月报表，并报财务部门审核。每年 1 月上旬，生产部门将上一年度的监控化学品数据形成年度报表，并报财务部门审核，审核通过后由安全环保部门在国家禁化武采集与宣布系统做数据申报。

接受国际视察情况

2023 年 11 月 20 日—22 日，企业顺利通过了禁化武组织的现场视察。

（**撰稿**　*颜志伟*）

浙江沙星科技股份有限公司

企业概况

浙江沙星科技股份有限公司始建于 1996 年 2 月 1 日，前身是浙江沙星医药化工有限公司，于 2022 年 12 月更名，是一家专业从事医药中间体生产及销售的企业。

企业厂区内建有 4 个生产车间，其中，二车间为生产含磷、硫、氟的第四类监控化学品车间，一、三、四车间为生产不含磷、硫、氟的第四类监控化学品车间。此外，还有 1 个机修车间。

履约日常工作

在工作机制方面，企业成立了禁化武履约工作领导小组，由总经理、企业法人代表担任组长，副总经理担任副组长和设施代表，下设数据组、工艺设备组、现场组和后勤接待组共 4 个小组，分别由质量总监、技术总监、工程总监和行政人事部经理担任小组组长。

在管理制度方面，企业制定了监控化学品相关管理制度及《接受禁化武组织现场视察工作预案》，每年不定期组织相关部门进行履约培训。

在数据统计申报方面，根据企业的管理情况，每日由生产车间及仓库确认原料的发放和储存以及产品的产、销、存数据。每月 8 日前，生产车间完成上个月的生产月报表，并报 EHS 部门审核。每年 1 月上旬，生产部门将上一年度的监控化学品数据形成年度报表，并报 EHS 部门审核，审核通过后由 EHS 部门在国家禁化武数据采集与宣布系统做在线申报。

接受国际视察情况

2023 年 11 月 23 日—24 日，企业顺利通过了禁化武组织的现场视察。

（撰稿　李雪玲）

永农生物科学有限公司

企业概况

永农生物科学有限公司始建于 2005 年，占地面积 20 万平方米，建筑面积 15 万平方米，是一家专业从事农药生产经营的民营企业。厂区内水、电、气、维修和三废处理等公用工程配套设施完善。

企业生产过程会消耗第二类监控化学品。企业产品中有 8 种第四类监控化学品，其中含磷、硫、氟第四类监控化学品 1 种。

厂区内建有 11 个生产车间和 1 个机修车间，其中，第二类监控化学品消耗车间 1 个，含磷、硫、氟第四类监控化学品生产车间 1 个，第四类监控化学品生产车间 9 个。

履约日常工作

企业高度重视禁化武履约工作，成立了以法人代表为组长，总经理以及分管生产设备管理、安全环保、行政人事和财务仓管的副总经理为副组长的领导小组，制定了《监控化学品管理制度》《接受禁化武组织现场视察工作预案》，明确了各职能部门以及有关人员的工作职责。

为确保履约工作的顺利开展，企业制定并每年更新《视察前情况介绍》。在数据统计方面，落实专人记录、核对和统计上报工作，并分类装订保存，年初和年末按规定完成年度宣布工作。

严格要求各岗位人员认真执行操作规程，及时填写领用和生产记录。生产管理部门定期检查生产记录填写情况，不定期抽查生产记录是否准确规范。车间、仓库之间物料移交手续完备，物料和产品流动的每一个环节都严格做好记录。

在日常管理中，企业定期召开内部监控化学品管理会议，积极宣传履约责任和义务，以提高员工履约的主动性，加强各岗位员工的业务技能和履约知识培训，不断提高企业履约的能力和水平。

企业认真对待各级履约主管部门的监督检查，全面把握迎检项目的具体要求，提前做好禁化武组织国际视察准备工作。在接受国际视察前，加大自查自纠的力度，对发现的问题，立行立改，以扎实的工作基础和良好的工作面貌接受国际视察。

接受国际视察情况

2023 年 12 月 4 日—6 日，企业顺利通过了禁化武组织的现场视察。

（撰稿　游建荣）

浙江医药股份有限公司昌海生物分公司

企业概况

浙江医药股份有限公司昌海生物分公司始建于2011年，是一家专业生产、经营维生素A、天然维生素E、维生素E和胡萝卜素的企业，占地面积38.2万平方米，建筑面积29.9万平方米，现有员工1332人，其中技术人员805人。企业生产的产品维生素A系列、天然维生素E系列、维生素E系列和胡萝卜素系列均为第四类监控化学品。企业已通过环境、职业健康安全管理体系和二级安全生产标准化认证。

履约日常工作

为切实履行《公约》义务，落实《条例》《细则》规定，企业成立了由总经理为组长，常务副总经理及分管安全环保的副总经理为副组长，生产部门、质管部门和仓储部门负责人为组员的履约工作领导小组，统筹协调各项履约工作。

企业制定了《监控化学品管理规程》和监控化学品生产使用管理制度、数据统计申报制度、接受国际视察预案等，明确各部门的职责和分工，细化各项管理措施。

认真做好数据申报工作。生产车间和仓库统计发放、使用和储存等生产数据，每月中旬生产车间完成上个月的生产月报表，每年1月上旬生产部门将上一年度的监控化学品数据形成年报表，审核通过后在国家禁化武数据采集与宣布系统做在线申报。

加强宣传和培训。企业将监控化学品管理纳入培训计划，不定期解读《条例》《细则》及相关工作规范，确保员工了解并落实各项管理规定。同时，积极参加省级、市级禁化武履约培训，进一步提升履约管理的水平。

接受国际视察情况

2023 年 12 月 7 日—8 日，企业顺利通过了禁化武组织的现场视察。

（撰稿　丁莹莹）

台州达辰药业有限公司

企业概况

台州达辰药业有限公司始建于 2017 年 11 月 9 日，是一家专业从事医药、农药的生产企业。企业厂区内建有 2 个生产车间，其中，车间一、车间二为含磷、硫、氟的第四类监控化学品和其他第四类监控化学品生产车间。此外，还有 1 个回收车间和 1 个机修车间。

履约日常工作

在工作机制方面，企业成立了禁化武履约工作领导小组，由企业法人代表担任组长，副总经理担任副组长和设施代表，下设数据组、工艺设备组、现场组和后勤接待组共 4 个小组，分别由生产部总监、生产部经理、生产部主任和行政部经理担任小组组长。

在管理制度方面，企业制定了监控化学品相关管理制度及《接受禁化武组织现场视察工作预案》，每年不定期组织相关部门进行培训。

在数据统计申报方面，根据企业的管理情况，每日由生产车间及仓库确认原料的发放和储存以及产品的产、销、存等数据。每月 15 日前，生产车间完成上个月的生产月报表，并报安环部审核。每年 1 月上旬，生产部将上一年度的监控化学品数据形成年度报表，并报安环部审核，审核通过后由安环部在国家禁化武数据采集与宣布系统做在线申报。

接受国际视察情况

2023 年 12 月 18 日—19 日，企业顺利通过了禁化武组织的现场视察。

（撰稿　谢建波）

浙江华海药业股份有限公司临海川南分公司

企业概况

浙江华海药业股份有限公司创立于 1989 年，2003 年在上海证券交易所上市，现有员工 7000 多人，在全球拥有 40 多家子公司，主营化学药、生物药、医药包装和贸易流通，形成以心血管类、中枢神经类和抗病毒类为主导的产品系列，为全球 100 多个国家和地区提供健康医疗产品。

临海川南分公司成立于 2005 年，是浙江华海药业股份有限公司旗下最大的原料药制造基地，主要从事原料药技术研发与生产服务，产品包括心血管、精神类等高端原料药，是全球最主要的沙坦类原料药生产基地。厂区内建有 10 个生产车间，其中，一、八、九车间为含磷、硫、氟的第四类监控化学品生产车间。此外，还有 2 个回收车间、1 个机修车间和 1 个在建生产车间。

履约日常工作

在工作机制方面，企业成立了禁化武履约工作领导小组，由公司总经理担任组长，常务副总经理担任副组长和设施代表，下设资料组、现场管控组、现场警戒组、通信组、应急抢修组和后勤接待组共 6 个小组，分别由生产运营总监、生产总监、工程高级总监、行政人事总监、保安部经理和办公室主任担任小组组长。

在管理制度方面，企业制定了监控化学品相关管理制度及《接受禁化武组织现场视察工作预案》，每年不定期组织相关部门进行培训。

在数据统计申报方面，根据企业的管理情况，每日由生产车间及仓库确认原料的发放和储存以及产品的产、销、存数据。每月 25 日前，生产车间完成上个月的生产月报表，并报安全环保部门审核。每年 1 月上旬，生产部门将上一年度的监控化学品数据形成年度报表，并报安全环保部门审核，审核通过后由安全环保部门在国家禁化武数据采集与宣布系统做在线申报。

接受国际视察情况

2023 年 12 月 20 日—21 日，企业顺利通过了禁化武组织的现场视察。

（**撰稿**　尤澈冰）

China

支撑篇

中国履行《禁止化学武器公约》报告（2023）

中国电子产品可靠性与环境试验研究所

单位概况

中国电子产品可靠性与环境试验研究所，又名工业和信息化部电子第五研究所（以下简称“电子五所”）、中国赛宝实验室，1955 年成立，主要从事基础科研和生产性服务业，是工业和信息化部直属事业单位和国内质量可靠性领域权威机构。电子五所坚持以“支撑政府的专业智库、服务行业的科技平台、提升质量的权威机构”为发展定位，为工业和信息化部的行业管理和地方政府提供各类支撑服务，为军民企业提供优质技术服务，可提供从材料到整机设备、从硬件到软件直至复杂大系统的认证计量、试验检测、分析评价、数据服务、软件评测、信息安全、技术培训、标准信息、工程监理、节能环保、专用设备和专用软件研发等技术服务。电子五所支撑服务军民融合、产业链自主可控、科技自立自强等国家战略，牵头承担国家重大研发计划、核心电子器件、高质量发展专项等一批重大项目，“十三五”期间获得省部级以上奖励 27 项。

履约支撑工作

一是支撑国家禁化武办编制和发行 2019—2021 年度《中国履行〈禁止化学武器公约〉报告》，编制《中国履行〈禁止化学武器公约〉报告（2022）》。自 2015 年以来，电子五所已连续 9 年编制年度报告，为履约宣传工作作出应有贡献。

二是继续推动低浓度监控化学品进出口豁免规定研究，支撑国家禁化武办赴上海市开展低浓度监控化学品三乙醇胺进出口情况调研，研提优化低浓度三乙醇胺进出口监管措施建议。

三是支撑广东省开展年度宣布和行政许可审查。2023 年 7 月 26 日，支撑广东省工业和信息化厅民爆处开展监控化学品年度宣布数据审核。

（撰稿　孙秀敏　苏健梅）

工业和信息化部国际经济技术合作中心

单位概况

工业和信息化部国际经济技术合作中心（以下简称“国合中心”）是工业和信息化部专门从事国际产业合作的直属事业单位，中国国际贸易促进委员会电子信息行业分会挂靠运行。

国合中心聚焦国际合作和智库研究两大业务，着力打造工业和信息化领域高水平国际合作执行平台、高端国际化研究智库和综合经贸服务机构，持续提升产业链、供应链的国际化发展水平，为服务中国特色大国外交、制造强国和网络强国建设提供有力支撑。

履约支撑工作

在新形势下，国合中心以服务国家履约工作和化工高质量发展为核心目标，以夯实履约基础、提升智力支撑能力为主线，依托能源资源环境研究所的人才优势，积极推动化工园区和企业的智能化、高端化和绿色化转型升级，全面支撑禁化武履约的各项工作。

一是做好履约政策研究工作。重点开展五审会立场研究，召开专题研讨会，重点围绕工业议题开展专题讨论，形成研究报告，供国家禁化武办参考。

二是做好履约信息跟踪及宣传工作。创建禁化武组织文献数据库并持续更新，建立较为完善的信息跟踪机制，密切关注各方履约的最新动态。

支撑禁化武办做好“4·29 国际禁止化学武器组织日”的宣传工作。

三是做好秘书处平台建设工作。组织召开专家委第二次全体会议，研究当前禁化武履约的工作重点，明确专家委的下一步工作。同时加强对企业的服务，组织专家委地方服务行活动，赴湖北省监控化学品企业开展国际视察演练。

（撰稿　宋晓明　李飞）

北京化工大学环境安全研究中心

单位概况

北京化工大学创办于1958年，原名北京化工学院，是新中国为“培养尖端科学发展所需的高级化工技术人才”而创建的一所高水平大学，是教育部直属的全国重点大学，国家“211工程”和“‘985’优势学科创新平台”重点建设院校，国家“双一流”建设高校。

北京化工大学环境安全研究中心（以下简称“中心”）成立于2020年12月，定位为落实总体国家安全观，推进我国生态文明建设，打造绿色发展的特色型高端智库和服务平台。中心依托学校化工、材料和生物等学科的科技优势，整合文法、经管等相关力量，从化工环境安全入手，开展“科技+政策+法律”的环境安全问题学科协同创新研究，积极拓展和利用校外社会资源，聚焦基于化学品和化工生产引发的生态安全、气候变化与能源安全、生物技术安全等领域跨学科研究中的法律重大问题、前沿问题和疑难问题，服务国家生态文明建设和绿色发展战略。中心主任作为国家履约专家委委员，带领中心研究团队积极参与国际视察演练、履约培训、人才培养及履约宣传等工作，发挥良好的支撑与示范作用。

履约支撑工作

认真履行专家委员职责，为禁化武工作建言献策。2023 年 3 月 9 日，专家委第二次全体会议在浙江省杭州市召开，中心主任带领团队成员积极参与会议筹办，并作“《海牙伦理准则》与我国化学科技伦理教育”专题报告。3 月 10 日，参加在浙江工业大学召开的加强禁化武履约人才培养专题研讨会。9 月 14 日—15 日，专家委赴湖北开展地方服务行活动，中心主任带领团队成员积极参与视察演练，查看现场并核对数据。9 月 25 日—27 日，国家禁化武办在宁夏回族自治区银川市举办了全国禁化武履约培训班，中心主任带领中心研究团队积极参与培训，并围绕“《中华人民共和国行政处罚法》解读”为学员做专题授课。

广泛开展履约宣传，加强履约人才培养。2023 年 4 月，中心主任多次组织开展“真人图书馆”活动，围绕“禁化武履约工作实践”为本科生、研究生宣传普及禁化武履约工作及相关人才需求，激发学生对禁化武履约工作的兴趣。指导北京化工大学文法学院、机电学院的本科生、研究生共同参与国家禁化武办主题海报的设计征集工作，其中两张获评为官方主题海报，一张入选优秀海报。

积极参与国际交流，关注最新国际动态。2023 年 11 月 20 日—21 日，禁止化学武器组织桌面演练活动在禁化武组织化学与技术中心举行，中心主任受邀赴荷兰海牙参加活动。

（撰稿　张建伟　刘宇轩）

河北省监控化学品协会

协会动态

河北省监控化学品协会成立于 2006 年 12 月，主要职责是为河北省监控化学品企业提供宣传、培训、生产技术和产品推介等服务，现有会员单位 76 家。

2023 年，河北省监控化学品协会召开理事长、副理事长、专家委员会会议，总结协会近 3 年工作，交流企业管理经验及做好接受国际视察的各项准备工作进展，商讨协会的下一步工作计划，并组织参观示范企业。

履约支撑工作

一是配合河北省禁化武办开展监控化学品行政许可现场考核工作。二是指导帮助监控化学品企业做好年度数据宣布工作。三是组织协会专家为企业接受国际视察提供技术支撑。四是协助河北省禁化武办组织举办全省监控化学品管理培训班。五是协助河北省禁化武办开展“4 • 29 国际禁止化学武器组织日”履约宣传活动。

（撰稿　张翠）

河北科技大学化学安全与履约技术研究中心

单位概况

河北科技大学坐落于河北省石家庄市，由原河北轻化工学院、河北机电学院、河北省纺织职工大学、河北纺织工业学校合并组建而成，是河北省首批重点建设的多科性骨干大学、河北省人民政府与国家国防科技工业局共建高校、河北省重点支持的国家一流大学建设高校、教育部“卓越工程师教育培养计划”高校。

化学安全与履约技术研究中心（以下简称“中心”）是设立在河北科技大学的《禁止化学武器公约》履约与决策相关的技术研究机构。该中心实行 PI 制，由万人计划科技创新领军人才、禁化武组织科学咨询委员会（由全球 193 个缔约国中 25 个来自不同国家的专家委员组成）唯一的中国专家委员、禁化武组织科学咨询委员会生物毒素（BIOTOXINS）分析工作组唯一的中国专家委员（全球 16 位成员）领衔。

中心工作强力支撑化学安全与履约相关领域的国家战略发展，是河北科技大学化学工程与技术学科和争取博士点建设的重要特色，连续 20 年为我国履约工作作出重要贡献，得到了相关领导的高度认可。2023 年 2 月中心作为非政府组织向禁化武组织第五次审议大会进行注册并申请认证。

履约支撑工作

为国家履约提供技术支撑。对我国监控化学品、生物毒素进行调研，提供基础数据，为民用化工及其相关企业接受国际视察提供技术支撑和政策咨询，为国家禁化武办的战略研究提供支撑和建议。

禁化武组织相关课题研究。针对禁化武组织提出的履约视察问题进行讨论，形成数据分析和建议，为我国关于工业视察机制改革的立场提供支撑。针对禁化武组织科学咨询委员会每年发布的化工可持续发展研究议题，开展大量的基础研究工作。

禁化武组织热点问题研究。紧跟禁化武组织热点问题，开展理论研究并制定履约措施。围绕高活性原料药、失能剂和附表新增化合物开展研究，为我国履约工作提供基础数据和信息。

（撰稿　孙凤霞）

辽宁省化工学会

单位概况

辽宁省化工学会成立于 1972 年，属于学术性、公益性和非营利法人社会团体，被评为辽宁省科协优秀科技社团、科技成果转移转化服务基地、辽宁省科协系统先进集体、承接政府转移职能与公共服务试点示范学会。

辽宁省化工学会 2023 年新设立学会服务站 8 家，学会累计发展个人会员 1060 人，单位会员 91 家。

履约支撑工作

2023 年 3 月 9 日，辽宁省化工学会理事长受邀参加国家履行《禁止化学武器公约》专家委员会第二次全体会议，并做专家委员会服务地方行（辽宁站）活动经验分享。6 月 14 日，赴东北制药集团股份有限公司核查第二类监控化学品使用许可。7 月 29 日，受邀参加辽宁省禁化武履约培训会，并为参会人员授课。8 月 9 日，赴营口昌成新材料科技有限公司参加第三类监控化学品生产设施竣工验收初审工作。9 月 8 日，组织辽宁省内禁化武履约专家参加由工业和信息化部国际经济技术合作中心举办的禁化武组织后备人才能力建设培训会。9 月 13 日—15 日，参加在湖北省武汉市举办的专家委地方服务行系列活动的“新形势下省级及以下履约主管部门工作机制及协会组织支撑作用研究”专题研讨会。11 月 24 日，赴恒力石化（大连）新材料科技有限公司参加第三类监控化学品生产设施竣工验收。

（撰稿　李爽）

福建省化工建设工程质量技术服务中心

单位概况

福建省化工建设工程质量技术服务中心（以下简称“中心”）成立于 2021 年，是福建省工业和信息化厅直属的公益一类事业单位，核定事业编制 24 名，主要职责是承担化工建设工程质量监督检查相关的技术性、事务性工作。

中心自成立起便支撑着福建省工业和信息化厅开展禁化武履约相关工作，并为监控化学品行政许可审查、日常监管、宣贯培训等提供技术支撑，承担国家禁化武办相关课题研究，得到国家禁化武办和福建省工业和信息化厅的肯定。

履约支撑工作

一是协助做好行政许可事项的技术审查。全年协助共完成不含磷、硫、氟的第四类监控化学品生产设施备案，第二类、第三类和含磷、硫、氟的第四类监控化学品的生产设施建设初审，第二类、第三类和含磷、硫、氟的第四类监控化学品的生产设施建设竣工验收初审及第二类监控化学品使用许可审查等共 25 项。

二是协助开展监控化学品监督检查。全年支撑对 3 家企业开展“双随机、一公开”执法检查，对 12 家企业开展日常监督检查，协助下发整改通知书 2 份，指导企业加强监控化学品日常生产、经营等管理工作。

三是协助组织开展禁化武履约普法宣传。以“4·29 国际禁化武组织日”为契机，协助组织举办各类宣传活动共 7 场，发放宣传资料 500 余份，协助组织 1800 余人参加国家禁化武办举办的在线禁化武履约普法知识竞赛，营造良好履约宣传氛围。

四是协助做好培训指导工作。协办福建省禁化武履约工作专题培训班，近 100 人参加，培训有效提高各级履约主管部门、重点履约企业的履约意识和能力，为接受禁化武组织国际视察打好基础。协助开展为期 8 个月的履约宣贯“敲门行动”，以“服务、宣传、培训”等线下现场指导为主要内容，送服务上门，有效减轻企业履约的负担，降低履约的风险。

（撰稿　邱模松）

湖北省监控化学品协会

协会动态

湖北省监控化学品协会（以下简称“协会”）成立于1997年12月，是湖北省境内依法注册的从事监控化学品生产、科研、经营的企业、事业单位和相关经济组织自愿组成的全省性、行业性、非营利性社会团体。协会现有会员单位108家，其中，理事单位36家，理事长1人，副理事长9人。

协会的宗旨是遵守宪法、法律法规和国家政策，遵守社会道德，积极贯彻执行国家有关监控化学品的方针政策，协助政府做好禁化武履约有关工作；做好行业协调、服务、规范工作，维护会员的合法权益，反映会员的期望和诉求；在政府和企业之间发挥桥梁纽带的作用，促进化工行业的发展，为国民经济的繁荣作贡献。

履约支撑工作

协助完成2次接受国际视察任务。选派专家指导洪湖市一泰科技有限公司、襄阳金达成精细化工有限公司做好接受禁化武组织现场视察的各项准备工作，组织专家进驻企业现场，帮助企业完善《视察前情况介绍》编制及翻译，梳理数据资料，进行物料衡算，准备视察现场，指导后勤安排，有力保障企业顺利通过国际视察。

开展监控化学品管理工作。一是派员参加国家禁化武办对甘肃省3家监控化学品企业的“双随机、一公开”执法检查并提供技术支撑。二是在国家禁化武办赴湖北省开展监控化学品生产特别许可监督检查及国家履约专家委地方服务行（湖北站）活动期间，派员全程参与，积极配合相关工作，获得国家禁化武办和专家委的高度评价。三是选派专家参加湖北省6家企业的监控化学品生产设施竣工验收及8家企业的监控化学品生产特别许可现场考核工作。四是支撑湖北省禁化武办赴荆州市、宜昌市的7家监控化学品企业开展专项监督检查。五是支撑武汉市、荆州市、襄阳市和宜昌市经信部门对当地县（区）的监控化学品管理工作人员、监控化学品企业开展履约培训。

协助开展禁化武履约宣传。一是协会专家利用项目评审、环保验收、安全评价评审验收等机会，对发现的未履行《公约》义务、不遵守《条例》《细则》的企业，现场宣贯相关法律法规，并将相关企业的信息反馈给湖北省禁化武办及相关地市。二是围绕“4·29国际禁止化学武器组织日”，协助湖北省禁化武办开展形式多样的宣传活动，在华中师范大学、武汉工程大学、武汉科技大学和湖北省化学和工业研究设计院等地开办宣传栏，并组织学生参与宣传海报的设计和履约知识竞赛。

协助举办禁化武履约培训。协助湖北省禁化武办在襄阳市举办全省禁化武履约工作业务培训班。针对企业履约工作不规范、工作人员变动频繁等具体问题，组织专家编写《〈监控化学品管理条例〉实施细则讲解》《视察前情况介绍》《湖北省禁化武履约工作手册》《数据采集》《物料衡算和生产能力核算及现场核查》《化工企业安全生产相关知识及要求》等培训教材，并在培训班上对相关内容进行详细讲解。

加强国内外履约信息报道。在湖北省禁化武办的指导下，出版发行2期《湖北履约简讯》，及时跟踪国际国内履约的新动态，介绍湖北省履约工作情况，突出报道监控化学品宣布、接受视察、监管、进出口管理和防扩散、化武销毁等方面的工作内容，搭建禁化武信息交流的平台，在省内外产生了一定的影响。

积极参加国家禁化武办组织的活动及有关课题的研究。协会在2023年2次派人员参加国家禁化武办举办的履约工作培训班、座谈会。开展国家禁化武办项目“新形势下省级及以下履约主管部门工作机制和方法及协会组织支撑作用研究”的相关研究工作。

（**撰稿**　陈道勇）

广东省循环经济和资源综合利用协会

协会动态

广东省循环经济和资源综合利用协会（以下简称“协会”）成立于2006年11月（2011年12月变更为现名），是具有省民政厅颁发的承接政府职能转移和购买服务资质的跨行业、跨部门、跨所有制的5A级全省性社会团体。协会以为企业服务、为政府服务，维护会员的合法权益，充分发挥政府与协会会员之间的桥梁和纽带作用为宗旨，广泛开展循环经济和资源综合利用领域的政策研究、咨询服务、技术推广、市场开发、专业培训和会议展览，以及国际交流与合作等，现有会员近500家。

协会于2023年8月发起成立监控化学品专业委员会，联合监控化学品生产、使用及从事监控化学品研究的企业、科研院所等单位，开展化学品安全与保障管理策略研究、监控化学品的供应链管理和禁化武相关专题研究等工作，旨在搭建监控化学品信息发布、经验交流、业务学习和普法宣传平台，助力监控化学品企业加快技术升级改造，提升管理水平。为保障中国履行《公约》，维护国家利益、人民安全和世界和平作出贡献。截至2023年年底，专业委员会共有8家成员单位，20余名专家。

履约支撑工作

监控化学品专业委员会成立后，发挥自身优势，开展多种形式的禁化武履约工作。

一是积极协助省、地市工信主管部门做好禁化武履约及监控化学品管理支撑工作，参与省内监控化学品检查及行政许可现场审核的专家指导工作，参与宣布数据审核等工作。

二是积极参与或组织多场国内外履约培训交流和会议活动，主要包括：组建 2 人代表团，首次以非政府组织身份参加 2023 年 11 月 27 日—12 月 2 日在荷兰海牙召开的禁化武组织第 28 届缔约国大会；派人员参加国家禁化武办在宁夏回族自治区银川市举办的全国禁化武履约综合培训班；协助广东省工业和信息化厅组织全省 2023 年过去活动年度宣布工作专题培训视频会议，并派专家做视察前情况介绍及参加禁化武组织第 28 届缔约国大会情况介绍；组织开展协会禁化武履约及监控化学品管理主题培训活动。

三是开展成员单位走访，现场走访了广东省内监控化学品企业，就企业发展和监控化学品管理等话题开展交流。同时，与各成员单位保持线上联系，随时为企业解决监控化学品的相关问题。

（**撰稿** 何力行 郑丽琼）

贵州省化工研究院

单位概况

贵州省化工研究院（以下简称“化工院”）成立于 1958 年，2000 年 7 月进行科技体制改革，是贵州省从事化工科研开发的转制科研院所。60 多年来，化工院在磷化工、煤化工、有机化工、无机化工、农药、化肥、黏合剂、塑料和橡胶助剂等方面取得了较为显著的科研成果。目前已发展为以化工技术开发、新材料新产品开发、生产应用、检验检测、环境影响评价、安全评价、节能评估、清洁生产审核、安全标准化考评和可行性研究等服务为主体的专业技术单位。

履约支撑工作

2023 年，在贵州省禁化武办的领导下，积极参与监控化学品日常监管、行政许可及专项监督检查等工作，帮助企业规范管理。6 月 21 日，协助对贵州威顿晶磷电子材料股份有限公司第三类监控化学品生产特别许可换证申请进行审查。8 月 22 日，协助对贵州璟和化学工业有限责任公司新建第三类监控化学品生产设施进行现场审核。10 月 18 日—19 日，协助对贵州红星发展股份有限公司、贵州赤天化桐梓化工有限公司开展“双随机、一公开”执法检查。

（撰稿　田娟　周昌平）

China

附 录

中国履行《禁止化学武器公约》报告（2023）

附录一 2023年中国履约大事记

1月

5日 中国常驻联合国代表团在联合国安理会就叙利亚化学武器问题举行的公开会上呼吁，对话协商解决叙利亚化学武器相关问题，并就禁化武组织总干事和叙利亚外长会晤、禁化武组织与叙利亚第25轮技术性磋商等阐述中方立场。

30日—2月1日 浙江科达新型建材有限公司的第二类监控化学品加工设施接受禁化武组织现场视察。

2月

7日 中国常驻联合国代表团在联合国安理会就叙利亚化学武器问题举行的公开会上呼吁，对话协商解决叙利亚化学武器相关问题，并就指称使用化学武器调查、叙利亚同禁化武组织合作、调查鉴定组涉叙报告等方面阐述中方立场。

8日 中、日、禁化武组织第37轮日遗化武问题三方磋商以视频方式举行。三方就日遗化武销毁进展、新销毁计划落实、恢复现场视察等交换意见。中方敦促日方尽快将污染土壤问题列入处理计划，并尽可能提供日遗化武埋藏信息。

13日 工业和信息化部部长主持召开党组会议，研究部署禁化武履约工作。

13日—16日 襄阳金达成精细化工有限公司的第二类监控化学品生产设施接受禁化武组织现场视察。

24日—3月18日 军事科学院军事医学研究院毒物分析实验室、防化研究院化学分析实验室参加禁化武组织第9次生物医学样品分析国际联试，并顺利通过。

27日—3月2日　山东滨农科技有限公司的第二类监控化学品生产、消耗设施接受禁化武组织现场视察。

3月

1日　国家禁化武办派员线上参加禁化武组织举办的工业磋商会议。会议就《公约》第六条视察次数的确定、附表2化学品设施视察情况和未来计划等议题进行了研讨。

5日—11日　中方赴黑龙江省伊春市、牡丹江市日遗化武埋藏点进行现场勘查，并与日方就2023年作业安排进行磋商。

6日—8日　原中央纪委驻工业和信息化部纪检组组长、专家委高级顾问金书波，工业和信息化部原副部长、十三届全国政协经济委员会副主任、专家委高级顾问刘利华赴浙江省调研石化化工产业发展和禁化武履约工作。

6日—26日　为日遗化武销毁目的，中方协助实施了黑龙江省鸡西市、佳木斯市、齐齐哈尔市至哈尔滨市，广东省清远市、江西省九江市至湖北省武汉市，内蒙古自治区巴彦淖尔市、山西省晋城市至太原市的日遗化武运输路线调查和风险评估作业。

9日　原中央纪委驻工业和信息化部纪检组组长、专家委高级顾问金书波，工业和信息化部原副部长、十三届全国政协经济委员会副主任、专家委高级顾问刘利华应邀出席在浙江省召开的国家履行《禁止化学武器公约》专家委员会第二次全体会议。

10日　工业和信息化部原副部长、十三届全国政协经济委员会副主任、专家委高级顾问刘利华出席在浙江工业大学举办的加强禁化武履约人才培养专题研讨会。

13日—17日　为日遗化武销毁目的，中方在内蒙古自治区巴彦淖尔市及云南省大理白族自治州实施日遗化武内部调查作业，确认巴彦淖尔市托管库存放日遗化武情况及其污染物状态，对大理白族自治州1枚不明弹药进行识别。

14日—16日　聊城氟尔新材料科技有限公司的第二类监控化学品生产、消耗设施接受禁化武组织现场视察。

14日—17日　中国驻荷兰大使兼常驻禁化武组织代表谈践率团出席禁化武组织在荷兰海牙召开的第102次执理会。谈践在一般性辩论发言中，就加快推进化武销毁进程、推动对话协商解决分歧、推进和平利用国际合作、为《公约》未来发展制定规划等问题阐述中方立场和主张。中国政府派员参加会议。

15日　按照《公约》有关规定，中国向禁化武组织提交第二类、第三类和第四类监控化学品2022年过去活动年度宣布。

15日　国家禁化武办印发《2023年履行〈禁止化学武器公约〉工作要点》，要求以做好新形势下接受禁化武组织视察工作为重点，严格履行《公约》义务，加强监督管理，加强宣传培训，加强国际合作，加强队伍建设，全面完成履约各项工作。

19日—21日　国家禁化武办派员现场参加禁化武组织在卡塔尔多哈举办的化学安全安保管理研讨会。

22日　中国向禁化武组织提交《中华人民共和国关于日本遗弃在华化学武器问题的立场文件》《关于在〈禁止化学武器公约〉框架下促进和平利用国际合作的工作文件》。

27日—30日　河南九势制药股份有限公司的第二类监控化学品生产、消耗设施及新乡市瑞丰新材料股份有限公司的第四类监控化学品生产设施接受禁化武组织现场视察。

30日　按照《公约》有关规定，中国向禁化武组织提交第一类监控化学品2022年过去活动年度宣布及2022年国家防备化学武器方案。

4月

4日　总召集人、工业和信息化部部长在北京主持召开履约工作部际联席会议第五次全体会议。副总召集人、工业和信息化部副部长徐晓兰，副总召集人、中央军委国际军事合作办公室副主任宋延超，联席会议成员国家移民管理局副局长刘海涛、中国国家铁路集团有限公司副总经理李文新等出席会议。

10日　中国向禁化武组织提交《中华人民共和国关于工业核查问题的立场文件》。

10日—12日　上海金力泰化工股份有限公司的第二类监控化学品消耗设施接受禁化武组织现场视察。

10日—17日　中国协助接待禁化武组织对湖北省武汉市日遗化武托管库及江西省九江市日遗化武托管库进行现场视察。此次视察为禁化武组织自2020年以来首次恢复对日遗化武设施的现场视察。

14日　国家禁化武办向禁化武组织推荐上海赛科石油化工有限责任公司、扬子石化—巴斯夫有限责任公司作为化工研修班项目实习企业。

16日—8月12日　中方监督协助日方在黑龙江省松花江佳木斯段水域实施日遗化武挖掘回收作业，挖掘废旧弹药40枚（件），确认日遗化武35枚（件）。上述日遗化武经密封包装后运至佳木斯日遗化武托管库安全看管。

17日—24日　国家禁化武办联合工业和信息化部新闻宣传中心开展第8个“国际禁止化学武器组织日”在线禁化武履约普法知识竞赛。

20日—12月10日　中方监督协助日方在吉林省敦化市哈尔巴岭实施日遗化武挖掘回收和销毁作业，挖掘回收日遗化武13901枚（件），销毁20605枚（件），处理废弃物392吨。

22日—28日　为日遗化武销毁目的，中方在吉林省通化市实施日遗化武内部调查作业，挖掘废旧弹药1枚，确认为疑似日遗化武。上述废旧弹药经密封包装后运至哈尔巴岭日遗化武托管库安全看管。

23日　国家禁化武办组织编撰的《中国履行〈禁止化学武器公约〉报告（2019—2021）》出版发行。

24 日—26 日 洪湖市一泰科技有限公司的第二类监控化学品生产、消耗设施接受禁化武组织现场视察。

28 日 国家禁化武办发布第 8 个国际禁止化学武器组织日主题宣传海报，并在工业和信息化部官网展出《地方履行〈禁止化学武器公约〉工作巡礼》。

5 月

4 日—6 日 国家禁化武办赴上海市调研禁化武组织化工研修项目实习企业准备工作落实情况。

6 日—6 月 11 日 为日遗化武销毁目的，中方协助实施了黑龙江省鸡西市、佳木斯市、齐齐哈尔市至哈尔滨市日遗化武运输作业，安全行驶 5600 千米，转运日遗化武 2320 枚（件），其中鸡西市 471 枚（件）、佳木斯市 550 枚（件）、齐齐哈尔市 1299 枚（件），并关闭鸡西日遗化武临时托管库。

8 日—10 日 江西名成科技发展有限公司的第二类监控化学品生产、消耗设施接受禁化武组织现场视察。

10 日—6 月 3 日 中方监督协助日方在黑龙江省尚志市帽儿山实施日遗化武挖掘回收作业，挖掘回收废旧弹药 155 枚（件），确认日遗化武 124 枚（件）。上述日遗化武经密封包装后运至哈尔滨日遗化武托管库安全看管。

14 日—21 日 中国政府派员参加五审会。中国代表团在一般性辩论发言中系统阐述对日遗化武、叙化武、化学科技和平利用、工业履约等问题的立场和主张，并与不结盟运动共同发言阐述对上述问题的共同立场。会间，中方举办了日遗化武专题展览，禁化武组织总干事、审议大会主席、50 余个缔约国常驻代表和官员、禁化武组织技秘处核查司和视察局负责人等 100 余人出席。中国向五审会提交了国家履约报告和关于日遗化武、工业核查问题的 2 份立场文件，与巴基斯坦等 14 国共同提交了关于在《公约》框架下促进和平利用国际合作的立场文件。外交部例行记者会于 15 日、

17日就五审会、日遗化武等问题表明中方立场。

16日—6月3日　中方监督协助日方在吉林省敦化市大桥乡实施日遗化武现场调查作业，挖掘回收日遗化武44枚（件）。上述日遗化武经密封包装后运至哈尔巴岭托管库安全看管。

21日—28日　国家禁化武办派员现场参加禁化武组织在荷兰海牙举办的女性化学师基础分析化学课程。

22日—26日　国家禁化武办派员现场参加禁化武组织在波兰华沙举办的实验室分析化学家课程。

22日—26日　齐鲁制药（内蒙古）有限公司呼伦贝尔分公司的第二类监控化学品消耗设施接受禁化武组织现场视察。

23日—25日　国家禁化武办派员现场参加禁化武组织在马来西亚吉隆坡举办的和平利用化学论坛。

23日—6月2日　中国协助接待禁化武组织对吉林省敦化市哈尔巴岭日遗化武挖掘回收、销毁作业及托管库进行现场视察。日方作为遗弃国派团参加了视察活动。

6月

2日—23日　国家禁化武办派员线上参加禁化武组织举办的亚洲地区化学防护援助初级培训班。

3日—26日　中方监督协助日方在吉林省珲春市实施日遗化武挖掘回收作业，含作业期间从周边回收的3枚（件）共挖掘废旧炮弹150枚（件），确认日遗化武150枚（件）。上述日遗化武与作业产生的12桶144.3千克的污染物经密封包装后运至珲春日遗化武托管库安全看管。

10日—13日　中央军委国际军事合作办公室主任李斌赴黑龙江省和吉林省日遗化武作业现场调研，勘察了珲春市、敦化市哈尔巴岭、哈尔滨市和佳木斯市4个作业点位，检查了珲春和哈尔滨日遗化武托管库，并与作业人员进行座谈。

12日—15日　山东国邦药业有限公司和山东普洛得邦医药有限公司的第四类监控化学品生产设施接受禁化武组织现场视察。

16日　国家禁化武办派员线上参加禁化武组织举办的工业磋商会议。会议就五审会对现行工业核查机制的审查情况进行了研讨。

18日—23日　中国协助接待禁化武组织对黑龙江省佳木斯市日遗化武挖掘回收作业及宁安市日遗化武托管库进行现场视察。日方作为遗弃国派团参加了视察活动。

26日—29日　国家禁化武办派员线上参加禁化武组织举办的国际化学防护与援助培训班。

26日—30日　内蒙古浩普科技有限公司的第二类监控化学品生产、消耗设施接受禁化武组织现场视察。

30日　根据《公约》有关规定，中国向禁化武组织提交日遗化武宣布。

7月

2日—23日　为日遗化武销毁目的，中方协助实施了广东省清远市、江西省九江市至湖北省武汉市日遗化武运输作业，安全行驶6192千米，转运日遗化武3375枚（件），其中清远市366枚（件）、九江市3009枚（件），并关闭九江日遗化武托管库。

10日　国家禁化武办派员现场参加禁化武组织在荷兰海牙举办的工业磋商会议。会议就启用新的视察报告模板、改进《公约》第六条核查机制、调整被视察厂区选择方法、附表2B04化学品等议题进行了研讨。

10日—14日　内蒙古灵圣作物科技有限公司的第二类监控化学品生产、消耗设施接受禁化武组织现场视察。

11日　中国常驻联合国代表团出席联合国安理会就叙利亚化学武器问题举行的公开会，呼吁对话协商解决叙利亚化学武器相关问题，欢迎叙利亚政府同禁化武组织进行更高级别磋商，并就二者沟通合作阐述中方立场。

11日—14日　中国驻荷兰大使兼常驻禁化武组织代表谈践率团出席

禁化武组织在荷兰海牙举行的第103次执理会。谈践在一般性辩论发言中，就加快推进化武销毁、推动热点问题解决重返正轨、坚持对话协商、促进国际合作等问题阐述中方立场和主张。中国政府派员参加会议。

18日—25日　中国协助接待禁化武组织对黑龙江省哈尔滨市日遗化武销毁作业及托管库进行现场视察。日方作为遗弃国派团参加了视察活动。

19日—21日　国家禁化武办对福建省开展监控化学品生产特别许可现场督查检查。

21日　根据《公约》有关规定，中国向禁化武组织提交吉林省珲春市、敦化市哈尔巴岭，黑龙江省哈尔滨市、鸡西市、佳木斯市、齐齐哈尔市等6地日遗化武宣布。

23日—28日　营口营新化工科技有限公司和山东宏旭化学股份有限公司的第三类监控化学品生产设施接受禁化武组织现场视察。

26日—9月9日　中方监督协助日方在黑龙江省牡丹江市实施日遗化武挖掘回收作业，挖掘回收废旧弹药3089枚（件），确认日遗化武3050枚（件）。上述日遗化武经密封包装后运至宁安日遗化武托管库安全看管。

8月

6日—9日　石家庄瑞凯化工有限公司宏润分公司的第二类监控化学品生产、消耗设施接受禁化武组织现场视察。

7日—9日　国家禁化武办赴上海市调研低浓度监控化学品三乙醇胺的进出口情况。

14日—17日　中方监督并协助日方在山西省太原市实施日遗化武现场调查作业，鉴别日遗化武7枚（件）。

16日—9月20日　为日遗化武销毁目的，中方协助实施了内蒙古自治区巴彦淖尔市、山西省晋城市至太原市日遗化武运输作业，安全行驶8643千米，转运带引信日遗化武4枚（件），其中巴彦淖尔市3枚（件），晋城市 1 枚（件），并关闭巴彦淖尔和晋城日遗化武托管库。

18 日—22 日　中方监督协助日方在天津市实施日遗化武现场调查作业，鉴别日遗化武 14 枚（件）。

18 日—9 月 1 日　国家禁化武办派员现场参加禁化武组织在柬埔寨举办的第 21 届亚洲地区国家履约主管部门会议。

21 日—25 日　河北威远生物化工有限公司的第二类监控化学品生产、消耗设施和山东海江化工有限公司的第三类监控化学品生产设施接受禁化武组织现场视察。

9 月

1 日—10 月 6 日　国家禁化武办派员参加禁化武组织在线举办的化学工业防爆与安全管理培训。

3 日—9 日　宁夏格瑞精细化工有限公司和宁夏东吴农化股份有限公司的第四类监控化学品生产设施接受禁化武组织现场视察。

7 日　按照《公约》有关规定，中国向禁化武组织提交第二类、第三类监控化学品 2024 年预计活动年度宣布。

11 日—13 日　国家禁化武办对湖北省开展监控化学品生产特别许可现场督查检查。

11 日—15 日　国家禁化武办派员现场参加禁化武组织在德国举办的国际化学防护与援助培训班。

14 日　按照《公约》有关规定，中国向禁化武组织提交第一类监控化学品 2024 年预计活动年度宣布。

14 日—15 日　原中央纪委驻工业和信息化部纪检组组长、专家委高级顾问金书波应邀出席专家委赴湖北省开展地方服务行活动并讲话。

18 日—21 日　江西理文化工有限公司的第二类监控化学品生产、消耗设施接受禁化武组织现场视察。

21 日　中、日、禁化武组织第 38 轮日遗化武问题三方磋商以视频方式举行。此次磋商正值中日达成2022年后日遗化武销毁计划1周年。三方就日遗化武销毁进展，黑龙江省佳木斯市、尚志市和吉林省珲春市三地日遗化武销毁计划及2024年日遗化武销毁计划制定等交换意见。

23日—28日　中方组织对天津市蓟州区，山西省太原市，吉林省珲春市、敦化市、辽源市，黑龙江省哈尔滨市、佳木斯市、牡丹江市，江苏省南京市，安徽省合肥市，湖北省武汉市等地的日遗化武托管库进行安全检查。

24日—27日　国家禁化武办在宁夏回族自治区银川市举办全国禁化武履约综合培训班。国家禁化武办通报了2023年全国履约工作主要情况，分析了当前履约工作面临的新情况、新问题，对做好下一步重点工作和本次培训提出了具体要求。外交部军控司介绍了禁化武组织动态和国际履约形势。

27日　国家禁化武办派员线上参加禁化武组织举办的工业磋商会议。会议就改进《公约》第六条核查机制、附表2化学品设施视察计划等议题进行研讨。

10月

2日—31日　国家禁化武办派员线上参加禁化武组织举办的国际化学防护与援助培训班。

8日—11月16日　中方监督协助日方在黑龙江省伊春市实施日遗化武挖掘回收作业，挖掘回收废旧弹药41枚（件），确认日遗化武10枚（件）。上述日遗化武经密封包装后运至伊春日遗化武托管库安全看管。

9日　国家禁化武办派员现场参加禁化武组织在荷兰海牙举办的工业磋商会议。会议就安全信息交换中心的使用、被视察厂区选择方法、附表2化学品设施视察计划等议题进行研讨。

9日—12日　潍坊加华化工有限公司和山东海利尔化工有限公司的第四类监控化学品生产设施接受禁化武组织现场视察。

10日—13日　中国代表团出席禁化武组织在荷兰海牙召开的第104次

执理会，在一般性辩论发言中，就推进化武销毁、维护《公约》权威性和有效性、促进和平利用国际合作、坚持务实高效合作等问题阐述中方立场。中国政府派员参加会议。

13 日　外交部副部长孙卫东一行赴吉林省敦化市哈尔巴岭日遗化武销毁作业现场考察调研。

16 日—19 日　国家禁化武办对广西壮族自治区开展监控化学品生产特别许可现场督查检查。其间，广西壮族自治区召开自治区履约工作座谈会，工业和信息化部原副部长、十三届全国政协经济委员会副主任、专家委高级顾问刘利华出席会议。

16 日—23 日　中国协助接待禁化武组织对吉林省敦化市哈尔巴岭日遗化武销毁作业及托管库进行现场视察。日方作为遗弃国派团参加了视察活动。

17 日—19 日　国家禁化武办派员现场参加禁化武组织在韩国首尔举办的和平发展与利用化学研讨会。

20 日—11 月 12 日　防化研究院化学分析实验室参加禁化武组织第 54 次环境样品分析国际联试，并顺利通过。

22 日—26 日　扬州晨化新材料股份有限公司的第二类监控化学品生产设施接受禁化武组织现场视察。

24 日—26 日　国家禁化武办派员现场参加禁化武组织在卡塔尔多哈举办的第十届化学工业和国家履约主管部门代表年会。

26 日—11 月 25 日　中方监督协助日方在黑龙江省哈尔滨市实施日遗化武鉴别包装作业，鉴别日遗化武 309 枚（件）。上述日遗化武已密封包装并安全看管。

31 日　按照《公约》有关规定，中国向禁化武组织提交吉林省敦化市哈尔巴岭日遗化武宣布。

11 月

1 日　国家禁化武办对甘肃省第二类监控化学品企业甘肃滨农科技有

限公司开展监控化学品专项执法检查。

2日　国家禁化武办对甘肃省白银市伊博化工科技有限公司开展监控化学品“双随机、一公开”执法检查。

6日—9日　淮安华源化工有限公司的第三类监控化学品生产设施和利民化学有限责任公司的第四类监控化学品生产设施接受禁化武组织现场视察。

7日—12日　中国协助接受禁化武组织对山西省太原市日遗化武托管库进行现场视察。日方作为遗弃国派团参加了视察活动。

13日—17日　国家禁化武办派员现场参加禁化武组织在巴基斯坦举办的国际化学防护与援助培训班。

17日　国家禁化武办在陕西省西安市召开接受禁化武组织现场视察工作座谈会。国家禁化武办通报了2023年全国履约工作情况，分析了当前履约工作面临的新形势，并就做好下一步工作特别是做好2024年接受禁化武组织视察工作提出了要求。省级禁化武办和履约专家委专家就禁化武组织电子视察报告（E-INS）模板及试用情况、接受视察及做好视察后勤安保工作、《视察前情况介绍》等进行了研讨交流。

18日　国家禁化武办在陕西省西安彩晶光电科技股份有限公司举办第12次禁化武组织国际视察演练，工业和信息化部原副部长、十三届全国政协经济委员会副主任、专家委高级顾问刘利华出席，外交部军控司、中央军委国际军事合作办公室、专家委有关同志到场观摩指导。

20日—21日　国家禁化武办派员现场参加禁化武组织在荷兰海牙举办的化学反恐桌面演习。

20日—24日　浙江万盛股份有限公司的第二类监控化学品加工设施和浙江沙星科技股份有限公司的第四类监控化学品生产设施接受禁化武组织现场视察。

22日—24日　国家禁化武办派员现场参加禁化武组织在荷兰海牙举办的第25届国家履约主管部门会议。

22日—24日　中日双方对山西省忻州市日遗化武销毁场地、周边交通、环境情况和医疗保障等情况进行考察。

26日—12月6日　中方监督协助日方在湖北省武汉市实施日遗化武鉴别包装作业，鉴别日遗化武66枚（件）。上述日遗化武已密封包装并安全看管。

27日—12月1日　中国驻荷兰大使兼常驻禁化武组织代表谈践率团出席禁化武组织在荷兰海牙召开的第28届缔约国大会。谈践在一般性辩论发言中，就建设“无化武世界”、促进化学经济科技发展、正确解决化武热点问题、加强缔约国团结协作等问题阐述中方立场和主张。中国政府派员参加会议。

12月

4日—8日　永农生物科学有限公司的第二类监控化学品消耗设施和浙江医药股份有限公司昌海生物分公司的第四类监控化学品生产设施接受禁化武组织现场视察。

12日—14日　国家禁化武办对辽宁省第二类监控化学品企业辽宁佳加隆新材料有限公司和朝阳鑫美高纯半导体材料有限公司开展监控化学品专项执法检查。

18日—21日　台州达辰药业有限公司和浙江华海药业股份有限公司临海川南分公司的第四类监控化学品生产设施接受禁化武组织现场视察。

19日—22日　中方对湖南省长沙市、衡阳市、岳阳市，甘肃省兰州市4地日遗化武线索开展内部调查，共鉴别包装疑似日遗化武9枚（件）。上述疑似日遗化武已密封包装并安全看管。

22日　中国常驻联合国代表团出席联合国安理会就叙利亚化学武器问题举行的公开会，呼吁对话协商解决叙化武相关问题，欢迎叙利亚政府和禁化武组织举行第25轮技术性磋商，并就指称化武使用事件的调查和追责阐述中方立场和主张。

附录二　2023年中国履约文件选编

国家禁化武办关于组织开展第 8 个国际禁止化学武器组织日宣传活动的通知

禁化武办发〔2023〕50 号

各省、自治区、直辖市及新疆生产建设兵团工业和信息化主管部门：

2023 年是《禁止化学武器公约》开放签署 30 周年，4 月 29 日是第 8 个国际禁止化学武器组织日。为广泛宣传《禁止化学武器公约》履约工作的重要意义和丰硕成果，提高全社会对履约工作的认知度，国家禁化武办决定在全国范围内开展第 8 个国际禁止化学武器组织日系列宣传活动。现将有关事项通知如下。

一、宣传主题

以第 8 个国际禁止化学武器组织日为重点，围绕“携手共创一个永无化学武器的世界”“化学领域成就完全用于造福人类”“4·29 国际禁止化学武器组织日”等主题，开展形式多样的宣传活动，宣传履约工作重要意义，展现我国履约工作成就，展示履约人风采。

二、活动安排

宣传活动采取国家禁化武办统一部署动员，各省（自治区、直辖市）及新疆生产建设兵团工业和信息化主管部门和有关单位分别组织落实的方式。

国家禁化武办将面向社会组织开展主题海报征集、在线履约普法知识竞赛活动，组织各省（自治区、直辖市）及新疆生产建设兵团工业和信息化主管部门举办“地方禁化武履约工作巡礼”在线展览。以上活动信息、活动成果将在工业和信息化部官网《履行禁止化学武器公约工作专栏》等平台发布。

各省（自治区、直辖市）及新疆生产建设兵团工业和信息化主管部门组织发动相关政府部门、协会、企业和科研院所，根据《2023年履行〈禁止化学武器公约〉工作要点》，结合本地实际，统筹宣传资源，创新宣传方式，在4月29日及前后开展宣传活动，广泛宣介《禁止化学武器公约》宗旨目标及对世界和平的重要意义和巨大贡献。

三、活动要求

（一）高度重视，加强组织领导。充分认识禁化武履约工作的重要意义，加强对监控化学品企业、行业协会、学校等重点单位参加征集活动的组织领导，充分调动广大履约相关人员积极性、主动性和创造性，确保活动取得良好效果。

（二）创新形式，注重宣传效果。结合本地禁化武履约工作实际和地区特点，充分利用各类新闻媒体和网络平台，策划开展群众参与度高、传播效果好的宣传活动。同时，组织推动在重点监控化学品企业、相关政府部门、高校和科研院所等单位场所，开展悬挂横幅、张贴海报、举办展览、专家讲座等活动，营造浓郁的履约宣传氛围。

（三）常抓不懈，加强宣传工作。履约宣传工作需要持之以恒，久久为功。积极探索履约宣传融入日常工作的新模式和新思路，充分利用行政规范性文件起草过程、办理监控化学品行政许可、监控化学品事中事后监管和履约业务培训，开展履约普法宣传，确保提高履约宣传实效。

国家履行《禁止化学武器公约》工作办公室

2023年3月24日

国家禁化武办关于开展监控化学品生产特别许可督查工作的通知

禁化武办发〔2023〕95号

各省、自治区、直辖市及新疆生产建设兵团工业和信息化主管部门：

为进一步规范监控化学品生产特别许可工作程序，加强对各地区实施行政许可行为的监督和指导，强化事中事后监管，根据中央办公厅和国务院办公厅的工作要求，我办自即日起开展监控化学品生产特别许可督查工作，具体要求如下：

一、督查内容

2022年6月1日—2023年5月31日期间监控化学品生产特别许可审批和备案情况。

二、督查安排

本次督查采取自查与抽查相结合方式进行。

（一）省级自查。自即日起至7月14日，各单位对照监控化学品生产特别许可督查事项表（见附件），完成本地区监控化学品生产特别许可自查，并形成自查书面材料。

（二）督查检查。8月14日至9月29日，我办根据各地区监控化学品生产特别许可开展情况，选取若干省份，组织督查组进行检查。

三、督查检查方式

（一）实地检查。组织督查组赴被抽查省份开展现场检查，工作时间为2个工作日，其中，查阅文件1个工作日，现场检查企业1个工作日。

督查组由我办工作人员及专家组成。

（二）书面检查。被抽查省份将监控化学品生产特别许可审批及备案相关材料寄送至工业和信息化部安全生产司（国家禁化武办），由我办组织书面审查。

被检查省份、检查方式、督查组人员情况及检查时间另行通知。

四、相关工作要求

（一）加强组织领导。各单位要充分认识本次督查检查的重要性，积极做好准备工作，成立工作小组配合督查，小组成员应至少包含承担禁化武履约和监控化学品行政许可的处室负责同志等，认真细致开展自查，收集整理汇总相关材料。

（二）狠抓工作落实。对自查过程中发现的问题要立行立改。自查形成的书面材料应当真实准确，不得弄虚作假。

（三）请各单位将自查报告，经主要领导审批、加盖公章后，于7月21日前报送至国家禁化武办。

国家履行《禁止化学武器公约》工作办公室

2023年6月12日

国家禁化武办关于开展2024年预计活动年度宣布工作的通知

禁化武办发〔2023〕119号

各省、自治区、直辖市及新疆生产建设兵团工业和信息化主管部门：

为履行《禁止化学武器公约》规定的宣布义务，根据《中华人民共和国统计法》《中华人民共和国监控化学品管理条例》《〈中华人民共和国监控化学品管理条例〉实施细则》以及《全国监控化学品统计调查制度》有关规定，现将2024年预计活动年度宣布有关事项通知如下：

一、宣布工作要求

加强组织领导。高度重视，充分认识宣布工作的重要性、严肃性和时效性，强化对预计宣布工作的组织领导，健全履约规章制度，加强审核把关，不断提高宣布工作质效，确保预计宣布工作顺利开展。

打牢宣布数据申报基础。宣布工作是一项专业性、技术性强的长期性工作。积极探索将宣布工作融入日常履约监管和企业生产管理工作中的新模式和新思路，充分利用监控化学品行政许可及事中事后监管，持之以恒加强对宣布工作的监督指导。围绕禁化武组织《宣布手册》，开展专题培训，组织企业重点学习、准确掌握宣布要求。深入企业开展数据核查，督促企业真实、准确、完整、按时填报宣布数据，切实解决宣布不全、不准等问题，坚决防范和惩治统计造假等行为。组织专家认真审核宣布数据，切实提高宣布信息的准确性。

规范宣布工作报告。宣布工作完成后，请将宣布工作、组织领导等情况以书面形式，经本单位负责同志批准后，报国家禁化武办，同时提交宣布厂区数量分类统计表、第二类、第三类监控化学品申报厂区一览表，以及2023年上半年拆除及永久停产的各类监控化学品厂区一览表，作为报告附件。

二、数据申报范围

（一）预计在2024年度生产、加工、消耗第二类监控化学品的厂区；

（二）预计在2024年度生产第三类监控化学品的厂区，其中《列入第三类监控化学品的新增品种清单》的氰化钾、氰化钠、五硫化二磷等10个第三类监控化学品除外。

三、数据申报时间

系统开放时间为2023年7月10日—28日。监控化学品企业网上填报、提交及各级禁化武办审核均须在此期间完成。数据及书面报告提交国家禁化武办截至2023年8月11日。

四、其他事项

请使用火狐浏览器通过禁化武数据采集与宣布系统在线申报2024年预计活动年度宣布。网上填报前，请组织辖区内监控化学品企业登录禁化武数据采集与宣布系统，下载《国家禁化武数据采集与宣布系统企业用户使用说明书》，并认真阅读，按要求完成新系统登录认证、手机号码绑定、账户信息确认及参数合法性检查等工作。

特此通知。

国家履行《禁止化学武器公约》工作办公室

2023年6月28日

国家禁化武办关于开展2023年过去活动年度宣布工作的通知

禁化武办发〔2023〕209号

各省、自治区、直辖市及新疆生产建设兵团工业和信息化主管部门：

为履行《禁止化学武器公约》规定的宣布义务，根据《中华人民共和国统计法》《中华人民共和国监控化学品管理条例》《〈中华人民共和国监控化学品管理条例〉实施细则》以及《全国监控化学品统计调查制度》有关规定，现将2023年过去活动年度宣布有关要求通知如下：

一、宣布工作要求

加强组织领导。高度重视，充分认识宣布工作的重要性、严肃性和时效性，强化对年度宣布工作的组织领导，健全履约规章制度，加强审核把关，不断提高宣布工作质效，确保预计宣布工作顺利开展。

打牢宣布数据申报基础。宣布工作是一项专业性、技术性强的长期工作。积极探索将宣布工作融入日常履约监管和企业生产管理工作中的新模式和新思路，充分利用监控化学品行政许可事中事后监管，持之以恒加强对宣布工作的监督指导。围绕禁化武组织《宣布手册》，开展专题培训，组织企业重点学习、准确掌握宣布要求。深入企业开展数据核查，督促企业真实、准确、完整、按时填报宣布数据，切实解决宣布不全、不准等问题，坚决防范和惩治统计造假等行为。组织专家认真审核宣布数据，切实提高宣布信息的准确性。

规范宣布工作。宣布工作完成后，请将宣布工作、组织领导等情况以书面形式，经本单位负责同志批准后，报国家禁化武办，同时提交宣布厂区数量分类统计表、第二类、第三类、第四类监控化学品申报厂区一览表，以及2023年下半年拆除及永久停产的各类监控化学品厂区一览表。作为报告附件。

二、数据申报范围

（一）在 2023 年度生产、加工、消耗第二类监控化学品的厂区。

（二）在 2023 年度生产第三类监控化学品的厂区，其中《列入第三类监控化学品的新增品种清单》的五硫化二磷豁免数据申报，氰化钾、氰化钠、二甲胺等其他 9 个化学品按第四类监控化学品有关要求申报生产数据。

（三）在 2023 年度生产第四类监控化学品的厂区。

三、数据申报时间

新增企业注册、企业及各级禁化武办修改验证手机号码时间：2023 年 12 月 18 日至 2023 年 12 月 22 日。

企业网上填报、提交及各级禁化武办审核时间：2023 年 12 月 25 日至 2024 年 1 月 12 日。于 2023 年 12 月 25 日完成生产任务的企业可正常填报，连续生产的企业应填报整个日历年的数据。

上报文件及数据提交国家禁化武办时间：2024 年 1 月 23 日前。

四、其他事项

请使用火狐浏览器通过禁化武数据采集与宣布系统在线申报 2023 年过去活动年度宣布。网上填报前，请组织辖区内监控化学品企业登录国家禁化武数据采集与宣布系统，下载《国家禁化武数据采集与宣布系统企业用户使用说明书》，并认真阅读，按要求完成新系统登录认证、手机号码绑定、账户信息确认及参数合法性检查等工作。

特此通知。

国家履行《禁止化学武器公约》工作办公室

2023 年 11 月 14 日

国家禁化武办关于表扬2023年度履行《禁止化学武器公约》工作先进集体和个人的通报

禁化武办发〔2023〕237号

各省、自治区、直辖市及新疆生产建设兵团工业和信息化主管部门：

2023年，在工业和信息化部党组的正确指导下，在各省、自治区、直辖市和新疆生产建设兵团党委政府的大力支持下，全国履约系统牢记初心使命，坚持以习近平新时代中国特色社会主义思想为指导，全面贯彻党的二十大精神，贯彻落实党中央、国务院决策部署，认真履行《禁止化学武器公约》核心义务，夯实禁化武履约工作基础，切实提升政务服务水平，积极开展履约宣传培训，主动推选履约人才，扎实推进履约各项工作，取得了新成绩、新进展，涌现出了一批履约战线先进集体和先进个人。

为表彰履约先进典型，弘扬履约优良传统，进一步激发广大履约工作者增强履约荣誉感、使命感，经《禁止化学武器公约》履约工作部际联席会议副总召集人徐晓兰副部长批准，国家履行《禁止化学武器公约》工作办公室决定对河北省禁化武办等12个先进集体、赵帅等15名先进个人予以通报表扬。

希望受到表扬的先进集体和个人再接再厉，继续发挥模范表率作用，以更加奋进的精神，更加务实的举措投入履约工作中，努力作出新贡献。全国各级履约主管部门和全体履约工作者要以先进集体和个人为榜样，积极履职尽责，做实做细禁化武履约监管各项工作，为奋力谱写新时代履约工作新篇章作出更大贡献。

附件：1. 先进集体名单

2. 先进个人名单

国家履行《禁止化学武器公约》工作办公室

2023 年 12 月 15 日

附件 1：

先进集体名单（共 12 个）

河北省禁化武办
山西省禁化武办
内蒙古自治区禁化武办
江苏省禁化武办
浙江省禁化武办
福建省禁化武办
江西省禁化武办
山东省禁化武办
湖北省禁化武办
广西壮族自治区禁化武办
陕西省禁化武办
宁夏回族自治区禁化武办

附件 2：

先进个人名单（共 15 名）

北京市禁化武办	赵　帅
内蒙古自治区禁化武办	丹　江
黑龙江省禁化武办	曹滨巍
上海市禁化武办	刘元东
江苏省禁化武办	陈忠明
浙江省禁化武办	朱小庆
山东省禁化武办	田晓慧
河南省禁化武办	刘国正
湖北省禁化武办	戴兰林
湖南省禁化武办	康文娟
广东省禁化武办	郑　威
四川省禁化武办	梁　虎
贵州省禁化武办	周　珊
陕西省禁化武办	赵亚茹
宁夏回族自治区禁化武办	张　颖

工业和信息化部办公厅 商务部办公厅 海关总署办公厅关于优化低浓度三乙醇胺混合物进出口监管措施的通知

工信厅联安全函〔2023〕394 号

各省、自治区、直辖市及新疆生产建设兵团工业和信息化主管部门、商务主管部门，各直属海关：

根据《中华人民共和国监控化学品管理条例》《〈中华人民共和国监控化学品管理条例〉实施细则》有关规定，为提升监控化学品进出口管理效能，现决定自 2024 年 2 月 1 日起优化部分低浓度三乙醇胺混合物进出口的监管措施。现将有关事项通知如下：

三乙醇胺含量较低的非医用消毒剂、合成洗涤粉、化妆品、墨水等消费类商品（详见附件），防扩散风险可控，不属于《两用物项和技术进出口许可证管理目录》中三乙醇胺（海关商品编号 2922150000）和三乙醇胺混合物（海关商品编号 3824999950）项下的管控物项，无须办理监控化学品进出口审批手续，无须办理两用物项和技术进出口许可。

执行过程中发现的问题，请及时报国家履行《禁止化学武器公约》工作办公室，以便根据实际情况动态调整监管措施。

附件：不属于《两用物项和技术进出口许可证管理目录》的低浓度三乙醇胺混合物产品清单

工业和信息化部办公厅

商务部办公厅

海关总署办公厅

2024 年 1 月 16 日

附件：

不属于《两用物项和技术进出口许可证管理目录》的
低浓度三乙醇胺混合物产品清单

序号	商品名称	备注	参考海关商品编号
1	非医用消毒剂	其他非医用消毒剂	3808940090
2	合成洗涤粉	零售包装的合成洗涤粉	3402501000
		其他零售包装有机表面活性剂制品	3402509000
3	洁肤用有机表面活性产品及制品（液状或膏状并制成零售包装的，不论是否含有肥皂）	洁肤用有机表面活性产品及制品	3401300090
		洁肤用有机表面活性产品及制品，液状或膏状并制成零售包装的，含有含汞亮肤肥皂（含汞量超过百万分之一）	3401300010
	香水及花露水	包装标注含量以重量计的香水及花露水	3303000010
		包装标注含量以体积计的香水及花露水	3303000020
	唇用化妆品	包装标注含量以重量计的含濒危物种成分唇用化妆品	3304100011
		包装标注含量以体积计的含濒危物种成分唇用化妆品	3304100012
		包装标注规格为“片”或“张”的含濒危物种成分唇用化妆品	3304100013
		包装标注含量以重量计的其他唇用化妆品	3304100091
		包装标注含量以体积计的其他唇用化妆品	3304100092
		包装标注规格为“片”或“张”的其他唇用化妆品	3304100093
	眼用化妆品	包装标注含量以重量计的含濒危物种成分眼用化妆品	3304200011
		包装标注含量以体积计的含濒危物种成分眼用化妆品	3304200012

续表

序号	商品名称	备注	参考海关商品编号
3	眼用化妆品	包装标注规格为“片”或“张”的含濒危物种成分眼用化妆品	3304200013
		包装标注含量以重量计的其他眼用化妆品	3304200091
		包装标注含量以体积计的其他眼用化妆品	3304200092
		包装标注含量以体积计的其他眼用化妆品	3304200093
	指（趾）甲化妆品	包装标注含量以重量计的指（趾）甲化妆品	3304300001
		包装标注含量以体积计的指（趾）甲化妆品	3304300002
		包装标注规格为“片”或“张”的指（趾）甲化妆品	3304300003
	粉，不论是否压紧	其他粉状化妆品，不论是否压紧	3304910090
	洗发剂（香波）	含濒危物种成分的洗发剂	3305100010
		其他洗发剂（香波）	3305100090
	其他护发品	其他护发品	3305900000
	剃须用制剂	剃须用制剂	3307100000
	香浴盐及其他泡澡用制剂	香浴盐及其他泡澡用制剂	3307300000
	其他盥洗用皂及有机表面活性产品（包括含有药物的产品、呈条状、块状或模制形状）（特殊化妆品功效香皂）	其他盥洗用皂及有机表面活性产品（包括含有药物的产品、呈条状、块状或模制形状）（特殊化妆品功效香皂）	3401110090
	其他按零售包装供私人使用或经包装供个人使用的美容品或化妆品或护肤品	包装标注含量以重量计含濒危物种成分的美容品或化妆品及护肤品（包括防晒油或晒黑油，但药品除外）	3304990021
		包装标注含量以重量计的其他美容品或化妆品及护肤品（包括防晒油或晒黑油，但药品除外）	3304990029
		包装标注含量以体积计含濒危物种成分的美容品或化妆品及护肤品（包括防晒油或晒黑油，但药品除外）	3304990031

续表

序号	商品名称	备注	参考海关商品编号
3	其他按零售包装供私人使用或经包装供个人使用的美容品或化妆品或护肤品	包装标注含量以体积计的其他美容品或化妆品及护肤品（包括防晒油或晒黑油，但药品除外）	3304990039
		包装标注规格为“片”或“张”的含濒危物种成分的美容品或化妆品及护肤品（包括防晒油或晒黑油，但药品除外）	3304990041
		包装标注规格为“片”或“张”的其他美容品或化妆品及护肤品（包括防晒油或晒黑油，但药品除外）	3304990049
		其他包装标注规格的含濒危物种成分的美容品或化妆品及护肤品（包括防晒油或晒黑油，但药品除外）	3304990091
		其他包装标注规格的其他含濒危物种成分的美容品或化妆品及护肤品（包括防晒油或晒黑油，但药品除外）	3304990099
4	水性喷墨墨水	水性喷墨墨水	3215902000
5	书写墨水	书写墨水（不论是否固体或浓缩）	3215901000

备注：清单中商品范围以商品名称及备注为准，海关商品编号仅供通关申报参考。

附录三　2023年监控化学品生产设施建设目录

序号	企业名称	所在省（自治区、直辖市）	类型
1	天津奥瑞芙生物医药有限公司	天津	含磷、硫、氟的第四类监控化学品
2	中国石油化工股份有限公司天津分公司	天津	第三类监控化学品
3	天津凯莱英制药有限公司	天津	含磷、硫、氟的第四类监控化学品
4	河北振兴化工橡胶有限公司	河北	含磷、硫、氟的第四类监控化学品
5	河北允升生物科技有限公司	河北	含磷、硫、氟的第四类监控化学品
6	河北冀衡药业股份有限公司	河北	含磷、硫、氟的第四类监控化学品
7	河北珈奥甘油化工有限公司	河北	第三类监控化学品
8	唐山三鼎化工有限公司	河北	含磷、硫、氟的第四类监控化学品
9	多氟多阳福新材料有限公司	山西	第三类监控化学品
10	山西裕英永旭新材料有限责任公司	山西	含磷、硫、氟的第四类监控化学品
11	内蒙古祁泰化学有限公司	内蒙古	含磷、硫、氟的第四类监控化学品
12	内蒙古世杰化工有限公司	内蒙古	含磷、硫、氟的第四类监控化学品
13	内蒙古鑫卫化工有限责任公司	内蒙古	含磷、硫、氟的第四类监控化学品
14	内蒙古兴发科技有限公司	内蒙古	第三类监控化学品 含磷、硫、氟的第四类监控化学品
15	内蒙古宇晨润医药科技有限公司	内蒙古	含磷、硫、氟的第四类监控化学品
16	内蒙古扬帆新材料有限公司	内蒙古	含磷、硫、氟的第四类监控化学品
17	内蒙古齐晖药业有限公司	内蒙古	含磷、硫、氟的第四类监控化学品
18	内蒙古中高化工有限公司	内蒙古	含磷、硫、氟的第四类监控化学品
19	内蒙古海泰科技有限公司	内蒙古	含磷、硫、氟的第四类监控化学品
20	内蒙古鲲鹏新材料有限公司	内蒙古	含磷、硫、氟的第四类监控化学品
21	内蒙古蓝科生物科技有限公司	内蒙古	含磷、硫、氟的第四类监控化学品
22	内蒙古佳瑞米精细化工有限公司	内蒙古	含磷、硫、氟的第四类监控化学品

续表

序号	企业名称	所在省（自治区、直辖市）	类型
23	内蒙古灵圣作物科技有限公司	内蒙古	第二类监控化学品 第三类监控化学品 含磷、硫、氟的第四类监控化学品
24	乌海青石化学有限公司	内蒙古	含磷、硫、氟的第四类监控化学品
25	内蒙古津盟化工有限公司	内蒙古	含磷、硫、氟的第四类监控化学品
26	内蒙古利元科技有限公司	内蒙古	含磷、硫、氟的第四类监控化学品
27	巴彦淖尔市金盛汇化工有限公司	内蒙古	含磷、硫、氟的第四类监控化学品
28	内蒙古源宏精细化工有限公司	内蒙古	含磷、硫、氟的第四类监控化学品
29	内蒙古联群化工科技有限公司	内蒙古	含磷、硫、氟的第四类监控化学品
30	内蒙古永太化学有限公司	内蒙古	含磷、硫、氟的第四类监控化学品
31	内蒙古明岳新材料有限公司	内蒙古	含磷、硫、氟的第四类监控化学品
32	内蒙古瑞鸿化工有限责任公司	内蒙古	含磷、硫、氟的第四类监控化学品
33	内蒙古常盛制药有限公司	内蒙古	含磷、硫、氟的第四类监控化学品
34	包头永和新材料有限公司	内蒙古	第二类监控化学品 含磷、硫、氟的第四类监控化学品
35	营口营新化工科技有限公司	辽宁	第三类监控化学品
36	锦州三丰科技有限公司	辽宁	含磷、硫、氟的第四类监控化学品
37	阜新金丰氟化工有限公司	辽宁	含磷、硫、氟的第四类监控化学品
38	恒力石化（大连）新材料科技有限公司	辽宁	第三类监控化学品（一）
39	恒力石化（大连）新材料科技有限公司	辽宁	第三类监控化学品（二）
40	吉林北沙制药有限公司	吉林	第三类监控化学品 含磷、硫、氟的第四类监控化学品
41	黑龙江豪运药业有限公司	黑龙江	第二类监控化学品
42	黑龙江亚尔迪新材料有限责任公司	黑龙江	含磷、硫、氟的第四类监控化学品
43	桦南生物科技有限公司	黑龙江	第二类监控化学品 含磷、硫、氟的第四类监控化学品
44	黑龙江省百纵新材料科技有限公司	黑龙江	含磷、硫、氟的第四类监控化学品
45	佳木斯黑龙农药有限公司	黑龙江	含磷、硫、氟的第四类监控化学品
46	上海奥威日化有限公司	上海	含磷、硫、氟的第四类监控化学品

续表

序号	企业名称	所在省（自治区、直辖市）	类型
47	江苏同禾药业有限公司	江苏	含磷、硫、氟的第四类监控化学品
48	安道麦安邦（江苏）有限公司麦道分公司	江苏	含磷、硫、氟的第四类监控化学品
49	江苏中丹化工技术有限公司	江苏	含磷、硫、氟的第四类监控化学品
50	连云港市三联化工有限公司	江苏	含磷、硫、氟的第四类监控化学品
51	大金新材料（常熟）有限公司	江苏	第二类监控化学品 含磷、硫、氟的第四类监控化学品
52	张家港北兴化工有限公司	江苏	含磷、硫、氟的第四类监控化学品
53	江苏长青农化股份有限公司	江苏	含磷、硫、氟的第四类监控化学品
54	托尔专用化学品（镇江）有限公司	江苏	含磷、硫、氟的第四类监控化学品
55	江苏永创医药科技股份有限公司	江苏	含磷、硫、氟的第四类监控化学品（一）
56	江苏永创医药科技股份有限公司	江苏	含磷、硫、氟的第四类监控化学品（二）
57	泰州百力化学股份有限公司	江苏	含磷、硫、氟的第四类监控化学品
58	泰兴市梅兰化工有限公司	江苏	含磷、硫、氟的第四类监控化学品
59	泰兴市远东化工有限公司	江苏	含磷、硫、氟的第四类监控化学品
60	镇江江南化工有限公司	江苏	含磷、硫、氟的第四类监控化学品
61	中化蓝天霍尼韦尔新材料有限公司	江苏	含磷、硫、氟的第四类监控化学品
62	苏州祺添新材料股份有限公司	江苏	含磷、硫、氟的第四类监控化学品
63	泰兴梅兰新材料有限公司	江苏	含磷、硫、氟的第四类监控化学品
64	淮安晨化新材料有限公司	江苏	含磷、硫、氟的第四类监控化学品
65	常熟三爱富氟化工有限责任公司	江苏	含磷、硫、氟的第四类监控化学品
66	江苏常隆农化有限公司	江苏	含磷、硫、氟的第四类监控化学品
67	江苏优士化学有限公司	江苏	含磷、硫、氟的第四类监控化学品
68	浙江神洲药业有限公司	浙江	第三类监控化学品 含磷、硫、氟的第四类监控化学品
69	浙江精进药业有限公司	浙江	含磷、硫、氟的第四类监控化学品
70	联化科技（台州）有限公司	浙江	第二类监控化学品 含磷、硫、氟的第四类监控化学品

续表

序号	企业名称	所在省（自治区、直辖市）	类型
71	万华化学（宁波）有限公司	浙江	第三类监控化学品
72	宁波龙欣精细化工有限公司	浙江	含磷、硫、氟的第四类监控化学品
73	浙江恒康药业股份有限公司	浙江	含磷、硫、氟的第四类监控化学品
74	临海市华南化工有限公司	浙江	含磷、硫、氟的第四类监控化学品
75	浙江圣达生物药业股份有限公司	浙江	含磷、硫、氟的第四类监控化学品
76	中化蓝天氟材料有限公司	浙江	含磷、硫、氟的第四类监控化学品（一）
77	中化蓝天氟材料有限公司	浙江	含磷、硫、氟的第四类监控化学品（二）
78	台州达辰药业有限公司	浙江	含磷、硫、氟的第四类监控化学品
79	衢州环新氟材料有限公司	浙江	含磷、硫、氟的第四类监控化学品
80	肯特催化材料股份有限公司	浙江	含磷、硫、氟的第四类监控化学品
81	浙江新潜阳环保科技有限公司	浙江	含磷、硫、氟的第四类监控化学品
82	奥锐特药业股份有限公司	浙江	含磷、硫、氟的第四类监控化学品
83	安徽省久江新能源科技有限公司	安徽	第三类监控化学品
84	安徽久易农业股份有限公司	安徽	含磷、硫、氟的第四类监控化学品
85	安徽宁亿泰科技有限公司	安徽	含磷、硫、氟的第四类监控化学品
86	福建智膦化学有限公司	福建	含磷、硫、氟的第四类监控化学品
87	福建舜跃科技股份有限公司	福建	含磷、硫、氟的第四类监控化学品
88	福建德尔科技股份有限公司	福建	含磷、硫、氟的第四类监控化学品（一）
89	福建德尔科技股份有限公司	福建	含磷、硫、氟的第四类监控化学品（二）
90	福建润华化工有限公司	福建	含磷、硫、氟的第四类监控化学品
91	福建省建阳金石氟业有限公司	福建	含磷、硫、氟的第四类监控化学品
92	三明市海斯福化工有限公司	福建	含磷、硫、氟的第四类监控化学品
93	福建华谊三爱富氟佑新材料有限公司	福建	含磷、硫、氟的第四类监控化学品
94	九江中星医药化工有限公司	江西	含磷、硫、氟的第四类监控化学品
95	江西胜垒实业有限公司	江西	含磷、硫、氟的第四类监控化学品

续表

序号	企业名称	所在省（自治区、直辖市）	类型
96	海利贵溪新材料科技有限公司	江西	含磷、硫、氟的第四类监控化学品（一）
97	海利贵溪新材料科技有限公司	江西	第三类监控化学品 含磷、硫、氟的第四类监控化学品（二）
98	江西维达药业有限公司	江西	第二类监控化学品
99	江西禾益化工股份有限公司	江西	含磷、硫、氟的第四类监控化学品
100	江西肯特化学有限公司	江西	含磷、硫、氟的第四类监控化学品
101	江西鑫淦三磷化工有限公司	江西	第三类监控化学品
102	山东瑞兴阻燃科技有限公司	山东	含磷、硫、氟的第四类监控化学品
103	山东尚舜化工有限公司	山东	含磷、硫、氟的第四类监控化学品
104	潍坊润安化学科技有限公司	山东	含磷、硫、氟的第四类监控化学品
105	山东合益丰生物科技有限公司	山东	第二类监控化学品
106	山东松川新材料有限公司	山东	含磷、硫、氟的第四类监控化学品
107	鲁北超能新材料产业（山东）有限公司	山东	第三类监控化学品
108	山东华氟化工有限责任公司	山东	含磷、硫、氟的第四类监控化学品（一）
109	山东华氟化工有限责任公司	山东	含磷、硫、氟的第四类监控化学品（二）
110	济南尚博生物科技有限公司	山东	第二类监控化学品 含磷、硫、氟的第四类监控化学品
111	潍坊滨海石油化工有限公司	山东	第三类监控化学品 含磷、硫、氟的第四类监控化学品
112	益丰新材料股份有限公司	山东	含磷、硫、氟的第四类监控化学品
113	山东同成医药股份有限公司	山东	含磷、硫、氟的第四类监控化学品
114	寿光诺盟化工有限公司	山东	含磷、硫、氟的第四类监控化学品
115	山东群鑫助剂有限公司	山东	含磷、硫、氟的第四类监控化学品
116	山东英合生物科技有限公司	山东	含磷、硫、氟的第四类监控化学品
117	泰安亚荣生物科技有限公司	山东	第三类监控化学品
118	山东亚蓉能源科技有限公司	山东	第三类监控化学品

续表

序号	企业名称	所在省（自治区、直辖市）	类型
119	淄博飞源化工有限公司	山东	含磷、硫、氟的第四类监控化学品
120	山东金城医药化工有限公司	山东	含磷、硫、氟的第四类监控化学品
121	山东新和成氨基酸有限公司	山东	含磷、硫、氟的第四类监控化学品
122	济南万兴达新材料科技有限公司	山东	含磷、硫、氟的第四类监控化学品
123	山东凯瑞化学有限公司	山东	含磷、硫、氟的第四类监控化学品
124	潍坊茂源生物科技有限公司	山东	含磷、硫、氟的第四类监控化学品
125	山东万盛新材料有限公司	山东	含磷、硫、氟的第四类监控化学品
126	山东华夏神舟新材料有限公司	山东	含磷、硫、氟的第四类监控化学品
127	山东亿盛实业股份有限公司	山东	第二类监控化学品 含磷、硫、氟的第四类监控化学品
128	济南万兴达化工有限公司	山东	含磷、硫、氟的第四类监控化学品
129	山东京博农化科技股份有限公司	山东	含磷、硫、氟的第四类监控化学品
130	山东旭锐新材有限公司	山东	含磷、硫、氟的第四类监控化学品
131	山东凯盛新材料股份有限公司	山东	含磷、硫、氟的第四类监控化学品
132	山东华鲁恒升（荆州）有限公司	山东	第三类监控化学品
133	美瑞科技（河南）有限公司	河南	第三类监控化学品
134	河南神马艾迪安化工有限公司	河南	第三类监控化学品
135	漯河市新旺化工有限公司	河南	第三类监控化学品 含磷、硫、氟的第四类监控化学品
136	天科（荆州）制药有限公司	湖北	含磷、硫、氟的第四类监控化学品
137	湖北中迅长青科技有限公司	湖北	含磷、硫、氟的第四类监控化学品
138	吉和昌新材料（荆门）有限公司	湖北	含磷、硫、氟的第四类监控化学品
139	湖北大闰化学科技有限公司	湖北	第二类监控化学品（一）
140	湖北大闰化学科技有限公司	湖北	第二类监控化学品（二） 第三类监控化学品
141	湖北易普乐生物科技股份有限公司	湖北	第三类监控化学品
142	荆州众一生物科技有限公司	湖北	含磷、硫、氟的第四类监控化学品
143	湖北金瑞景生物科技有限公司	湖北	第三类监控化学品
144	荆州三才堂化工科技有限公司	湖北	第三类监控化学品

续表

序号	企业名称	所在省（自治区、直辖市）	类型
145	湖北达兴新材料科技有限公司	湖北	第三类监控化学品
146	湖北达一化工科技有限公司	湖北	含磷、硫、氟的第四类监控化学品
147	湖北松石新材料有限公司	湖北	含磷、硫、氟的第四类监控化学品
148	广州龙沙制药有限公司	广东	含磷、硫、氟的第四类监控化学品
149	广东众和高新科技有限公司天行分公司	广东	第二类监控化学品 含磷、硫、氟的第四类监控化学品
150	广西金源生物化工实业有限公司	广西	第三类监控化学品 含磷、硫、氟的第四类监控化学品
151	贵州璟和化学工业有限公司	贵州	第三类监控化学品
152	贵州红星发展股份有限公司	贵州	含磷、硫、氟的第四类监控化学品
153	陕西中化蓝天化工新材料有限公司	陕西	含磷、硫、氟的第四类监控化学品
154	陕西瑞科新材料股份有限公司	陕西	含磷、硫、氟的第四类监控化学品
155	宁夏格瑞精细化工有限公司	宁夏	含磷、硫、氟的第四类监控化学品（一）
156	宁夏格瑞精细化工有限公司	宁夏	含磷、硫、氟的第四类监控化学品（二）
157	宁夏伟创药业有限公司	宁夏	含磷、硫、氟的第四类监控化学品
158	新疆梅花氨基酸有限责任公司	新疆	第三类监控化学品 含磷、硫、氟的第四类监控化学品

附录四　2023年监控化学品生产特别许可证发放目录

序号	企业名称	所在省（自治区、直辖市）	生产特别许可证书编号
1	天津力生化工有限公司	天津	HW-12T0010
2	天津信谊津津药业有限公司	天津	HW-12T0593
3	天津信谊津津药业有限公司	天津	HW-12T0594
4	科迈化工股份有限公司	天津	HW-12T0109
5	天津凯莱英制药有限公司	天津	HW-12T0577
6	津药药业股份有限公司	天津	HW-12T0369
7	天象生物药业邢台有限责任公司	河北	HW-13C0026
8	河北临港化工有限公司	河北	HW-13J0038
9	沧州大化股份有限公司聚海分公司	河北	HW-13J0039
10	石家庄市和合化工化肥有限公司	河北	HW-13A0100
11	山西鸿生化工股份有限公司	山西	HW-C14E0001
12	山西玉龙化工有限公司	山西	HW-14F0001
13	万荣县百盛精细化工有限公司	山西	HW-14K0015
14	内蒙古灵圣作物科技有限公司	内蒙古	HW-C150009
15	内蒙古科迈化工有限公司	内蒙古	HW-15E0003
16	齐鲁制药（内蒙古）有限公司呼伦贝尔分公司	内蒙古	HW-15G0007
17	内蒙古沙洲化学科技有限公司	内蒙古	HW-15C0011
18	辽宁佳加隆新材料有限公司	辽宁	HW-21L0033
19	中国石油天然气股份有限公司抚顺石化分公司洗涤剂化工厂	辽宁	HW-21D0022
20	抚顺浩源化工有限公司	辽宁	HW-21D0038
21	沈阳科创化学品有限公司	辽宁	HW-21A0030
22	朝阳鑫美高纯半导体材料有限公司	辽宁	HW-21N0010
23	营口昌成新材料科技有限公司	辽宁	HW-21H0051

续表

序号	企业名称	所在省（自治区、直辖市）	生产特别许可证书编号
24	辽宁金发科技有限公司	辽宁	HW-21M0033
25	佳木斯市恺乐农药有限公司	黑龙江	HW-23D0006
26	中国石油天然气股份有限公司大庆石化分公司化工运行二部	黑龙江	HW-23E0002
27	中国石油天然气股份有限公司大庆炼化分公司	黑龙江	HW-23E0005
28	佳木斯黑龙农药有限公司	黑龙江	HW-23D0007
29	赢创特种化学（上海）有限公司	上海	HW-31Z0011
30	南通泰禾化工股份有限公司	江苏	HW-32G0103
31	南通江山农药化工股份有限公司	江苏	HW-32G0001
32	江苏蓝丰生物化工股份有限公司	江苏	HW-32J0003
33	江苏丰山生化科技有限公司	江苏	HW-32H0014
34	南通宝叶化工有限公司	江苏	HW-32G0010
35	徐州永利精细化工有限公司	江苏	HW-32J0031
36	先尼科化工（泰兴）有限公司	江苏	HW-32L0084
37	泰兴梅兰新材料有限公司	江苏	HW-32L0085
38	金桐石油化工有限公司	江苏	HW-32L0086
39	江苏中旗科技股份有限公司	江苏	HW-32L0087
40	无锡南方石油添加剂有限公司	江苏	HW-32D0087
41	江苏雅克科技股份有限公司	江苏	HW-32D0148
42	金城化学（江苏）有限公司	江苏	HW-32A0242
43	江苏斯尔邦石化有限公司	江苏	HW-32K0033
44	江苏剑牌农化股份有限公司	江苏	HW-32H0007
45	徐州宏达新材料科技有限公司	江苏	HW-32J0088
46	大金新材料（常熟）有限公司	江苏	HW-32E1046
47	常州制药厂有限公司	江苏	HW-32C0020
48	江苏永创医药科技股份有限公司	江苏	HW-32I0023
49	泰兴市兴安精细化工有限公司	江苏	HW-32L0080
50	泰兴市申龙化工有限公司	江苏	HW-32L0078
51	镇江江南化工有限公司	江苏	HW-32B0001

续表

序号	企业名称	所在省（自治区、直辖市）	生产特别许可证书编号
52	扬州晨化新材料股份有限公司	江苏	HW-32F0058
53	江苏好收成韦恩农化股份有限公司	江苏	HW-32G0074
54	南通宝凯药业有限公司	江苏	HW-32G0112
55	江苏宝灵化工股份有限公司	江苏	HW-32G0009
56	利民化学有限责任公司	江苏	HW-32J0020
57	宁波现代精细化工有限公司	浙江	HW-33B0079
58	杭州华东医药集团浙江华义制药有限公司	浙江	HW-33J0025
59	浙江兰溪巨化氟化学有限公司	浙江	HW-33J0062
60	浙江新安化工集团股份有限公司建德农药厂	浙江	HW-33A0131
61	宁波锦莱化工股份有限公司	浙江	HW-33B0102
62	杭州百合辉柏赫颜料有限公司	浙江	HW-33A0103
63	浙江司太立制药股份有限公司	浙江	HW-33H0067
64	浙江沙星科技股份有限公司	浙江	HW-33H0020
65	浙江海翔川南药业有限公司	浙江	HW-33H0154
66	浙江海洲制药有限公司	浙江	HW-33H0037
67	浙江燎原药业有限公司	浙江	HW-33H0073
68	浙江闰土股份有限公司	浙江	HW-33F0014
69	台州市前进化工有限公司	浙江	HW-33H0029
70	浙江永宁药业股份有限公司	浙江	HW-33H0019
71	浙江传化华洋化工有限公司	浙江	HW-33A0070
72	浙江大洋生物科技集团股份有限公司	浙江	HW-33A0048
73	衢州凯沃化工有限公司	浙江	HW-33K0040
74	杭州吉华江东化工有限公司	浙江	HW-33A0066
75	诺力昂化学品（宁波）有限公司	浙江	HW-33B0088
76	宁波远利化工有限公司	浙江	HW-33B0106
77	衢州康鹏化学有限公司	浙江	HW-33K0041
78	浙江中硝康鹏化学有限公司	浙江	HW-33K0044
79	浙江精进药业有限公司	浙江	HW-33H0119

续表

序号	企业名称	所在省（自治区、直辖市）	生产特别许可证书编号
80	安徽金轩科技有限公司	安徽	HW-34D0001
81	安徽东至广信农化有限公司	安徽	HW-34H0003
82	安徽省久江新能源科技有限公司	安徽	HW-34M000
83	南平铭正医药化学有限公司	福建	HW-35E0034
84	福建省邵武金塘安晟祺化工有限公司	福建	HW-35E0018
85	福建舜跃科技股份有限公司	福建	HW-35E0038
86	福建德尔科技股份有限公司	福建	HW-35I0010
87	福建永晶科技股份有限公司	福建	HW-35E0037
88	江西省驰邦药业有限公司	江西	HW-36J0010
89	江西宏泽化工有限公司	江西	HW-36C0017
90	江西扬帆新材料有限公司	江西	HW-36D0020
91	海利贵溪新材料科技有限公司	江西	HW-36F0001
92	江西鸿久新材料科技有限公司	江西	HW-36I0027
93	九江中星医药化工有限公司	江西	HW-36D0023
94	江西维达药业有限公司	江西	HW-36I0026
95	江西兴氟中蓝新材料有限公司	江西	HW-36J0013
96	江西理文化工有限公司	江西	HW-36D0021
97	江西禾益化工股份有限公司	江西	HW-36D0018
98	山东新龙集团生物科技有限公司	山东	HW-37G0220
99	寿光诺盟化工有限公司	山东	HW-37G0204
100	寿光市海盟化工有限公司	山东	HW-37G0247
101	寿光卫东化工有限公司	山东	HW-37G0185
102	潍坊滨海石油化工有限公司	山东	HW-37G0067
103	潍坊世华化工有限公司	山东	HW-37G0110
104	威海建新橡塑科技有限公司	山东	HW-37J0004
105	荣成市化工总厂有限公司	山东	HW-37J0002
106	山东尚舜化工有限公司	山东	HW-37Q0007
107	东明万海氯碱化工有限公司	山东	HW-37Q0022
108	山东东岳化工有限公司	山东	HW-37C0029
109	山东京博农化科技股份有限公司	山东	HW-37M0031

续表

序号	企业名称	所在省（自治区、直辖市）	生产特别许可证书编号
110	潍坊密恩化工有限公司	山东	HW-37G0062
111	潍坊新绿化工有限公司	山东	HW-37G0085
112	山东华夏神舟新材料有限公司	山东	HW-37C0106
113	山东东岳未来氢能材料股份有限公司	山东	HW-37C0169
114	山东新和成氨基酸有限公司	山东	HW-37G0070
115	山东大成生物化工有限公司	山东	HW-37C0170
116	济源清源水处理有限公司	河南	HW-41R0009
117	河南新天地药业有限公司	河南	HW-41J0006
118	河南九势制药股份有限公司	河南	HW-41F0029
119	兰博尔开封科技有限公司	河南	HW- 41C3030
120	中国平煤神马集团开封兴华精细化工有限公司	河南	HW-41C0011
121	濮阳圣凯环保新材料科技股份有限公司	河南	HW-41G0045
122	濮阳蔚林新材料科技股份有限公司	河南	HW-41G0046
123	三门峡奥科化工有限公司	河南	HW-41P0014
124	湖南恒光科技股份有限公司	湖南	HW- 43I0007
125	湖北航欧新材料科技有限公司	湖北	HW-42B0023
126	湖北犇星新材料股份有限公司	湖北	HW-42L0005
127	华中药业股份有限公司	湖北	HW-42D0013
128	长青（湖北）生物科技有限公司	湖北	HW-42B0022
129	湖北大闰化学科技有限公司	湖北	HW-42L0006
130	湖北仙隆化工股份有限公司	湖北	HW-42M0001
131	湖北金瑞景生物科技有限公司	湖北	HW-42I0068
132	广东广康生化科技股份有限公司	广东	HW-44P0003
133	广东立威化工有限公司	广东	HW-44I0010
134	广东先导徽电子科技有限公司	广东	HW-44P0005
135	广东丽臣奥威实业有限公司	广东	HW-44S0001
136	广州龙沙制药有限公司	广东	HW-44A0052
137	南宁赢创美诗药业有限公司	广西	HW-D45A0052
138	四川润尔科技有限公司	四川	HW-51T0001

续表

序号	企业名称	所在省（自治区、直辖市）	生产特别许可证书编号
139	成都科美特特种气体有限公司	四川	HW-51A0023
140	福华通达化学有限公司	四川	HW-51K0009
141	广安诚信化工有限责任公司	四川	HW-51W0001
142	贵州威顿晶磷电子材料股份有限公司	贵州	HW-52A0006
143	青海西矿同鑫化工有限公司	青海	HW-63C0001
144	宁夏振岭化工有限公司	宁夏	HW-64D0013
145	宁夏格瑞精细化工有限公司	宁夏	HW-64B0011
146	利安隆（中卫）新材料有限公司	宁夏	HW-64D0017
147	新疆和山巨力化工有限公司	新疆	HW-65F0002

附录五　2023年中国接受《公约》第六条视察一览表

序号	民用工业累计视察次数	类别	日期	被视察设施名称
1	443	第二类	1月30日—2月1日	浙江科达新型建材有限公司
2	444	第二类	2月13日—2月16日	襄阳金达成精细化工有限公司
3	445	第二类	2月27日—3月2日	山东滨农科技有限公司
4	446	第二类	3月14日—3月16日	聊城氟尔新材料科技有限公司
5	447	第二类	3月27日—3月30日	河南九势制药股份有限公司
6	448	第四类		新乡市瑞丰新材料股份有限公司
7	449	第二类	4月10日—4月12日	上海金力泰化工股份有限公司
8	450	第二类	4月24日—4月26日	洪湖市一泰科技有限公司
9	451	第二类	5月8日—5月10日	江西名成科技发展有限公司
10	452	第二类	5月22日—5月26日	齐鲁制药（内蒙古）有限公司呼伦贝尔分公司
11	453	第四类	6月12日—6月15日	山东国邦药业有限公司
12	454	第四类		山东普洛得邦医药有限公司
13	455	第二类	6月26日—6月30日	内蒙古浩普科技有限公司
14	456	第二类	7月10日—7月14日	内蒙古灵圣作物科技有限公司
15	457	第三类	7月23日—7月28日	营口营新化工科技有限公司
16	458	第三类		山东宏旭化学股份有限公司
17	459	第二类	8月6日—8月9日	石家庄瑞凯化工有限公司宏润分公司
18	460	第二类	8月21日—8月25日	河北威远生物化工有限公司
19	461	第三类		山东海江化工有限公司
20	462	第四类	9月3日—9月9日	宁夏格瑞精细化工有限公司
21	463	第四类		宁夏东吴农化股份有限公司
22	464	第二类	9月18日—9月21日	江西理文化工有限公司
23	465	第四类	10月9日—10月12日	潍坊加华化工有限公司
24	466	第四类		山东海利尔化工有限公司

续表

序号	民用工业累计视察次数	类别	日期	被视察设施名称
25	467	第二类	10月22日—10月26日	扬州晨化新材料股份有限公司
26	468	第三类	11月6日—11月9日	淮安华源化工有限公司
27	469	第四类		利民化学有限责任公司
28	470	第二类	11月20日—11月24日	浙江万盛股份有限公司
29	471	第四类		浙江沙星科技股份有限公司
30	472	第二类	12月4日—12月8日	永农生物科学有限公司
31	473	第四类		浙江医药股份有限公司昌海生物分公司
32	474	第四类	12月18日—12月21日	台州达辰药业有限公司
33	475	第四类		浙江华海药业股份有限公司临海川南分公司

附录六　2023年中国接受禁止化学武器组织日遗化武视察一览表

序号	累计视察次数	日期	被视察设施名称
1	145～146	4月10日—4月17日	江西省九江市、湖北省武汉市新洲市临时保管库托管库
2	147～149	5月23日—6月2日	吉林省敦化市哈尔巴岭挖掘作业、保管库托管库、销毁设施
3	150～151	6月18日—6月24日	黑龙江省宁安市保管库托管库、佳木斯市水域挖掘作业
4	152～153	7月18日—7月25日	黑龙江省哈尔滨市保管库托管库、销毁设施
5	154～155	10月16日—10月23日	吉林省敦化市哈尔巴岭销毁设施、保管库托管库
6	156	11月7日—11月12日	山西省太原市临时保管库托管库

附录七　《公约》第五次审议大会国家履约立场文件

中华人民共和国

关于履行《禁止化学武器公约》的报告

（RC-5/MAT.2、2023 年 5 月 11 日）

《禁止化学武器公约》（以下简称“《公约》”）是全球安全治理体系的重要支柱，对维护国际和平与安全、促进化学领域和平利用科技发挥了重要作用。中国是化学武器受害国，一贯主张全面禁止和彻底销毁包括化学武器在内所有大规模杀伤性武器，坚决反对化学武器及其技术的扩散。作为《公约》原始缔约国，中国坚定支持《公约》的宗旨和目标，认真履行各项义务，致力于维护《公约》的权威性和有效性，为促进化学领域安全治理作出积极贡献。

2022 年 4 月，中国国家主席习近平提出全球安全倡议，倡导以团结精神适应深刻调整的国际格局，以共赢思维应对复杂交织的安全挑战。中方将继续以此为指引，促进国际社会团结协作，在化武领域化解风险、消弭政治对抗，推动《公约》得到持续、全面、有效落实。现将中国的履约进展及相关立场主张向第五次审议大会[①]报告如下。

1. 履约立法、组织和管理体系

1.1　根据《公约》规定和本国国情，中国政府不断完善履约法律体系

① 全称《公约》第五次审议大会，每五年召开一次，明确未来五年工作重点和方向，评估过去五年核查机制效能。

和组织管理体系。

法律体系

1.2　自1996年全国人大常委会通过关于批准《公约》的决定以来，中国颁布、实施、修订了一系列法律法规，包括《中华人民共和国监控化学品管理条例》（2011年修订）、《〈中华人民共和国监控化学品管理条例〉实施细则》（2018年修订）、《各类监控化学品名录》（2020年修订）等，对附表化学品的生产、经营、使用、储存和进出口等进行严格管理和监督，依法打击违法行为。2022年，中国还修订了《有关化学品及相关设备和技术出口管制办法》管制清单，进一步完善对附表外两用化学品、设备和技术的出口管制。

1.3　2020年，中国颁布《中华人民共和国出口管制法》，对出口管制体制、管制措施及国际合作等作出明确规定，进一步完善了出口管制制度体系。此外，2001年全国人大常委会通过《中华人民共和国刑法》修正案，将非法制造、运输、储存或投放毒害性物质等危害公共安全的行为定为犯罪，并规定相应的刑事处罚。根据《中华人民共和国反恐怖主义法》，中国依法防范和打击包括化学恐怖主义在内的一切恐怖主义活动。

组织管理体系

1.4　中国建立并完善了中央和地方两级履约工作机制。在中央层面，建立由16个政府部门组成的《禁止化学武器公约》履约工作部际联席会议制度，负责研究国内重大履约问题，协调处理履约重要事项，研提制定和调整履约法律法规的意见，协调接受禁化武组织核查，并指导全国监控化学品管理工作。在地方层面，相关省（自治区、直辖市）政府设立了履约领导和办事机构，部分化学工业发达地区还建立了市、县级履约机构。在工业和信息化部设立国家履行《禁止化学武器公约》工作办公室，负责日常组织协调。中国各级履约机构积极贯彻依法治国基本方略，依法实施监控化学品设施建设、生产、进出口等行政许可，开展监督检查，督促和帮助企业严格履行《公约》义务。加强《公约》和履约相关法规宣传，提高社会履行《公约》意识。

1.5　按照“一国两制”原则和香港特别行政区、澳门特别行政区基本法，中央政府确立了《公约》在港、澳特区适用的模式，确保《公约》在港、澳特区得到全面有效执行。香港特别行政区、澳门特别行政区分别制定、颁布政府条例、行政命令等，对《公约》涉及的化学品生产和贸易等活动进行严格监管，并按时通过中央政府向禁化武组织提交各类宣布。

2. 日本遗弃在华化学武器问题

2.1　日遗化武问题是《公约》框架下最严重的历史遗留问题。侵华日军在1945年战败前夕秘密将大量化学武器掩埋或遗弃在中国。截至目前，已在中国18个省（自治区、直辖市）120多个地点发现日遗化武，严重威胁危害中国人民的生命财产和生态环境安全，也对实现《公约》的宗旨和目标构成重大挑战。《公约》生效后，中、日于1999年、2012年两度签署关于销毁日遗化武的备忘录。中国克服极大困难，同意日方在中国境内销毁日遗化武，并向日方提供适当合作。中国外交部设立“处理日本遗弃在华化学武器问题办公室”，专门负责处理日遗化武工作。中国政府开展大量内部调查并协助日方完成数百次现场挖掘、鉴别和回收作业，为日遗化武安全存放、集中运输、销毁技术选定、销毁场地选址及设施建设等付出了巨大努力。

2.2　中国于1997年5月提交了日遗化武的初始宣布，并及时提交后续宣布。截至2023年4月，中国共提交了59次日遗化武宣布。南京、石家庄、武汉移动式销毁作业已完成。2014年吉林敦化哈尔巴岭销毁作业启动，2019年哈尔滨移动式销毁作业启动。受新冠疫情影响，两地销毁作业一度暂停。哈尔巴岭销毁作业于2021年重启，2022年追加销毁设施建成并启动实弹销毁。哈尔滨移动式销毁作业于2022年重启。

2.3　截至2023年3月31日，共销毁日遗化武65903枚。其中，自2018年1月至2023年1月，中方共协助日方在哈尔巴岭挖掘回收日遗化武 29358 枚，销毁日遗化武 12705 枚；在哈尔巴岭以外地区进行了 27 次调查，挖掘回收日遗化武 6631 枚；在哈尔滨销毁日遗化武 3582 枚。受日方委托，中方对待销毁的 3.23 万枚日遗化武进行安全看管。新冠疫情以来，中方高效统筹疫情防控和处理日遗化武工作，制定科学作业和疫情防控方案，加强应急演练和日常防控，为日方来华作业人员入境、转运、入场、回国以及器材设备运输等最大限度提供便利，协调治疗日方感染者，有力保障了作业顺利开展和中、日人员健康安全。2022 年 11 月以来，中方持续优化调整疫情防控措施，进一步保障了处理日遗化武作业需要。

2.4　自 2013 年起，中方同日方联合邀请禁化武组织技术秘书处（以下简称“技秘处”）总干事和执行理事会（以下简称“执理会”）代表团来华访问日遗化武销毁设施，迄今已接待来访 5 次。2022 年 9 月，阿里亚斯总干事和执理会代表团首次以视频形式访华，各方均强调应尽早彻底完成日遗化武销毁，构建“无化武世界”。自 2005 年起，中、日和技秘处就日遗化武问题举行了 37 轮三方磋商，对监督销毁进程发挥重要作用。截至 2023 年 4 月，中国接受禁化武组织对日遗化武设施及作业现场视察共计 146 次。为克服疫情影响，中国于 2022 年 10 月以线上方式接受视察，2023 年 4 月接受疫情以来首次现场视察。

2.5　《公约》历次审议大会、缔约国大会会议、执理会会议审议遗弃化武问题，反复强调彻底完成销毁的重要性和紧迫性，并对销毁时限提出明确要求。中方迄今已向执理会提交 53 份日遗化武销毁进展报告。由于日方重视不够投入不足，销毁进程多次逾期。中方秉持建设性态度，同日方多次达成新销毁方案，并提交第 46 次、67 次、84 次执理会会议审议通过（EC-46/DEC.4，2006 年 7 月 5 日；EC-67/DEC.6，2012 年 2 月 15 日；及 EC-84/2）。2022 年，由于日方再次未在规定期限内完成销毁，中方同日方达成 2022 年后销毁计划，并提交同年 10 月举行的第 101 届执理会会议审议通过（EC-101/DEC.2）。

2.6　中国已向《公约》第五次审议大会提交《中华人民共和国关于日本遗弃在华化学武器问题的立场文件》，全面阐释对有关问题的立场主张，敦促日方认真对待中方和国际社会关切，履行政治承诺和法律义务，全面、完整、准确落实新销毁计划，切实加大投入，全面加快销毁进程，早日彻底清除日遗化武遗毒。中方主张第五次审议大会采取以下行动：全面审议日遗化武销毁情况，对日方第四次未按期完成销毁表示严重关切；根据《公约》规定及执理会决定，重申销毁所有日遗化武的重要性和紧迫性；要求日方全面、完整、准确落实第101次执理会会议审议通过的新销毁计划，早日彻底完成日遗化武销毁；强调日方应全力搜集并及时向中方提供日遗化武相关信息，积极配合中方做好线索排查和确认；呼吁各方关注日遗化武污染水和土壤现实威胁，敦促日方切实承担责任、妥善解决，授权禁化武组织科学咨询委员会研究相关问题；重申审议大会、缔约国大会和执理会在审议日遗化武问题方面的重要作用；重申执理会和禁化武组织对日遗化武销毁设施开展访问和核查的重要性，强调禁化武组织应确保用于销毁视察的资源。

3. 宣布与核查

3.1　中国是化工业规模最大的国家，也是宣布化工设施最多的国家，一贯认真履行宣布、核查等义务。

提交宣布

3.2　《公约》生效26年来，中国按时提交附表1、附表2、附表3及其他化学生产设施相关的初始宣布、年度宣布。自2002年起，中国每年提交国家防护方案。截至2023年4月，中国共提交了53次化工设施年度宣布。2023年中国提交的2022年过去活动年度宣布厂区共1450个，其中达到视察阈值的厂区1390个，约占各缔约国应视察设施总数的28%。中国国家履约机构建设了“禁化武数据采集和宣布系统”，实现了网上实时宣布，不断提高宣布效率和管理水平。

接受核查

3.3　截至2023年4月，中国共接受621次现场视察，其中第六条视察468次，居世界首位。自2018年以来，中国共接受第六条视察77次。2019年6月，禁化武组织对中方军事科学院防化研究院单一小规模设施进行了技术访问。中国政府和企业克服视察次数多、分布范围广等困难，全力向视察组提供配合和便利。历次视察均确认中国严格履行《公约》义务，视察组高度评价中方所作努力。新冠疫情暴发后，中国统筹疫情防控和履行核查义务，于2022年初与禁化武组织技秘处就疫情背景下开展视察达成临时安排，全年完成14次附表2视察、1次附表1视察。2023年以来，各项视察已全面恢复疫情前安排。

3.4　中国已向第五次审议大会提交了《关于工业核查问题的立场文件》，强调改进优化工业视察措施应以不额外增加工业界负担为原则、以提高视察效果效率为目的，充分考虑地域平衡原则，加强对科技发展问题的研究，并结合实际情况评估设施风险，细化宣布和进出口申报等相关标准和指南。中方希望审议大会对工业视察机制进行全面审议，在优化视察磋商、提高视察效率、确保视察资源分布地域平衡等方面取得积极进展，并授权工业问题工作组就解决视察任务积压、应对其他化学生产设施“临界点”等开展进一步讨论。

4. 处理化武热点问题

4.1　中国一贯坚决反对任何国家、任何组织、任何个人在任何情况下研发或使用化学武器，始终秉持客观公正立场，致力于推动通过政治外交手段解决化武热点问题。中方一贯坚定维护以联合国为核心的国际体系，以国际法为基础的国际秩序，以联合国宪章宗旨和原则为基础的国际关系基本准则，主张《公约》是处理化武热点问题的准绳和依据，按照《公约》规定处理相关问题是唯一正确途径。

4.2　关于叙利亚化武问题。在联合国安理会和禁化武组织缔约国大会、执理会相关讨论中，中国始终坚持对话是解决叙化武问题的唯一正确途径，要求按照《公约》规定的程序，开展全面、客观、公正的调查，基于确凿证据得出经得起历史和事实检验的结论，坚决反对有关国家利用叙化武问题进行政治操弄。中方认为，成立“调查鉴定组”不符合《公约》规定，没有体现全面、客观、公正的原则，无从得出经得起历史和事实检验的结论。

4.3　基于一贯立场，中国在2018年6月《公约》第四次特别缔约国大会会议上同其他23个缔约国一道，对“应对使用化武威胁”决定投了反对票。在2020年7月第94次执理会会议、2021年4月第25届缔约国大会会议上，投票反对“处理叙利亚拥有及使用化学武器”决定。2018年以来，中国连续5年对含叙化武追责费用的禁化武组织预算投反对票。中方并对联合国大会“联合国同禁止化学武器组织的合作”“《禁止化学武器公约》的执行情况”等决议投反对票。中方主张，对指称使用化武事件的处置应尽早回归到《公约》框架，严格根据《公约》及其核查附件开展工作。

4.4　2023年2月，中国发布《关于政治解决乌克兰危机的中国立场》，其中明确反对任何国家在任何情况下研发、使用生化武器。在联合国安理会、禁化武组织缔约国大会、执理会等场合，中方多次阐述在乌克兰局势及化武相关问题上的立场，强调各方都应严格遵守《公约》，避免火上浇油、激化矛盾，并鼓励有关当事方在《公约》框架下，通过对话协商妥善处理相关问题。

5. 和平利用国际合作和化武防护援助

5.1　出于和平目的利用化工领域科学技术并开展国际合作是《公约》赋予缔约国不容剥夺的权利。在历次审议大会、缔约国大会会议、执理会会议等场合，中国同不结盟国家等一道，反复呼吁加强和平利用及国际合作，制定落实《公约》第十一条的行动计划。中国同不结盟国家共同推动2005年、2007年、2009年第十届、第十二届、第十四届缔约国大会会议就全面落实第十一条通过 3 份决定（C-10/DEC.14，C-12/DEC.10，C-14/DEC.11）。2011 年推动第十六届缔约国大会会议进一步通过《全面实施第十一条商定框架的构成要素》决定（C-16/DEC.10），提出落实第十一条的具体措施。2007 年、2013 年，不结盟国家和中国提交了《全面实施第十一条行动计划的指示性要素》（C-12/NAT.1）和《全面实施第十一条行动计划的建议》（RC-3/NAT.8）两份工作文件，提出制定第十一条行动计划的基本要素。中国和不结盟国家在缔约国大会、执理会等场合多次做共同发言，反复呼吁采取实际行动加强和平利用国际合作，制定第十一条行动计划。

5.2　2021 年、2022 年，第七十六届、第七十七届联合国大会会议通过中国及立场相近国家提交的“在国际安全领域促进和平利用国际合作”决议，强调和平利用科技对可持续发展至关重要、国际法赋予各国和平利用科技的权利不容剥夺，敦促有关国家取消对发展中国家的过度管制，并鼓励就此开展对话合作。这份决议体现了国际社会特别是广大发展中国家的共同立场。中方将继续推动该决议得到全面、有效落实，维护国际社会的共同利益，呼吁所有国家支持该决议并积极参与后续进程。

5.3　上述决议同《公约》第十一条以及审议大会相关成果文件、缔约国大会相关决定一脉相承。决议中特别指出，欢迎旨在促进和平利用国际合作的各种倡议，包括通过制定行动计划以充分执行第十一条。全面、有效落实上述决议将为促进第十一条执行凝聚新共识、注入新动力。

5.4　中国已向第五次审议大会提交《关于在〈禁止化学武器公约〉框架下促进和平利用国际合作的立场文件》，呼吁将落实上述联大决议同规划落实《公约》第十一条结合起来，将发展中国家长期关注的和平利用和发展问题置于更加优先位置，开辟落实第十一条的新思路和新局面。中国将继续推进相关工作。

5.5　中国以实际行动促进和平利用国际合作。自 1999 年承诺向禁化武组织提供个人防护和侦检、洗消器材以来，中国建设了专用援助器材库，并进行定期更新和日常管理。《公约》生效以来，中国与禁化武组织联合举办了8次防化援助培训、2次医学援助培训。2018年，在北京举办防化高级培训班，对来自巴林、保加利亚、科特迪瓦、古巴等15国的18名代表进行化学防护培训。2019年，在西安举办防化医学培训班，来自阿根廷、孟加拉国、希腊、肯尼亚等19个国家的26名专业技术人员参与培训。2018年和2019年，中国为禁化武组织研修项目提供实习企业，每年接受2名学员来华实习。中国积极支持化学技术中心建设和运营。2019年，中国向禁化武组织捐款3万美元，用于建设化学技术中心。2023年，中国决定将从向禁化武组织捐款结余中划拨5万欧元用于化学技术中心联合研究项目，并在化学技术中心联合举办海关实验室培训项目。

6. 与禁化武组织的合作

中国是禁化武组织的第二大会费缴纳国，会费比额从《公约》生效之初的0.8%升至2023年的15.254%。2018年至2022年，中国累计缴纳会费超过3900万欧元，为禁化武组织的正常运行提供了最强有力的保障。中国还向禁化武组织捐款累计近30万美元。中国一贯积极支持总干事和技秘处工作。包括现任总干事阿里亚斯在内历任总干事来华访问11次。中国政府积极选送优秀人才到技秘处任职，并派专家参与科学咨询委员会、保密委员会、教育和外联咨询委员会等工作机构和专家会议。中国防化研究院分析化学实验室和军事医学科学院毒物分析实验室已成为禁化武组织指定实验室，自1997年以来参加禁化武组织指定实验室环境样品水平测试，2016年开始参加生物医学样品水平测试，并取得良好成绩。中方实验室还积极协助其他缔约国实验室加强能力建设。

中华人民共和国关于工业核查问题的立场文件

（RC-5/WP.13、2023 年 5 月 30 日）

《禁止化学武器公约》（以下简称“《公约》”）工业核查机制是确保实现《公约》宗旨和目标的重要手段。自《公约》第四次审议大会（以下简称“四审会”）以来，禁止化学武器组织核查制度总体运行有效，对监督库存化武销毁、防止化武再现和增进缔约国间信任发挥了重要作用。

四审会以来，中国不断完善国内履约法规和制度建设，修订施行《〈监控化学品管理条例〉实施细则》《各类监控化学品名录》及相关配套法规文件，依法加强《公约》相关附表和非附表化学品管理。加强履约业务培训和检查指导，提升地方政府和企业履约能力建设水平。广泛开展《公约》知识教育普及，提高社会履约认知度。每年组织全国开展《公约》生效纪念日和国际禁化武组织日宣传活动。2022 年，中国履约主管部门召开纪念《公约》生效 25 周年大会，组织多种形式的履约纪念活动，直接参与者达 22 万余人。

中国作为《公约》第六条下宣布和接受工业视察最多的国家，自 2018 年以来，按时提交了 12 次国家宣布，接受了 75 次工业视察（截至 2022 年 12 月 31 日）。视察结果表明，中国诚实认真履行了《公约》义务。特别是在新冠疫情大流行的情况下，中国尽最大努力支持和协助技术秘书处（以下简称“技秘处”）工作，打破多项惯例，例如，接受连续两周现场视察、接受长距离跨省附表 2 连续视察、新增 5 个临时入境点，以及视察组在中国法定节假日期间入境等，体现了最大灵活度，帮助技秘处尽快解决视察任务积压问题，为技秘处提高视察效率、节约视察经费作出了突出贡献。

同时，中国也注意到，工业核查在宣布、现场视察、政策制定和执行措施等方面面临一些问题和挑战。现将中国关于这些问题的立场阐述如下。

1. 充分、有效和非歧视性地执行《公约》第六条，进一步增强工业核查机制的有效性。应以不额外增加工业界负担为原则，以提高视察效果和效率为目的，改进优化工业核查措施，简化视察流程，特别是后续视察流程，提升视察的标准化水平，压缩视察结果判定的模糊地带和自由裁量空间，完善分歧解决机制，尽量减少对企业正常生产经营等活动的干扰和影响。技秘处实行临时性措施应符合《公约》规定，并应按照《公约》法定程序，经过执行理事会（以下简称“执理会”）乃至缔约国大会等决策机构授权。

2.《公约》生效 26 年以来，化工产业与科技发展日新月异，部分附表 2 化学品的商业用途不断拓展并广泛应用于建筑、纺织、农药、医药等多个行业，商业生产量不断增加。关于附表 2“未为本公约不加禁止的目的进行大批量商业生产”的准则已不再适用于部分附表 2 化学品。缔约国和技秘处应统筹发展和安全，进一步加强对《公约》附表 2 化学品与科学技术发展问题的研究，并落实《公约》第十一条关于“避免阻碍各缔约国的经济或技术发展”的规定，更好地使化学领域的成就完全用于造福人类。

3. 从视察结果看，附表化学品的车间主要活动、车间每一种宣布的附表 2 化学品生产能力、特定有机化学品的产品族类代码、厂区内生产特定有机化学品车间的大约数目、厂区内的磷硫氟车间数目等内容是缔约国宣布信息易错项目。中方建议，除继续修订完善《宣布手册》外，技秘处应采取实际行动，与缔约国进行密切协商，细化宣布相关标准与指南，以利于提高宣布信息的准确性。例如，制定附表化学品车间主要活动填报指南、附表 2 化学品生产能力标定方法，明确常见特定有机化学品的产品族类代码和特定有机化学品车间划分标准等，以减少因对宣布要求的不同理解而造成的企业宣布信息错误。

4. 如何正确判断特定有机化学品并准确宣布其他化学生产设施（OCPF），是企业宣布中常见的难点问题。为有效提高企业宣布的准确性，中方近年来进行了不懈的努力与尝试。2018 年，中方编制了近 9000 个特定有机化学品的名录，主要内容包括化学品名称、化学俗名（如果有）、化学文摘号、产品族类代码、分子式、是否含磷硫氟、结构式和主要用途等内容。经与技秘处共同核对，2019 年，中国国家主管部门正式公开发布《部分特定有机化学品名录》，作为履约公共产品，供国内外免费下载使用，作为宣布参考，受到普遍欢迎。中方建议，技术秘书处应统一考虑建立可供所有缔约国使用的特定有机化学品内部数据库，帮助缔约国增强化学品甄别能力，提高宣布的准确性和完整性。

5. 众多禁化武组织的研讨会、专家会议和工业磋商均认为，缔约国之间之所以出现进出口转让差异，并不是由于相关缔约国的疏忽或故意虚假宣布，而是由于缔约国关于进出口合计数据国家执行程序的千差万别。中方建议，技秘处应进一步明确细化供各缔约国参考的进出口数据收集程序和宣布标准，统一附表化学品出口目的国、中转国的划分标准，以及缔约国之间岁末年初的附表化学品进出口申报标准，从源头上解决因技术问题导致的大量附表化学品进出口转让数据差异。同时，技秘处应鼓励缔约国之间协商解决进出口转让数据差异，并为缔约国提供交流合作平台，如在国家主管部门会议、地区会议上增加进出口转让数据差异磋商议题。

6. 根据技秘处的评估，近年来，受市场变化和人们对卤代阻燃剂在环境保护及健康方面关切的影响，附表 2B04 化学品相关设施出现了较快增长，其宣布数量占附表 2 设施宣布总数的 60% ～ 70%，已对禁化武组织视察计划与活动产生明显影响。中方建议，技秘处应按照《公约》核查附件第七部分第 20 条规定，对其目前采用的附表 2 设施风险评估方法进行审议，根据附表 2 设施的不同风险等级，确定适宜的后续视察频率，以建立解决附表 2 视察任务积压问题的有效机制。同时，中方强调，附表 2 厂区进行后续视察的选择方法，应区别于附表 3 和 OCPF 采用“以随机方式选定”被视察厂区的方法，严格遵循《公约》确定的风险评估原则。考虑到部分附表 2B04 化学品日益广泛的民用用途，中方建议应根据实际情况合理评估此类化学品相关设施的风险，并适当降低对此类设施的后续视察频率。

7. 根据技秘处的评估，OCPF 视察将在未来 5 ～ 8 年出现“临界点”

问题。届时，拥有未接受初始视察 OCPF 的缔约国将从 50 个锐减至 30 个，即将影响到对 OCPF 视察的选择，并将使视察地域分布失衡问题更加突出。按照《公约》第六条第 6 款的规定，每一缔约国应按照核查附件第九部分的规定，将核查附件该部分中规定的设施置于数据监测和最后的现场核查之下，除非缔约国大会根据核查附件第九部分第 22 款另有决定。按照《公约》核查附件第九部分第 11 款规定，“视察的公平地域分布”是以随机方式选定 OCPF 视察厂区的首要因素。中方认为，上述规定均应严格遵守。根据执理会通过的“关于用以确定第六条视察数目的政策指导方针的决定”（EC-66/DEC.10，2011 年 10 月 7 日）明确规定的“在任一缔约国两次第六条视察的时间间隔应不超过大约八年”，中方认为，接受初始视察时间超过一定期限的 OCPF 厂区可考虑视同未接受初始视察的厂区进行选择。鉴于此，中方建议技秘处应继续优化 OCPF 视察选择方法，综合考虑每个厂区的风险度和地域平衡原则，制定合理有效的视察计划，在优先视察未接受过视察，包括初始视察超过一定时限的 OCPF 厂区的同时，后续视察可侧重于初始视察中出现不确定问题、需进一步注意事项的厂区或化学品产量、车间数目发生较大变化的厂区。

8. 技秘处应密切跟踪新一代现场分析技术的发展，提升采样和分析能力水平，提升附带现场分析视察的效率。考虑到所需设备及试剂的运输成本较高，附带现场分析视察应优先考虑风险程度较高且《公约》规定应进行采样和分析的附表 2 设施。

9. 技秘处应充分利用化学与技术中心，向缔约国提供更多履约能力提升培训项目，提高缔约国接待现场分析视察的能力。

中华人民共和国

白俄罗斯、玻利维亚多民族国、布隆迪、柬埔寨、
中国、古巴、老挝人民民主共和国、马来西亚、尼加拉瓜、
巴基斯坦、俄罗斯联邦、巴勒斯坦国、阿拉伯叙利亚共和国、
委内瑞拉玻利瓦尔共和国、津巴布韦

关于在《禁止化学武器公约》框架下促进和平利用国际合作的工作文件

（RC-5/WP.10、2023 年 5 月 17 日）

1. 出于和平目的利用化工领域科学技术并开展国际合作是《禁止化学武器公约》（以下简称“《公约》”）赋予缔约国不容剥夺的权利。《公约》第十一条规定:“执行《公约》各条款应避免妨碍缔约国的经济或技术发展，以及为《公约》不加禁止的目的而进行的化学活动方面的国际合作，包括为《公约》不加禁止的目的而进行生产、加工或使用化学品方面的科学和技术资料以及化学品和设备的国际交流。”

《公约》历次审议大会均重申和平利用国际合作的重要性，强调全面、有效和非歧视性落实第十一条对实现《公约》宗旨和目标至关重要，对缔约国经济技术发展具有重要意义。2005 年、2007 年、2009 年《公约》第 10 届、第 12 届、第 14 届缔约国大会分别就全面落实第十一条通过 3 个决定（C-10/DEC.14、C-12/DEC.10 和 C-14/DEC.11）。2011 年，第 16 届缔约国大会进一步通过《全面实施第十一条商定框架的构成要素》决定（C-16/DEC.10），提出加强缔约国在化学品的研究、发展、储存、生产及安全使用相关能力建设；促进科学界、学术机构、化工协会、非政府组织及区域和国际组织的交流；加强国际合作项目的有效性；促进缔约国化学品、设备、

科技信息的交流等措施，要求为落实上述措施提供资金支持，加强缔约国会和执理会对落实国际合作的监督。禁化武组织执理会根据缔约国会相关决定，建立全面落实第十一条的开放性磋商机制。

2. 不结盟运动和中国始终致力于在《公约》框架下推动和平利用国际合作。2007 年、2013 年不结盟运动和中国提交了《全面实施第十一条行动计划的指示性要素》（C-12/NAT.1）和《全面实施第十一条行动计划的建议》（RC-3/NAT.8）两份工作文件，呼吁制订落实第十一条的行动计划，并提出行动计划的基本要素。在历次审议大会、缔约国大会、执理会等场合，不结盟运动和中国反复呼吁切实加强和平利用国际合作，包括制定上述行动计划。

3.《公约》生效 26 年来，在缔约国和技秘处的共同努力下，落实《公约》第十一条取得积极进展。技秘处同缔约国和世界海关组织、联合国环境规划署、国际科学基金、世界卫生组织等国际和地区组织密切合作，聚焦化学综合管理、实验室能力建设和化学知识交流普及 3 方面重点领域，开展能力建设培训、履约研讨会、视察员培训、防化与援助培训、实验室结对合作、奖学金项目等，就国际合作、国家履约、化工安全与安保、援助与化武防护等开展了广泛的交流与合作，惠及缔约国政府、研究机构、企业、实验室等大量化学相关从业者。通过开展“非洲项目”，为非洲国家能力建设提供重要支持。

4. 化学领域和平利用国际合作仍面临严峻挑战。许多国家，特别是发展中国家获取用于和平目的的材料、设备和技术仍然遭到包括单边强制经济措施在内的过度限制。个别国家出于意识形态目的，泛化国家安全概念、滥用防扩散出口管制，严重损害和平利用及相关国际合作。发展中国家所呼吁的制定落实第十一条行动计划迟迟未能实现。落实第 16 届缔约国大会通过的《全面实施第十一条商定框架的构成要素》决定（C-16/DEC.10）仍存在显著差距，自 2011 年以来缔约国大会未通过新的落实第十一条的决定。禁化武组织工作严重极化和政治化，国际合作面临动力不足和投入不足等问题。这些情况加剧了许多国家，特别是发展中国家对和平利用权利无从保障的担忧，阻碍了关于促进和平利用及相关国际合作的讨论。

5. 2022 年，第 77 届联合国大会第二次通过“在国际安全领域促进和平利用国际合作”决议（以下简称“和平利用决议或决议”）。决议强调和平利用科技对可持续发展至关重要、国际法赋予各国和平利用科技的权利不容剥夺，敦促有关国家取消对发展中国家的过度管制，并鼓励就此开展对话合作。这份决议体现了国际社会特别是广大发展中国家的共同立场。中方将继续推动该决议得到全面、有效落实，维护国际社会的共同利益，呼吁所有国家支持该决议并积极参与后续进程。

6. 上述决议同《公约》第十一条以及审议大会相关成果文件、缔约国大会相关决定一脉相承。决议中特别指出，欢迎旨在促进和平利用国际合作的各种倡议，包括通过制定行动计划以充分执行第十一条。全面、有效落实上述决议将为促进第十一条执行凝聚新共识、注入新动力。

7. 我们呼吁缔约国以《公约》第五次审议大会为契机，将落实联大和平利用决议同规划落实《公约》第十一条结合起来，充分考虑联合国秘书长根据和平利用决议要求所提交的报告和所载的意见和建议，聚焦许多国家，特别是发展中国家长期关注的问题，将和平利用和发展问题置于更加优先位置，开辟落实第十一条的新思路和新局面。中方主张审议大会采取以下行动。

（a）重申全面、有效和非歧视性落实《公约》第十一条的政治承诺。

（b）强调各国在包括《公约》等框架下承担裁军和防扩散义务，同时享有和平利用科技的权利，所有国家都有促进和平利用及相关国际合作的义务，这三方面同等重要。进一步指出，和平利用科技的根本目的是促进可持续发展，根据《发展权利宣言》的精神，和平利用权理应是发展权的重要方面，进而是一项不容剥夺的基本人权。

（c）敦促各国在不影响其所承担的防扩散义务的前提下，采取切实措施促进化学领域的和平利用及国际合作。取消所有过度限制，包括违反《公约》精神的单边强制性制裁措施以及限制或妨碍和平利用科技贸易交流的措施。

（d）要求缔约国大会授权建立开放式工作组等对话机制，围绕促进化学领域和平利用及相关国际合作，开展缔约国普遍参与的、以结果为导向的对话，包括厘清存在的阻碍、差距、挑战、过度限制、加强合作的设想和方案等。在此基础上，请技秘处就全面、有效、非歧视性落实第十一条，特别是存在的阻碍、差距、挑战和过度限制，起草报告并提交缔约国大会审议。

（e）要求执理会讨论制定落实第十一条的具体措施和建议，在此基础上制定切实可行的行动计划，提交缔约国大会审议。要求缔约国大会建立审查机制，审查缔约国拒绝批准向其他缔约国转让化学领域材料、设备、技术的情况。

（f）鼓励缔约国采取旨在促进和平利用国际合作的建立信任措施，包括审查本国关于化学领域材料、设备、技术转让法规，确保其符合第十一条规定；梳理各自促进化学领域技术转让和国际合作的实际举措，定期向缔约国会提交报告；梳理各自拒绝批准向其他缔约国转让化学领域材料、设备、技术的情况，以及与有关国家就此类拒批沟通的情况，定期向缔约国会提交报告。在此方面，拥有先进化学工业和技术的发达国家应作出表率。

（g）要求禁化武组织确保对第十一条相关活动的预算投入，并向发展中国家倾斜。建立由技秘处管理、与缔约国协调的国际合作基金，鼓励缔约国自愿捐款。支持禁化武组织化学和技术中心在国际合作方面发挥重要作用。

中华人民共和国关于日本遗弃在华化学武器问题的立场文件

2023年3月22日，中国向《禁止化学武器公约》（以下简称“《公约》”）第五次审议大会（以下简称“五审会”）提交了《中华人民共和国关于日本遗弃在华化学武器问题的立场文件》。全文如下。

一、尽快彻底完成日本遗弃在华化学武器（以下简称“日遗化武”）销毁，是践行《公约》宗旨、实现“无化武世界”目标的重要方面。

《公约》明确规定，“缔约国承诺按照本公约的规定销毁其遗留在另一缔约国领土上的所有化学武器”“为销毁遗留的化学武器，遗留缔约国应提供一切必要的财政、技术、专家、设施及其他资源”。《公约》还规定了销毁遗弃化武的时间框架。上述条款构成处理日遗化武问题的国际法依据。

《公约》历次审议大会和缔约国大会均对遗弃化武销毁相关问题进行审议，并在相关报告中强调彻底完成销毁的重要性和紧迫性。禁止化学武器组织第46次、67次、84次、101次执理会以决定或报告的形式（EC-46/DEC.4、EC-67/DEC.6、EC-84/2，EC-101/DEC.2），对彻底销毁日遗化武和销毁时限提出明确要求。

作为遗弃国，日方应切实承担起国际义务和政治责任，按照《公约》有关条款和禁化武组织执理会决定，在禁化武组织有效核查下，早日彻底销毁日遗化武。

二、日遗化武问题是《公约》框架下最严重的历史遗留问题，也是最严重的现实威胁和挑战之一。

第二次世界大战期间，日本军国主义秘密生产大量化学武器，并违反国际法在侵华战争中使用，仅记录在案的多达1241次，造成中国军民伤亡20余万人。1945年战败前夕，侵华日军为掩盖罪行，将大量化学武器就地掩埋或弃于中国江河湖泊之中。截至目前，已在中国18个省（自治区、直辖市）120多个地点发现日遗化武。日本侵华战争已结束78年，《公约》

已生效26年，但日遗化武仍严重威胁和危害着中国人民生命财产及生态环境安全。据不完全统计，第二次世界大战结束至今日遗化武已造成中国民众2000余人伤亡。早日全面、干净、彻底销毁日遗化武刻不容缓。

迄今日遗化武销毁虽取得一定进展，但仍面临严峻、突出挑战。一是销毁进程严重滞后。《公约》规定日方应于2007年内完成日遗化武销毁，同时设定了5年宽限期。由于重视不足、投入不够，日方于2007年、2012年、2016年、2022年四次逾期。二是日方迄今未提供全面、翔实、准确的日遗化武线索信息。日遗化武只能被动发现、紧急处置，极大增加了伤人风险，也迟滞了处置进度。三是难点问题的解决进度缓慢。佳木斯、尚志、珲春等地区挖掘回收极其缓慢，辽源日遗化武销毁技术和设备仍未确定。对于水域探测回收、地下探测等技术瓶颈，日方迄今未拿出足够的政治决心予以突破。四是污染土壤处理问题悬而未决。日遗化武埋藏地下数十年，多数弹体锈蚀，因毒剂泄漏或毒气筒破损碎裂等原因，对土壤、水等造成严重污染，日方应承担责任、予以解决。

三、中国政府高度重视日遗化武销毁问题。作为领土国，中国认真履行《公约》规定，克服极大困难，同意日方在中国境内销毁日遗化武，并积极向日方提供协助。中国政府组织专家和技术人员，开展大量内部调查并协助日方完成数百次现场挖掘、鉴别和回收作业，为日遗化武的安全存放、集中运输、销毁技术选定、销毁场地选址及设施建设等付出巨大努力。新冠疫情暴发以来，中方克服困难、多措并举，积极探索视频访问、远程视察等新模式，有效统筹疫情防控和日遗化武销毁工作，全力保障各项作业的需要和中日双方人员的健康安全。

四、2022年10月，禁化武组织第101次执理会通过了关于新的销毁计划的决定，要点包括2027年内完成哈尔巴岭和2022年底之前已向禁化武组织宣布的日遗化武销毁，2026年尽快开始辽源日遗化武销毁并尽早完成；力争2025年内完成牡丹江、伊春和敦化日遗化武挖掘回收，2023年内制定佳木斯、尚志和珲春日遗化武中长期挖掘回收计划并全力落实；日方将提高挖掘回收效率，积极研究提升水域、地下探测和挖掘回收技术，全力搜集并及时提供日遗化武线索信息；中日双方将推进托管库标准化、集约化。

中方再次敦促日方全面、完整、准确落实新销毁计划，积极匹配资源、加大投入，早日彻底销毁日遗化武。

五、《公约》第五次审议大会应对日遗化武问题进行全面审议，并就下一阶段处理日遗化武问题作出决定。中方主张将以下内容写入审议大会成果文件。

（一）根据《公约》规定及执理会决定，重申销毁所有日遗化武的重要性和紧迫性，强调日方应切实承担相关义务。

（二）全面审议日遗化武销毁情况。对日方第四次未按期完成销毁表示严重关切。推进中、日提交并由禁化武组织第 101 次执理会通过的新销毁计划，要求日方全面、完整、准确落实，早日彻底完成日遗化武销毁。

在此方面，敦促日方采取切实措施，尽快解决处理日遗化武过程中存在的投入不充足不平衡、工作效率不高、一些地点未制订有效作业计划、水域和地下探测及挖掘回收面临技术瓶颈等问题，为全面加快销毁进程创造条件。

（三）强调根据禁化武组织第 101 次执理会决定和中、日提交的新销毁计划，日方应全力搜集并及时向中方提供日遗化武相关信息，积极配合中方做好线索排查和确认工作。

（四）考虑到《公约》的宗旨，呼吁各方关注日遗化武污染水和土壤现实威胁，敦促日方切实承担责任、妥善解决，授权禁化武组织科学咨询委员会研究上述问题。

（五）重申审议大会、缔约国大会和执理会在审议日遗化武问题方面的重要作用。重申执理会和禁化武组织对日遗化武销毁设施开展访问和核查的重要性，强调禁化武组织应确保用于销毁视察的资源。欢迎本轮审议周期内执理会和总干事于 2019 年和 2022 年两次访问销毁设施。

附录八　2023年中国在禁止化学武器组织重要会议上的发言选编

中国代表团团长谈践大使在禁化武组织第102次执理会一般性辩论中的发言

（2023年3月14日，海牙）

主席先生，

请允许我代表中国代表团欢迎你再次主持执理会。中方希望你充分利用外交经验和技巧，改善执理会工作和氛围，维护协商一致传统，推动本届执理会顺利进行。中国代表团将积极支持你的工作。

中方认真听取了总干事所作发言和几位副主席的报告，赞同阿塞拜疆大使拉赫曼·穆斯塔法耶夫阁下代表不结盟运动和中国所作的发言。下面，请允许我进一步阐述中方立场。

当前，百年变局加速演进，地区安全热点问题此起彼伏，局部冲突和动荡频发，全球战略平衡与稳定面临严峻挑战。在此背景下，中方发布了《全球安全倡议概念文件》，呼吁各方坚持共同、综合、合作、可持续的安全观，践行真正的多边主义，坚定维护以联合国为核心的国际体系和以国际法为基础的国际秩序，坚持通过对话协商解决分歧和争端。中方上述倡议同样适用于禁化武组织工作。今年将迎来《禁止化学武器公约》（以下简称“《公约》”）第五次审议大会。各方应以此为契机，发扬多边主义，加强对话沟通，改善政治化氛围，回归协商一致传统。中方有以下几点主张。

一是坚决发挥《公约》化武裁军作用，加快推进化武销毁进程。全面、彻底销毁化武是《公约》的核心目标，关乎“无化武世界”的实现。中方注意到近年来库存化武销毁所取得的进展，敦促唯一化武拥有国尽快完成销毁。当前，日遗化武销毁的重要性和紧迫性愈加突出，日方销毁已四次逾期，何时最终完成销毁仍是未知数。中方对此深表不满，敦促日方加大投入，全面、完整、准确落实新销毁计划，提供日遗化武埋藏线索，并尽快解决污染土壤问题。中方将一如既往地提供必要协助。中方将于近期向五审会提交中方关于日遗化武问题的立场文件，完整阐述有关问题的历史经纬、现实危害、问题挑战及中方立场。

二是坚定维护《公约》权威性和有效性，推动对话协商解决分歧。近年来禁化武组织内政治化严重，一些国家出于地缘政治目的，强行推动以投票方式通过“应对使用化武威胁决定”、成立“调查鉴定组”。上述决定及机制超出《公约》授权，侵蚀《公约》权威性和有效性。中方认为应严格按照《公约》规定，客观、公正地开展对指称使用化武事件的调查。在查明真相前，不无端指责、不有罪推定、不激化矛盾，努力通过协商和对话处理分歧。

三是坚持促进各国共同发展，推进和平利用国际合作。中方呼吁各方全面落实联大通过的“在国际安全领域促进和平利用国际合作”决议，在《公约》框架下开展广泛合作，促进化学领域和平利用、提升各国履约以及化武防护等方面能力水平。化学技术中心即将投入使用，中方鼓励技秘处做好规划，期待中心为缔约国能力建设发挥积极作用。同时，中方关切地注意到个别缔约国泛化“国家安全”概念，滥用出口管制措施，实施单边制裁，有悖《公约》规定和精神。中方主张要统筹安全与发展，确保缔约国充分享受和平利用的合法权利。

四是坚守“无化武世界”初心，为《公约》未来发展制定规划。《公约》五审会筹备工作正在有序开展，中方呼吁各方发挥建设性作用，从维护《公约》宗旨和目标出发，聚焦共识，妥处分歧，努力以协商一致方式为《公约》及禁化武组织未来发展制定切实有效的战略规划，为维护国际和平与安全贡献积极力量。中方期待主席团继续履行职责，以开放、透明、包容的方式开展工作，推动五审会取得积极成果。

中国代表团要求将此发言作为会议正式文件散发，并刊载于禁化武组织公众网和内网。

谢谢主席先生。

中国代表团在《禁止化学武器公约》第五次审议大会一般性辩论中的发言

（2023年5月15日，海牙）

主席先生，

我代表中国代表团，对你当选《禁止化学武器公约》（以下简称“《公约》”）第五次审议大会（以下简称“五审会”）主席表示祝贺。中国代表团将全力支持你的工作，并同主席团和各国代表团密切合作，坚持协商一致原则，推动五审会取得积极成果。借此机会，我也对筹备工作组所做工作表示感谢。荷兰政府作为东道国，为禁化武组织各项工作作出了巨大贡献，中方对此表示赞赏。

主席先生，

当今世界变乱交织、动荡不安，国际社会面临前所未有的挑战。中国国家主席习近平提出全球安全倡议，倡导坚持共同、综合、合作、可持续的安全观，推动国际社会秉持团结精神和共赢思维，携手完善安全治理、解决安全难题、消弭安全赤字，实现世界持久和平与发展。中方将继续以此为遵循，践行真正的多边主义，深入参与《公约》履约和审议进程，坚定维护《公约》的宗旨和目标。

《公约》是全球安全治理体系的重要支柱，对维护国际和平与安全、促进化学领域科技和平利用发挥了重要作用。中方主张通过此次五审会，全面、客观评估《公约》执行情况，既肯定成绩，又直面问题，规划好未来五年乃至更长远的工作。中方已向五审会提交了履约国家报告以及关于日本遗弃在华化学武器（以下简称“日遗化武”）、和平利用及国际合作、工业核查等问题的立场文件。我愿进一步阐述中方的立场和主张：

第一，坚持缔约初心，不断向无化武世界目标迈进。26 年来，全球 99% 以上的库存化武已销毁，8 个宣布库存化武的国家有 7 个已完成任务。今年库存化武销毁有望画上句号，这是具有里程碑意义的成就。希望唯一仍有库存化武的国家切实履行义务，在今年的规定期限内完成销毁。

随着库存化武销毁接近完成，日遗化武已成为实现无化武世界最现实的挑战。近年来，日遗化武销毁虽取得一定进展，但销毁进程仍严重滞后。中方将在五审会期间举办展览，全面介绍日遗化武的历史经纬和现实危害，欢迎各缔约国积极参加。展览中有一张对比图，《公约》生效 26 年来，全球库存化武销毁了 99% 以上，而日遗化武仅销毁了已知总量的不到五分之一。同时，相关挖掘、销毁工作还存在埋藏线索缺失、水土污染严重等突出问题。

我要强调的是，销毁日遗化武是日方应尽的历史责任和国际义务，而不是什么“付出和贡献”。衡量日方履约情况的标准是销毁多不多、进度快不快，而不是投入了多少人力物力。中方高度赞赏国际社会和禁化武组织为促进日遗化武销毁所作的努力，希望禁化武组织保持对日方的监督、核查力度。日遗化武未完成销毁，无化武世界的目标就无法实现，禁化武组织作为政府间军控与裁军机构的属性就不能弱化。

第二，维护《公约》权威，探索热点问题解决之道。在国际社会的共同努力下，2012 年联合国安理会及禁化武组织先后通过决议，取得了叙利亚加入《公约》、销毁化武的重要进展。令人遗憾的是，部分国家出于地缘政治私利，将叙化武问题乃至整个中东局势推向了错误的轨道。

中国古人讲，“道私者乱，道法者治”。《公约》是解决化武热点问题的依据和准绳。当前局面的症结不在于《公约》过时了，而恰恰在于《公约》被过时的冷战思维政治化了。有些国家无视《公约》及核查附件明确规定，绕开缔约国协商一致谈判达成的指称使用化武调查等既有机制和程序，强行投票成立“调查鉴定组”，炮制一系列基于无法确保证据链完整性“证据”的调查报告，并推动所谓“问责”。这些国家以维护《公约》之名，行破坏《公约》之实，中方对此严重关切。

世界上只有一个秩序，就是以国际法为基础的国际秩序；只有一套规则，就是以联合国宪章宗旨和原则为基础的国际关系基本准则。中东地区近期一系列互动充分说明，求和平、谋发展是人心所向、大势所趋，地区国家有意愿、有能力掌握地区和平与发展主导权。中方呼吁缔约国总结经验教训，按照《公约》规定，努力回到对话协商的轨道，为解决叙化武问题及其他化武热点问题、维护国际和地区和平稳定创造良好条件。

第三，全面平衡履约，为和平利用与国际合作注入新动力。发展权是各国不可剥夺的权利。《公约》第十一条明确规定，各国都享有和平利用化学技术的权利，同时承担促进和平利用及相关国际合作的义务，执行《公约》不得妨碍各国经济和技术发展。上述权利和义务与禁止化学武器、防止化学武器扩散同等重要。

《公约》生效26年来，在缔约国和技秘处共同努力下，落实第十一条取得积极进展。另外，化学领域的和平利用及国际合作仍面临严峻挑战。发展中国家所呼吁的制定落实第十一条行动计划迟迟未能实现，自2011年以来缔约国大会未通过新的落实第十一条的决定。个别国家出于意识形态和地缘政治目的，泛化安全概念、滥用出口管制工具，严重损害和平利用及相关国际合作。

联合国大会已连续两年通过“在国际安全领域促进和平利用国际合作”决议，强调和平利用科技对可持续发展至关重要、国际法赋予各国和平利用科技的权利不容剥夺，敦促有关国家取消对发展中国家的过度管制，并鼓励开展对话合作。这体现了国际社会特别是广大发展中国家的共同立场。中方呼吁五审会将落实上述决议同落实第十一条结合起来，聚焦发展中国家长期关注的问题，将促进和平利用国际合作与发展问题置于更优先位置，并采取切实有效的行动。

第四，坚持团结合作，维护协商一致原则。禁化武组织处于转型发展的重要节点，肩负完善化学领域安全治理的重任。然而，个别国家利用化武热点问题进行政治操弄，引发禁化武组织陷入严重的政治对抗，对话合作的共识和基础日益削弱。

个别国家将动辄强推投票的错误做法推行到《公约》各个领域，连续5年强行表决禁化武组织预算草案，强行推动通过中枢神经作用剂决定，将完全可以协商一致的技术问题政治化，甚至技秘处人事任命也被强行付诸表决。不仅如此，美国还将中国的禁化武组织指定实验室列入所谓“军事最终用户清单”，严重影响中方实验室及禁化武组织正常履行职责。

任何一个领域的全球治理都必须坚持共商共建共享，任何一个国际组织的正常运转都离不开对话、协商、合作。中方呼吁缔约国以五审会为契机，扭转政治操弄的逆流，尽最大努力推动禁化武组织回归正确轨道，避免国际禁化武体系受到进一步损害甚至陷于崩塌。五审会成果文件是一个试金石。个别国家声称将付诸表决，中方对此坚决反对。希望各方展现最大诚意，全力推动协商一致达成成果文件。

第五，统筹安全发展，优化完善工业履约机制。化学领域科学技术的进步，对工业履约带来新的机遇和挑战。经过前段时间的讨论，改进宣布与核查机制已具有广泛共识，可成为此次五审会成果的重要内容。

中方主张以不额外增加工业界负担为原则，确保视察资源均衡分配；加强科学技术发展对《公约》附表化学品影响的研究，继续修订完善《宣布手册》等相关标准和技术指引；授权工业问题工作组就解决视察任务积压，应对其他化学生产设施视察“临界点”等问题开展进一步讨论。

主席先生，

作为《公约》原始缔约国和第二大会费国，中国一贯严格履行义务，深入参与禁化武组织工作。2018年至2022年，中国累计缴纳会费超过3900万欧元，为禁化武组织的正常运行提供了最强有力的保障。作为化工业规模最大的国家、宣布化工设施最多的国家，中国已接受621次现场视察，居世界首位。

中国一贯坚决反对任何国家、任何组织、任何个人在任何情况下研发或使用化学武器，始终秉持客观公正立场，致力于推动通过政治外交手段解决化武热点问题。2023 年 2 月，中国发布《关于政治解决乌克兰危机的中国立场》，明确反对研发、使用生化武器。在联合国安理会、禁化武组织缔约国大会、执理会等场合，中方多次阐述在乌克兰局势及化武相关问题上的立场，强调各方都应严格遵守《公约》，避免火上浇油、激化矛盾，并鼓励有关当事方通过对话协商妥善处理相关问题。

中方致力于全面、有效落实《公约》第十一条，积极开展多边、双边合作，促进化学领域和平利用。中方支持禁化武组织化学和技术中心在国际合作方面发挥重要作用，高度赞赏技秘处特别是阿里亚斯总干事以及荷兰政府所做的重要贡献。中方将进一步为化学技术中心提供资金、人力等各方面支持，包括开展联合研究项目以及海关实验室培训项目。

主席先生，

中国共产党第二十次全国代表大会对未来 5 年乃至更长一个时期国家发展战略做出规划，提出走中国式现代化道路，在坚定维护世界和平与发展中谋求自身发展，又以自身发展更好地维护世界和平与发展。在新起点上，中方愿同各方同舟共济、携手共进，为完善军控与防扩散领域全球治理，早日实现无化武世界宏伟目标作出不懈努力。

谢谢主席先生。

中国代表团团长谈践大使在禁化武组织第103次执理会一般性辩论中的发言

（2023年7月11日，海牙）

主席先生，

首先，请允许我代表中国代表团，对你当选执理会主席表示祝贺。中国代表团将积极支持你的工作，同主席团和各国代表密切合作，坚持协商一致原则，推动本次执理会取得积极成果。

中方认真听取了总干事所作的发言和几位副主席的报告，赞同阿塞拜疆大使拉赫曼·穆斯塔法阁下代表不结盟运动和中国所作的发言。下面，请允许我进一步阐述中方立场。

主席先生，

当前，百年变局加速演进，地区安全热点问题此起彼伏，局部冲突和动荡频发，国际社会面临前所未有的严峻挑战。中国国家主席习近平提出全球安全倡议，倡导坚持共同、综合、合作、可持续的安全观，推动国际社会秉持团结精神和共赢思维，携手完善安全治理、解决安全难题、消弭安全赤字，实现世界持久和平与发展。

近日，上海合作组织成员国领导人发表《新德里宣言》，呼吁各方全面履行《禁止化学武器公约》（以下简称“《公约》”），使其成为裁军和防扩散领域的有效法律文书；呼吁尽快销毁所有已宣布的库存化武；重申支持禁化武组织，支持通过协商决策弥合分歧，确保该组织完整性并根据《公约》有效开展工作。

中方将以全球安全倡议为遵循，与各方一道，践行真正的多边主义，坚定推进《公约》宗旨目标，共同维护《公约》权威性和有效性。中国愿与各方进一步分享以下几点主张：

第一，坚守《公约》初心，加快推进化武销毁。全面、彻底销毁化武是《公约》的核心目标。当前，库存化武销毁宣告结束，日本遗弃在华化学武器（以下简称“日遗化武”）已成为实现“无化武世界”最现实的挑战。近年来，日遗化武销毁虽取得一定进展，但销毁进程仍严重滞后。当前日遗化武仅销毁了已知总量的不到五分之一，日遗化武销毁计划已四次逾期。根据日方当前销毁效率，要在十分遥远的未来才能完成日遗化武销毁。同时，相关工作还面临埋藏线索缺失、水土污染严重等突出问题。在日遗化武完成销毁前，“后化武销毁时代”不会到来，“无化武世界”也不会实现。中方敦促日方全面、完整、准确落实新销毁计划，尽快完成日遗化武销毁，并妥善解决污染土壤等问题。中方赞赏国际社会和禁化武组织为促进日遗化武销毁所作努力，希望禁化武组织坚持裁军与军控机构属性，加大对日遗化武销毁的监督核查力度。

第二，维护《公约》权威，推动热点问题解决重返正轨。《公约》是全球安全治理体系的重要支柱，《公约》规定的核查与调查机制是解决化武问题的依据和准绳。近年来，部分国家出于地缘政治私利，无视《公约》及核查附件的明确规定，绕开《公约》既有机制和调查程序，强推投票通过所谓“追责决定”，成立超出《公约》授权的“调查鉴定组”，炮制一系列证据未经证实、证据链不完整的调查报告，进而推动所谓追责，造成禁化武组织内激烈政治对抗，严重损害《公约》权威性和有效性。当前局面的症结不在于《公约》过时了，恰恰在于公约被冷战思维裹挟，政治化问题日益突出，而严重影响《公约》的有效执行。中方愿与各方一道，推动指称使用化武调查重返正轨，坚持以《公约》为准绳，以事实为依据，得出经得起历史和时间检验的结论。

第三，坚持对话协商，回归协商一致传统。任何领域的全球治理都应秉持共商共建共享，任何国际组织的正常运作都离不开对话协商合作。禁化武组织是政府间化武军控与裁军机构，肩负化武军控领域全球治理重任。但近年来，个别国家动辄强推投票表决，甚至关于技术性、常规性议题的审议讨论也受到地缘政治干扰，严重削弱对话合作基础。中方呼吁各方重拾协商一致传统，通过对话协商解决分歧，共同抵制政治操弄逆流，反对通过集团化、意识形态化和对抗性思维解决国际和地区问题，避免进一步损害国际化武裁军与军控体系。

第四，加大资源投入，注入国际合作新动力。联合国大会已连续两年通过“在国际安全领域促进和平利用国际合作”决议。今年召开的《公约》第五次审议大会（以下简称“五审会”）期间，中方代表15个缔约国提交了“关于在《禁止化学武器公约》框架下促进和平利用国际合作”的工作文件。上述决议和文件强调和平利用科技对可持续发展至关重要、国际法赋予各国和平利用科技的权利不容剥夺。中方敦促有关国家取消对发展中国家的过度限制，呼吁禁化武组织持续完善国际合作机制和框架，丰富国际合作工具箱，加大资源投入，使化学领域的科学技术成果切实惠及广大发展中国家。中方赞赏总干事和技秘处在化学和技术中心建设方面作出的大量努力。中方将充分发挥自身优势，积极参与有关项目合作。

第五，延续对话势头，开启合作新篇章。尽管五审会未通过成果文件，但在近一年的筹备进程中，各方理念、立场和诉求不断碰撞，在复杂矛盾分歧中寻求共识，这对思考当前化武领域以及国际裁军与军控体系面临的新形势、新挑战具有重要意义。特别是经过广泛深入讨论，各方就工业视察、组织管理等议题取得广泛共识，可以此为基础推进《公约》和禁化武组织下一步工作。在工业视察问题上，中方主张以不额外增加工业界负担为原则，推动视察资源合理均衡分布。中方愿建设性参与视察机制改革进程，支持各方加强关于科学技术发展对《公约》附表化学品影响的研究，就解决视察任务积压、应对其他化学生产设施视察“临界点”等问题开展进一步讨论。在组织管理问题上，中方认为，确保广泛地域代表性是《公约》规定的重要组织管理原则。中方一贯支持提高发展中国家职员在禁化武组织中的代表性，期待各方加大关注和投入，推动上述原则切实有效执行。

谢谢主席先生。

中国代表团在禁化武组织第104次执理会一般性辩论中的发言

（2023年10月10日，海牙）

主席先生，

首先，请允许我代表中国代表团欢迎你再次主持执理会。中方将与各方一道积极支持你的工作，坚持协商一致原则，改善执理会工作和氛围，推动本次执理会取得积极成果。

中方认真听取了总干事所作发言和几位副主席的报告，赞同阿塞拜疆代表不结盟运动和中国所作的发言。下面，请允许我进一步阐述中方立场。

主席先生，

当前，世界之变、时代之变、历史之变正以前所未有的方式展开，热点问题频发，地缘冲突加剧，单边霸凌肆虐，国际社会比以往任何时候都更需要团结与合作、公平与正义。中国国家主席习近平提出全球安全倡议，倡导坚持共同、综合、合作、可持续的安全观，共同构建人类安全共同体。日前，中国发布《关于全球治理变革和建设的中国方案》，呼吁国际社会践行真正的多边主义，承担起推动加强和完善全球治理体系的共同任务。

今年是《禁止化学武器公约》（以下简称“《公约》”）开放签署30周年。30年来，禁化武组织在建立严格有效核查机制、提高普遍性、推进化武裁军与防扩散等方面取得了长足发展。各方应珍视来之不易的成果，以团结精神应对挑战，维护协商一致传统，共同维护《公约》的权威性和有效性。中方愿分享以下几点主张。

一是坚持裁军属性，加快推进化武销毁。当前全球已宣布库存化武销毁完成，但“无化武世界”远未到来。日本遗弃在华化学武器（以下简称“日遗化武”）现实危害远大于库存化武，销毁进程四次逾期、严重滞后，是实现“无化武世界”的最大障碍。中方敦促日方切实履行遗弃国责任，全面、完整、准确落实销毁计划，加快推进销毁进程，早日干净彻底销毁日遗化武，并妥善解决污染土壤等问题。中方希望禁化武组织加大对日遗化武销毁的监督核查力度。

二是坚持团结合作，维护《公约》权威性和有效性。近年来，受地缘政治干扰，禁化武组织对立对抗氛围严重，个别国家动辄强推投票表决，技术性、常规性议题的审议讨论亦受到政治操弄。这有违协商一致传统和共同建设“无化武世界”初心。中方倡导坚持真正的多边主义，以对话代替对立、以团结代替分裂、以协商代替投票。《公约》是解决化武相关问题的依据和准绳，按照《公约》规定处理问题是唯一正确途径，指称使用化武调查应回归《公约》框架。

三是坚持全面履约，促进化学领域和平利用国际合作。国际合作是《公约》重要支柱，要统筹安全与发展，切实促进国际合作，确保缔约国特别是发展中国家充分享受和平利用的合法权利。化学技术中心为开展国际合作、提高能力建设等搭建了很好平台，技秘处应加大整合各方资源、充分挖掘能力和潜力，不断丰富国际合作工具箱，努力将化学技术中心打造成国际合作高地。中方高度重视国际合作，《公约》第五次审议大会（以下简称“五审会”）期间，中方代表15国提交了“关于在《禁止化学武器公约》框架下促进和平利用国际合作”的工作文件，中方将继续积极支持技秘处开展各类国际合作活动。

四是坚持务实高效，开启合作新篇章。各方在此前特别是五审会讨论基础上，就工业视察、组织管理等议题取得广泛共识和一定进展。中方主张以不额外增加工业界负担为原则，加快推进工业视察机制改革，推动视察资源合理均衡分布。确保广泛地域代表性是《公约》规定的重要组织管理原则，提高发展中国家职员在禁化武组织的代表性对确保组织健康、可持续发展至关重要。各方应延续上述对话势头，加大协商与合作，尽早推动相关工作取得可视成果。本次执理会将审议禁化武组织第二个双年度项目和预算。技秘处应以此为契机，全面总结以往特别是第一个双年度项目和预算经验，优化预算制定、管理及使用，提高资源分配透明度，为禁化武组织未来发展制定切实有效的战略规划。

主席先生，

中方高度重视履约工作，始终严格履行《公约》义务，按时高效提交国家宣布，依法加强附表化学品进出口管理。中方是禁化武组织第二大会费国，始终按时足额缴纳会费，为禁化武组织良好运作作出巨大贡献。中方是宣布和视察设施最多的国家，一贯按时准确提交各类宣布，高效严格接待视察，累计接待超过600次视察。中方将继续积极、建设性参与禁化武组织各类活动，为《公约》全面有效实施作出更大贡献。

中国代表团要求将此发言作为会议正式文件散发，并刊载于禁化武组织公众网和内网。

谢谢主席先生。

中国代表团团长谈践大使在《禁止化学武器公约》第28届缔约国大会一般性辩论中的发言

（2023年11月29日，海牙）

主席先生，

祝贺你当选《禁止化学武器公约》（以下简称“《公约》”）第28届缔约国大会主席。中国代表团愿与你和各国代表团充分合作，推动大会取得积极成果。中方赞同委内瑞拉代表不结盟运动和中国所作发言，我愿进一步阐述中方立场。

主席先生，

面对百年未有之大变局，中方主张坚持共同、综合、合作、可持续的安全观，践行共商共建共享的全球治理观，坚持真正的多边主义，推进国际关系民主化，推动全球治理朝着更加公正合理的方向发展，共同构建人类命运共同体。《公约》是全球安全治理重要支柱之一，也是促进化学经济和技术发展的重要国际法基础。中方呼吁缔约国以此次大会为契机，坚守《公约》宗旨和目标，维护团结合作，完善治理机制，避免《公约》权威受到更大挑战。中方愿提出四点意见：

第一，我们要为构建“无化武世界”凝聚更大合力。

尽管全球库存化武已完成销毁，但国际社会迈向“无化武世界”目标仍面临严峻挑战，最突出的是日遗化武问题。日遗化武已埋藏数十年，数量巨大，地点不明，多数是在生产生活过程中偶然发现，其现实危害性、销毁紧迫性远大于库存化武。

今年日遗化武销毁进程加快，全年销毁量已超过2万枚。技秘处全面重启现场视察，全年共开展12次视察，覆盖挖掘回收、销毁、托管库等设施，明年视察次数还将进一步增加。中方对技秘处和缔约国的支持表示高度赞赏。中方愿同日方共同探讨，邀请总干事和执理会代表团2024年再次访华，视察日遗化武销毁进展。

为尽快推进销毁日遗化武，中方同意在中国境内销毁日遗化武。过去26年来，中方为此投入了大量人力物力，包括销毁设施土地、配套作业和工程施工人员等，日方人员设备通关、在华交通食宿、医疗等均由中方提供保障。以今年为例，仅参加现场作业中方人员达3000人次，而相关人员和资源本可以用于发展经济、改善民生等更有用的领域。

销毁遗弃化武是遗弃国应尽的国际义务和历史责任。在政治欠账和现实危害面前，遗弃国妄谈所谓投入和贡献，是苍白无力的。26年来缔约国完成了72304吨库存化武销毁，这充分表明化武销毁症结不是技术问题。日方应以更加坚定的政治意愿，更加扎实的投入，落实销毁计划，解决难点问题。

第二，我们要为化学经济和技术发展采取更多实质行动。

安全与发展是《公约》的两大属性，应统筹推进。《公约》生效以来，缔约国和技秘处在促进和平利用及国际合作方面开展了大量工作，取得显著成果。化学和技术中心投入运营具有里程碑意义，中方对此表示赞赏。本月中国派出4名专家，依托化学和技术中心，为发展中国家开展海关实验室人员培训，取得良好效果。

另外，化学领域和平利用仍面临严峻挑战。个别国家泛化安全概念，滥用出口管制，大搞单边制裁，阻碍了化学等各领域科技和平利用，也阻碍了正常经贸往来。发展中国家呼吁制定落实《公约》第十一条行动计划未能实现，自2011年以来缔约国大会未能就落实第十一条通过新的决定。这充分说明，和平利用仍是全面、有效落实《公约》的短板弱项。我想强调的是，“遵约能力建设”只是国际合作的一方面。缔约国应按照《公约》规定，坚持问题导向，把广大发展中国家突出诉求摆在重点位置，聚焦和平利用采取切实举措。

今年5月，中方与14个缔约国共同向《公约》第五次审议大会提交《在禁止化学武器公约框架下促进和平利用国际合作》工作文件，呼吁结合执行第77届联大通过的“在国际安全领域促进和平利用国际合作”决议，为化学领域和平利用凝聚新共识、注入新动力。今年第78届联大一委期间，中方和共提国作共同发言，重申和平利用是各国不可剥夺的权利，敦促有关国家落实决议要求，取消过度限制。中方和共提国将向2024年第79届联大再次提交决议，欢迎所有缔约国积极参与联大后续进程。

第三，我们要为解决热点问题找到正确途径。

今年2月，中方发布《全球安全倡议概念文件》，全面阐释全球安全倡议核心理念和行动方向。在国际和地区热点问题上，中方一贯主张以劝和促谈为主要方式，以公平务实为主要态度，以标本兼治为主要思路，坚持对话谈判、政治解决。

“防止化武再现”的治本之策是维护《公约》权威，用好《公约》规定的核查机制，照顾各方合理合法关切，通过对话协商妥善解决问题，构建均衡、有效、可持续的安全架构。“调查鉴定组”是政治操弄的产物，事实证明既不符合《公约》，无法解决问题，也无法实现“防止化武再现”的目标。

叙利亚化武问题延宕至今，症结不是《公约》过时了，恰恰是《公约》权威未得到有效维护。今年以来，叙政府与技秘处合作取得积极进展。中方对此表示欢迎，鼓励双方持续开展建设性合作，为解决问题创造良好条件。中方也支持地区国家从改善关系、共建和平、共谋发展的大局出发，在叙化武问题解决进程中发挥更大作用。

第四，我们要为缔约国团结协作注入正能量。

团结协作是禁化武组织工作行稳致远的金钥匙。第103次执理会协商一致通过地域平衡决定，支持增强国际职员地域代表性，给予发展中国家更多代表性和发言权，给禁化武组织工作注入新的正能量，中方对此表示欢迎。

近年来，个别国家出于一己私利，利用化武问题进行政治操弄，严重阻碍禁化武组织健康可持续发展。个别国家罔顾积极进展，在未经协商的情况下，执意向此次大会提交叙化武问题新决定草案并强推表决，中方对此严重关切。

执理会是禁化武组织重要决策机构。按照《公约》规定，作为一项基本原则，各个地区组中具有最重要的本国化学工业的缔约国应成为执理会成员。部分国家寻求推翻这一基本原则，将严重影响《公约》的宗旨和目标，不符合缔约国共同利益。

2020 年，美国将中国军事科学院列入“军事最终用户”清单，中方对此坚决反对。美方非法单边制裁已严重影响中方指定实验室正常活动，严重干扰禁化武组织和使用生化武器事件联合国秘书长调查机制相关工作。中方敦促美方立即纠正错误做法，取消非法单边制裁。

总之，一个被个别国家政治操弄所绑架的国际组织是不可持续的。中方呼吁有关缔约国本着负责任态度，妥善处理相关问题，寻求协商一致解决方案。

主席先生，作为化工业规模最大的国家，中方一贯高度重视履约工作。今年全年中国将接受 30 余次视察，其中附表二视察约 17 次，占全球视察总数的 35%，是接受视察最多的国家。中方国家履约机构连续 26 年开展禁化武组织宣传活动，通过举办履约普法知识竞赛和线上展览等方式加强宣传，面向地方政府和企业开展履约培训。中国政府指导香港、澳门特区政府，不断完善履约立法，及时提交宣布，加强附表化学品贸易管理。

主席先生，

今年是中国国家主席习近平提出构建人类命运共同体重大理念十周年。近年来，习近平主席提出全球发展倡议、全球安全倡议、全球文明倡议，进一步丰富了构建人类命运共同体理念的内涵和实施路径。中国将继续秉持人类命运共同体理念，与禁化武组织技秘处和缔约国一道，为实现“无化武世界”目标作出不懈努力。

谢谢主席先生！

附录九　2023年禁止化学武器组织主要工作情况

2023年
《关于禁止发展、生产、储存和使用化学武器及销毁此种武器的公约》的履行状况（节选）[①]

（C-29/4、2024年11月25日）

导言

1. 在2023年，继续在下列工作领域取得了进展：处理有关使用化学武器的事件；销毁剩余的已宣布的化学武器库存；开展并加强工业核查；进行国际合作和援助；应对化学恐怖主义构成的挑战；拓展和维持禁化武组织在教育和外联方面的工作。

2. 最后一个拥有尚待销毁的已宣布化学武器的缔约国——美利坚合众国——在2023年7月销毁完了其剩余的化学武器库存。

3. 关于已宣布化学武器在2023年间的销毁进展，经技术秘书处（以下简称“技秘处”）核实，已经销毁了358.293吨第1类化学武器。

4. 从《禁止化学武器公约》（以下简称“《公约》”）生效至2023年12月31日，经技秘处核实，已销毁了70493.640吨[②]宣布的第1类化学武器，占宣布制剂总量的100%。因此，这标志8个拥有缔约国宣布的化学武器库存已被全部消除。

5. 中国和日本就日本遗弃在中国领土上的化学武器的销毁、挖掘和回

① 本报告来源于禁止化学武器组织网站，于2024年11月第29届缔约国大会上审议通过。
② 该数目包括根据《公约》的《核查附件》第六部分第2款（d）项取出用于《公约》不加禁止的目的的2.913吨附表1化学品。

收问题继续进行了双边合作。于 2023 年 4 月恢复了有关遗弃化学武器（以下简称“遗弃化武”）的现场视察，并总共进行了 12 次视察。经与有关缔约国协商，技秘处对老化学武器（以下简称“老化武”）进行了 4 次视察。

6. 2023 年，禁化武组织进行了 196 次工业设施视察。由于存在技秘处掌控之外的行动制约因素，无法完成 2023 年方案和预算中构想的全部 200 次第六条视察。

7. 继续进行了下列工作：澄清阿拉伯叙利亚共和国的初始宣布；处理在该国发生的使用化学武器的情况。宣布评估组（以下简称“宣评组”）的工作在 2023 年全年继续进行，以期澄清与阿拉伯叙利亚共和国的初始宣布和后来提交的宣布相关的所有尚未解决的问题。以执行理事会（以下简称“执理会”）的相关决定和联合国安全理事会的有关决议为指南，禁化武组织派往叙利亚的事实调查组还在 2023 年继续开展了其活动。技秘处还集中精力落实以下两项决定：缔约国大会（以下简称“大会”）第四次特别会议通过的决定（C-SS-4/DEC.3，2018 年 6 月 27 日），其中包括根据上述决定成立的调查和鉴定组（以下简称“调鉴组”）的行动；大会第二十五届会议通过的有关决定（C-25/DEC.9，2021 年 4 月 21 日）。

8. 2023 年 5 月 12 日，在荷兰威廉·亚历山大国王陛下、派恩纳克－诺多普市市长、大会主席和执理会主席、各缔约国代表和其他利益攸关方的见证下，禁化武组织化学与技术中心（以下简称“化技中心”）揭幕启用。该中心在年内全面投入运行。

9. 2023 年，技秘处继续实施了旨在协助缔约国履行《公约》的能力建设方案。技秘处为来自各个地区组的 2200 名专家举办了 79 项活动和方案。

10. 五审会于 2023 年 5 月 15 日至 19 日在海牙召开。此前开展了会议筹备工作，其不限成员名额五审会筹备工作组（以下简称“五审会筹备工作组”）在 2023 年 1 月至 4 月举行了有关会议。

11. 全面而有效地履行《公约》仍然是禁化武组织为全球反恐事业做贡献的基石。执理会的不限成员名额反恐工作组（以下简称“反恐工作组”）举行了 3 次会议，还进行了一次模仿发生化学恐怖主义袭击各阶段的桌面演练。

12. 禁化武组织的 3 个咨询机构——科学咨询委员会（以下简称“科咨委”）、行政和财务问题咨询机构（以下简称“行财咨机构”）以及教育和外联咨询委员会（以下简称“教咨委”）——继续根据各自的授权向禁化武组织提供咨询意见。

13. 公众对禁化武组织工作的兴趣仍然高涨。2023 年，禁化武组织的各社交媒体平台的阅读量平均增长率为 8%。在继续接待人员实地到访的同时，技秘处还运用了多种数字化外联工具。

14. 2023 年，《公约》的缔约国数目保持在 193 个上。在《公约》的普适性行动计划框架内，技秘处在这一年中继续主动接触了剩余的非缔约国。

1. 核查

1.1　在 2023 年完成的视察见表 1。禁化武组织在 2023 年进行了 248 次视察，而其中 21% 为化学武器方面的视察。与非例行任务相关的行动占了 740 个视察员日。

表 1　在 2023 年完成的视察

设施种类	视察次数	被视察设施或现场数	视察员日数
与化学武器相关的视察			
化武销毁设施	31	3①	2572
化武储存设施	4	2	72
化武生产设施	0	0	0
老化武	4	4	54
遗弃化武②	13	11	236
非例行任务	不适用		740

① 所有设施都在美利坚合众国。
② 包括遗弃化武储存和销毁设施。

续表

设施种类	视察次数	被视察设施或现场数	视察员日数
小计	52	20	3674
第六条视察			
附表 1	11	11	202
附表 2	49	49	808
附表 3	8	8	82
其他化学生产设施	128	128	1142
小计	196	196	2234
总计	248	216	5908

1.2　截至 2023 年 12 月 31 日，8 个缔约国（某缔约国①、阿尔巴尼亚、印度、伊拉克、利比亚、俄罗斯联邦、阿拉伯叙利亚共和国和美利坚合众国）宣布的化学武器合计为 72304.343 吨②第 1 和第 2 类化学武器；417833 枚第 3 类化学武器。本报告的附件 3 提供了更多有关资料。

1.3　在老化武方面继续取得了进展。宣布了拥有老化武的缔约国继续努力以安全而有效的方式销毁这类武器。

1.4　根据执理会第 67 次会议通过的决定（EC-67/DEC.6，2012 年 2 月 15 日），中国和日本继续在遗弃化武及其销毁方面进行了合作。此外，2023 年，中国和日本继续合作执行了向执理会第 101 次会议提交的“2022 年以后中华人民共和国境内日本遗弃化学武器销毁计划”（EC-101/NAT.4*，2022 年 9 月 30 日），其中包含了关于销毁设施的资料以及销毁的时间安排。

化学武器的销毁

1.5　在报告期内，3 个位于美利坚合众国的化武销毁设施进行了第 1 类化学武器的销毁。通过视察员的驻扎、利用监测和专用录像设备以及查看有关的文献资料，技秘处在 2023 年核实了 358.293 吨第 1 类化学武器的

① 由于有关缔约国要求将其国名视为高度保护级资料，故为了本报告，在下文中将其称为“某缔约国”。

② 该总量不包括俄罗斯联邦宣布的黏稠剂或伊拉克宣布的残留化学武器的重量。

销毁。

1.6　2023 年 6 月 22 日，普埃布洛化学剂销毁中试车间（以下简称“普埃布洛设施”）销毁了最后一枚弹药。普埃布洛设施中的所有系统核查活动均已终止。2023 年 7 月 7 日，布鲁格拉斯化学剂销毁中试车间（以下简称“布鲁格拉斯设施”）处理完最后一枚弹药，这标志着美利坚合众国已经彻底消除了其化学武器库存。虽然化学武器销毁已经完成，但在布鲁格拉斯设施的非毗邻静态引爆室（以下简称“静爆室”）2000 号现场继续处置化学武器组件的废弃物。

1.7　技秘处还核实了如下情况：在位于阿拉巴马州安尼斯顿军械库的静爆室现场销毁了从普埃布洛设施拆除的高能组分；在位于得克萨斯州阿瑟港的非毗邻的 Veolia 处理、储存和处置设施中销毁了来自布鲁格拉斯设施的水解产物；在位于布鲁格拉斯设施的安尼斯顿非毗邻静爆室销毁了火箭发动机。此外，经技秘处核实，在亚拉巴马州雷德斯顿军械库的原型爆破和销毁设施中销毁了 3 枚带有运载和发射管端盖的火箭发动机。这些火箭发动机是从布鲁格拉斯设施中装填有 GB 的火箭上拆卸下来的。

1.8　截至 2023 年 12 月 31 日，经技秘处核实，美利坚合众国共计销毁了其宣布的 27769.831 吨第 1 类化学剂，占其宣布库存的 100%。此前已核实美利坚合众国销毁了全部第 2 类和第 3 类化学武器。

1.9　从《公约》生效至2023年12月31日，技秘处核实的销毁情况如下：宣布的第 1 类化学武器，70493.640 吨（或 100%）；宣布的第 2 类化学武器，1810.703 吨（或 100%）；宣布的第 3 类化学武器，417833 吨（或 100%）。本报告附件 3 载有更多的相关资料。

1.10　美利坚合众国在 2023 年提交了下述资料：

（a）对化学武器初始宣布的修订（第 78 号更新）；

（b）对化学武器初始宣布的修订（第 79 号更新）；

（c）对化学武器初始宣布的修订（第 80 号更新）；

（d）对化学武器初始宣布的修订（第 81 号更新）；

（e）对化学武器初始宣布的修订（第 82 号更新）；

（f）对化学武器初始宣布的修订（第 83 号更新）；

（g）布鲁格拉斯设施详细设施资料的增补 4，卷 1，修订 1，其有关改变 SDC 2000 号覆土库的用途以在其中进行火箭分离活动；

（h）布鲁格拉斯设施详细设施资料的增补 4，卷 2 补编，其有关用于进行火箭分离活动的 SDC 2000 号覆土库的示意图；

（i）布鲁格拉斯设施的设施协定和议定详细核查计划（载有对增设火箭分离活动所必需的修订和修改）；

（j）普埃布洛设施协议关停计划；

（k）布鲁格拉斯设施协议关停计划；

（l）关停普埃布罗化学仓库化武储存设施的通知；

（m）关于布鲁格拉斯化学活动化武储存设施的通知；

（n）关于普埃布洛设施完成化学武器销毁活动的宣布；

（o）关于布鲁格拉斯设施完成化学武器销毁活动的宣布；

（p）关于在布鲁格拉斯设施继续消除火箭组件废弃物并接受核查的通知；

（q）终止对化学转运设施 / 弹药评估和处理系统的系统视察；

（r）终止对回收化学武器销毁设施的系统视察；

（s）终止对原型引爆测试和销毁设施的系统视察；

（t）2022 年化学武器销毁情况的年报。

化学武器储存设施

1.11　2023 年，技秘处对美利坚合众国的两个化学武器储存设施（以下简称“化武储存设施”）进行了 4 次视察。美国宣布已将所有的化学武器从这些化武储存设施中运走，而技秘处开展的有关视察证实了其中已没有化学武器。因此，在这些设施中进行的所有系统核查均已终止。

化学武器生产设施

1.12　截至 2023 年 12 月 31 日，总干事已对下列设施颁发了有关认证证书：由 14 个缔约国向禁化武组织宣布的全部 97 个化学武器生产设施（以下简称“化武生产设施”）已销毁或已改装用于《公约》不加禁止的目的（74 个被认证为已销毁，23 个被认证为已改装）。

1.13　2023 年，受利比亚和伊拉克局势影响，无法按原计划开展对这两个国家改装后的化武生产设施进行 4 次视察。

遗弃化学武器

1.14　自《公约》生效以来，有 4 个缔约国报告了其领土上有遗弃化武。一个缔约国（日本）报告了其在另一缔约国（中国）的领土上的遗弃化武。

1.15　技秘处继续与中日两国就遗弃化武事宜进行互动。在 2023 年举行了两次三方会议，目的如下：确保透明度；讨论技术和实践事项；按照适当的核查措施来落实有关项目；为今后活动进行规划。

1.16　截至 2023 年 12 月 31 日，中国宣布了 115741 枚遗弃化武，而日本则宣布了 115520 枚这类弹药。已销毁了宣布的中国境内的 88155 枚遗弃化武弹药。由于 4 个大型控制引爆室已投入运行，在中国哈尔巴岭的遗弃化武销毁速度在 2023 年达到最高水平。

老化学武器

1.17　截至 2023 年 12 月 31 日，有 19 个缔约国宣布了 153431 枚老化武，这些老化武或生产于 1925 年以前，或生产于 1925—1946 年。据报告，其中约 78% 已被销毁。2023 年，技秘处在比利时、法国、德国和意大利进行了 4 次老化武视察。

质疑性视察和指称使用调查

1.18　2023 年，没有收到有关《公约》规定的质疑性视察或指称使用调查的请求。技秘处将其培训重点放在了加强进行指称使用调查的常备状态上，具体而言，即在实地环境中侦查、记录和采样程序的方法和执行。

宣布评估组

1.19　2023 年，根据《公约》、执理会 EC-M-33/DEC.1 号决定（2013 年 9 月 27 日）第一段、执理会 EC-81/DEC.4 号决定（2016 年 3 月 23 日）

第三段、执理会 EC-83/DEC.5 号决定（2016 年 11 月 11 日）第六段和执理会 EC-94/DEC.2 号决定（2020 年 7 月 9 日）第五段，技秘处继续开展工作，以核实阿拉伯叙利亚共和国是否履行了全部的宣布要求。在技秘处收到足够的资料用以研判这些问题是否得到解决之前，已向叙利亚国家主管部门提出了在这些宣布中发现的缺陷，而这些缺陷即为未决问题。

1.20　技秘处与叙利亚国家主管部门自 2014 年起就宣布进行了磋商，截至 2023 年年底，阿拉伯叙利亚共和国一共提交了 19 项对其初始宣布的修改。这些修改含有以前未曾宣布的内容，其中包括：一个额外的化武生产设施；4 个附加的化学武器研究和开发设施；涉及 5 种以前未宣布的化学战剂的活动；大量以前未宣布的化学弹药；有关叙利亚化学武器方案所有部分的其他补充资料。

1.21　自 2014 年以来，技秘处已提出并报告了 24 个未决问题，其中 4 个已经解决[①]。2021 年 4 月，在叙利亚国家主管部门提供了关于在阿拉伯叙利亚共和国宣布的那个从未用于生产化武战剂的化武生产设施内的大容量储存容器中有这种战剂一事的不充分解释之后，技秘处新增了一个最新问题。在本报告期内继续就此事进行着澄清。

1.22　到 2023 年年底，对于依然存在的 20 个问题，其实质内容牵涉大量可能未被宣布或者未经核实的化学剂和化学弹药。此外，阿拉伯叙利亚共和国尚未完成执理会第 EC-94/DEC.2 号决定第 5 段所制定的任何与其宣布的相关措施。

1.23　2021 年 4 月—2023 年 10 月，技秘处组织的宣评组与叙利亚国家主管部门进行的第二十五轮磋商未果，这主要是因为阿拉伯叙利亚共和国拒绝向宣评组的首席技术专家发放签证。

1.24　鉴于此，技秘处提出了几个替代方案，其中包括部署日期和进行有限磋商的会晤地点。所有这些尝试都因为阿拉伯叙利亚共和国设置的

① 技秘处报告称在 2024 年又解决了 3 个未决事项。这将在禁化武组织 2024 年的年报中予以反映。

签证问题或资金条件未果。

1.25　2023 年 1 月和 4 日，技秘处向阿拉伯叙利亚共和国部署了一个由几名宣评组成员组成的缩编小组，以便开展有限的境内活动。在进行这两次有限的境内活动期间，这个缩编小组开展了面询、现场查访并收集了样本。在部署有限的境内活动期间，双方专家没有进行技术讨论。有关这两次有限的境内活动部署的结果，已通过总干事关于宣布组的工作报告向执理会第 102 次和 103 次会议做了汇报①。

1.26　2023 年 6 月，阿拉伯叙利亚共和国和技秘处的代表团在贝鲁特进行了会晤，在此期间，双方经过讨论认为应重启包括宣评组全体专家在内的磋商，这是解决阿拉伯叙利亚共和国初始宣布中存在的差异、不一致和数据出入的最好的推进方式。

1.27　作为上述在贝鲁特进行会晤的后续，技秘处告叙利亚国家主管部门其拟向大马士革部署宣布组的全员，以开展第二十五轮磋商。对于在 2023 年 10 月举行第二十五轮磋商且宣评组全员参会一事，叙利亚国家主管部门表示欢迎。

1.28　在第二十五轮磋商期间，审查了所有未决事项的现状和解决这些事项的行动计划。

1.29　通过其在执理会第 102 次、第 103 次和第 104 次会议上向执理会分发的说明，总干事继续报告了关于叙利亚的宣布和有关提交资料中的所有未解决的问题。在 2023 年发布的关于此事的最近一份说明（EC-104/HP/DG.2/Add.2）中，总干事得出以下结论：“技秘处经评估认定：根据《公约》、执理会 EC-M-33/DEC.1 号决定（2013 年 9 月 27 日）、EC-81/DEC.4（2016 年 3 月 23 日）、EC-83/DEC.5（2016 年 11 月 11 日）和 EC-94/DEC.2 号决定（2020 年 7 月 9 日）、大会 C-SS-4/DEC.3 号决定（2018 年 6 月 27 日）

① EC-102/HP/DG.1（2023 年 3 月 6 日）和 EC-103/HP/DG.1（2023 年 7 月 6 日）。关于宣评组工作的更多报告已提交执理会第 104 次会议：EC-104/HP/DG.2（2023 年 9 月 25 日），及其 Add.1（2023 年 10 月 27 日）和 Add.2（2023 年 11 月 22 日）。

以及联合国安全理事会第 2118（2013）号决议，阿拉伯叙利亚共和国提交的宣布仍然不能被视为是准确和完备的”。

叙利亚科学研究中心

1.30　根据执理会第 EC-83/DEC.5 号决定第 11 段，技秘处将“对叙利亚科学研究中心的巴尔扎赫设施每年进行两次视察，并对叙利亚科学研究中心（以下简称“叙利亚科研中心”）的贾姆拉亚赫设施每年进行两次视察，且这些视察应附带取样和分析；进行视察时应充分和不受限制地察看上述设施内的所有建筑物以及这些建筑物中的全部房间；且进行视察的日期将由技秘处确定”。

1.31　2023 年 12 月，技秘处对叙利亚科研中心的巴尔扎赫设施和贾姆拉亚赫设施进行了第十轮视察。

1.32　有关于 2018 年 11 月在叙利亚科研中心的巴尔扎赫设施进行的第三轮视察时发现有附表第 2.B.04 号化学品一事，技秘处主要通过互换普通照会来与阿拉伯叙利亚共和国进行互动。在 2023 年 12 月进行的第十轮视察期间讨论了该问题。视察组未收到任何新的能使技秘处能够解决这一问题的技术资料。

1.33　在 2022 年 9 月进行的上一轮视察期间，视察组发现这里使用过一种具有双重用途的化学品并拟了解其来源，为此，视察组与叙利亚国家主管部门在第十轮视察期间讨论了此事。在这次讨论期间，叙利亚国家主管部门未提供任何新资料。技秘处将继续就此事与叙利亚国家主管部门进行互动。

1.34　2022 年 4 月，叙利亚国家主管部门告技秘处计划建造一个焚烧单元以销毁叙利亚科研中心的化学废弃物，关于此事，视察组请叙利亚国家主管部门提供最新进展。叙利亚国家主管部门报告视察组：由于费用增加，该项目已搁置。

禁化武组织派往叙利亚的事实调查组

1.35　事实调查组对于 2017 年 7 月 7 日和 8 月 4 日在阿拉伯叙利亚共

和国哈尔比特马萨斯内发生的指称使用事件进行了调查。在此基础上，技秘处发布了一份题为“禁化武组织事实调查组关于在阿拉伯叙利亚共和国的哈尔比特马萨斯内发生的将有毒化学品用作武器的指称事件（2017 年 7 月 7 日和 8 月 4 日）的报告”（S/2186/2023，2023 年 6 月 28 日）。

1.36 事实调查组收集了在阿拉伯叙利亚共和国发生的将有毒化学品用作武器的指称使用事件的有关事实，但获得并分析的相关资料无法提供合理的依据，事实调查组得以认定：在 2017 年 7 月 7 日和 8 月 4 日，据报在哈尔比特马萨斯内发生的有关事件中有人将有毒化学品用作了武器。

1.37 事实调查组已继续调查被评估为可信的指称使用事件。自 2022 年第二十七届大会以来，事实调查组进行了 5 次部署，以便收集有关正在审查的指控的更多资料，且已就此于 2023 年 3 月 8 日、7 月 3 日和 9 月 28 日向缔约国做了通报。

1.38 在一份说明（S/2232/2023，2023 年 12 月 21 日）中，技秘处对事实调查组在 2023 年开展的活动的最新情况做了概述。

落实 C-SS-4/DEC.3 号大会决定

1.39 调鉴组继续对带有以下标题的说明（EC-91/S/3，2019 年 6 月 28 日）的附件 2 所确定的几起事件进行调查：“根据 C-SS-4/DEC.3 号决定（2018 年 6 月 27 日）成立的调查和鉴定小组的工作。”

1.40 2023 年 1 月 27 日，调鉴组发布了第三份报告（S/2125/2023），其关注重点是有人于 2018 年 4 月 7 日在杜马镇（大马士革）使用了氯气。根据调鉴组获得并分析的所有资料，报告得出了如下结论：有合理的依据可以认为在 2018 年 4 月 7 日 19 时 10 分到 19 时 40 分（协调世界时 +3）之间，至少 1 架阿拉伯叙利亚空军的米 -8/17 直升机在老虎部队的控制下开展行动，并投下了两个装有氯气的黄色气瓶，其命中了该市中心区域的两座住宅楼。43 人身亡，还有数十人中毒。调鉴组于 2023 年 2 月 2 日向执理会简要介绍了该报告，同时应联合国安全理事会主席的邀请，于 2023 年 2 月 7 日向安理会简要介绍了该报告。

1.41　尽管有如下情况，但调鉴组仍被拒绝与阿拉伯叙利亚共和国的代表进行接触和直接互动，而且还被拒绝进入相关地点：

（a）技秘处向其提出了各项请求；

（b）根据《公约》第七条第 7 款，阿拉伯叙利亚共和国有与技秘处进行合作的义务；

（c）根据联合国安全理事会第 2118（2013）号决议，阿拉伯叙利亚共和国有义务与禁化武组织进行充分合作，即向由禁化武组织指定的人员提供立即和不受限制地进入任何地点以及接触任何人的机会。

1.42　2023 年 12 月 11 日，阿拉伯叙利亚共和国给技秘处发来了一份普通照会，以对后者请求获得与调鉴组正在进行调查的相关资料做出答复。

1.43　根据 C-SS-4/DEC.3 第 12 条和禁化武组织与“协助调查和起诉应对自 2011 年 3 月以来在阿拉伯叙利亚共和国发生的国际法所定义的最严重罪行负责的肇事者的国际公正和独立机制（IIIM）”达成的关于提供资料和证据的获取、存储和处理的谅解备忘录，调鉴组保管并与 IIIM 分享有关资料。

1.44　根据 C-SS-4/DEC.3 号决定第 20 条的规定，调鉴组的人员进一步向技秘处的其他部门和办公室传授知识和专业技能。这包含加强技秘处为缔约国提供专业技能的法证和调查能力，以便通过此种专业技能来查明在将化学品用作武器的事件中的肇事者、组织者、赞助者或其他方式的涉事者。

工业核查

1.45　《公约》的缔约国提交关于《公约》的《关于化学品的附件》的 3 个化学品附表所载的化学品的生产、进口、出口、加工和消耗情况的宣布，并提交有关《公约》不加禁止的目的生产特定有机化学品的其他化学生产设施的宣布。截至 2023 年 12 月 31 日应宣布的各类设施见表 2。

表 2　截至 2023 年 12 月 31 日应宣布的各类设施

设施类型	宣布的设施数	须接受视察的设施数①	申报了应宣布设施的缔约国数②	拥有须接受视察设施的缔约国数
附表 1	28	28	24	24
附表 2	462	226	36	25
附表 3	385	362	33	32
其他化学生产设施	4526	4356	81	81
总计	5401	5152③	81④	81⑤

1.46　技秘处在 2023 年进行了 196 次第六条视察。技秘处由于存在掌控范围外的行动制约，无法完成 2023 年方案和预算中构想的全部 200 次第六条视察。因此，有两次其他化学生产设施视察和两次附表 3 视察未能进行。第六条视察见表 3。

表 3　第六条视察

2015 年	2016 年	2017 年	2018 年	2019 年	2020 年	2021 年	2022 年	2023 年
241	241	241	241	241	82	80	160	196

1.47　上文提到的 196 次视察包括：对附表 1 设施进行的 11 次视察；对附表 2 厂区进行的 49 次视察；对附表 3 厂区进行的 8 次视察；对其他化学生产设施进行的 128 次视察（上述几类视察分别占可视察设施总数的 39%、22%、2% 和 3%）。在视察期间，没有记录到任何不确定因素。但有 10 次视察留下了须予以进一步关注的事项，并有 116 次视察建议在宣布中提供进一步的资料。此外，由于有关宣布出现了误差，有 2 次其他化学生产设施视察是对不必视察的设施进行的。

① 因超过阈值而须接受通过现场视察而进行的核查。
② 包括预计活动年度宣布和过去活动年度宣布。
③ 原文“4972”有误，已更正为“5152”。
④ 有 81 个缔约国宣布了拥有至少有一个第六条设施。
⑤ 有 81 个缔约国宣布了拥有至少有一个可视察的第六条设施。

1.48　关于在2023年接受视察的其他化学生产设施和附表3厂区，厂区的选取是根据“在混合型厂区进行核查的替代方法”（S/1202/2014，2014年7月23日）一文所述的方法进行的。如果一个附表3或其他化学生产设施混合型厂区已经在一种第六条核查制度下接受过视察，为了随机选取附表3或其他化学生产设施厂区供视察，该厂区将被视为此前已接受过视察。因此，从统计上来讲，该厂区被选中供视察的频率应会降低。

1.49　2023年，在缔约国的支持下，技秘处继续为优化资源而尽可能地增加进行连续视察的次数。因此，与2022年相比，2023年视察计划中的连续视察次数有所增加。连续视察见表4，其中，48次连续视察在21个不同的国家中进行，包括在9个不同国家中进行的14次长时间的工业视察。39次连续任务是国内视察，另外9次是长时间跨国视察。

表4　连续视察

2015年	2016年	2017年	2018年	2019年	2020年	2021年	2022年	2023年
59	54	58	58	60	20	21	34	48

1.50　2023年，技秘处继续开展跨司小组的工作，以对视察做法、视察报告表格、视察工具和视察培训进行一次全面的审查，从而查明进一步优化视察的选项。例如，技秘处在2023年采用了新的电子视察工具，并修订了视察报告模板（见下文1.62段）。

1.51　2023年，技秘处进行了一次包括采样和分析活动在内的视察。各年的附带采样和分析的视察数见表5。

表5　各年的附带采样和分析的视察数

2015年	2016年	2017年	2018年	2019年	2020年	2021年	2022年	2023年
11	11	10	9	6	1	0	0	1

宣布

1.52　2023年，在85个提交了过去活动年度宣布的缔约国中，有68

个（80%）是按照《公约》规定的期限提交的。在报告年内，在拥有应宣布的其他化学生产设施的缔约国中，94% 在其过去活动年度宣布中更新了其他化学生产设施的清单，从而使应宣布的其他化学生产设施的更新率达到 99.3%。通过提供有关其他化学生产设施清单的年度更新资料，相关缔约国为核查机制的运行提供了极大的便利。

附表化学品的转让

1.53　5 个缔约国在其 2022 年过去活动年度宣布中宣布了 10 项附表 1 化学品转让。在这些转让中，发送和接收缔约国均做了通知和宣布的有 9 项，有 1 项转让由接收缔约国做了通知和宣布。

1.54　2022 年过去活动年度宣布显示：55 个缔约国参与了大约 6283 吨的附表 2 化学品的转让，123 个缔约国参与了大约 539577 吨的附表 3 化学品的转让。

1.55　7 个缔约国宣布向 3 个非缔约国出口了 4 种附表 3 化学品。

转让数据差异

1.56　2023 年，2022 年过去活动年度宣布显示共有 1679 起缔约国之间的附表 2 和附表 3 化学品的转让。其中，宣布的 835 起转让的数量超过了宣布阈值，其中又有涉及 94 个缔约国的 592 起转让出现了彼此的数据存在差异的现象。

1.57　在此方面，技秘处继续与缔约国进行后续联系，并与其他利益攸关方密切合作，以协助缔约国减少和解决这些转让数据差异的问题。

控暴剂

1.58　至报告期终了时，有 137 个缔约国宣布拥有控暴剂（主要是催泪瓦斯），并有 53 个缔约国宣布其不拥有此种化学剂。有 1 个缔约国尚未提交初始宣布，另外 2 个缔约国尚未在其初始宣布中提供有关控暴剂的详细资料。本报告的附件 4 载有更多关于拥有控暴剂情况的资料。

电子宣布和资料安全交换系统

1.59　2023 年，技秘处查明了电子宣布信息系统软件应用和文件需要进行完善的领域。对该资料的收集主要是在与缔约国开展培训和磋商期间进行的。这些改动将被添加到暂定于2024年发布的新版电子宣布信息系统中。至报告期终了时，有63个缔约国的119名用户已注册使用了资料安全交换系统。

1.60　2023年，技秘处提供了电子宣布信息系统培训，作为第六条相关培训活动的一部分。此外，技秘处还为提出请求的缔约国提供了有关电子宣布信息系统和资料安全交换系统的培训和咨询。

分析平台和业务智能化

1.61　技秘处正在建立一个新的分析平台，其中包含一个数据仓库软件应用（WhereScape）和一个业务情报软件应用（Qlik Sense）。Qlik Sense将替代旧的业务情报软件应用（Cognos），开发工作定于2024年完成。

电子视察工具

1.62　电子视察（eINS）软件应用程序已于2023年使用，以简化视察流程并使其数字化。该工具是跨司第六条优化项目的一部分，旨在提高当前核查过程的各方面的工作效率。

核查信息系统

1.63　2023年，技秘处批准了核查信息系统——工业现代化项目。该项目选定了一个供应商，同时聘用了一名项目经理。项目组正在进行开发工作，该项目将于2025年年底完工。

非正式磋商

1.64　2023年，进行了5轮关于第六条核查和视察的非正式磋商（工业系列磋商）。会议以混合形式进行。缔约国就一些与核查相关的事宜进行了磋商，其中包括：

（a）根据确定的第六条视察数量的政策指导大纲落实结果；

（b）2022年外部审计员报告中的建议；

（c）附表2视察——当前积压的任务和未来；

（d）完善厂区筛选的算法；

（e）其他化学生产设施的厂区筛选的使用情况。

禁化武组织效能水平测试和指定实验室

1.65　禁化武组织每年都为有意加入禁化武组织分析实验室网络的机构举办效能水平测试。在报告期内，完成了第52次，举行和完成了第53次并开始了第54次禁化武组织环境分析正式效能水平测试。此外，举行了禁化武组织第八次生物医学正式效能水平测试。至报告期终了时，已有来自21个缔约国的26个实验室被指定可进行环境分析，并有14个缔约国的19个实验室被指定可进行生物医学样品分析。本报告的附件5介绍了截至2023年12月31日每个指定实验室的状况。

将禁化武组织实验室和设备仓库升格为一个化学与技术中心的项目

1.66　化技中心于2023年5月12日举行了落成典礼并全面投入运行。荷兰威廉•亚历山大国王陛下、派恩纳克－诺多普市市长、大会和执理会主席、各缔约国代表和利益攸关方参加了典礼。57个国家、欧洲联盟和其他捐助方为该中心的建造项目筹集了3460万欧元的资金。

1.67　通过有关说明介绍了项目进度的最新情况：S/2136/2023（2023年2月17日）和S/2193/2023（2023年7月20日），标题均为“将禁化武组织实验室和设备仓库升格为一个化学与技术中心的项目的进展情况”。

禁化武组织中央分析数据库

1.68　过去5年间禁化武组织中央分析数据库收录的化学品种类的数目见表6。在现场分析中仅使用气相色谱（保留指数）和质谱数据。

表6　过去5年间禁化武组织中央分析数据库收录的化学品种类的数目

技术	2019年	2020年	2021年	2022年	2023年
红外	775	775	794	805	826
气相色谱（保留指数）	4482	4543	4588	4596	4609
核磁共振	298	300	300	300	300
质谱	4602	4647	4673	4682	4697
串联质谱	不适用	38	68	68	68

视察局提供的培训

1.69　2023年，视察局的能力建设和紧急应对规划分队协调或开办了

31 门单项培训课程，这些课程在比利时、德国、荷兰、塞尔维亚和大不列颠及北爱尔兰联合王国进行。在技秘处其他部门的支持下，能力建设和紧急应对规划分队继续开办了视察员必修培训及专业课程，这些课程包括职业健康和安全、禁化武组织保密制度、弹药培训、战争的爆炸残余物、移动式实验室的部署、分析化学师许可等。

1.70　为 69 名技秘处的工作人员举办了关于危险废物作业和紧急应对的 1 期初始课程和 3 期进修课程。美利坚合众国为此提供了支持和资助。

1.71　大不列颠及北爱尔兰联合王国举办了 4 期课程支持和资助：1 期关于职业健康和安全的课程；3 期面向离岸医疗人员的进修课。此外，资助了在禁化武组织总部大楼为 12 名技秘处工作人员举办的 1 期外交技能课程。

1.72　德国资助并举办了 2 期“野外环境中的安全和安保方法”课程。135 名可能需要到高危地区工作的技秘处工作人员接受了培训。

1.73　2023 年，在塞尔维亚举办了 2 期有毒化学品培训课程，培训后有 35 名技秘处工作人员获得了证书。

1.74　2023 年 9 月，一组由 7 人组成的新视察员组（V 组）加入了禁化武组织。在技秘处其他部门的协作下，能力建设和紧急应对规划分队协调开展了为期 12 周的强制初始培训，目的是准备好担任视察员这一重要角色。

2. 国际合作和援助

2.1　2023 年，技秘处继续通过能力建设方案来提供技术援助，以支持各缔约国履行《公约》。技秘处举办了 79 次活动，使来自各地区的 2200 余名专家受益。这些活动包括线上、混合模式和现场参与的活动。此外，技秘处继续实施 4 个常设方案，即研究金方案、研究项目支持和资助方案、大会支持和资助方案及设备交换方案。

2.2　此外，自化技中心于 2023 年 5 月揭幕启用以来，技秘处加大利用该中心的性能以更好地满足缔约国在培训和交流专长方面的需求。在本年度的审查期内，化技中心举办了 13 期能力建设活动，使来自各地区组的学员受益，并覆盖了全部任务授权领域。

国家履约和技术援助

2.3　2023 年，技秘处继续加强了缔约国全面和有效履行《公约》的国家能力。来自各地区的 654 名参与者参加了 15 项技术援助活动，这些活动重点关注了加强机构能力以履行其《公约》义务。

2.4　截至 2023 年 12 月 31 日，在《公约》193 个缔约国中，已有 161 个报告称通过了国家履约立法，其中，128 个缔约国报告称有涵盖所有初步措施的立法，33 个缔约国报告称有涵盖部分初步措施的立法，32 个缔约国尚未报告履约立法的通过情况或向技秘处提交有关资料。在技秘处的年度报告中载有关于《公约》第七条履行状况的详细资料[①]。

2.5　2023 年，技秘处与缅甸国家主管部门（1 月 27 日）和吉布提国家主管部门（5 月 30 日）合办了 2 期国家立法审查论坛。在上述论坛举办期间，技秘处与相应缔约国的代表一同审查了其关于《公约》的国家立法框架的范围，同时技秘处就履约的各种立法及监管方式提供了专门的建议。

2.6　技秘处与世界海关组织合作，于 2023 年 5 月 23 日至 25 日在刚果开办了关于对有毒化学品贸易开展有效的海关执法管控区域大会。此次区域大会有来自 27 个非洲缔约国的 53 名与会人员出席。会议为海关机构和国家主管部门举办了论坛，以分享对化学品贸易进行有效管控的最佳做法。2023 年 10 月 10 日至 12 日，技秘处在肯尼亚为海关培训机构开办了业内培训，并在此期间就履行《公约》附表化学品的转让制度为海关机构

① 2023 年关于《公约》第七条履行状况的年度报告：EC-104/DG.8 C-28/DG.7（2023 年 9 月 6 日）、EC-104/DG.9 C-28/DG.8（2023 年 9 月 6 日）和 EC-104/DG.10 C-28/DG.9（2023 年 9 月 6 日）。

提供了进一步培训。培训使来自13个非洲缔约国的41名学员得以强化了相关知识和技能，同时发挥了平台作用，以促进海关培训机构之间联络关系和协同合作。

2.7　2023年10月3日至5日，在巴巴多斯举办了面向加勒比缔约国的《公约》国家履约次区域论坛。此次论坛有来自11个缔约国的48名与会者出席，使技秘处与该区域重新恢复了互动，同时通过共享经验和良好做法，鼓励与会缔约国围绕《公约》履约开展更广泛的合作和互动。

2.8　2023年7月和8月举行了4次《公约》缔约国国家主管部门的区域会议。在会议期间，国家主管部门介绍了有关国家履行《公约》的最新情况，讨论了各种挑战，并分享了经验教训。代表们还就与加强《公约》第六、第七、第十和第十一条规定的国家能力有关的一系列问题与技秘处进行了交流，并听取了关于技秘处的技术援助和能力建设议程的介绍。为非洲、亚洲、东欧以及拉丁美洲和加勒比地区举行了会议。

2.9　2023年6月27日至29日，技秘处在多米尼加共和国为拉丁美洲和加勒比组的缔约国国家主管部门及利益攸关方举办了关于《公约》的一般性培训课程。学员们增进了对《公约》规定的理解，并提高了相关技能。来自24个缔约国的53名学员参加了该课程。

2.10　2023年10月24日至26日，技秘处在卡塔尔多哈举行了《公约》缔约国化学工业和国家主管部门代表第十届年会。国家主管部门和行业代表就国家、区域和全球层面的《公约》履约分享了经验、发展情况、良好做法和挑战。会上，26个缔约国的50名与会人员增强了对重要履约事项的意识，同时认识到需要采取全面的履约立法以指导工业宣布和遵守《公约》规定的义务。

2.11　《公约》缔约国国家主管部门第二十五次年度会议于2023年11月22日至24日在海牙禁化武组织总部大楼举行。国家主管部门分享了与履行《公约》和加强化学安保有关的经验、知识和良好做法。国家主管部门在年会上了解了上一年的能力培养活动中的亮点和进展的最新情况。来自各地区的123个缔约国的200多名代表参加了会议。

援助和防护

2.12　2023年，有39个缔约国根据第十条第4款提交了针对使用化学武器的国家防护方案的年度资料。

2.13　乌克兰的局势增加了包括化学武器在内的大规模毁灭性武器所带来的威胁。在此方面，应乌克兰的请求，技秘处继续根据第十条的规定向其提供了援助和防护。为紧急应对人员提供了线上和线下的能力建设课程，使其更好地保持常备状态，以应对使用化学武器的威胁和涉及化学工业设施的事件。

2.14　技秘处还向乌克兰的紧急应对人员提供了必要的化学品侦检设备，并举办了有关指导使用这些设备的培训活动和能力建设课程。缔约国捐助的实施第十条信托基金已用于资助这些采购的费用。截至2023年年底，已为此承付了140万欧元。

2.15　2023年，技秘处继续密切关注乌克兰境内在履行《公约》方面的情况，并随时向缔约国通报任何相关事态发展。这包括维持一份供缔约国分享的有关乌克兰通信的简编，该简编可在禁化武组织的网站上公开查阅。该资源不仅有助于缔约国了解相关发展，而且技秘处可以根据需要对其进行更新。

2.16　技秘处继续推动使用一款用户友好型在线工具，以方便收集和提交第十条第4款所规定的资料。该在线工具已被纳入援助与防护数据库（援防数据库）的更新版本中。缔约国现在可以通过外部服务器“Catalyst”访问援防数据库。

2.17　在报告期内，技秘处继续根据第十条开展能力建设活动，为此举办了36场能力建设活动，使来自各地区的805名紧急应对人员获益。技秘处根据第十条开展的能力建设活动采用了新形式，其以由5个部分构成的混合培训周期为基础，其中包括2期覆盖理论知识的线上课程；2场培养实操技能的现场活动（基础课程、高阶课程及演练综合课程）；1期后续的网络研讨会。

2.18　技秘处开办了 16 期量身定制的专业培训课程，以满足各缔约国的防护需求。技秘处还借助其教员培养和交流方案来支持开发和开展线上培训。该方案涉及国际专业知识交流和最佳实践的培训，旨在加强各缔约国在国家、次区域和地区层级的应对能力。该方案还继续加强了禁化武组织响应援助请求的常备状态。

2.19　2023 年，技秘处分别为亚洲和拉丁美洲及加勒比地区的缔约国举办了两个周期的援助和防护培训。这是加强缔约国应对涉及有毒化学品事件能力的重要手段。部分培训周期方案跨越了 2023 年和 2024 年，计划在 2024 年下半年完成。阿根廷、厄瓜多尔、德国、马来西亚、摩洛哥、巴基斯坦、大韩民国、瑞士和赞比亚为这些培训周期提供了支持和资助。

2.20　在拉丁美洲和加勒比地区，技秘处举办了 9 场线上和线下的能力建设活动。其中包括在区域培训周期下进行的关于紧急应对涉及化武战剂或有毒工业化学品事件的混合模式课程。此外，在巴巴多斯、墨西哥和西班牙的支持下，还开办了以下专业课程，包括入院前护理、医院常备状态、在非常规环境下出现有毒化学品的紧急应对，以及在该地区举办了一期关于在线自评估工具的讲习班。

2.21　在禁化武组织就《公约》同非洲加强合作方案（非洲方案）的第六阶段，在建立和加强国家及区域应对涉及化武战剂和有毒工业化学品的事件的能力方面取得了进一步的进展。

2.22　2023 年 9 月 23 日至 10 月 5 日，技秘处和阿尔及利亚在阿尔及尔联合举办了首期泛非洲“非洲地区化学紧急应对能力建设演练”（以下简称“CHEMEX 非洲”），并得到了加拿大的资助。

2.23　作为此次活动的一部分，来自西非国家经济共同体、中非国家经济共同体和南部非洲发展共同体的紧急应对人员小组接受了东非共同体教员提供的培训，后者得到了北非和萨赫勒地区的技术团队及东非政府间发展组织提供的支持。

2.24 来自33个非洲缔约国的81名紧急应对人员参与了“CHEMEX非洲”演练。此外，捷克共和国、大不列颠及北爱尔兰联合王国、美利坚合众国和欧洲联盟化生放核风险减缓示范中心的相关专家以不同身份（督导、观察员和评估员）参与了演练。

2.25 2023年10月3日，阿尔及利亚人民国民军参谋长萨义德·常格里亚将军主持了贵宾日活动，并有阿尔及利亚总统阿卜杜勒马吉德·特本亲临参加。当日活动包括一场重要演练，模拟了在发生涉及有毒化学剂的恐怖袭击时的协调应对，还举办了国际设备展。

2.26 此外，为对非洲的区域和次区域能力和专业知识予以最佳利用，技秘处继续与区域经济共同体合作，以便向每一个区域的缔约国提供能力建设支持。能力建设活动遵循培训周期方法，侧重于具体需求的专门活动，例如培养能够应对化学紧急情况的事件指挥官的技能。

2.27 在化学武器受害者国际支援网络中继续开展工作以支持该网络的目标。此外，根据大会的相关决定（C-16/DEC.13，2011年12月2日），为支持未来项目而供资予以鼓励。2023年，技秘处继续与国际专家组合作，以起草面向医疗从业人员的第二份指南，而其关注重点是受害者的长期护理。该指南已处于最后的起草阶段，将于2024年出版。

2.28 受害者信托基金的余额为98728欧元。有关自愿援助基金，根据《公约》第十条第7款（a）项设立了基金，其余额现为1594085欧元。根据第十条第7款（c）项而向其提供援助的缔约国数量达到47个。

国际合作和技术发展

2.29 2023年，技秘处继续完成能力建设方案，并继续为国际合作提供便利，以推动化学的和平利用。根据第十一条以线上、线下和混合模式开展的有关方案涉及化学品综合管理、增强实验室能力和推广并交流化学知识3个专题领域。

2.30 2023年，技秘处为750名学员举办了28项能力建设活动。

2.31 “充分实施第十一条一事商定框架的构成要素”（C-16/DEC.10，

2011 年 12 月 1 日）审查和评价讲习班促进了缔约国和利益攸关方之间的讨论和意见交流，以进一步全面履行《公约》的第十一条。2023 年 11 月 20 日，该讲习班以混合模式举办了第八期，来自 26 个缔约国的 40 名人员与会。讲习班审查了第十一条下正在开展的能力建设工作，对相关方案和活动的影响进行了讨论，还包括对进展和缺陷的审议。

2.32 技秘处于 7 月 21 日至 9 月 22 日举办了第二十四期禁化武组织研修方案，其内容包括：在禁化武组织总部大楼开展培训，其主题包括核查制度、视察程序、国家主管部门的作用、国际合作和援助；在大不列颠及北爱尔兰联合王国萨里大学进行学习，以培养工业环境下在化工厂的作业技能和化学工程理论；学习工业领域相关技能，以便在各种工业作业中获得实操接触和培训。共有 31 名学员代表 31 个缔约国参加了这一期方案。至报告期终了时，研修方案校友网络由来自 122 个缔约国的 576 名校友组成。

2.33 在化学品综合管理领域，技秘处组织了 12 场关于化学品安全和安保的全球和区域能力建设系列活动，其中 7 场为在线下进行的活动，举办地在意大利、马来西亚、墨西哥、荷兰、大韩民国、卡塔尔、阿联酋和大不列颠及北爱尔兰联合王国。这些活动包括：上文提到的研修方案；以化学安全和安保管理为关注重点的一系列全球和区域研讨会；培训和网络学习活动，以在化学设施和实验室中推广安全和安保标准，从而最大程度地降低事件发生的风险。

2.34 2023 年，进行化学安全和安保工具开发方案的第二阶段。在报告期内，举办了 2 期讲习班以编制公路运输危险化学品的示意性导则（一期于 2 月 21 日至 24 日在吉隆坡举办，另一期于 11 月 13 日在线上举办）。预计导则将在 2024 年发布。在增强分析实验室能力的框架内，于 2023 年举办了 9 期《公约》相关化学品分析和禁化武组织效能水平测试的培训课程。这些线上培训课程由芬兰、印度、西班牙及南非的有关实验室承办，并在化技中心开设。这包括有关基础分析化学和专门的效能水平测试线上培训。

此外，2023 年 7 月 11 日至 13 日，化技中心还举办了旨在加强女性专家在分析《公约》相关化学品方面知识和实操技能的基础化学分析课程。

2.35 在实验室结对和援助方案下，2023 年开展了以下 3 个结对项目：一个在阿尔及利亚（受援实验室）和德国（施援实验室）之间；另一个在南非（受援实验室）和荷兰（施援实验室）之间；还有一个在塞尔维亚（受援实验室）和芬兰（施援实验室）之间。塞尔维亚项目于 2023 年年底顺利结项。这些项目旨在加强受援实验室的能力，使其顺利完成为获得禁化武组织指定地位而必需的禁化武组织效能水平测试。

2.36 为进一步提高非洲和拉丁美洲及加勒比的实验室的能力，“评估和增强非洲和拉加成员国的分析实验室的能力的项目：为获得禁化武组织的指定资格而努力”的第四阶段于 2023 年 3 月 31 日完成。该项目得到了大不列颠及北爱尔兰联合王国自愿捐款资助，且已于 2023 年 8 月延期，直至 2024 年 3 月 31 日。项目活动继续侧重于提升位于巴西、智利、肯尼亚和尼日利亚的 4 间分析实验室的能力。

2.37 一个为期 5 年的项目从 2023 年 2 月开始，旨在构建西语系实验室网络来分析《公约》包含的有关化学品。2023 年，西班牙的指定实验室——化学武器核查实验室（LAVEMA）作为技秘处执行该项目的合作伙伴，为该项目启动了候选实验室调研。

2.38 本报告期内，在德国提供的自愿捐助的支持下，“为非洲成员国分析实验室强化能力”项目开展了首批活动。该项目计划从 2023 年至 2025 年，涉及一系列活动，包括为非洲海关实验室提供化学武器相关分析的培训；加强非洲实验室在设备维护方面的能力；根据结对计划采取定制行动，以协助一间试图获得禁化武组织指定地位的非洲实验室。

2.39 在设备交换方案框架内，技秘处在 2023 年促成德国向坦桑尼亚联合共和国姆旺戈大学进行捐赠。此后还培训了坦桑尼亚的 15 名专家。此外，2023 年 7 月，技秘处促成德国的一间实验室向肯尼亚国家主管部门转让了 2 台实验室设备。

2.40 本报告期内，技秘处继续在利益攸关方群体中推广化学知识。2023 年 5 月 23 日至 25 日，在马来西亚吉隆坡举办了化学和平利用年度论坛，其重点是增强与会人员对化学安全和安保管理的意识并深化对此的理解，同时推广绿色和可持续化学。2023 年 6 月 19 日至 20 日，在化技中心召开了化学界的女性研讨会。该研讨会由法国提供自愿捐款，汇聚了全球的专家、科学家和研究员来讨论并解决女性在科学领域面临的挑战，尤其是在化学领域。

2.41 2023 年 6 月 21 日至 23 日，技秘处在化技中心恢复举办了“面向科学家的政策和外交”讲习班。该讲习班侧重于在化学和生化科学领域推广尽责研究做法，包括科学研究的双重用途、科技发展对国际安全的影响、科学和学术界在降低化学风险方面发挥的作用。

2.42 在研究金方案的框架内，技秘处继续促进机构间的科学技术信息交流，同时通过能力建设和促进科学领域的国际合作，来支持目标国家的科学研究并强化其有关机构。在 2023 年共完成 12 个研究金项目：6 人来自喀麦隆（由法国、德国、罗马尼亚和西班牙主办）；1 人来自肯尼亚（由德国主办）；1 人来自菲律宾（由瑞典主办）；2 人来自塞尔维亚（由芬兰和匈牙利主办）；2 人来自乌克兰（由芬兰和波兰主办）。

2.43 在研究项目支持和资助方案的框架内，技秘处继续将其支持和资助拓展到缔约国的小型研究项目，以协助促进工业、农业、研究、医疗、制药和其他与《公约》相关的和平目的在化学方面的科学技术知识的发展。截至 2023 年年底，技秘处继续支持和资助了 20 个正在进行的研究项目。

2.44 2023 年，加强能力建设需求的评估十分重要。技秘处邀请缔约国自愿提交对其化学安全和安保管理的特定需求的评估，以及提交有关化学管理中现有工具、指南和最佳做法的信息。为获得进一步的反馈，技秘处对调查问卷进行了修改和更新，以更好地关注成员国在能力建设以及对相关领域（包括有害化学品运输）的工具和指导大纲的需求，同时对缔约国扩大外联。为此，技秘处收到 55 个缔约国发来的答复，通过更全面的分析，将相关结论用于指导正在开展的方案和活动。

2.45 本报告期内，方案审查和吸取经验教训的方法和技术已进一步制度化。2023 年，技秘处对 2019 年至 2022 年开展的分析技能培养方案进行了审查。从中获得的经验和结论有助于指导和加强 2024 年及今后计划开展的有关课程。

2.46 2023 年 5 月 4 日，技秘处举行了一次线上信息介绍会，以使各缔约国意识到其在第十一条下广泛开展的各类服务和能力建设方案，其中还包括对第七条和第十条下的类似方案的简要综述。来自 59 个缔约国的 145 名人员参加了此次介绍会，会上详细介绍了定制培训，以及这些领域现有的技术支持。

禁化武组织非洲方案

2.47 本报告期内，技秘处通过非洲方案继续积极地解决非洲地区与《公约》有关的特定需求。启动了方案第六阶段（2023—2025 年）的实施，并在 2023 年持续取得了进展。技秘处在全年组织了 55 期能力建设活动，使来自 45 个非洲缔约国的 850 余名学员获益。这些活动包括专门为非洲地区举办的 22 期活动。

2.48 根据第六阶段的目标，相关活动的关注重点涉及以下内容：加强《公约》的国家履约；完善对附表化学品跨境转让的控制；发展针对化学紧急情况的防护和援助能力；推动化学安全和安保管理；升级整个非洲大陆的实验室能力。

2.49 2023 年，在化技中心举办了上文提到的若干项活动。本报告期内，技秘处为 6 项研究基金和非洲科学家开展的 12 个研究项目提供了资助。在大会支持和资助方案下，技秘处还为在意大利、芬兰和毛里求斯（线上）举行的 3 场国际科学活动提供了参会资助，这些会议承接了 101 名来自非洲的科学家。技秘处还促成了德国向肯尼亚及向坦桑尼亚联合共和国分别转让实验室设备。

2.50 2023 年，技秘处与合作伙伴共同协调开展了有针对性的培训和结对项目，以加强那些感兴趣且符合资质的非洲实验室的能力，使其能通过禁化武组织的效能水平测试，从而获得禁化武组织的指定地位。

2.51　对2023年在非洲方案的框架内进行的活动，技秘处继续通过禁化武组织的常规预算来供资，而且动用了更多自愿捐款来进一步实现方案的目标。本报告期内，在该方案框架下，动用预算外资金开展了以下的关键性专门项目："关于对非洲有毒化学品贸易开展有效的海关执法管控区域大会"（刚果布拉柴维尔，2023年5月23日至25日）；"CHEMEX非洲"演练（阿尔及利亚阿尔及尔，2023年9月23日至10月5日）；面向非洲海关培训机构的同行对同行培训课程（肯尼亚内罗毕，2023年10月10日至12日）。

2.52　"CHEMEX非洲"演练是在《公约》背景下举办的首个泛非洲的化学紧急情况应对能力建设演练。活动表明了禁化武组织致力于进一步促进南南合作，同时在向成员国提供能力建设支持和资助中采取教员培训的方式。为纪念该活动对禁化武组织的重要意义，总干事和副总干事一同出席了该活动的贵宾日活动。贵宾日包括一场模拟在发生涉及有毒化学剂的恐怖袭击时进行协同应对的重大演练，以及一场国际设备展。

2.53　作为强化相关伙伴关系的一部分，总干事于2023年4月13日接见了到访的非洲联盟政治事务、和平与安全专员班克勒•阿德耶大使。双方进行了富有成效的交流，并同意重振两个组织之间的合作，目的是进一步推动《公约》的普遍性和其在非洲的本地化，同时重新恢复两个组织于2006年签署的谅解备忘录。作为此次会晤的后续，技秘处向非洲联盟委员会提供了一份拟开展行动项的修订清单，双方在此背景下一直保持联络。

2.54　2023年，非洲方案指导委员会继续监督并支持方案的落实。委员会成员包括阿尔及利亚、安哥拉、喀麦隆（主席）、乍得、加纳、肯尼亚、摩洛哥、塞内加尔、南非和苏丹。委员会的观察员（方案捐助国）包括加拿大、捷克共和国、法国、德国、瑞士、大不列颠及北爱尔兰联合王国、美利坚合众国和欧洲联盟。

2.55　在喀麦隆大使玛德琳·理古默·奥多那大使的主持下，指导委员会于2023年6月26日和11月20日分别召开了会议，以便详细审查方案近期取得的进展。

3. 决策机构

缔约国大会的活动

五审会

3.1　2023年5月15日至19日，五审会在海牙召开。共有137个《公约》缔约国出席了大会，另外还有一个签署国和一个非签署国出席。注册参会的还包括14个国际组织和专门机构、74个非政府组织和代表全球化工行业和科学界的3个机构。联合国副秘书长、裁军事务高级代表中满泉女士向大会发来致辞。

3.2　根据《公约》第八条第22款的规定，五审会对《公约》各项条款的履行情况进行了审议，同时考虑到相关的一切科技发展情况。科咨委主席古德尔·波佛顿博士向五审会简要介绍了该委员会关于科技发展的报告（RC-5/DG.1，2023年2月22日），其中重点强调了科学审查流程、值得考虑的专题领域和有关建议。根据第C-16/DEC.11号决定（2011年12月1日），五审会对已宣布的剩余化学武器库存的销毁和为实现计划的完成日期而取得的进展进行了全面的审议。

3.3　五审会通过了一份纪实性报告（RC-5/3，2023年6月7日）。

3.4　在执理会第103次会议上分发了“五审会主席亨克·考尔·范德卡斯特大使关于五审会的成果的思考”（EC-103/WP.1，2023年6月26日）。如下文相关章节所述那样，执理会和大会审议了五审会的后续工作，并在此方面开展了几项行动。

大会第二十八届会议

3.5　大会第二十八届会议于2023年11月27日至12月1日举行。有143个缔约国、1个签约国、1个非签约国和8个国际组织、专门机构和其他国际机构的代表参加。106 个非政府组织和代表全球化学工业和科学界的 3 个机构也注册与会。

3.6　2023年11月29日，缔约国在化学战受害者纪念日举行了纪念活动。

3.7　大会第二十八届会议审议了《公约》在各方面的履行现状，其中包括化学裁军、与销毁相关的事项、国家履约措施、防护和援助、国际合作、教咨委的活动以及与防范化学武器卷土重来有关的各项活动。缔约国就在非洲方案指引下开展的有关活动的报告进行了讨论，还审议了禁化武组织在与化工行业和科学界开展互动方面的工作进展。

3.8　大会第二十八届会议通过的决定包括[①]：

（a）“禁化武组织参加联合国合办工作人员养恤基金”（C-28/DEC.8，2023 年 11 月 27 日）；

（b）“禁化武组织 2024—2025 年方案和预算”（C-28/DEC.9，2023 年 11 月 29 日）；

（c）“对禁化武组织任期政策的修订”（C-28/DEC.10，2023 年 11 月 30 日）；

（d）“地域代表性行动计划”（C-28/DEC.11，2023 年 11 月 30 日）；

（e）“应对使用化学武器构成的威胁及其未来的威胁使用”（C-28/DEC.12，2023 年 11 月 30 日）。

执行理事会的活动

3.9　2023 年，执理会审议了技秘处关于《公约》履行现状的若干份报告，其内容包括核查活动以及第六条、第七条、第十条和第十一条的履行情况。

3.10　执理会还：

（a）审查落实了关于化学武器销毁的决定所取得的进展；

（b）讨论了阿拉伯叙利亚共和国使用化学武器一事；

（c）审查了宣评组的工作；

① 其他（非机密性）决定可在禁化武组织的公共网站上查阅。

（d）讨论了事实调查组的一份报告（S/2186/2023）；

（e）审查了大会 C-SS-4/DEC.3 号决定的执行进展情况，并收到了调鉴组的一份报告（S/2125/2023）；

（f）核准了对禁化武组织与一个缔约国之间关于设施协定和议定的详细核查计划的修订；

（g）通过了关于新通过验证的附表化学品数据的清单的决定（EC-102/DEC.1，2023 年 3 月 14 日），以及拟纳入中央数据库的新通过验证的《公约》相关非附表化学品数据的清单的决定（EC-102/DEC.2，2023 年 3 月 14 日）；

（h）审议了在非洲方案背景下完成的有关工作；

（i）审议了内部监察办公室的 2022 年度报告（EC-103/DG.8C-28/DG.3，2023 年 6 月 1 日）；

（j）通过了关于设立地域代表性工作组的决定（EC-103/DEC.1，2023 年 7 月 12 日）；

（k）通过了关于允许在特殊情况下召开执理会会议或届会的决定（EC-102/DEC.6，2023 年 3 月 16 日）；

（l）通过了关于行政和财务事项的有关决定；

（m）将其关于若干事项的建议提交大会第二十八届会议。

附属机构的活动

3.11　解决保密争端委员会于 2023 年 5 月 31 日至 6 月 2 日举行了第二十五届会议（CC-25/1，2023 年 6 月 2 日）。

3.12　行财咨机构于 2023 年 6 月 6 日至 8 日举行了第五十四届会议（ABAF-54/1，2023 年 6 月 8 日），并于 2023 年 7 月 25 日至 27 日举办了第五十五届会议（ABAF-55/1，2023 年 7 月 27 日）。

3.13　科咨委于 2023 年 8 月 28 日至 9 月 1 日举行了第三十七届会议（SAB-37/1，2023 年 9 月 1 日）。

3.14　教咨委于 2023 年 2 月 7 日至 9 日举行了第十四届会议（ABEO-14/1，2023 年 2 月 9 日），并于 2023 年 6 月 20 日至 22 日举行了第十五届会议（ABEO-15/1，2023 年 6 月 22 日）。

3.15　执理会主席、罗马尼亚大使吕西安·法图向大会第二十八届会议报告了与东道国关系委员会的工作状况。为了改进对决策机构的支持，技秘处：

（a）购置并维护了多语言网络会议服务平台 KUDO，为禁化武组织全部 6 种正式语言提供实时口译服务，以便根据第 EC-102/DEC.6 号决定的要求远程召开执理会届会和会议；

（b）完成了将决策机构及其附属机构的有关届会和会议的音 / 视频记录档案迁移到 Connected Views 5.0 云端系统这一工作，从而确保决策机构的各项记录得以被长期且安全地保存和使用；

（c）进一步升级了禁化武组织的外部服务器 Catalyst，以便获得各国在特定届会上的国家发言；

（d）维持了在届会前通过非正式磋商进程来审议非争议性议程项目这一模式，这也是一种具有最佳做法的工具，借以推动对大会和执理会届会的高效和及时管理。

4. 对外关系

普遍性

4.1　2023 年，《公约》的缔约国数目仍然为 193 个。以色列已签署但尚未批准《公约》；朝鲜人民民主共和国、埃及和南苏丹既未签署也未加入《公约》。

4.2　在《公约》普遍性行动计划的框架内，技秘处在 2023 年继续接触剩余的非缔约国。技秘处仍保持惯例，即邀请非缔约国和签署国的代表参加选定的禁化武组织的相关活动，其中包括五审会和大会第二十八届会议。本报告期内，技秘处还利用各种机会与非缔约国代表进行了互动，包括在海牙和国际大会间隙。

4.3　关于签署国，技秘处在 2023 年与以色列驻荷兰使馆保持了定期联系。以色列代表团出席了五审会和大会第二十八届会议，且以色列大使还在2场活动中做了发言。

4.4 在阿尔及尔举办的“CHEMEX非洲”演练活动的间隙，总干事与南苏丹外交事务和国际合作部长詹姆斯·皮蒂亚·摩根先生进行了会晤。在会晤期间，双方签署了一份联合公报，同意开展合作，以尽快完成南苏丹的加入进程。技秘处与南苏丹驻荷比卢国家及欧洲联盟大使馆维持定期联系。南苏丹代表团出席了五审会，其外交部多边事务司长里克·普克·里克先生在会上做了发言。南苏丹代表团还出席了大会第二十八届会议。此外，1名代表还参加了于11月在化技中心举行的针对不设在海牙的常驻代表机构的情况介绍，并与总干事进行了会晤。

4.5 在与非缔约国代表、缔约国高级官员的接触以及与国际组织、学术机构和智库的互动中，总干事强调了实现普遍性的重要意义。

与外界的互动和外联活动

4.6 2023年，总干事和副总干事会见了来自各缔约国的高级别官员，以及其他国际组织的高级官员，在禁化武组织总部大楼接待了33次这类来访。

4.7 技秘处开展活动以加强与联合国的伙伴关系，并加强与其他国际组织的关系，目的是推动对禁化武组织有现实意义的裁军和不扩散议题。

4.8 总干事与荷兰外交部的官员进行了会晤，以讨论本组织与荷兰王国之间关于落实禁化武组织总部协定（于1997年5月22日在海牙签署）的相关事宜。

总干事和副总干事的出访与情况介绍

4.9 2023年，总干事出访了阿尔及利亚、芬兰、卡塔尔、阿拉伯联合酋长国和美利坚合众国。在访问期间，他与高层政府官员进行了会晤，包括有关部长和副部长。总干事还向科学界、政府机构和化工行业的代表致辞。

4.10 2023年2月7日，在调鉴组的第三份报告发布之后，总干事以线上方式向联合国安全理事会做了情况介绍。

4.11　2023 年，总干事还在一些活动中致辞，包括在阿尔及利亚阿尔及尔举办的“CHEMEX 非洲活动”；在卡塔尔多哈举办的化工行业和《公约》缔约国国家主管部门第十届年会；在芬兰赫尔辛基举办的化武战剂分析国际讲习班，以纪念芬兰《公约》核查研究所成立 50 周年；在美利坚合众国华盛顿特区举办的纪念美国销毁完成已宣布化学武器的仪式。

4.12　2023 年，副总干事陪同总干事分别访问了阿尔及利亚（9 月）和卡塔尔（10 月）。

禁化武组织——海牙奖

4.14　2023 年，禁化武组织——海牙奖的获奖者包括瑞士施皮茨实验室的孟加拉国萨伊达·苏尔塔纳·拉吉博士、加纳的胡伯特·K. 弗伊先生。

其他活动

4.15　2023 年 5 月 12 日，禁化武组织举办了化技中心的落成典礼，荷兰威廉·亚历山大国王陛下莅临出席。在典礼进行期间，威廉·亚历山大国王陛下为该中心揭牌；来自不同国家的高级别代表、常驻代表和其他宾客出席了该活动。

4.16　2023 年 9 月 27 日，举办了第 23 期新任外交官讲习班，共有 99 名代表报名参加。

4.17　2023 年 9 月 19 日至 20 日，禁化武组织接待了联合国裁军研究金方案下的 25 名研究人员，他们听取了技秘处的有关专家为期一天的情况介绍，并参访了化技中心。这是该方案的第 24 期活动。

4.18　11 月 3 日，总干事在化技中心向那些派驻在海牙以外的常驻代表们做了一次情况介绍。来自 23 个成员国的常驻代表和其他外交人员出席了此次情况介绍活动。

公共事务和媒体知名度

公共外联

4.19　禁化武组织参加了海牙国际开放日（2023 年 9 月 24 日），在禁化武组织总部大楼接待了 350 多名人员，使其了解《公约》和本组织的工作。

公共事务处和视察局做了介绍和演示。来宾们还看到了按《公约》规定销毁的化学武器的模型、了解了视察任务中使用的不同类型的防护设备，并参观了展出的诺贝尔和平奖。在代表休息区播放了“禁化武组织基础知识”视频，同时邀请了孩子们在“化学用于和平”涂色区游玩。

4.20　本报告期内，公共事务处组织了80场外联活动，其中77场是禁化武组织团组参访方案的一部分。此外，公共事务处组织禁化武组织参加了3场现场外的外联活动，包括在国际纯粹与应用化学联合会年会上设立展台；在德国化学学会青年化学家网络大会上做介绍；在特伦托大学关于武器转让和军控的冬令营上做介绍。通过这些活动，禁化武组织与共计2667名参与人员进行了直接互动。

与民间社团的外联

T.M.C.Asser研究所

4.21　2023年9月18日至23日，技秘处举办了第14期T.M.C. Asser研究所关于大规模杀伤性武器裁军和不扩散的培训方案。来自23个缔约国的30名处于职业初期和中期的专业人员参与其中，以增加对化学武器裁军和不扩散的外交、法律和技术的了解。副总干事向该方案的学员做了致辞。利用欧洲联盟提供的资助，禁化武组织将3份奖学金授予了该方案中来自刚果民主共和国、肯尼亚和乌干达的参与人员。

五审会

4.22　74个民间社团组织获准出席五审会。民间社团组织的参会方式包括在全体会议上做了10次发言；围绕与《公约》有关的主题举办了一系列会间活动。

大会第二十八届会议

4.23　106个民间团体组织获准参加了大会第二十八届会议。与会的民间社团组织举办了会间活动，同时在全体会议上就《公约》相关主题做了8次发言。在欧洲联盟的支持下，禁化武组织为来自发展中经济体或经济转型国的民间社团的4名与会代表提供了一定的资金支持。

社交媒体

4.24　技秘处提供了大会第二十八届会议的实时网络直播，这吸引了4669名观众。在技秘处的官方社交媒体渠道对大会进行了广泛的报道，包括重大决定的细节和对会间活动的介绍。

4.25　2023年，根据关于社交媒体平台的统计数据表，技秘处的数字受众继续增加。社交媒体增长情况见表7。

表7　社交媒体增长情况

社交媒体	2022年	2023年	2022—2023年的变化
脸书关注者	20936	22087	5.5%
X关注者	37882	39055	3.1%
油管关注者	2582	2942	14%
领英关注者	29157	33579	15.2%

4.26　技秘处的社交媒体战略确保相关帖子和宣传均旨在增强意识，并增强利益攸关方对与本组织及与《公约》有关的工作和活动的了解。2023年，值得注意的社交媒体宣传活动包括：

（a）报道调鉴组和事实调查组的报告；

（b）报道五审会和大会第二十八届会议；

（c）科学沟通意识，包括科咨委报告、不限成员名额工作组和教育/意识材料；

（d）报道禁化武组织——海牙奖。

4.27　除上文所述外，社交媒体的宣传还包括几个国际日和纪念活动，诸如，国际妇女儿童科学日和全体化学战受害者纪念日。X（前身为推特）于2023年改变了企业政策，使用户模式和平台动态随之变化。为缓解任何单一的社交媒体网络因不稳定而可能造成的中断，技秘处在社交媒体网络Mastodon上开设了账户。总体上，禁化武组织社交媒体平台在2023年有8%的综合增长率。

5. 执行管理和行政

战略和政策

筹备五审会

5.34　五审会筹备工作组于2023年1月至4月定期举行了会议，以便为五审会奠定基础。2022年6月至2023年4月，五审会筹备工作组就四审会以来与《公约》履行有关的一系列事宜举行了非正式磋商。2023年2月至4月，工作组重点审议了将要提交给五审会审议的临时案文草案。工作方案还包含了与民间社团及化工协会的代表进行交流的内容。

打击化学恐怖主义

5.35　2023年，反恐工作组仍然是缔约国与国际专家互动并就恐怖主义构成的挑战；禁化武组织如何通过全面且有效的《公约》履行来进一步应对等交换意见的主要平台。技秘处为3次反恐工作组会议的召开、在反恐工作组主持下举行的一次桌面演习提供了协助。

5.36　2023年，反恐工作组的讨论重点如下：科学技术的发展；为与其他国际组织合作开展的“CHEMEX非洲”演练做规划；筹备反恐工作组的桌面演练。反恐工作组于3月6日、7月6日和9月30日举行了3次会议。所有会议均由南非大使武西木兹・菲利蒙・马东瑟拉主持。

5.37　2023年11月20日和21日，反恐工作组的桌面演练在化技中心举行。此次演练是在欧洲联盟的支持和资助下举行的，来自24个缔约国的48人参加。参加者包括国家主管部门、科学界、执法界、应急管理界、国防和决策当局的代表。利用一个预设场景模拟了化学恐怖主义袭击的3个阶段（袭击前、事件应对和调查）。邀请参与者合作和处理不足之处，并提出建议。反恐工作组将在2024年对演练的结果进行审议。

5.38　2023年，禁化武组织继续积极参与了“联合国全球打击恐怖主义协调契约”（于2018年成为其签署方）。在该契约的倡导下，本组织被评选为新组建的关于新兴威胁和关键基础设施防护工作组的副主席（国际刑警组织担任主席）。在该框架下，禁化武组织完成了在发生化学或生物袭击事件时加强机构间对接和公共沟通项目的第三阶段的实施，该工作是与联合国反恐办事处、联合国人道主义事务协调厅、世卫组织、国际刑警组织、联合国区域间犯罪和司法研究所以及《禁止生物武器公约》履约支持和资助股共同开展的。作为这项工作的一部分，禁化武组织于2023年3月27日和28日在海牙开办了一个信息交流讲习班；国际刑警组织于2023年5月5日在法国里昂开办了一个关于紧急行动中心的讲习班；禁化武组织于2023年6月26日和27日在化技中心开办了一个有关部署的讲习班。

5.39　技秘处和根据联合国安全理事会1540（2004）号决议建立的委员会专家组继续在强化缔约国对其相关义务的意识方面开展合作，并在《公约》和联合国安全理事会1540（2004）号决议有关领域，即国家立法、化学安保、海关和边境管控等提供实际援助。

与化学工业协会的互动

5.40　禁化武组织继续与全球化工界进行互动，后者是履行《公约》的关键利益攸关方。本报告期内，技秘处为国家主管部门与化工界之间的对话提供了便利，还与国际化学协会理事会和国际化学品贸易协会进行了定期磋商。本报告期内，化工行业协调小组召开了第14次和第15次会议。与会人员讨论了诸如全球化工行业的当前趋势和挑战以及工业核查制度的调整等事项，并就能力培养活动展开了交流，重点讨论了推广化学安全和安保领域中的最佳做法。

5.41　2023年，化学协会国际理事会和国际化学品贸易协会的代表参加了技秘处的一系列活动。总干事向大会第二十八届会议提交了题为“使化工协会参与其中”的说明（C-28/DG.15，2023年11月6日），其中详细介绍了自大会上届会议以来禁化武组织与行业协会的互动。该说明涵盖了与核查、教育和外联、各国的《公约》履约以及化学安全和安保有关的活动。

教育和外联

5.42　2023年，教咨委分别于2月7日至9日和6月20日至22日召开了两次现场会议。教咨委主席代表委员会参加了五审会的一般性辩论。在辩论中，缔约国强调了教育和外联在防止重新使用化学武器方面发挥的日益重要的作用。此外，2023 年 5 月 15 日，在五审会期间举办了一场会外活动，以讨论教育和外联在当前快速发展的国际环境中的作用。缔约国、化工界、学术机构和非政府组织的代表参加了该活动。2023 年，教咨委向缔约国介绍了其各项活动和未来的优先事项，并参加了第二十八届会议的一般性辩论，以便介绍有关其活动的最新情况。

5.43　2023 年，教咨委开展了多项与教育以及提高对禁化武组织和《公约》了解有关的活动。教咨委继续就加强技秘处在教育领域提供的内容一事提出咨询意见，其中特别侧重于电子学习资源；鉴于全部已宣布的化学武器已销毁，将要更新教咨委的战略计划。教咨会就与各学术机构铺设网络一事提供了专家咨询，并编制了一份在禁化武组织的教育和外联活动领域可发挥协同增效作用的相关国际组织清单。此外，教咨委与国际合作与援助司继续合作。总干事鼓励教咨委推动和促进化技中心的各项活动和方案，并考虑将工作重点更多地放在妇女和青年等特定目标受众上。

6. 科学和技术

禁化武组织科学咨询委员会

6.1　为了支持五审会的召开，科咨委于 2023 年年初完成了关于科学和技术发展的科学报告（RC-5/DG.1）。报告载有概要和各项建议，涉及可能影响《公约》履行和技秘处工作的科技进步有关的事宜。总干事发布了对该报告的回复（RC-5/DG.2，2023 年 2 月 22 日）。此外，科咨委主席古恩特·波沃顿先生在审议大会中做了发言。

6.2　科咨委于 2023 年 8 月举行了第三十七次会议（报告以 SAB-37/1 文号发布）。除讨论科咨委的相关业务外，科咨委还听取了由外聘发言者的 6 次介绍，其主题包括 3D 生物打印、医疗对策和治疗、高通量实验和生物标志物等。此外，科咨委还听取了技秘处各个部门作的简要介绍，以便丰富其科学讨论的内容。另外，还提出了一些建议供总干事考虑，其中包括成立一个新的临时工作组。总干事对科咨委第三十七次会议报告的回复已以 EC-104/DG.22（2023 年 9 月 27 日）的文号发布。总干事在其中表示将成立一个新的关于化学取证的工作组，而且将与科咨委主席合作确定该工作组的人员构成及职权范围。

6.3　生物毒素分析临时工作组于 2023 年 1 月举行了第七次也是最后一次会议，目的是拟定其任务结束报告。此后，该报告于 2023 年 4 月 20 日发布（SAB/REP/1/23），并最终获得了第三十七次会议的认可。该报告载录了向总干事和禁化武组织提出的 23 项建议。

6.4　2023 年，科咨委与科学界继续深入合作。科咨委委员主持、参加出席了多场会议，并在专业化学学会内发挥领导作用，而且与国际化联开展合作，同时发表科学文章。特别是在国际化联第四十九届世界化学大会（2023 年 8 月）上，科咨委发挥了突出的作用。科咨委参与这类活动可确保技秘处紧跟化学领域的发展趋势，并在科学家中保持紧密的联系和信誉，同时进行科学实践和支持教育的外联活动。

与科学界的互动

6.5　技秘处与全球科学界的互动在 2023 年继续进行。技秘处的工作人员参与了国际化联各个委员会的工作。

6.6　2023 年，技秘处在各个技术界中保持了显著的影响力，并参加了以下会议和活动：2023 年戈登化学和生物防御研究会议（2023 年 3 月）、全球化学安全和新出现的威胁大会（2023 年 10 月）、为纪念芬兰核查研究所成立 50 周年而举办的化学战剂分析国际研讨会（2023 年 11 月）。技秘处还在以下会议上做了演示介绍：化学武器非军事化会议（2023 年 5 月）、禁核试组织科学和技术大会（2023 年 6 月）、国际化联第四十九届世界化学大会（2023 年 8 月）、联合国秘书长调查指称使用化学和生物武器机制讲习班（2023 年 9 月）以及斯德哥尔摩国际和平研究所关于加强《公约》的讲习班（2023 年 11 月）。此外，科学政策顾问主持了首届戈登防扩散、反扩散和裁军科学研究大会（2023 年 7 月），并在同行评审的《自然》杂志上发表了一篇专栏文章，该文章探讨了可获取的科学数据如何防范化学武器的死灰复燃。

6.7　植物的生物标志物挑战赛于 2023 年结束。为了进行该挑战赛，各个研究团队获得了调查各种方法或系统的资金，以便达到以下目的：使特定类型的植被可以用作一种接触到对人类或动物有毒的化学物质的标识。在 6 个研究小组中，有 5 个在科咨委第三十七次会议上介绍了其工作。这项挑战赛由欧盟资助，现已促成了一篇经同行评审的科学文章的发表，且预计在未来 1 ～ 2 年内还会再发表几篇。

6.8　技秘处继续与国际组织合作伙伴互动，以参与科学和技术讨论。其中包括国际化联、国际刑警组织、禁核试条约组织、联合国裁军事务厅和《禁止生物武器公约》履行支持和资助股等组织。此外，在 T.M.C.Asser 研究所的“关于大规模杀伤性武器裁军和不扩散的年度培训方案”（2023 年 9 月）期间以及禁化武组织的第二十三期新任外交人员讲习班上，均做了科学介绍。

附件①

附件 5

截至 2023 年 12 月 31 日禁化武组织的指定实验室一览表
（环境分析）

序号	缔约国	实验室名称	获指定日期
1	澳大利亚	防务科技集团	2021 年 3 月 25 日
2	比利时	防备实验室（DLD）	2004 年 5 月 12 日
3	巴西	陆军技术中心分析化学实验室	2021 年 8 月 31 日
4	中国	防化研究院分析化学实验室	1998 年 11 月 17 日
5	中国	军事医学科学院毒物药物研究所毒物分析实验室	2007 年 9 月 14 日
6	芬兰	芬兰《化学武器公约》的核查研究所	2017 年 3 月 29 日
7	法国	核生化辐控制军备总署化学分析室	1999 年 6 月 29 日
8	德国	联邦国防军防护技术和化生辐核防护研究所	1999 年 6 月 29 日
9	印度	防务研究和发展机构 VERTOX 实验室	2006 年 4 月 18 日
10	印度	印度化学技术研究院化学毒素分析中心	—
11	伊朗伊斯兰共和国	防化研究实验室	2011 年 8 月 3 日
12	荷兰	TNO 防务、安保和安全实验室	1998 年 11 月 17 日
13	挪威	挪威防务研究机构（FFI）化学威胁剂分析实验室	2021 年 3 月 25 日
14	巴基斯坦	防务科学技术组织分析实验室	2018 年 4 月 18 日
15	大韩民国	防务开发署化生辐总司化学分析实验室	2011 年 8 月 3 日
16	大韩民国	大韩民国国防司令部国防化生辐核研究所	2022 年 8 月 15 日
17	罗马尼亚	核生化辐防护及生态研究与创新中心化学分析实验室	2018 年 4 月 18 日
18	俄罗斯联邦	军事研究中心化学和分析控制实验室	2000 年 8 月 4 日

① 附件部分仅节选附件 5。

续表

序号	缔约国	实验室名称	获指定日期
19	俄罗斯联邦	“有机化学和技术国立科学研究所”联邦国立单一企业中央化学武器销毁分析实验室	2015 年 4 月 15 日
20	新加坡	DSO 国立实验中心国防医学和环境研究所核查实验室	2003 年 4 月 14 日
21	西班牙	“La Marañosa”技术研究所化学武器核查实验室	2004 年 9 月 8 日
22	瑞典	瑞典防务研究所生化辐核防卫安全部，FOI	1998 年 11 月 17 日
23	瑞士	瑞士核生化防务所施皮茨实验室	1998 年 11 月 17 日
24	大不列颠及北爱尔兰联合王国	波顿达恩防务科技实验室	1999 年 6 月 29 日
25	美利坚合众国	DEVCOM 化学生物中心取证分析实验室	1998 年 11 月 17 日
26	美利坚合众国	劳伦斯利佛摩尔国家实验室	2003 年 4 月 14 日

截至 2023 年 12 月 31 日禁化武组织的指定实验室一览表

（生物医学分析）

序号	缔约国	实验室名称	获指定日期
1	澳大利亚	防务科技集团	2016 年 8 月 1 日
2	中国	防化研究院分析化学实验室	2016 年 8 月 1 日
3	中国	军事医学科学院毒物药物研究所毒物分析实验室	2016 年 8 月 1 日
4	芬兰	芬兰《化学武器公约》核查研究所	2016 年 8 月 1 日
5	法国	核生化辐控制军备总署化学分析室	2016 年 8 月 1 日
6	德国	联邦国防军药物学与毒物学研究所	2016 年 8 月 1 日
7	印度	防务研究和开发机构生物医学核查司	2016 年 8 月 1 日
8	伊朗伊斯兰共和国	防化研究实验室（DCRL）	2021 年 8 月 31 日
9	荷兰	TNO 防务、安保和安全实验室	2016 年 8 月 1 日
10	大韩民国	防务开发署化生辐总司化学分析实验室	2021 年 8 月 31 日
11	俄罗斯联邦	军事研究中心化学和分析控制实验室	2016 年 8 月 1 日
12	俄罗斯联邦	卫生、职业病理学和人类生态学研究所化学分析控制和生物试验实验室	2016 年 8 月 1 日
13	新加坡	DSO 国立实验中心国防医学和环境研究所核查实验室	2016 年 8 月 1 日

续表

序号	缔约国	实验室名称	获指定日期
14	瑞典	瑞典防务研究所生化辐核防卫安全部，FOI	2016 年 8 月 1 日
15	大不列颠及北爱尔兰联合王国	波顿达恩国防科技实验室	2016 年 8 月 1 日
16	美利坚合众国	疾病防控中心	2017 年 7 月 11 日
17	美利坚合众国	埃奇伍德化学和生物法证分析中心	2016 年 8 月 1 日
18	美利坚合众国	劳伦斯利弗摩尔国家实验室	2016 年 8 月 1 日
19	美利坚合众国	美国陆军化学防护医疗研究所	2019 年 8 月 19 日

总干事的说明
2023 核查活动总结（节选）①

（S/2336/2024、2024 年 11 月 15 日）

“从透明度的角度并为了让缔约国不断地得到遵约的保证出发”，第二次审议大会重申技术秘书处（以下简称“技秘处”）提供关于核查结果的纪实性报告的重要性（RC-2/4，第 9.51 段，2008 年 4 月 18 日）。此外，技秘处曾为第三次审议大会印发了关于“对第二次审议大会以来的《禁止化学武器公约》（以下简称“《公约》”）实施状况的审查”的说明（RC-3/S/1，2013 年 3 月 12 日；及其 Corr.1，2013 年 3 月 20 日），该说明第 3.187 和第 3.188 段表示：“在技秘处有关核查的纪实性报告方面的近期发展进一步改善了缔约国的履约状况的透明度及对其之持续保证。……技秘处将继续努力改进报告核查结果的方式。”

据此，技秘处编制了本文所附的 2023 年禁化武组织核查活动总结，以介绍技秘处当年开展的核查工作。

这份总结尤其为在海牙不设代表机构的缔约国提供了关于技秘处核查活动的有价值的汇报。从公众外联的角度来看，这符合禁化武组织《媒介和公共事务政策》（C-I/DEC.55/Rev.1，2017 年 11 月 30 日），并为广大公众提供了有关这方面工作的相关信息。

本总结的结构与以往年度的核查总结相似，且不包含任何保密资料。

① 本文来源于禁止化学武器组织网站。

附件 1

禁化武组织 2023 年核查总结

1. 综合概要

概述

1.1　截至 2023 年 12 月 31 日，共有 193 个《公约》缔约国。由 8 个缔约国宣布的所有化学武器经核实均已被销毁。另经核实，所有宣布的化学武器生产设施（以下简称“化武生产设施”）均已被销毁或者已被改装用于《公约》不加禁止的目的；10 个缔约国有尚待销毁或尚未报告销毁的老化学武器（以下简称“老化武”）库存；两个缔约国境内有已回收的确认或疑似遗弃化学武器（以下简称“遗弃化武”）。关于《公约》第六条和在 2023 年收到的关于 2022 年过去活动年度宣布的资料，经技秘处评估，有 85 个缔约国在其境内有应宣布的活动（其中 81 个有至少 1 处应宣布设施）。

1.2　在非缔约国中尚有 1 个签署国（以色列）和 3 个非签署国（朝鲜人民民主共和国、埃及和南苏丹），而对这些国家无法进行任何核查活动。2023 年，没有国家加入《公约》。

1.3　截至 2023 年年底，在 193 个缔约国中，尚有 1 个缔约国未根据《公约》提交其初始宣布。技秘处未能完成对该缔约国进行的核查活动。

1.4　在裁军和防止扩散方面，虽然技秘处一直在阿拉伯叙利亚共和国境内开展行动，但技秘处在 2023 年进行了 248 次视察 / 轮换；共在 38 个缔约国的 217 处地点投入了 5168 个视察员日。在此总数中，52 次视察或轮换涉及《公约》第四和第五条所规定的化学武器非军事化；196 次视察涉及《公约》第六条所规定的工业核查。此外，2023 年，技秘处在非例行核查活动中另行投入了 740 个视察日。

1.5　2023 年，在化学武器方面共投入了 3376 个视察员日（占总数的

62%），其中包括在阿拉伯叙利亚共和国的视察员日；根据第六条投入了2234个视察员日（38%）。

1.6　2023年没有收到任何有关质疑性视察和指称使用调查的请求。

核查行动

1.7　技秘处在2023年进行的所有视察均达到视察任务授权所规定的要求。在10次第六条视察中，记录了需要予以进一步注意的有关问题。

化学武器核查

1.8　2023年，经技秘处核实，共销毁了358.293吨第1类化学武器。在美利坚合众国境内的3处化学武器销毁设施（以下简称"化武销毁设施"）中进行了销毁作业。2023年7月7日，作为唯一的拥有国，美利坚合众国销毁了剩余的化学武器库存。

1.9　至报告期终了时，技秘处核实了在销毁化学战剂方面的以下状况：

（a）在宣布的72304.343吨化学武器库存中，经核实已销毁72304.343吨（其中包括为《公约》不加禁止的目的而从化学武器库存中取出的化学武器），占宣布总量的100.00%。

（b）所有第2和第3类化学武器在本报告期之前均已销毁。

1.10　截至2023年12月31日，经总干事核实，全部97个已宣布的化武生产设施均已被销毁（74处）或已改装（23处）。2023年没有对化武生产设施进行视察。

1.11　2023年，技秘处对美利坚合众国的2处化学武器储存设施（以下简称"化武储存设施"）进行了4次视察。对普埃布罗化学军械库的化武储存设施和布鲁格拉斯化学活动中心的化武储存设施进行了2次最后视察，并证实了在这些储存现场已没有任何化学武器。在审查期终了时，没有化武储存设施需接受系统性核查。

1.12　日本遗弃在中国境内的化学武器的销毁继续进行，其依据为：根据执行理事会（以下简称"执理会"）的决定（EC-101/DEC.2，2022年10月4日；并将其作为执理会第EC-67/DEC.6号决定（2012年2月15日）

的附件 3 而附于其后）以及根据《公约》的有关条款，中日双方联合提交给执理会的销毁计划（EC-101/NAT.4*，2022 年 9 月 30 日）。受新冠疫情影响，对中国境内的日本遗弃化学武器进行的现场视察均被暂停，后于 2023 年 4 月重启。技秘处在 2023 年进行了 12 次视察。

1.13　自《公约》生效以来，已有 19 个缔约国宣布了老化武。其中，14 个缔约国宣布了在 1925 年至 1946 年间生产的老化武；11 个宣布了在 1925 年以前生产的老化武。2023 年，技秘处对比利时、法国、德国和意大利进行了 4 次老化武视察。多处的销毁作业均取得了可观的进展，但大量老化武的回收仍在继续进行。

第六条核查

1.14　在《公约》的第六条方面，技秘处于 2023 年核实了 38 个缔约国宣布的在 196 处设施和厂区进行的活动。由于存在技秘处掌控之外的行动方面的限制，无法完成在 2023 年方案和预算（C-26/DEC.11，2021 年 12 月 1 日）中构想的全部 200 次第六条视察。已完成的视察包括附表 1 设施 11 处（占视察计划的 100%）、附表 2 厂区 49 处（占视察计划的 100%）、附表 3 厂区 8 处（占视察计划的 80%）和其他化学生产设施厂区 128 处（占视察计划的 98.5%）。

1.15　17 个缔约国报称在 2023 年将作为出口国或进口国参与在缔约国之间进行的 28 起附表 1 化学品的转让。在 2023 年收到的宣布显示，2022 年，55 个缔约国转让了 6283 吨的附表 2 化学品；123 个缔约国转让了 539577 吨的附表 3 化学品。2022 年，没有任何关于附表 1 化学品转让的报告，也没有报告任何向非缔约国进行的附表 2 化学品的转让。

优化核查制度

1.16　资料安全交换系统为宣布相关的数据提供了安全的电子渠道，以便在缔约国与技秘处之间交换包括机密性资料在内的电子宣布和其他资料。截至 2023 年 12 月 31 日，共有 63 个缔约国的 119 个用户已在资料安全交换系统中注册，并正在积极使用该系统。

1.17　不提交或逾期提交宣布的情况对技秘处高效和有效地行使核查职责的能力造成了不利影响。技秘处与有关缔约国进行了持续互动，以改进这方面的工作效果。

1.18　2023年，技秘处一共处理了760份（共计5171页）缔约国来文、宣布及其他与核查相关的文件。

2. 视察活动

概述

2.1　2023年，技秘处进行了248次视察/轮换（与阿拉伯叙利亚共和国或其他缔约国相关联的其他核查活动不计算在内）；在38个缔约国的217个设施投入了5168个视察员日。如算上投入与阿拉伯叙利亚共和国或其他缔约国相关的其他行动的视察员日，则2023年的视察员日总计为5908天。

2.2　2023年的视察活动见表1，自《公约》生效以来进行的视察活动见表2。

表1　2023年的视察活动

设施种类	可视察或运行中的设施①	完成的视察②	所视察的设施或现场	视察员日
与化学武器相关的视察				
化武销毁设施	3	31	3	2572
化武储存设施	2	4	2	72
化武生产设施	9	0	0	0
老化武	10	4	4	54
遗弃化武③	16	13	11	236
小计	40	52	20	2934

① 对化武销毁设施而言，在2023年处于运转中的设施数；对化武储存设施、化武生产设施和老化武而言，2023年的可视察设施；对第六条设施而言，2023年的可视察设施。

② 由于技秘处在阿拉伯叙利亚共和国的任务具有独特性，故此列未包含在该缔约国境内进行的视察。这里报告的数字可能与下文各节陈述的内容略有差异，因为在下文中尽可能地涵盖了在叙利亚的行动。

③ 其中包括遗弃化武销毁设施。

续表

设施种类	可视察或运行中的设施	完成的视察	所视察的设施或现场	视察员日
与阿拉伯叙利亚共和国或其他缔约国相关的行动的视察员日				740
与化学武器相关的视察员日总数				3674
第六条视察				
附表 1	28	11	11	202
附表 2	226	49	49	808
附表 3	362	8	8	82
其他化学生产设施	4356	128	128	1142
小计	**4972**	**196**	**196**	**2234**
总计	**5012**	**248**	**216**	**5168**
视察员日的总计数，包含与阿拉伯叙利亚共和国或其他缔约国相关的行动所使用的视察员日数				5908

表 2　自《公约》生效以来进行的视察活动①

设施种类	完成的视察数	所视察的设施或现场数	视察员日数
与化学武器相关的视察			
化武销毁设施	2052	46	236098
化武储存设施	529	37	15637
化武生产设施	523	82	9444
老化武	178	41	2672
遗弃化武	163	55	4022
高危化武的销毁 / 化武的紧急销毁	25	不适用	1734
小计	**3470**	**261**	**269607**
与应急行动相关联的视察员日			17823
与化学武器相关的视察员日总数			287430
第六条视察			
附表 1	356	40	6346
附表 2	1046	452	23296
附表 3	532	425	7798

① 对于化武储存设施，与所视察设施的数量相关的数字不包括被宣布为“化武销毁设施中的化武储存设施”的设施，原因是此类设施已被确认为相应化武销毁设施的组成部分，而非单独实体。对于化武生产设施，塞尔维亚与波斯尼亚和黑塞哥维那均单独宣布了一处设施。

续表

设施种类	完成的视察数	所视察的设施或现场数	视察员日数
其他化学生产设施	2628	2307	30548
小计	4562	3224	67988
总计	8032	3485	337595
包含与应急行动相关联的视察员日在内的总计数			355418

第六条视察的分布

2.3　2023年，有38个缔约国接受了第六条视察。已对过去10年第六条视察的分布情况见表3，2023年第六条视察在各区域的分布情况见表4。

表3　过去10年第六条视察的分布情况

	2014年	2015年	2016年	2017年	2018年	2019年	2020年	2021年	2022年	2023年
视察数	241	241	241	241	241	241	82	80	160	196
被视察缔约国数	50	43	50	48	43	41	31	30	36	38
占了全部视察的一半的缔约国数	7	6	7	6	7	6	8	6	6	5

表4　2023年第六条视察在各区域的分布情况

区域组	工业视察数	占总数的比例	可视察厂区的比例
非洲	1	0.5%	1%
亚洲	103	52.6%	60%
东欧	9	4.6%	4%
拉丁美洲和加勒比	14	7.1%	5%
西欧和其他国家	69	35.2%	30%

质疑性视察和指称使用调查

2.4　2023年，没有接到任何根据《公约》提出的进行质疑性视察或指称使用调查的请求。然而，根据执理会第EC-83/DEC.5号决定（2016年11月11日），技秘处部署了若干次禁化武组织派往叙利亚的事实调查组和几次非例行任务。

视察员培训

2.5　2023年，能力建设和应急规划分队为342名学员开办了31个培训课程，总计达到1552个培训日，占视察员培训日的83%和非视察员培训日的17%。在比利时、德国、荷兰、塞尔维亚和大不列颠及北爱尔兰联合王国举办了培训课程。能力建设和应急规划分队提供了必修的视察员进修课程和针对新擢升的视察组组长的专业课程。

2.6　美利坚合众国资助了共有85名学员参加的5期危险废物作业和紧急应对线上培训。德国资助并主办了关于在实地环境中运用安全保障方法（SSAFE）课程。33名需要在高风险地区工作的技秘处工作人员接受了培训。此外，大不列颠及北爱尔兰联合王国资助了1期外交技能课程，有13名学员参加。

2.7　2023年9月，由不同背景的7人组成的一组新视察员（V组）加入了禁化武组织。能力建设和应急规划分队协调进行了为期12周的必修初始培训方案，旨在他们准备好承担作为视察员的重要职责。2023年12月8日，为6名视察员举办了一场结业仪式。

3. 化学武器

3.1　技秘处派员常驻在所有运转中的化武销毁设施内，以对库存的化学武器的销毁进行核查，从而监督正在进行的已宣布活动。这可以通过现场仪器（包括专供视察员使用的设备）和审查有关文件资料进行直接的实地观察。为了达到核查目的，视察员获准不受妨碍地进行察看，以便能够监测工艺参数。此外，通过采样和分析活动，技秘处得以核实所销毁的是何种化学战剂。通过观察销毁过程，并通过对所产生的副产品的取样分析和在适用情况下对已抽空并已洗消的弹体进行热处理和切割，技秘处得以核实宣布的化学武器量已经彻底销毁以及无化学武器被转用。另外，技秘处还视察了化武储存设施，以确保除符合《公约》规定外不存在未被发现的转移化学武器的情形。

3.2　2023 年，在化武销毁设施视察中投入了 2572 个视察员日（2022 年为 4284 个）；在化武储存设施的视察活动中共使用了 72 个视察员日（2022 年为 120 个）。

3.3　2023 年，经技秘处核实，共销毁了 358.293 吨第 1 类化学武器（这是余下待销毁的总量）。

3.4　至报告期终了时，经核实已销毁的第 1 类和第 2 类化学武器总量（其中包括为《公约》不加禁止的目的从库存中取出的化学武器）共计 72304.343 吨，占宣布的化学武器的 100.00%。1998—2023 年经核实已销毁的化学武器累计总量如图 1 所示。

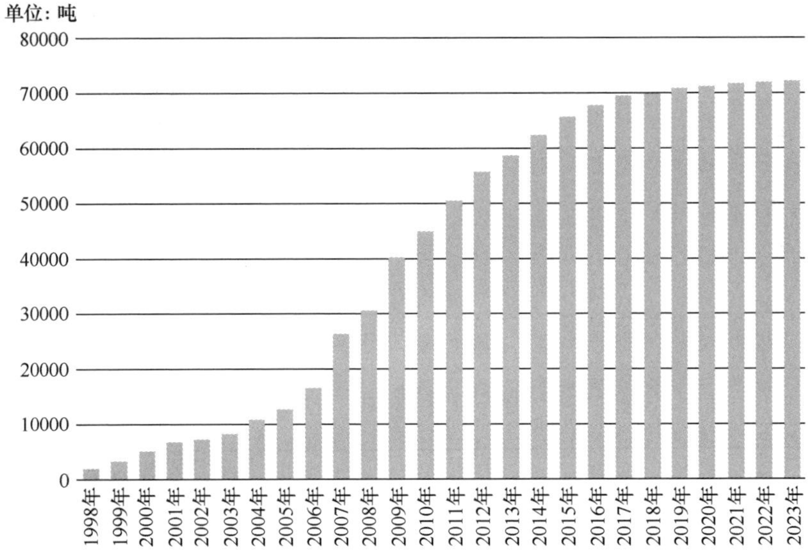

图 1　1998—2023 年经核实已销毁的化学武器累计总量

3.5　2023 年，在 3 处在役化武销毁设施进行了销毁活动：2 处涉及销毁剩余库存的第 1 类化学武器，其中一个设施——位于阿拉巴马州红石军械库的原型爆破试验和销毁设施，涉及对从化学武器上分离出来的火箭发动机进行试销毁。2023 年处于运行或在建的化学武器销毁设施见表 5。

表 5　2023 年处于运行或在建的化学武器销毁设施

美利坚合众国	1. 普埃布洛化学剂销毁中试车间（PCAPP） 2. 布鲁格拉斯化学剂销毁中试车间（BGCAPP） 3. 回收的化学武器销毁设施（RCWDF）* 4. 原型引爆测试和销毁设施（PDTDF） 5. 化学转装设施 / 弹药评估处理系统（CTF/MAPS）*

* 设施在 2023 年未进行任何销毁。

3.6　2023 年 7 月 7 日，美利坚合众国销毁了已宣布的化学武器的余留库存。

遵守销毁义务方面的进展

3.7　至报告期终了时，某缔约国①、阿尔巴尼亚、印度、利比亚、俄罗斯联邦、阿拉伯叙利亚共和国和美利坚合众国共宣布了 72304.343②吨的化学武器（70493.640 吨的第 1 类化学武器和 1810.703 吨的第 2 类化学武器），这些化学武器的载体为 8270595 枚（件）弹药和容器。总体上，截至 2023 年 12 月 31 日，上述化学武器 100.00% 已核实销毁或从化学武器库存中取出用于《公约》不加禁止的目的③。拥有缔约国也已宣布了 417833 件第 3 类化学武器，但这类化学武器已在 2015 年年底全部销毁。

按类别取得的进展

3.8　截至 2023 年 12 月 31 日，经禁化武组织视察员核实，上文第 3.7 段提到的 7 个宣布拥有化学武器库存的缔约国的化学武器销毁量如下。

（a）第 1 类化学武器：经技秘处核实，已销毁约 70493.640 吨此类化学武器。此外，根据《公约》第六条和《公约》的《核查附件》第六部分第 2 款（d）项，合计取出了 2.913 吨第 1 类化学武器。在上述合计数量中，68230.973 吨为一元化学武器（在 2023 年销毁了其中的 358.293 吨），其中包括路易氏剂、沙林（GB）、硫芥气（包括 H、HT、HD）、塔崩（GA）、

① 该缔约国要求将其国名列为高度保护级的资料。因此，将之称为“某缔约国”。
② 该数量采用了凑整规则。
③ 此合计数量包含 2.913 吨为《公约》不加禁止的目的而从某一缔约国、俄罗斯联邦和美利坚合众国的第 1 类化学武器库存中取出的附表 1 化学品［见《公约》之《核查附件》第六部分第 2 款（d）项］。

带消泡剂（UCON）的塔崩®、梭曼（GD）和黏性梭曼（GD）、VX 以及一种不明化学剂。装有上述化学战剂的载体为 8216.824 枚（件）弹药和容器［在 2023 年销毁了其中的 105740 枚（件）］、体积小于 2 立方米的其他储存器皿以及更大容量的储存罐。另有 2262.667 吨为二元化学武器（在 2023 年之前已全部销毁），其中包括甲基膦酰二氟（DF）、甲基亚膦酸乙基 -2- 二异丙氨基乙酯（QL）、异丙醇和异丙胺的混合物（OPA）、甲基硫代磷酸钠、六胺、二异丙基氨基乙基氯盐酸盐、二乙基氨基乙基氯盐酸盐和异丙醇。经技秘处核实已销毁的二元弹药合计为 785066 枚（件），其中有 415108 枚炮弹、另行宣布的 369958 个 DF 和 OPA 滤毒罐以及 306 个其他二元组分容器。

（b）第 2 类化学武器：经技秘处核实，已销毁了 1810.703 吨第 2 类化学武器，其中包括 CNS、硫二酣醇（TDG）、二氯乙醇（2-CE）、光气、硫化钠、氟化钠、氯苯乙酮（CN）、亚当氏剂（DM）、三氯氧磷、三氯化磷、五氯化磷、氟化氢、盐酸、单异丙胺、二异丙基氨基乙醇、亚硫酰氯、三乙胺、亚磷酸三甲酯、二甲酯、丁醇、甲醇、频哪基醇和三丁胺以及 3847 枚炮弹。

（c）第 3 类化学武器：经技秘处核实已销毁了向禁化武组织宣布的 417833 件第 3 类化学武器。

执行理事会的代表进行的访问

3.9　缔约国大会（以下简称“大会”）第十六届会议通过了一项决定（C-16/DEC.11，2011 年 12 月 1 日），其内容涉及由执理会代表对运行或在建的化武销毁设施进行访问。根据该决定，此种访问用以解决与一个缔约国关于在其延长的期限内履行销毁化学武器有关问题或关切。

3.10　根据第 C-16/DEC.11 号决定，2023 年 6 月 12 日至 14 日，执理会代表团对位于美利坚合众国肯塔基州里士满的布鲁格拉斯设施进行了访问，目的是审查销毁进展。有关详细报告已提交给执理会第 104 次会议（EC-104/2，2023 年 10 月 5 日）。

阿拉伯叙利亚共和国

宣布

3.11　根据执理会第 EC-M-33/DEC.1 号决定（2013 年 9 月 27 日），向该缔约国提供了所有相关资料。

销毁

3.12　经技秘处核实，已经销毁了所有已宣布的化学武器和化武生产设施。

宣布评估组

3.13　技秘处通过宣布评估组（以下简称“宣评组”）继续与阿拉伯叙利亚共和国保持互动，以澄清在其初始宣布和提交的相关资料中发现的所有差异、数据出入和前后不一致的情况。2014 年 4 月到 2023 年 12 月 31 日，宣评组共进行了 25 轮磋商，并为开展有限的境内活动而在该国部署了 2 次磋商。

3.14　通过这些磋商，技秘处获得了关于阿拉伯叙利亚共和国化学武器更多的信息，其中包括此前未宣布的有关情况，例如，1 个额外的化武生产设施；4 个额外的化学武器研发设施；涉及 5 种此前未宣布的化武战剂的有关活动；大量此前未宣布的化学弹药；其他关于阿拉伯叙利亚共和国化学武器方案各领域的补充资料。

3.15　如此前所报的那样，根据阿拉伯叙利亚共和国提供的资料，技秘处得以对一共 4 个未决问题予以结项，但截至 2023 年 12 月 31 日，还有 20 个问题尚待解决。

3.16　2020 年 10 月，技秘处向阿拉伯叙利亚共和国介绍了对该缔约国宣布的从未用作化学武器生产的 1 个化武生产设施的评估。还对宣评组自 2014 年以来收集到的所有资料和其他材料（其中包括样品）进行了审查，结果表明该设施曾进行过化武神经剂的生产或武器化。因此，技秘处请阿拉伯叙利亚共和国按照《公约》的相关条款，对在该受审查现场生产或武器化的化学剂的准确类型和数量做出宣布。阿拉伯叙利亚共和国在 2023

年没有提交该宣布。

3.17　截至2023年12月31日，阿拉伯叙利亚共和国尚未按执理会第EC-94/DEC.2号决定（2020年7月9日）第5(a)和5(b)分段的要求提交有关宣布。此外，阿拉伯叙利亚共和国未按第EC-94/DEC.2号决定第5(c)分段的要求解决有关其化学武器库存和方案的初始宣布方面的问题。

3.18　应执理会的要求（EC-81/DEC.4，2016年3月23日），总干事继续就关于叙利亚宣布及其相关提交资料中的所有未决问题做出报告。2023年，总干事向执理会分发了3份这类报告（EC-102/HP/DG.1，2023年3月6日；EC-103/HP/DG.1，2023年7月6日；EC-104/HP/DG.2，2023年9月25日；及其Add.1，2023年10月27日；及其Add.2，2023年11月22日）。在2023年发布的最后一份报告（EC-104/HP/DG.2）中，总干事得出的结论一如关于此事的前几份报告一样，即"根据《公约》、执理会第EC-M-33/DEC.1号决定、第EC-81/DEC.4号决定、第EC-83/DEC.5号决定、第EC-94/DEC.2号决定、大会第C-SS-4/DEC.3号决定和联合国安全理事会第2118(2013)号决议，技秘处经评估认为阿拉伯叙利亚共和国提交的宣布仍无法被视为准确或完整"。

美利坚合众国

宣布

3.19　2023年，美利坚合众国提交了8份对其初始宣布的修订，其中6份记载了有关把专门的空的圆顶储存容器从布鲁格拉斯化学活动化武储存设施转移到布鲁格拉斯设施的资料。其他2份修订介绍了有关资料，内容涉及新发现的已回收的化学武器；2枚化学武器弹药被重新评估为老化武。

销毁

3.20　根据大会第C-16/DEC.11号决定，美利坚合众国通过年度或定期报告的形式向执理会和大会通报了关于在2012年4月29日最后延长期限之后彻底销毁剩余化学武器方面取得的进展。2023年，已按照上述决定的规定按时向技秘处提交了所有必需的报告[①]。在提交给大会的最新进度报告中，美国告技秘处其已销毁了自《公约》生效以来宣布的所有化学武器。该缔约国还告技秘处，火箭组件废弃物的处置工作将继续进行，将每季度对处置活动进行核查，直至所有废弃物都被消除。

3.21　2023 年 6 月 22 日，普埃布洛设施的化武销毁设施完成了销毁作业，此后该设施被关停，故在该现场的所有核查活动均停止。2023 年 7 月 7 日，布鲁格拉斯设施的化武销毁设施处理了最后的化学武器弹药。虽然化学武器销毁已完成，但对化学武器组件废弃物的处置将在非毗邻的 1200 号静态引爆室和 2000 号静爆室中继续进行，同时将在非毗邻的安妮斯顿静爆室现场处置火箭发动机。并将通过每季度视察来继续核查这些活动。

3.22　除上述情况外，美利坚合众国在 2023 年提交了以下资料：

（a）对化学武器初始数据宣布的修订（第 78 次更新）；

（b）对化学武器初始数据宣布的修订（第 79 次更新）；

（c）对化学武器初始数据宣布的修订（第 80 次更新）；

（d）对化学武器初始数据宣布的修订（第 81 次更新）；

（e）对化学武器初始数据宣布的修订（第 82 次更新）；

（f）对化学武器初始数据宣布的修订（第 83 次更新）；

（g）布鲁格拉斯设施详细设施资料之增补 4，第 1 卷，第 1 修订，关于重新设定 2000 号静爆室覆土库的用途以在其中进行火箭分离活动；

（h）布鲁格拉斯设施详细设施资料之增补 4，第 2 卷补编，关于用以进行火箭分离活动的 2000 号静爆室覆土库的示意图；

（i）布鲁格拉斯设施的设施协定和议定的详细核查计划，其中载有关于增设火箭分离活动所必需的修订和修改；

（j）普埃布洛设施协议关停计划；

① EC-102/NAT.2（2023 年 2 月 24 日）、EC-103/NAT.2（2023 年 6 月 22 日）、EC-104/NAT.5（2023 年 9 月 20 日）和 C-28/NAT.2（2023 年 11 月 6 日）。

（k）布鲁格拉斯设施协议关停计划；

（l）普埃布洛化学军械库化武储存设施的关停通知；

（m）布鲁格拉斯化学活动中心化武储存设施的关停通知；

（n）关于普埃布洛完成化学武器销毁活动的宣布；

（o）关于布鲁格拉斯完成化学武器销毁活动的宣布；

（p）关于布鲁格拉斯设施继续消除火箭组件废弃物（需接受核查）的通知；

（q）关于终止对化学转移设施 / 弹药评估和处理系统化武销毁设施进行系统性视察；

（r）关于终止对已回收的化武销毁设施进行系统性视察；

（s）关于终止对原型引爆测试和销毁设施的系统性视察；

（t）关于 2022 年化学武器销毁的年度报告；

（u）关于 2024 年老化学武器销毁的年度计划。

3.23　截至 2023 年 12 月 31 日，经技秘处核实，美利坚合众国已销毁的或为《公约》不加禁止的目的取出的第 1 类化学武器达到 27769.831 吨，占其宣布的此类库存总量的 100.00%。该缔约国此前已经完成了对其宣布的第 2 类化学武器（0.010 吨）和全部 81020 枚第 3 类化学武器的销毁。

3.24　2023 年，技秘处对在美利坚合众国的 358.293 吨第 1 类化学武器的销毁进行了核查。这包括在位于科罗拉多州的普埃布洛设施中销毁的装填在 52366 枚弹药中的 142.446 吨 HD 硫芥子气，以及在 19375 枚弹药中装填的 50.962 吨 HT；在位于肯塔基州里士满的布鲁格拉斯设施销毁的装填在 33997 枚弹药中的 164.885 吨 GB。

3.25　在进行销毁作业的同时，技秘处已核实了以下情况：在位于亚拉巴马州的安尼斯顿军械库的普埃布洛设施的非毗邻静爆室现场销毁了取出的高能组分；向位于亚拉巴马州安尼斯顿的布鲁格拉斯设施的非毗邻的安尼斯顿军械库静爆室运送了火箭发动机；在位于得克萨斯州的阿瑟港的布鲁格拉斯设施的非毗邻的 Veolia 处理、储存和处置设施销毁了水解产物和端盖。此外，技秘处核实了以下情况：在测试活动期间，在亚拉巴马州红石军械库的原型爆破和销毁设施中销毁了 3 个 M67 火箭发动机以及 M441 的运载管和发射管端盖。这些带有端盖的火箭发动机是从布鲁格拉斯设施中装填有 GB 的 M55 火箭上分离出来的。

4. 化武储存设施

在从普埃布洛和布鲁格拉斯化武储存设施运走了所有的化学武器之后，美利坚合众国便提交了有关后续宣布。技秘处进行了视察以核实有关宣布，并证实了在有关储存现场已没有化学武器。在这些化武储存设施中的所有系统性核查活动均已终止。至报告期终了时，已没有任何化武储存设施仍在接受系统性核查。

5. 优化在化武储存设施和化武销毁设施的核查活动

为响应大会第七届会议（C-7/5 第 13.7 和第 13.8 段，2002 年 10 月 11 日）和一审会（RC-1/5 第 7.37 段，2003 年 5 月 9 日）的要求，技秘处在 2023 年继续寻找机会以优化其核查活动。

6. 化学武器生产设施

在 2023 年以前，经总干事核证，已向禁化武组织宣布的全部 97 处化武生产设施均已被销毁或改装。已核证销毁的这类设施为 74 处，而已为《公约》不加禁止目的改装的为 23 处。2023 年没有进行视察。

7. 老化学武器和遗弃化学武器

7.1　在老化武方面，技秘处的核查工作包括对宣布有老化武弹药的缔约国所宣布的储存设施进行视察，以检查年度宣布或临时宣布以及其他通知所报告的任何变化（回收、销毁或重新列报）是否一致。

7.2　在遗弃化武方面，技秘处的核查工作包括对已宣布的日本遗弃在中国境内的化学武器储存和销毁现场进行视察，以便核实任何发生的变化（回收、销毁或重新分类）是否与年度宣布或临时宣布以及其他通知有关。此外，本报告期内，技秘处对德国宣布为遗弃化武的弹药进行了初始视察。

7.3 2023年，技秘处在4个缔约国进行了4次老化武视察。6个缔约国宣布了发现的已确认或疑似老化武为1338枚（其中1327枚老化武在1925年以前生产，11枚老化武在1925年至1946年生产）；6个缔约国报告了已销毁的老化武为1818枚（1329枚老化武在1925年以前生产，489枚老化武在1925年至1946年生产）。

7.4 2023年，已报告的新回收或经鉴定的日本于1946年以前生产并遗弃在中国境内的遗弃化武为18102枚，同时按日本的宣布，有22261枚遗弃化武已报告被销毁。日本遗弃在中国境内的化学武器应按照2012年4月29日的期限予以销毁（EC-46/DEC.4，2006年7月5日）。根据执理会第EC-67/DEC.6号决定，日本遗弃在中国境内的化学武器的销毁在2012年4月29日后将按照2016年以后的销毁计划（EC-84/NAT.6）和《公约》的规定继续进行。此外，2022年9月，中国和日本向执理会第102次会议提交了一份联合国家文件（EC-101/NAT.4*），其中详细介绍了2022年以后的销毁情况。执理会通过了该销毁计划（EC-101/DEC.2），将其作为附件3附于执理会关于“2012年4月29日的时限以及日本遗弃在中华人民共和国境内化学武器的未来销毁”的决定（EC-67/DEC.6），并相应地对该决定做了修订。

7.5 2023年，在哈尔巴岭和哈尔滨遗弃化武销毁设施中继续进行销毁作业。在哈尔巴岭、哈尔滨、尚志、珲春、牡丹江、伊春、佳木斯和武汉进行了挖掘和回收作业。于2023年4月对日本遗弃在中国境内的化学武器重启实地视察。技秘处计划并进行了12次视察。

7.6 通过第25/2023号普通照会（2023年5月26日），德国提交了一项遗弃化学武器宣布。2023年6月，技秘处对宣布的有关弹药进行了初始视察。鉴于该视察，技秘处注意到没有充足的资料来确定遗弃国为哪一国。技秘处向执理会第 105 次会议提交了关于赴德国进行初始视察的报告（EC-105/S/5，2024 年 2 月 26 日）。

宣布的库存

7.7　从《公约》生效至 2023 年 12 月 31 日，19 个缔约国宣布了其境内有老化武。其中，14 个缔约国宣布了 75184 枚在 1925 年至 1946 年生产的老化武；11 个缔约国宣布了 78247 枚在 1925 年以前生产的老化武。根据《公约》有关条款，所有这些缔约国均已向技秘处提供了有关回收和销毁作业的资料以及有关为销毁或处置老化武而采取的步骤的必需的资料。

7.8　2023 年，比利时、加拿大、法国、德国、意大利、大不列颠及北爱尔兰联合王国和美利坚合众国向技秘处提交了与老化武有关的若干文件。

7.9　截至 2023 年 12 月 31 日，10 个缔约国（比利时、爱沙尼亚、法国、德国、意大利、拉脱维亚、荷兰、所罗门群岛、大不列颠及北爱尔兰联合王国和美利坚合众国）的境内仍有老化武或疑似老化武，且有约 33700 枚老化武尚待销毁或予以另行处置。

7.10　截至 2023 年 12 月 31 日，有 2 个缔约国宣布了其境内有确认的遗弃化武。特别是如遗弃缔约国自加入《公约》以来所宣布的那样，已发现 115641 枚日本遗弃在中国境内的化学武器，同时报告已销毁的遗弃化武总数为 88155 枚。此外，德国宣布在其境内的遗弃化武，但没有确认遗弃缔约国为哪一国。

8. 工业核查

8.1　至报告期终了时，按照第六条核查制度在全球范围内宣布的设施共计 5475 个，其中，4972 个须接受系统核查。2023 年，技秘处对 38 个缔约国的 196 个设施和厂区的宣布的活动进行了核查。故此，2023 年共进行了 11 次附表 1 设施视察、49 次附表 2 厂区视察、8 次附表 3 厂区视察和 128 次其他化学生产设施厂区视察。截至 2023 年 12 月 31 日根据第六条宣布的设施见表 6。

表 6　截至 2023 年 12 月 31 日根据第六条宣布的设施

制度	附表 1	附表 2	附表 3	其他化学生产设施	总计
宣布数	28	517	396	4534	5475
应宣布数	28	462	385	4526	5401
可视察数	28	226	362	4356	4972
缔约国数	24	36	34	81	82

8.2　2023 年，进行的 10 次第六条视察留下了 26 个有关须予以进一步关注的问题的记录，其中，1 次附表 1 视察、6 次附表 2 视察和 3 次其他化学生产设施视察。2023 年进行的任何视察中均没有报告不确定性问题。另外，在“收集进一步资料”的项下，记录了 116 项视察（6 次附表 1、29 次附表 2、3 次附表 3 和 78 次其他化学生产设施）意见（宣布事项通常不算作须予以进一步关注的问题）。

8.3　与 2022 年相比，2023 年视察计划中的连续视察的数量有所增加。部分原因是选取的厂区的地理位置便捷，部分是因为有关被视察缔约国接受了进行连续视察或长时间的工业视察任务。

8.4　2023 年，事后发现有 2 次其他化学生产设施视察和 1 次附表 2 视察是对不必视察的设施进行的。

附表化学品的转让

在 2022 年过去活动年度宣布中附表 1 化学品转让的情况

8.5　5 个缔约国在 2022 年过去活动年度宣布中宣布了 10 次附表 1 化学品转让。截至 2023 年 12 月 31 日，在这些转让中，发送缔约国和接收缔约国对其中的 9 次转让都做了通知和宣布，另一次转让只有接受缔约国做了通知和宣布。2022 年的过去活动年度宣布中共宣布了 4 克附表 1 化学品的转让。

2022 年过去活动年度宣布中在缔约国之间进行附表 2 和附表 3 化学品

转让的情况

8.6　根据2023年收到的2022年过去活动年度宣布，124个缔约国参与了附表2或附表3化学品的转让。55个缔约国在2022年参与了附表2化学品的转让（总量为6283吨），123个缔约国在2022年参与了附表3化学品的转让（总量为539577吨）。

2022年过去活动年度宣布中向非《公约》缔约国转让附表2和附表3化学品的情况

8.7　根据2023年收到的2022年过去活动年度宣布，没有关于向非缔约国转让附表2化学品的报告。7个缔约国向3个非缔约国出口了4种附表3化学品。

第六条视察制度的优化

8.8　2023年，技秘处优化了第六条视察制度的效力和效率。例如，技秘处使用新的电子工具（电子视察），并修订了视察报告模板。

8.9　视察组的规模与在2022年进行同类视察时相当。技秘处根据视察经验，进一步评价和再评估视察组的规模，确保效力和效率尽可能达到最佳水平。

8.10　2023年，技秘处努力将连续视察[①]和长时间工业视察任务[②]的数量最大化，将之作为优化人力和物力资源利用并使已完成的视察数量最大化的一种方式。连续视察和长时间工业视察任务是提高视察工作效率的重要工具。如有更多缔约国同意在其境内进行连续视察，特别是那些每年接受大量第六条视察的缔约国，将会进一步节约资源。2023年进行了48次连续视察或长时间工业视察。其中，在16个缔约国进行了34次连续视察，并在9个缔约国进行了14次长时间工业视察任务。此外，有21个缔约国在其领土上接受了国内连续视察。技秘处的差旅费节省了约71万欧元（主

---

① 连续视察是将两个其他化学生产设施视察或附表3视察组合成一个任务而在一周内进行。

② 长时间工业视察任务是在一个任务期间将分属于不同视察制度下的两个或更多的视察合并进行，为期超过一周。

要来自机票费用）。过去10年进行的连续视察的数量见表7。

表7　连续视察

2013年	2014年	2015年	2016年	2017年	2018年	2019年	2020年	2021年	2022年	2023年
57	51	59	54	58	57	62	19	22	34	48

8.11　2023年进行了1次附带采样和分析的视察（见表8）。迄今为止，附带采样和分析的第六条视察的总数为121次。

表8　第六条厂区的附带采样和分析的视察

2013年	2014年	2015年	2016年	2017年	2018年	2019年	2020年	2021年	2022年	2023年
8	9	11	11	10	9	6	1	0	0	1

8.12　经小组验证和执理会核准的分析数据不断被纳入禁化武组织中央分析数据库（中央数据库）。执理会关于增列非附表化学品的衍生物的决定（EC-86/DEC.10，2017年10月13日）是为改进中央数据库而采取的重要步骤。

对不必视察的第六条厂区的视察

8.13　2023年，事后发现一共有3次第六条厂区视察是对不必视察的设施进行的，1次为附表2厂区，2次为其他化学生产设施厂区。该数字与前几年记录的平均数目一致。近年来，技秘处已设法通过多种方式解决不必视察的问题，其中包括双边磋商和发出澄清请求、内部分析与核对、为国家主管部门举办培训课程和研讨班。此外，开发了网络学习模块以支持缔约国对宣布要求的理解。对不必接受视察的厂区进行的视察数见表9。

表9　对不必接受视察的厂区进行的视察数

2013年	2014年	2015年	2016年	2017年	2018年	2019年	2020年	2021年	2022年	2023年
7	8	7	4	9	5	3	2	4	2	3

技秘处对工业和其他第六条事宜磋商的协助

8.14　2023年3月、6月、7月、9月和10月举行了5次非正式磋商。

缔约国就核查相关议题开展了磋商，其中包括：

（a）实施据以确定第六条视察数量的政策指导方针的结果；

（b）2022 年外部审计员报告的有关建议；

（c）附表 2 视察——目前积压和今后情况；

（d）完善厂区选择的算法；

（e）其他化学生产设施厂区选择的实施情况。

9. 与核查有关的其他活动

履约事宜

9.1 本节介绍了对技秘处有效行使核查职责能力构成了挑战的事项。所列内容并非全部内容。

初始宣布中存在的未决问题

进展和现状

9.2 截至 2023 年 12 月 31 日，在 193 个缔约国中已有 192 个提交了其完整的初始宣布。

9.3 2023 年，技秘处仍没有从汤加这个唯一余下的缔约国收到其尚未提交的《公约》第三条和第六条规定的初始宣布（到期日：2003 年 7 月 28 日）。技秘处已通过各种方式提醒汤加提交其初始宣布的义务，并将与汤加就此进行合作，以促其提交拖欠的初始宣布。

9.4 截至 2023 年 12 月 31 日，技秘处一直未收到阿拉伯叙利亚共和国提交的充分资料，以解决涉及其初始宣布的 20 个问题。技秘处通过宣评组继续与阿拉伯叙利亚共和国合作以解决这些问题。

拖欠或逾期提交年度宣布

9.5 为使技秘处有效地完成核查任务，缔约国及时提交过去活动年度宣布和预计活动年度宣布是非常有必要的。如果资料已经过时，不仅会导致选错厂区，还会使不必视察的厂区进行视察的次数上升，这两种情况都会损害视察资源的使用效率。不仅如此，逾期提交全国合计数据的缔约国可能会造成转让数据出入。

后续行动

9.6 关于及时提交宣布一事，技秘处在 2023 年继续向各缔约国提供技术援助。

进展和现状

9.7 自执理会关于及时提交第六条宣布的第 EC-51/DEC.1 号决定（2007 年 11 月 27 日）以来，已定期请技秘处为执理会编写关于该决定执行情况的现状报告。技秘处在 2023 年提供了 2 份此类报告①。此外，2023 年发布了关于 2022 年过去活动年度宣布和截至 2023 年 12 月 31 日的 2024 年预计活动年度宣布的现状报告（EC-105/DG.7，2024 年 1 月 26 日）。

9.8 总体来说，有 85 个拥有应宣布设施或活动的缔约国提交了 2022 年过去活动年度宣布。其中，68 个缔约国按 2023 年 3 月 31 日这一时限至少提交了一部分规定的宣布，而 17 个缔约国在期限过后提交了其 2022 年过去活动年度宣布。

9.9 2023 年，有 41 个拥有应宣布设施或活动的缔约国提交了 2024 年预计活动年度宣布，其中 39 个在截止日期前做了提交。对于 2024 年附表 1 化学品和设施的预计活动年度宣布，24 个有关缔约国中的 23 个遵守了截止日期（2023 年 10 月 2 日）；对于 2024 年附表 2 和附表 3 化学品和设施的预计活动年度宣布，38 个有关缔约国中的 36 个遵守了截止日期（2023 年 11 月 1 日）。

9.10 按照总干事的说明（EC-53/DG.11，2008 年 6 月 17 日），技秘处继续通过双边会议、讲习班上的演示介绍以及年度核对函等渠道和手段，向缔约国强调有必要审查其应宣布的其他化学生产设施清单。因此，截至 2023 年 12 月 31 日，在 81 个有关缔约国中，76 个（94%）在 2022 年过去活动年度宣布中全面更新了其他化学生产设施清单，其结果是在 4526 个

① EC-102/DG.5，2023 年 1 月 24 日和 EC-103/DG.10，2023 年 6 月 16 日。

应宣布的其他化学生产设施，有4493个得到了更新（99.3%）。

关于附表2和附表3化学品的转让数据出入

9.11　虽然技秘处采取了后续行动，但根据2022年过去活动年度宣布，仍然有相当的附表2和附表3转让数据出入问题①，这与上一年度的情况相同。尤其是在缔约国之间的附表2和附表3化学品转让总次数（8335起）中，有71%（592起）的转让量超过了宣布阈值，造成了转让数据出入。2022年的过去活动年度宣布显示：上述592起附表2和附表3化学品的转让数据出入涉及94个缔约国。在这592起转让数据出入中，166起涉及附表2化学品，426起涉及附表3化学品。

规定的宣布的现状

控暴剂

9.12　按照以往年度采取的做法，技秘处利用一切机会（除其他外），例如双边磋商和后续函件等，向缔约国强调更新其有关控暴剂的宣布的必要性。截至2023年12月31日，有关按制剂类型宣布控暴剂的缔约国数目如图2所示。

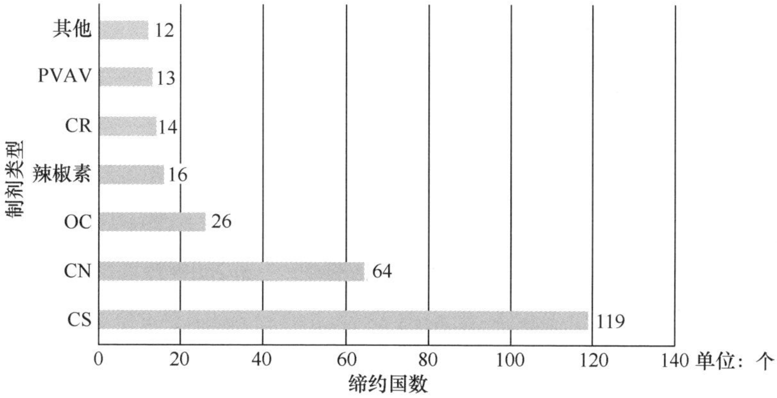

图2　宣布控暴剂的缔约国数目——按制剂类型显示

① 当进口缔约国和出口缔约国各自宣布的附表2或附表3化学品转让数量之间的差异超过了《公约》的《核查附件》第七部分第3款或第八部分第3款为该化学品规定的相关阈值时，就会产生转让数据出入。

宣布的处理

对宣布的澄清

9.13　在第 EC-36/DEC.7 号决定（2004 年 3 月 26 日）中，执理会促请缔约国对澄清请求从速做出反应，并制定了应在此请求发出后 90 天内做出反应的时限，同时还建议：若无法判定某设施是否为可视察设施，技秘处应采取后续行动。

9.14　2023 年，技秘处未就设施的可视察发出任何澄清请求。本报告期内，发现了少量与可视察的相关问题，但这些问题的每一种情况都通过在技秘处和所涉缔约国之间的商谈而迅速得以解决，因此无须发出澄清请求。至本报告期终了时，没有任何此种未决问题。

宣布的处理

9.15　2023 年，技秘处收到了缔约国提交的 760 份文件（纸质和电子版），共计 5171 页。这些包括 98 项 2022 年过去活动年度宣布，44 项 2024 年预计活动年度宣布文件。总共有 53% 的文件和 66% 的页数带有密级（相比之下，2022 年有 46% 的文件和 70% 的页数）。技秘处继续确保所有文件的处理均严格按照禁化武组织的保密制度进行。同时，技秘处鼓励缔约国审慎评估其文件的密级，以尽可能地减少带密级的文件数量。

电子宣布

9.16　有 51 个缔约国完全以或另外又以电子格式提交了 2022 年过去活动年度宣布（前一年为 54 个缔约国）。共有 33 个缔约国以电子格式提交了 2024 年预计活动年度宣布（前一年为 34 个缔约国）。

9.17　在缔约国使用电子宣布信息系统提交其电子宣布时，技秘处继续向缔约国提供了支持。技秘处举办了关于电子宣布的课程，以作为国际合作和援助司的能力建设活动的一部分。2023 年，技秘处举办了更多的双边支持会议，以协助国家主管部门设定并开始使用电子宣布信息系统。

9.18　2023 年，技秘处观察到与上一年相比，缔约国之间使用资料安全交换系统的情况与之类似。资料安全交换系统于 2014 年 7 月向各缔约国发布（S/1192/2014，2014年7月1日），它提供了一个安全的电子交换渠道，可用于在缔约国与技秘处之间交换电子宣布和其他资料，包括机密级的此种宣布和资料。截至2023年12月31日，共有来自63个缔约国的119名用户注册了资料安全交换系统并在系统保持活跃状态（相比而言，2022年有来自62个缔约国的120名用户进行了注册）。该系统的作用是使国家主管部门能够开展关于宣布的工作，并且一直持续到截止日期之前的几天，而不用考虑将涉密信息以非电子方式送交技秘处所需要的时间。2023年，技秘处对资料安全交换系统进行了修改，以简化资料安全交换系统的用户所使用的多因素认证。

缔约国执行关于含附表2A和2A*化学品的化学品混合物的低浓度阈值的2009年大会决定的情况

9.19 大会第十四届会议批准了有关含附表2A和2A*化学品的混合物的低浓度阈值的准则的决定（C-14/DEC.4，2009年12月2日）。这项决定要求缔约国按实际可能尽快执行准则。

9.20 该决定也要求技秘处最迟从2012年1月1日起报告缔约国执行该决定的进展情况。为收集用于编写该报告的资料，总共进行了13次调查：2011年（S/948/2011，2011年7月6日）；2012年（S/1040/2012，2012年9月18日）；2013年（S/1125/2013，2013年9月17日）；2014年（S/1213/2014，2014年9月12日）；2015年（S/1310/2015，2015年9月15日）；2016年（S/1420/2016，2016年9月13日）；2017年（S/1531/2017，2017年9月4日）；2018年（S/1668/2018，2018年9月3日）；2019年（S/1790/2019，2019年8月30日）；2020年（S/1894/2020，2020年9月2日）；2021年（S/1982/2021，2021年8月12日）；2022年（S/2085/2022，2022年7月28日）；及2023年（S/2199/2023，2023年8月7日）。

9.21 截至2023年12月31日，对13次调查回复的总体情况显示：在193个缔约国中，有67个至少对13次调查中的1次做了回复。在这67个缔约国中，有46个已执行了该决定，而其余21个尚未执行。

10. 对核查活动的技术支持

为核查目的进行的采样和分析

10.1 虽然已从莱兹维克搬至位于派恩纳克－诺多普的禁化武组织化学与技术中心，但禁化武组织实验室在2023年依然维持常备状态。2023年进行了1次附带采样和分析的视察任务，而禁化武组织实验室为分析化学师视察员提供了协助和支持，其中包括备齐模拟工序流所需的化学品，同时提供关于结果分析方法的咨询。

禁化武组织正式效能水平测试

10.2 禁化武组织每年为希望参加禁化武组织指定实验室网络的机构举办效能水平测试。在本审查年期间，完成了第五十二次禁化武组织关于环境分析的正式效能水平测试，并进行了第五十三次测试，同时开始了第五十四次测试。此外，还进行了第八次生物医学正式效能水平测试。2023年禁化武组织效能水平测试概览见表10。

表10　2023年禁化武组织效能水平测试概览

	第五十二次效能水平测试	第五十三次效能水平测试	第五十四次效能水平测试	第八次生物医学效能水平测试
样品制备	禁化武组织实验室	德国联邦国防军防护技术和核生化防护研究所	CSIR印度化学技术研究所化学毒素分析中心	澳大利亚防务科技集团
成绩评定	美利坚合众国利物摩尔国家实验室	瑞典国防研究院（FOI）	荷兰TNO防务、安保和安全实验室	德国联邦国防军实验室药物学和毒理学研究所
报名数[①]	26	19	29	29
成绩	15项A 5项B 3项C 2项D 1名试参与人员	7项A 2项B 6项D 2名试参与人员 1名被提名实验室退出	在2024年公布	18项A 3项B 1项C 1项D 2项F 5名试参与人员，其中1人退出

① 包括进行样品制备/评估的实验室。

10.3 至报告期终了时，共有 21 个缔约国的 26 所实验室被指定进行环境样品分析；14 个缔约国的 19 所实验室被指定进行生物医学样品分析。本报告的附件 2 概述了截至 2023 年 12 月 31 日时的指定实验室（环境或生物医学样品）的情况。

禁化武组织中央分析数据库

10.4 验证小组在 2023 年召开了 2 次会议，并从技术上核准了 86 套新分析数据集。对从 2022 年验证小组会议中获得的数据进行了处理，然后将其提交执理会核准。

10.5 2023 年，执理会批准的总计 54 项新的分析数据集（其中包括大会第二十四届会议近来通过的 14 项①新增列附表化学品）已被纳入新版的中央数据库（第 25 版）。这些数据已得到内部监察办公室（以下简称“监察办”）认证，并已于 2023 年 5 月向各缔约国发布。

10.6 禁化武组织中央分析数据库的内容见表 11。

表 11 禁化武组织中央分析数据库的内容

中央分析数据库的分析数据量（前 5 个版本）					
	21 版	22 版	23 版	24 版	25 版
质谱	6117	6187	6217	6230	6249
红外分光	1033	1033	1052	1063	1074
核磁共振光谱	1392	1396	1396	1396	1396
气相色谱（保留值）	5292	5357	5417	5429	5444
串联质谱仪	0	138	303	303	303
中央数据库的化学品种类（独立化学品的数量）					
	21 版	22 版	23 版	24 版	25 版
质谱	4602	4647	4673	4682	4697
红外分光	775	775	794	805	816
核磁共振光谱	299	300	300	300	300
气相色谱（保留值）	4482	4543	4588	4596	4609

① 附表 1.A.13、附表 1.A.14 和附表 1.A.15。

续表

中央数据库的化学品种类（独立化学品的数量）					
	21 版	22 版	23 版	24 版	25 版
串联质谱仪	0	38	68	68	68

禁化武组织实验室的资质认可

10.7　2023 年，监察办对禁化武组织实验室的 3 个已获认证的活动领域进行了 2 次内部审计，此外，荷兰认证理事会在 2023 年 5 月进行了一次外部审计，从而确认实验室一直遵循国际标准化组织的 ISO 17025 和 ISO 17043 标准。

多功能培训设施

10.8　2023 年，在多功能培训设施举办了面向女性化学师的基础分析化学课程、面向海关分析师的分析化学课程和线上基础分析技能课程。

缔约国大会审议《禁止化学武器公约》的履行状况第五次特别会议（五审会）的报告（节选）[①]

（RC-5/3、2023 年 6 月 7 日）

1. 议程项目一：五审会开幕

1.1　缔约国大会审议《禁止化学武器公约》（以下简称"《公约》"）的履行状况第五次特别会议（以下简称"五审会"）由缔约国大会（以下简称"大会"）第二十七届会议主席、南非大使福西姆斯·费勒蒙·马东塞拉于 2023 年 5 月 15 日 10 时 12 分在世界论坛会议中心的威廉·亚历山大国王剧场宣布开幕。

1.2　以下 137 个缔约国参加了五审会：阿尔巴尼亚、阿尔及利亚、安道尔、安哥拉、阿根廷、亚美尼亚、澳大利亚、奥地利、阿塞拜疆、巴林、孟加拉国、白俄罗斯、比利时、玻利维亚多民族国、波斯尼亚和黑塞哥维那、博茨瓦纳、巴西、保加利亚、布基纳法索、布隆迪、柬埔寨、喀麦隆、加拿大、智利、中国、哥伦比亚、哥斯达黎加、科特迪瓦、克罗地亚、古巴、塞浦路斯、捷克共和国、丹麦、多米尼加共和国、厄瓜多尔、萨尔瓦多、爱沙尼亚、埃塞俄比亚、斐济、芬兰、法国、冈比亚、格鲁吉亚、德国、加纳、希腊、危地马拉、罗马教廷、洪都拉斯、匈牙利、印度、印度尼西亚、伊朗伊斯兰共和国、伊拉克、爱尔兰、意大利、牙买加、日本、约旦、哈萨克斯坦、肯尼亚、科威特、吉尔吉斯斯坦、老挝人民民主共和国、拉脱维亚、黎巴嫩、利比亚、列支敦士登、立陶宛、卢森堡、马来西亚、马耳他、

① 本文来源于禁止化学武器组织网站。

墨西哥、摩纳哥、蒙古国、黑山、摩洛哥、莫桑比克、缅甸[①]、纳米比亚、尼泊尔、荷兰、新西兰、尼加拉瓜、尼日尔、尼日利亚、北马其顿、挪威、阿曼、巴基斯坦、巴拿马、巴拉圭、秘鲁、菲律宾、波兰、葡萄牙、卡塔尔、大韩民国、摩尔多瓦共和国、罗马尼亚、俄罗斯联邦、卢旺达、萨摩亚、圣马力诺、沙特阿拉伯、塞内加尔、塞尔维亚、新加坡、斯洛伐克、斯洛文尼亚、南非、西班牙、斯里兰卡、巴勒斯坦国、苏丹、瑞典、瑞士、阿拉伯叙利亚共和国、塔吉克斯坦、泰国、多哥、特立尼达和多巴哥、突尼斯、土耳其、土库曼斯坦、乌干达、乌克兰、阿拉伯联合酋长国、大不列颠及北爱尔兰联合王国、坦桑尼亚联合共和国、美利坚合众国、乌拉圭、委内瑞拉玻利瓦尔共和国、越南、也门、赞比亚和津巴布韦。

1.3 根据大会《议事规则》第 29 条，签约国以色列作为观察员列席了五审会。

1.4 根据大会《议事规则》第 30 条，并根据五审会关于此事的一项决定（RC-5/DEC.1，2023 年 5 月 15 日），非签约国南苏丹被授予了观察员地位。

1.5 根据《议事规则》第 31 条和第 32 条，并根据五审会关于此事的一项决定（RC-5/DEC.2，2023 年 5 月 15 日），14 个国际组织、专门机构和其他国际组织出席了五审会。

1.6 根据缔约国大会审议《公约》的履行状况第三次特别会议的有关建议（RC-3/3*，2013 年 4 月 19 日），并根据五审会关于此事的一项决定（RC-5/DEC.3，2023 年 5 月 15 日），五审会邀请了全球化工行业和科学界的有关代表出席了五审会。

1.7 根据《议事规则》第 33 条，并根据五审会关于此事的一项决定（RC-5/DEC.4，2023 年 5 月 15 日），五审会邀请了 74 个非政府组织亲自或通过远程接入以及通过预录制发言的方式出席并参加了五审会。

1.8 德国常驻代表代表以下国家宣读了一份联合声明，内容涉及与非

① 见 RC-5/2/Rev.1（2023 年 5 月 18 日）第 2（d）分段和第 3.1（c）分段已经五审会于 2023 年 5 月 19 日核准。

政府组织合作以及后者参与禁化武组织的工作，其中包括出席大会的有关届会：阿尔巴尼亚、安道尔、澳大利亚、奥地利、比利时、巴西、保加利亚、加拿大、智利、哥伦比亚、哥斯达黎加、克罗地亚、塞浦路斯、捷克共和国、丹麦、厄瓜多尔、爱沙尼亚、芬兰、法国、格鲁吉亚、德国、希腊、匈牙利、冰岛、爱尔兰、意大利、拉脱维亚、列支敦士登、立陶宛、卢森堡、马耳他、墨西哥、摩纳哥、黑山、荷兰、新西兰、北马其顿、挪威、秘鲁、波兰、葡萄牙、摩尔多瓦共和国、罗马尼亚、圣马力诺、斯洛伐克、斯洛文尼亚、西班牙、瑞典、瑞士、乌克兰、大不列颠及北爱尔兰联合王国和美利坚合众国。

1.9　土耳其、俄罗斯联邦、爱尔兰和伊朗伊斯兰共和国代表团在该环节做了发言。

2. 议程项目二：选举主席

根据大会《议事规则》第 8 条（b）项，五审会以鼓掌通过的方式选举了荷兰大使亨克・考尔・范德卡斯特担任大会主席。

3. 议程项目三：选举副主席和主席团其他成员

3.1　根据大会《议事规则》第 8 条（b）项，五审会以鼓掌通过的方式选举了阿尔及利亚、安哥拉、澳大利亚、玻利维亚多民族国、塞浦路斯、萨尔瓦多、德国和日本 8 个缔约国的代表担任大会副主席。

3.2　对于涉及东欧组的两个席位，立陶宛、北马其顿和俄罗斯联邦代表团介绍了各自的候选人。

3.3　根据大会《议事规则》第 79 条，拉脱维亚代表团代表以下国家要求采用无记名投票进行表决，以填补涉及东欧组的 2 个席位：阿尔巴尼亚、波斯尼亚和黑塞哥维那、保加利亚、克罗地亚、捷克共和国、爱沙尼亚、格鲁吉亚、匈牙利、拉脱维亚、立陶宛、黑山、北马其顿、波兰、摩尔多瓦共和国、罗马尼亚、斯洛伐克、斯洛文尼亚和乌克兰。俄罗斯联邦代表团也在该环节做了发言。

3.4　五审会从东欧组中选举了立陶宛和北马其顿两个缔约国担任五审会的副主席。

3.5　根据大会《议事规则》第8条（b）项，五审会选举了墨西哥大使何塞·安东尼奥·扎波尔戈迪亚·特莱赫担任全体委员会主席。

5. 议程项目五：组织工作和建立附属机构

5.1　五审会审议并通过了总务委员会根据大会《议事规则》第43（b）条所报告的各项建议。

任命全权证书委员会

5.2　根据大会《议事规则》第27条，五审会按照大会主席的建议任命了智利、哥伦比亚、捷克共和国、希腊、伊拉克、摩洛哥、尼日利亚、菲律宾、斯洛伐克和大不列颠及北爱尔兰联合王国10个全权证书委员会成员。

9. 议程项目九：根据第八条第22款的规定，考虑到任何相关的科学技术发展，审查《公约》的实施情况

9.1　不限成员名额五审会筹备工作组（以下简称“五审会筹备工作组”）主席、爱沙尼亚大使劳里·库兹向五审会报告了五审会筹备工作组的工作（RC-5/WP.9，2023年5月15日），并向五审会提交了关于五审会临时议程之议程项目九的主席临时案文草案（WGRC-5/2 RC-5/CRP.1，2023年5月2日）。

9.2　科学咨询委员会主席古恩特·波沃登博士向五审会简要介绍了该委员会关于科技发展的报告（RC-5/DG.1，2023年2月22日），其中重点强调了科学审查程序、审议的专题领域和有关建议（该发言已上传至禁化武组织的外部服务器）。

分议题9（a）《公约》在促进国际和平与安全方面以及在实现《公约》序言所载目标方面的作用

分议题 9（b）确保《公约》的普遍性

9.3　伊朗伊斯兰共和国、危地马拉、大韩民国、日本、巴勒斯坦国、阿拉伯叙利亚共和国和加纳代表团在该环节做了发言。

分议题 9（c）《公约》条款在以下方面做执行情况

核查相关事项

（i）一般义务和有关的宣布义务。

（ii）总干事关于销毁相关问题的各项报告。

（iii）化学武器的销毁，包括缔约国大会和执行理事会关于销毁相关问题的各项决定的执行情况。

（iv）化学武器生产设施的销毁或改装。

（v）禁化武组织的核查活动。

（vi）《公约》不加禁止的活动。

（vii）协商、合作和事实调查。

9.4　伊朗伊斯兰共和国、美利坚合众国、日本、中国、德国、委内瑞拉玻利瓦尔共和国、阿拉伯叙利亚共和国、俄罗斯联邦、巴基斯坦和大不列颠及北爱尔兰联合王国代表团在该环节做了发言。

加强国际合作与援助

（viii）国家履约措施。

（ix）援助和化学武器防护。

（x）经济技术发展。

9.5　伊朗伊斯兰共和国、古巴、乌克兰、摩洛哥、巴勒斯坦国、阿拉伯叙利亚共和国、美利坚合众国、中国、巴西、加纳、大不列颠及北爱尔兰联合王国、阿尔及利亚、加拿大（代表澳大利亚、比利时、加拿大、智利、捷克共和国、芬兰、法国、德国、匈牙利、爱尔兰、意大利、日本、哈萨克斯坦、墨西哥、荷兰、新西兰、挪威、菲律宾、波兰、葡萄牙、大韩民国、西班牙、瑞典、瑞士、大不列颠及北爱尔兰联合王国、美利坚合众国和欧洲联盟）、印度尼西亚、法国、也门、阿根廷和俄罗斯联邦代表团在该环节做了发言。

9.6　根据 RC-5/DEC.2，欧洲联盟在该环节做了发言。

组织管治

（i）第十二至第十五条和最后条款。

（ii）机密资料的保护。

分议题 9（d）禁化武组织的总体运作

9.7　巴西、马来西亚（代表阿尔巴尼亚、安道尔、澳大利亚、奥地利、孟加拉国、比利时、波斯尼亚和黑塞哥维那、博茨瓦纳、巴西、保加利亚、柬埔寨、加拿大、智利、哥伦比亚、哥斯达黎加、克罗地亚、塞浦路斯、捷克共和国、丹麦、多米尼加共和国、厄瓜多尔、萨尔瓦多、爱沙尼亚、芬兰、格鲁吉亚、德国、加纳、希腊、洪都拉斯、冰岛、爱尔兰、意大利、日本、拉脱维亚、列支敦士登、立陶宛、卢森堡、马来西亚、马耳他、墨西哥、黑山、荷兰、新西兰、尼日利亚、北马其顿、巴拿马、秘鲁、葡萄牙、大韩民国、摩尔多瓦共和国、罗马尼亚、卢旺达、圣马力诺、塞尔维亚、斯洛文尼亚、西班牙、瑞典、瑞士、泰国、土耳其和乌拉圭）、加拿大、爱尔兰、大不列颠及北爱尔兰联合王国、加纳、孟加拉国、阿尔及利亚和阿根廷代表团在该环节做了发言。

9.8　根据 RC-5/DEC.2，欧洲联盟在该环节做了发言。

10. 议程项目十：附属机构的报告

全体委员会

10.1　五审会注意到全体委员会主席关于根据总务委员会的建议向其交付的议程项目的审查结果的报告（RC-5/CoW.1，2023 年 5 月 18 日），并在需要时采取了适当行动。

总务委员会

10.2　五审会注意到总务委员会的报告，并视情况采取了适当行动。

全权证书委员会

10.3　五审会审议并通过由全权证书委员会主席、捷克共和国常驻副代表玛蒂娜·菲力比奥瓦主席女士所做的全权证书委员会的汇报（RC-5/2/Rev.1，2023年5月18日）。

10.4　五审会进一步通过了主席的以下口头汇报：在全权证书委员会会议结束之后，又收到了布基纳法索、哥斯达黎加、科威特、蒙古国和卡塔尔提交的全权证书的原件。

12. 议程项目十二：通过五审会最后文件

12.1　大会审议并通过了五审会的纪实性报告。

12.2　没有就通过五审会的最后文件达成协商一致。

缔约国大会第二十八届会议的报告（节选）[①]

（C-28/5、2023 年 12 月 1 日）

1. 议程项目一：会议开幕

1.1　缔约国大会（以下简称“大会”）第二十八届会议于 2023 年 11 月 27 日 10 时 11 分在世界论坛会议中心的威廉·亚历山大国王剧场由南非大使弗希姆兹·费勒蒙·马东塞拉主持开幕。

1.2　以下 143 个缔约国出席了第二十八届会议：阿富汗、阿尔巴尼亚、阿尔及利亚、安道尔、安哥拉、阿根廷、亚美尼亚、澳大利亚、奥地利、阿塞拜疆、巴哈马、巴林、孟加拉国、白俄罗斯、比利时、不丹、玻利维亚多民族国、波斯尼亚和黑塞哥维那、博茨瓦纳、巴西、文莱达鲁萨兰国、保加利亚、布基纳法索、布隆迪、柬埔寨、喀麦隆、加拿大、智利、中国、哥伦比亚、哥斯达黎加、科特迪瓦、克罗地亚、古巴、塞浦路斯、捷克共和国、丹麦、吉布提、多米尼加共和国、厄瓜多尔、萨尔瓦多、厄立特里亚、爱沙尼亚、埃塞俄比亚、芬兰、法国、冈比亚、格鲁吉亚、德国、加纳、希腊、危地马拉、罗马教廷、匈牙利、冰岛、印度、印度尼西亚、伊朗伊斯兰共和国、伊拉克、爱尔兰、意大利、牙买加、日本、约旦、哈萨克斯坦、肯尼亚、科威特、吉尔吉斯斯坦、老挝人民民主共和国、拉脱维亚、黎巴嫩、莱索托、利比亚、列支敦士登、立陶宛、卢森堡、马来西亚、马里、马耳他、毛里塔尼亚、毛里求斯、墨西哥、摩纳哥、蒙古国、黑山、摩洛哥、莫桑比克、尼泊尔、荷兰、新西兰、尼加拉瓜、尼日利亚、北马其顿、挪威、阿曼、巴基斯坦、帕劳、巴拿马、巴拉圭、秘鲁、菲律宾、波兰、葡

① 本文来源于禁止化学武器组织网站。

萄牙、卡塔尔、大韩民国、摩尔多瓦共和国、罗马尼亚、俄罗斯联邦、卢旺达、圣马力诺、沙特阿拉伯、塞内加尔、塞尔维亚、新加坡、斯洛伐克、斯洛文尼亚、南非、西班牙、斯里兰卡、巴勒斯坦国、苏丹、瑞典、瑞士、阿拉伯叙利亚共和国、塔吉克斯坦、泰国、多哥、突尼斯、土耳其、土库曼斯坦、乌干达、乌克兰、阿拉伯联合酋长国、大不列颠及北爱尔兰联合王国、坦桑尼亚联合共和国、美利坚合众国、乌拉圭、乌兹别克斯坦、委内瑞拉玻利瓦尔共和国、越南、也门、赞比亚和津巴布韦。

1.3　根据《议事规则》第 29 条，签署国以色列以观察员身份列席了大会本次会议。

1.4　根据《议事规则》第 30 条，并根据大会就此事项做出的决定（C-28/DEC.1，2023 年 11 月 27 日），非签署国南苏丹被授予了观察员身份。

1.5　根据《议事规则》第 31 条和第 32 条，并根据大会就此事做出的决定（C-28/DEC.2，2023 年 11 月 27 日），8 个国际组织、专门机构和其他国际机构出席了第二十八届会议。

1.6　根据三审会的建议（RC-3/3*，2013 年 4 月 19 日），并根据大会就此事项做出的决定（C-28/DEC.3，2023 年 11 月 27 日），大会邀请了全球化工界和科学界的代表出席第二十八届会议。

1.7　根据《议事规则》第 33 条，并根据大会就此事项做出的决定（C-28/DEC.4，2023 年 11 月 27 日），106 个非政府组织应邀出席并参加了第二十八届会议。

2. 议程项目二：选举主席

根据《议事规则》第 34 条和第 35 条，大会选举了巴基斯坦大使苏鲁克•穆斯坦撒・塔拉尔为大会主席，任期至大会下次例会选出其继任者为止。

3. 议程项目三：选举副主席和主席团其他成员

3.1　根据《议事规则》第 34 条和第 35 条，大会选举了澳大利亚、玻利维亚多民族国、塞浦路斯、捷克共和国、萨尔瓦多、爱沙尼亚、伊朗伊斯兰共和国、摩洛哥、荷兰和卢旺达 10 个缔约国为大会副主席，任期至大会下次例会选出其继任者为止。

3.2 还根据《议事规则》第 34 条和第 35 条，大会选举了阿尔及利亚大使萨利马 • 阿布德拉克担任全体委员会主席，任期至大会下次例会选出其继任者为止。

5. 议程项目五：工作安排及设立附属机构

5.1 大会审议并通过了总务委员会根据《议事规则》第 43 条（b）项向大会报告的建议。

5.2 俄罗斯联邦、加纳（代表非洲组）、伊朗伊斯兰共和国和阿拉伯叙利亚共和国代表团在该环节做了发言。

6. 议程项目六：任命全权证书委员会

根据《议事规则》第 27 条，大会根据主席的建议委任了全权证书委员会——哥伦比亚、厄瓜多尔、德国、伊拉克、马来西亚、荷兰、俄罗斯联邦、斯洛文尼亚、突尼斯和坦桑尼亚联合共和国 10 位成员，任期至大会下次例会任命新成员为止。

9. 议程项目九：《公约》的履行现状

分项目 9（a）：履行第七条义务行动计划的执行进展报告

9.1 根据大会第十四届会议关于履行第七条义务的决定（C-14/DEC.12，2009 年 12 月 4 日），大会审议并注意到以下报告：总干事关于“截至 2023 年 7 月 31 日《公约》第七条实施现状综述”的报告（EC-104/DG.8 C-28/DG.7，2023 年 9 月 6 日）；总干事关于“截至 2023 年 7 月 31 日《公约》第七条实施状况报告：初步措施”的报告（EC-104/DG.9 C-28/DG.8，2023 年 9 月 6 日）以及总干事关于“截至 2023 年 7 月 31 日《公约》第七条实施状况报告：针对拥有《公约》规定应宣布工业设施的缔约国的补充措施”的报告（EC-104/DG.10 C-28/DG.9，2023 年 9 月 6 日）。

分项目 9（b）：技术秘书处 2022 年处理保密资料的制度的执行情况

9.2　大会审议并注意到总干事关于技术秘书处（以下简称“技秘处”）在 2022 年处理保密资料的制度的执行情况报告（EC-102/DG.8 C-28/DG.1，2023 年 2 月 9 日）。

分项目 9（c）：缔约国大会和执理会关于销毁相关事项的决定的执行情况

9.3　根据大会第十六届会议的决定（C-16/DEC.11 第 3（f）段，2011 年 12 月 1 日），大会对该决定的执行情况进行了年度审查。

9.4　根据大会第十六届会议的同一决定（C-16/DEC.11），大会注意到美利坚合众国的年度报告（C-28/NAT.2，2023 年 11 月 6 日）和该国就其与销毁相关的活动所做的年度通报，其中包括关于销毁其已宣布的所有化学武器库存的通报。

9.5　根据大会第十六届会议的同一决定（C-16/DEC.11）第 3（g）分段，总干事向大会提交了关于销毁剩余化学武器库存的总体进展的书面年度报告（C-28/DG.17，2023 年 11 月 23 日），其中包括关于所有已宣布的化学武器库存完成销毁的报告。

9.6　大会对美利坚合众国销毁其已宣布的化学武器库存这一成果表示赞赏。根据第 C-16/DEC.11 号决定，依据技秘处从本组织的核查活动获取的独立资料，现在可认为拥有国已宣布的剩余化学武器库存完成了销毁。

9.7　大会欢迎执理会第 67 次会议的决定（EC-67/DEC.6，2012 年 2 月 15 日）及执理会第 101 次会议通过的作为其附件 3 的关于 2022 年以后中国境内日本遗弃化学武器销毁计划（EC-101/DEC.2，2022 年 10 月 4 日），同时意识到销毁进度未达到附于关于“2012 年 4 月 29 日的时限以及日本遗弃在中华人民共和国境内化学武器的未来销毁”的决定（EC-67/DEC.6）

的此前提交的销毁计划的预期，并鼓励中国和日本继续合作以执行第 EC-67/DEC.6 号决定。

9.8 大会忆及《公约》关于遗弃缔约国承诺销毁其遗弃在另一缔约国领土上的所有化学武器并应提供一切必要的财政、技术、专家、设施及其他资源的规定；表示决心继续关注此事，并敦促遗弃缔约国继续全力以赴，以忠实地按照执理会的决定（EC-67/DEC.6）及其附件 3 尽早销毁完成日本遗弃在中国领土上的化学武器，同时解决有关难题，其中包括确保人民的安全并保护环境。大会重申领土缔约国应提供适当的合作。

9.9 大会还重申遗弃缔约国有义务根据《公约》的有关规定而提供所有可获得的资料，其中应尽可能包括有关地点、类型、数量和遗弃情况的资料，以便为日本加快销毁遗弃在中国境内的化学武器提供方便。

9.10 大会忆及“2022 年以后中华人民共和国境内日本遗弃化学武器销毁计划”（EC-101/DEC.2）规定的情况：使用移动销毁设施来销毁遗弃化学武器（以下简称“遗弃化武”）；在（吉林省）哈尔巴岭销毁遗弃化武；销毁其他遗弃化武，其中包括就制定中长期遗弃化武挖掘计划开展磋商；合并遗弃化武托管库；遗弃缔约国继续尽全力收集并提供关于遗弃化武的线索和资料并继续进行磋商，同时相关缔约国共同确认将加快各项销毁进程并确认将尽最大努力以尽早完成遗弃化武的销毁。

9.11 大会回顾了以下情况：三审会和三审会报告（RC-3/3*）对遗弃化武销毁的审查情况表示了欢迎，同时重申了执理会、大会和审议大会在《公约》的条款和执理会的有关决定（EC-67/DEC.6）所界定的与销毁遗弃化武有关的问题方面所发挥的作用。大会四审会对此事的审查表示了欢迎，并注意到五审会上有关此事进行的建设性讨论。

9.12 大会对 2023 年顺利进行的 12 次遗弃化武设施的现场视察表示肯定。

9.13 日本和中国代表团向大会介绍了各自与销毁相关活动的最新情况。

分项目 9（d）：应对使用化学武器所构成的威胁

9.15　大会第四次特别会议通过了题为“应对使用化学武器所构成的威胁”的决定（C-SS-4/DEC.3，2018 年 6 月 27 日）。自大会上次例会以来，根据上述决定第 24 段，已向执理会分发了以下文件：EC-102/DG.15（2023 年 2 月 27 日）；EC-103/DG.13，2023 年 6 月 26 日；EC-104/DG.20（2023 年 9 月 25 日）。

消除叙利亚化学武器方案

9.16　大会第二十五届会议通过了“处理阿拉伯叙利亚共和国拥有并使用化学武器的问题”决定（C-25/DEC.9，2021 年 4 月 21 日）。

9.17　技秘处分发了题为“阿拉伯叙利亚共和国加入《公约》：十年以后”的说明（S/2213/2023，2023 年 9 月 27 日）。

9.18　技秘处分发了由以下国家共同提出的题为“应对使用化学武器构成的威胁及其未来的威胁使用”的决定草案（C-28/DEC/CRP.12，2023 年 11 月 24 日）：阿尔巴尼亚、安道尔、澳大利亚、奥地利、比利时、波斯尼亚和黑塞哥维那、保加利亚、加拿大、哥斯达黎加、克罗地亚、塞浦路斯、捷克共和国、丹麦、厄瓜多尔、爱沙尼亚、芬兰、法国、格鲁吉亚、德国、希腊、匈牙利、冰岛、爱尔兰、意大利、日本、拉脱维亚、立陶宛、卢森堡、马耳他、墨西哥、摩纳哥、黑山、荷兰、新西兰、北马其顿、挪威、巴拿马、波兰、葡萄牙、大韩民国、摩尔多瓦共和国、罗马尼亚、圣马力诺、斯洛伐克、斯洛文尼亚、西班牙、瑞典、瑞士、土耳其、乌克兰、大不列颠及北爱尔兰联合王国和美利坚合众国。

9.19　根据《禁化武组织财务条例和细则》第 4.9 条，技秘处分发了总干事关于上述提案所涉及的财务、行政以及方案和预算影响的报告（C-28/DG.19，2023 年 11 月 24 日）。

9.20　挪威代表团代表上述联合提案国发表了一份联合声明。

9.21　法国、大不列颠及北爱尔兰联合王国、德国、加拿大（代表澳大利亚、加拿大和新西兰）、瑞士、俄罗斯联邦、阿拉伯叙利亚共和国、古巴、中国、爱尔兰、委内瑞拉玻利瓦尔共和国、比利时、伊朗伊斯兰共和国、意大利、美利坚合众国、荷兰、印度和圣马力诺代表团在该环节做了发言。

9.24 根据《议事规则》第69条和第72条，就题为“应对使用化学武器构成的威胁及其未来的威胁使用”的决定草案（C-28/DEC/CRP.12）进行了表决。表决结果如下：69票赞成（阿尔巴尼亚、安道尔、阿根廷、澳大利亚、奥地利、巴哈马、比利时、波斯尼亚和黑塞哥维那、保加利亚、加拿大、智利、哥伦比亚、哥斯达黎加、克罗地亚、塞浦路斯、捷克共和国、丹麦、厄瓜多尔、萨尔瓦多、爱沙尼亚、芬兰、法国、冈比亚、格鲁吉亚、德国、希腊、危地马拉、匈牙利、冰岛、爱尔兰、意大利、日本、科威特、拉脱维亚、列支敦士登、立陶宛、卢森堡、马耳他、毛里求斯、墨西哥、摩纳哥、黑山、荷兰、新西兰、北马其顿、挪威、帕劳、巴拉圭、秘鲁、波兰、葡萄牙、卡塔尔、大韩民国、摩尔多瓦共和国、罗马尼亚、圣马力诺、沙特阿拉伯、塞内加尔、新加坡、斯洛伐克、斯洛文尼亚、西班牙、瑞典、瑞士、土耳其、乌克兰、大不列颠及北爱尔兰联合王国、美利坚合众国和赞比亚）；10票反对（白俄罗斯、中国、厄立特里亚、伊朗伊斯兰共和国、尼加拉瓜、巴基斯坦、俄罗斯联邦、南非、斯里兰卡和巴勒斯坦国）；45票弃权（阿富汗、阿尔及利亚、安哥拉、亚美尼亚、巴林、孟加拉国、不丹、玻利维亚多民族国、博茨瓦纳、巴西、文莱达鲁萨兰国、布基纳法索、布隆迪、柬埔寨、喀麦隆、科特迪瓦、埃塞俄比亚、加纳、印度、印度尼西亚、伊拉克、约旦、哈萨克斯坦、肯尼亚、老挝人民民主共和国、黎巴嫩、马来西亚、马里、毛里塔尼亚、蒙古国、摩洛哥、莫桑比克、尼泊尔、尼日利亚、菲律宾、卢旺达、苏丹、泰国、突尼斯、乌干达、阿拉伯联合酋长国、坦桑尼亚联合共和国、乌拉圭、越南和津巴布韦）。鉴于该结果，通过了该决定（C-28/DEC.12，2023年11月30日）。

9.25 沙特阿拉伯、玻利维亚多民族国、危地马拉、中国、巴基斯坦、马来西亚、俄罗斯联邦、巴勒斯坦国、伊朗伊斯兰共和国和孟加拉国代表团解释了其表决的理由。

分项目 9(e)：化学武器受害者国际支援网络的实施状况

9.31　大会第十六届会议通过了关于建立化学武器受害者国际支持和资助网络和为此目的设立自愿信托基金的建议（C-16/DEC.13，2011 年 12 月 2 日）。大会请总干事每两年通过执理会向大会例会报告本决定的执行情况。

9.32　执理会第 104 次会议注意到总干事关于化学武器受害者国际支持和资助网络的落实状况的报告（EC-104/DG.15 C-28/DG.12，2023 年 9 月 14 日），大会注意到这份报告。

10. 议程项目十：禁化武组织关于 2022 年的《公约》履行状况的年度报告

10.1　大会审议了执理会第 103 次会议和关于 2022 年的《公约》履行状况的禁化武组织报告草案（EC-103/3 C-28/CRP.1，2023 年 7 月 12 日；及其 Corr.1，2023 年 11 月 23 日）。

10.2　俄罗斯联邦、阿拉伯叙利亚共和国、中国、古巴和美利坚合众国代表团在该环节做了发言。

10.3　大会通过了上述报告（C-28/3，2023 年 11 月 27 日）。

10.4　对于通过现有形式的上述报告，中国、伊朗伊斯兰共和国和俄罗斯联邦代表团不参与。

11. 议程项目十一：执理会关于 2022 年 7 月 9 日—2023 年 7 月 14 日活动开展情况的年度报告

大会注意到执理会关于 2022 年 7 月 9 日—2023 年 7 月 14 日活动开展情况的报告、题为“技术秘书处的说明：日本遗弃在中华人民共和国境内化学武器的销毁”的该报告的附文以及题为“缔约国大会第二十七届会议针对执理会提出的建议所采取的各项行动”的该报告的附件（EC-104/4 C-28/2，2023 年 10 月 10 日）。该报告由执理会主席罗马尼亚大使吕西安•法图做了介绍，其还向大会通报了在该报告的截稿日之后的事态发展。

12. 议程项目十二：选举成员国担任执理会成员

12.1　按照《公约》第八条第23款以及《议事规则》第83条的规定，大会以鼓掌的方式选举了以下17位执理会成员，任期自2024年5月12日起，为期两年。为确保执理会的构成符合《公约》第八条第23款的规定，补足的选任空缺的地域分布情况如下所述。

非洲：阿尔及利亚、加纳、尼日利亚、南非。

亚洲和太平洋：孟加拉国、伊朗伊斯兰共和国、马来西亚、巴基斯坦。

拉丁美洲和加勒比：智利、厄瓜多尔、萨尔瓦多、危地马拉。

西欧地区和其他国家：比利时、丹麦、希腊、新西兰、西班牙。

12.2　立陶宛、波兰、俄罗斯联邦和乌克兰代表团就关于东欧组的3个选任空缺介绍了各自的候选人。

12.3　根据《议事规则》第79条和第80条，大会以无记名投票的方式选举了来自东欧组立陶宛、波兰和乌克兰3个缔约国担任执理会成员，任期自2024年5月12日起，为期两年。

17. 议程项目十七：促进化学活动领域为了和平目的的国际合作

17.1　大会第十六届会议通过了关于充分实施《公约》第十一条一事商定框架的构成要素的决定（C-16/DEC.10，2011年12月1日），并请技秘处向大会各次例会报告为执行该项决定采取的各项具体措施的进展情况以及第十一条的履约现状。

17.2　大会注意到总干事关于2022年8月26日至2023年8月25日履行《公约》第十一条的进展及对履行现状的审查的报告（EC-104/DG.14 C-28/DG.11，2023年9月13日）。

17.3　大会听取了关于第十一条事宜的磋商召集人巴基斯坦的法蒂玛·哈姆迪亚·坦维尔有关在休会期内进行活动的报告（该报告已上载到禁化武组织的对外服务器）。

17.4　古巴、墨西哥、伊朗伊斯兰共和国（代表白俄罗斯、玻利维亚多民族国、中国、古巴、伊朗伊斯兰共和国、尼加拉瓜、俄罗斯联邦、阿拉伯叙利亚共和国和委内瑞拉玻利瓦尔共和国）、阿拉伯叙利亚共和国、中国、阿尔及利亚、俄罗斯联邦、委内瑞拉玻利瓦尔共和国、美利坚合众国、肯尼亚、巴勒斯坦国和奥地利代表团在该环节做了发言。

17.5　根据第 C-28/DEC.2 号决定，欧洲联盟在该环节做了发言。

17.6　俄罗斯联邦和中国代表团以行使答复权的方式做了发言。

18. 议程项目十八：确保《公约》的普遍性

18.1　执理会第 23 次会议通过了一项争取《公约》普遍性的行动计划（EC-M-23/DEC.3，2003 年 10 月 24 日）。该计划要求总干事除其他外，向大会的各次例会提交该项行动计划的年度执行报告，并定期向执理会通报，以便大会和执理会有效地审查相关进展并监测此项计划的执行情况。

18.2　大会注意到总干事关于报告争取《公约》普遍性行动计划在 2022 年 8 月 16 日至 2023 年 8 月 15 日的执行情况的年度说明（EC-104/DG.23 C-28/DG.14，2023 年 9 月 28 日）。

18.3　阿拉伯叙利亚共和国、伊朗伊斯兰共和国和巴勒斯坦国代表团在该环节做了发言。

19. 议程项目十九：禁化武组织非洲方案

19.1　大会注意到总干事关于加强与非洲就《公约》进行的合作方案的说明（EC-104/DG.13 C-28/DG.10，2023 年 9 月 13 日）。

19.2　加纳代表团代表非洲组在该环节做了发言。

22. 议程项目二十二：审议大会的后续活动

22.1　向执理会第 103 次会议分发了题为“五审会主席亨克 • 考尔 • 范德卡斯特大使关于五审会的成果的思考”的工作文件，文号为 EC-103/

WP.1（2023 年 6 月 26 日）。

地域代表性

22.2　执理会第 103 次会议设立了关于地域代表性的工作组（EC-103/DEC.1，2023 年 7 月 12 日），要求其就工作组的有关活动向大会第二十八届会议报告，并向大会提交一份行动计划和有关结论。

22.3　分发了题为“地域代表性行动计划”的决定草案（文号为 C-28/DEC/CRP.11，2023 年 11 月 24 日）。本决定草案的解释性备忘录也已分发（C-28/WP.2，2023 年 11 月 9 日）。

22.4　根据《禁化武组织财务条例和细则》第 4.9 条，技秘处分发了总干事关于该提案所涉及的财务、行政以及方案和预算问题的报告（C-28/DG.18，2023 年 11 月 24 日）。

22.5　根据第 EC-103/DEC.1 号决定第一段，工作组主席智利大使佳米•阿雷克斯・莫斯科索・瓦伦瑞拉向大会报告了工作组的有关活动，并向大会提交了一份行动计划及其结论。

22.6　大会审议并通过了该决定（C-28/DEC.11，2023 年 11 月 30 日）。

22.7　孟加拉国和中国代表团在该环节做了发言。

与民间社团的互动

22.8　在执理会第 103 次会议上，德国提交了题为“缔约国大会审查《公约》履行状况第五次特别会议的后续工作——与民间社团的互动”的工作文件（EC-103/WP.2，2023 年 7 月 4 日）。

22.9　德国代表团和厄瓜多尔代表团向大会介绍了正在进行的与民间社团开展互动的最新磋商情况。

22.10　大会注意到围绕与民间社团的互动而持续进行的磋商。

22.11　俄罗斯联邦、土耳其、中国和阿拉伯叙利亚共和国代表团在该环节做了发言。

性别平等

22.12　加纳和墨西哥代表团代表以下国家做了联合发言：阿尔巴尼亚、

安道尔、阿根廷、亚美尼亚、澳大利亚、奥地利、孟加拉国、比利时、波斯尼亚和黑塞哥维那、博茨瓦纳、巴西、保加利亚、加拿大、智利、哥伦比亚、哥斯达黎加、克罗地亚、塞浦路斯、捷克共和国、丹麦、多米尼加共和国、厄瓜多尔、萨尔瓦多、爱沙尼亚、芬兰、法国、格鲁吉亚、德国、加纳、希腊、匈牙利、冰岛、爱尔兰、意大利、日本、拉脱维亚、黎巴嫩、列支敦士登、立陶宛、卢森堡、马来西亚、马耳他、墨西哥、摩纳哥、黑山、荷兰、新西兰、北马其顿、挪威、巴拿马、秘鲁、菲律宾、波兰、葡萄牙、大韩民国、摩尔多瓦共和国、罗马尼亚、卢旺达、圣马力诺、塞尔维亚、斯洛伐克、斯洛文尼亚、西班牙、巴勒斯坦国、瑞典、瑞士、泰国、土耳其、乌干达、乌克兰、大不列颠及北爱尔兰联合王国、美利坚合众国和乌拉圭。

决定
应对使用化学武器构成的威胁及其未来的威胁使用[①]

（C-28/DEC.12、2023 年 11 月 30 日）

缔约国大会，

重申《关于禁止发展、生产、储存和使用化学武器及销毁此种武器的公约》（以下简称“《公约》”）。

决心为了全人类，通过履行《公约》各条款以彻底消除使用化学武器的可能性。

忆及无论是任何人发展、生产、获取、拥有、储存、保有、转让和使用或威胁使用化学武器，均对《公约》的目标和宗旨以及对缔造一个永无化学武器的世界构成威胁；同时忆及对从事此种活动的责任人必须将其绳之以法。

对使用化学武器的威胁持续存在深表关切。

忆及缔约国大会（以下简称“大会”）第四次特别会议题为“应对使用化学武器构成的威胁”的决定（C-SS-4/DEC.3，2018 年 6 月 27 日）。

赞赏宣布评估组（于 2014 年 4 月成立）、禁化武组织派往叙利亚的事实调查组（于 2014 年 4 月 29 日成立）、调查和鉴定组（以下简称“调鉴组”）（如 2019 年 6 月 28 日的第 EC-91/S/3 号决定所述，根据第 C-SS-4/DEC.3 号决定成立）正在进行的工作包括：查实阿拉伯叙利亚共和国提交的关于其化学武器方案的宣布是否准确且完整；查清有关在阿拉伯叙利亚共和国发生的化学武器指称使用事件的所有事实；查明在阿拉伯叙利亚共和国境内使用化学武器的具体事件的肇事者。

① 本文来源于禁止化学武器组织网站。

进一步对以下情况深表关切：禁化武组织—联合国联合调查机制（S/2016/738/Rev.1，2016 年 8 月 24 日；S/2016/888，2016 年 10 月 21 日；S/2017/904，2017 年 10 月 26 日）和调鉴组（S/1867/2020，2020 年 4 月 8 日；S/1943/2021，2021 年 4 月 12 日；S/2125/2023，2023 年 1 月 27 日）所记录的在阿拉伯叙利亚共和国发生的化学武器使用事件；禁化武组织—联合国联合调查机制所记录的恐怖组织所使用化学武器的事件；阿拉伯叙利亚共和国问题独立国际调查委员会报告过的化学武器使用事件（A/HRC/46/54，2021 年 1 月 21 日）。

忆及禁化武器组织执行理事会（以下简称“执理会”）题为“应对非国家行为方使用化学武器所构成的威胁”的决定（EC-86/DEC.9，2017 年 10 月 13 日）；以及各国根据联合国安全理事会第 1540（2004）号决议所承担的义务，即不向企图发展、获取、制造、拥有、运输、转让或使用化学武器及其运载工具的非国家行为方提供任何形式的支持。

强调不限成员名额反恐工作组（以下简称“反恐工作组”）正在开展的工作的重要性，以表明缔约国直面使用化学武器构成威胁这一共同承诺。

充分认识到以下工作的重要作用：提供援助来支持能力建设，以加强各国履行《公约》规定的义务，并支持缔约国发展保护其安全以免受化学武器的威胁的能力。

注意到需要继续加强技术秘书处（以下简称“技秘处”）的能力和常备状态，以根据《公约》第八条提供技术援助；根据《公约》第十条应一缔约国的请求部署紧急措施和其他措施；根据《公约》第九条、第十条以及《公约》的《关于执行和核查的附件》（以下简称“《核查附件》”）第十部分和第十一部分加强技秘处进行质疑性视察和指称使用调查的常备状态。

认识到根据《公约》第八条第 20 款，大会应审查《公约》的遵守情况；还认识到根据《公约》第八条第 21 款（k）项，大会应按照第十二条的规定，采取必要措施以确保《公约》得到遵守，并纠正和补救与《公约》条款相违背的任何情况，并进一步认识到履行上述职责对于本组织根据第八条第 1 款实现其任务所发挥的关键作用，即实现《公约》的宗旨和目标并确保其各项条款得到履行。

忆及《公约》第十二条第 3 款规定如下：如果《公约》且尤其是第一条所禁止的活动可能对《公约》的宗旨和目标造成严重损害，大会可建议缔约国采取符合国际法的集体措施。

还忆及《公约》第十二条第 4 款规定如下：如果情节特别严重，大会应提请联合国大会和联合国安全理事会注意该问题，包括有关资料和结论。

强调《公约》第七条第 1 款（a）项规定如下：一缔约国有义务禁止其领土上任何地方或国际法承认在其管辖下的任何其他地方的自然人和法人进行《公约》禁止一缔约国进行的任何活动，包括针对此种活动制定刑事立法。

忆及《核查附件》第六、第七和第八部分对缔约国转让《公约》的《关于化学品的附件》中的附表所列的化学品设定了具体的限制和宣布义务。

表示全力支持缔约国根据《公约》和国际法开展工作，以管控向缔约国的国家管辖范围以外的任何目的地转让可能以任何方式有助于发展、生产、获取、储存、保留、转让或使用化学武器的材料、设备、技术和软件。

对以下情况深表关切：根据大会第 C-25/DEC.9 号决定（2021 年 4 月 21 日），总干事报告了（最新情况载于第 EC-105/DG.2 号文件，2023 年 11 月 24 日）阿拉伯叙利亚共和国尚未完成执理会第 EC-94/DEC.2 号决定（2020 年 7 月 9 日）第 5 段所载的任何措施；并重申其要求阿拉伯叙利亚共和国应按照联合国安全理事会第 2118（2013）号决议的要求与技秘处充分合作，其中包括遵守禁化武组织和联合国的相关建议；接受禁化武组织或联合国指定的人员；保障并确保这些人员开展活动时的安全；使这些人员即时且不受阻碍地进出任何地点并让其在履行职责时拥有视察这些地点的权利；按照联合国安全理事会第 2118（2013）号决议第 7 段的要求，允许即时且不受阻碍地接触禁化武组织有理由认为对其完成任务授权至关重要的人员。

忆及根据《公约》第七条第7款，《公约》每一缔约国均有义务在禁化武组织行使其所有职能时给予合作，特别是向技秘处提供协助；重申其决心继续采取行动来应对在阿拉伯叙利亚共和国和其他地方与化学武器有关的威胁。

特此，

1. 最强烈地谴责任何人在任何情况下使用化学武器的行径，并强调任何人在任何时间、任何地点及在任何情况下使用任何化学武器都是不可接受的，而且此种行径违反了国际规范和标准。

2. 请技秘处在履行其《公约》规定的任务授权时，继续努力保持和加强其调查化学武器指称使用的能力，包括通过以下办法：进一步开发与取证、证人面询、证据收集、监管链等有关的工具和方法；规划和开展定期培训和其他相关演练；整合和保留先前开展任务所积累的知识、技能和专长；采取总干事认为必要和适当的任何其他办法。

3. 鼓励所有缔约国加强合作，以防范包括恐怖分子在内的非国家行为方生产、获取和使用化学武器。

4. 请技秘处加强其相关的能力建设方案并向执理会各届例会予以报告，以促进在以下领域分享最佳做法：制定国家措施以防止有毒化学品及其前体、其潜在运载方式和相关材料被转让，在这些情况下进行的此类转让可能有支持化学武器的使用或发展或支持任何其他与《公约》不符的活动的风险。

5. 鼓励各缔约国根据其国内法律通过反恐工作组酌情分享关于旨在防止发展、生产、获取、储存、保有、转让或使用化学武器的国家措施的资料以及关于已完成的涉及化学武器的国内调查的资料，其中包括有关已进行的任何后续的刑事诉讼或其他法律诉讼程序的资料，以便从经验教训中获益并形成最佳做法。

6. 请技秘处在《公约》及其《保密附件》和禁化武组织保密政策的框架内，审查并向执理会报告其可向各缔约国提供的合作和援助的类型，以协助后者制定用以防止有毒化学品及其前体、其潜在运载工具和相关材料被转让的国家措施，在这些情况下进行的此类转让可能有支持化学武器的使用或发展或支持任何其他与《公约》不符的活动的风险。

7. 决定以下情况对《公约》的宗旨和目标造成了严重损害：阿拉伯叙利亚共和国在叙利亚境内继续拥有和使用化学武器，其未能提交准确且完整的宣布，同时未能销毁其所有未宣布的化学武器和生产设施，还决定根据《公约》第八条第21款（k）项和第十二条第3款，建议各缔约国根据其国内法律采取以下具体措施。

（a）防止通过其本国领土或经由其国民或使用悬挂其国旗的舰船或航空器（无论是否始发于本国领土），直接或间接地向阿拉伯叙利亚共和国提供、销售或转让联合国第S/2006/853* 号文件的附件（2006年11月7日）及其Corr.1（2006年11月14日）所包括的化学品前体、双重用途化学品制造设施和设备及相关技术。

（b）对于向阿拉伯叙利亚共和国转让《公约》的《关于化学品的附件》中的附表所列出的可能有助于发展、生产、获取、拥有、储存、保有、转让和使用或威胁使用化学武器的有毒化学品及其前体，以及潜在的运载工具和相关材料，采取其认为有必要且与《公约》相符的其他适当措施。

（c）对于根据国际法就阿拉伯叙利亚共和国境内发生的化学武器袭击开展的刑事调查或刑事诉讼程序，尽最大可能提供协助，并为相关的国家和国际问责工作提供相应支持，其中包括根据联合国大会第71/248（2016）号决议设立的国际公正独立机制。

8. 进一步决定总干事应每年在定期召开的执理会的一次例会上向执理会和各缔约国报告技秘处为执行本决定所做的工作，以及报告总干事所掌握的关于缔约国向阿拉伯叙利亚共和国转让附表化学品的资料，并进一步决定对于禁化武组织查明缔约国为肇事者或缔约国对今后发生的化学武器使用另负有责任的任何情况，总干事还应向执理会报告其所掌握的关于向所查明的缔约国转让附表化学品的资料。

9. 进一步决定，鉴于情节特别严重，根据《公约》第十二条第 4 款，总干事应向联合国秘书长提供本决定的副本，以提请联合国大会和联合国安全理事会关注以下情况：尽管《公约》和安全理事会第 2118（2013）号决议规定了阿拉伯叙利亚共和国应尽的有关义务，但其仍拥有和使用化学武器并且未能提交准确和完整的宣布，同时未能销毁其未宣布的化学武器和生产设施，由此构成了持续的威胁，并敦促大会和安全理事会采取适当行动，以处理这一情况并推动问责。

10. 决定持续关注此事。

总干事的说明
美利坚合众国化学武器库存销毁的完成①

（EC-104/DG.25、2023 年 10 月 6 日）

1. 在第 EC-104/DG.24 号报告（2023 年 10 月 5 日）中，总干事向执行理事会做了以下报告：美利坚合众国已于 2023 年 7 月 7 日完成了对其第 1 类化学武器库存的销毁。这些库存包括以下部分。

（a）1997 年 8 月至 2001 年 1 月，在约翰斯顿岛化学战剂处理系统销毁了 639.578 吨化学剂。

（b）1997 年 4 月至 2012 年 1 月，在图埃勒化学剂处置设施销毁了 12118.826 吨化学剂（包括在化学战剂弹药处置系统销毁的部分沙林和 VX）。

（c）1998 年 11 月至 2005 年 4 月，在其他各个设施销毁了主要与紧急销毁活动相关的 0.044 吨化学剂。

（d）2001 年 9 月至 2011 年 6 月，在原型爆破试验和销毁设施销毁了 0.027 吨化学剂。

（e）2003 年 7 月至 2011 年 10 月，在安尼斯顿化学战剂处置设施销毁了 2044.829 吨化学剂。

（f）2004 年 5 月至 2011 年 11 月，在尤马蒂拉化学战剂处置设施销毁了 3374.340 吨化学剂。

（g）2003 年 2 月至 2006 年 3 月，在阿伯丁化学战剂处置设施销毁了 1471.255 吨化学剂。

（h）2005 年 3 月至 2010 年 11 月，在派恩布拉夫化学战剂处置设施销

---

① 本文来源于禁止化学武器组织网站。

毁了 3493.387 吨化学剂。

（i）1997 年 7 月至 2005 年 4 月，在化学战剂弹药处置系统销毁了 2.218 吨化学剂。

（j）1997 年 10 月至 2010 年 2 月，在化学品转送设施销毁了 3.156 吨化学剂。

（k）2004 年 7 月至 2009 年 7 月，在杜格威试验场爆炸物销毁系统销毁了 0.136 吨化学剂。

（l）2006 年 7 月至 2010 年 4 月，在派恩布拉夫爆炸物销毁系统销毁了 2.682 吨化学剂。

（m）2005 年 8 月至 2023 年 7 月，在回收后化学武器销毁设施销毁了 1.008 吨化学剂。

（n）1997 年 10 月至 2002 年 3 月，在霍索恩西部地区非军事化设施的 M687 非军事化系统销毁了 457.630 吨化学剂。

（o）2005 年 5 月至 2009 年 2 月，在新港化学战剂处置设施销毁了 1152.184 吨化学剂。

（p）2005 年 12 月至 2007 年 12 月，在派恩布拉夫二元销毁设施销毁了 160.438 吨化学剂。

（q）2015 年 3 月至 2018 年 12 月，在普埃布洛化学剂销毁中试车间爆炸物销毁系统销毁了 3.469 吨化学剂。

（r）2016 年 9 月至 2023 年 6 月，在普埃布洛化学剂销毁中试车间销毁了 2367.166 吨化学剂。

（s）2019 年 6 月至 2021 年 9 月，在布鲁格拉斯化学剂销毁中试车间静态引爆室销毁了 82.269 吨化学剂。

（t）2020 年 1 月至 2023 年 7 月，在布鲁格拉斯化学剂销毁中试车间销毁了 392.507 吨化学剂。

2. 此外，1997 年至 2011 年，从化学武器库存中总共取出了 2.682 吨化学剂用于《禁止化学武器公约》不加禁止的目的。

3. 将以上各个部分的总数相加，便得出了美利坚合众国从 1997 年 4 月至 2023 年 7 月销毁的第 1 类化学剂的合计总量，即 27769.831 吨。

4. 美利坚合众国已于 2008 年 7 月至 2008 年 8 月完成了对其第 2 类化学武器（0.010 吨）的销毁。此外，还于 1997 年至 2012 年完成了对其第 3 类化学武器（81020 枚）的销毁。

5. 技术秘书处核实了对化学武器销毁设施中的所有化学制剂和弹药的销毁，并系统地确认了以上销毁数量包含在相关化学武器储存设施中的全部已宣布化学武器。鉴于此，总干事报告美利坚合众国已完成了对其全部化学武器库存的销毁。

技术秘书处的说明
禁止化学武器组织的中期计划 2024 年至 2028 年[①]

（EC-104/S/1、C-28/S/1、2023 年 8 月 14 日）

导言

1. 本中期计划是为 2024 年至 2028 年这个时间段编写的。我们的意图是使该计划延续下去，直至作为下次缔约国大会审查《禁止化学武器公约》（以下简称"《公约》"）的履行状况特别会议的后续行动来予以修订为止，除非出现了以下情况而不得不加以修订：外部情况变化提出了其他要求，或者本组织的决策机构采取了决定。本中期计划取代 2020 年至 2024 年的计划（EC-92/S/1 C-24/S/1，2019 年 7 月 22 日），而且为年度规划进程指明了方向。根据禁化武组织《财务条例》中的 3.9，本中期计划为禁化武组织 2024 年至 2025 年以及此后各双年期方案和预算的随附文件，直到对其做出必要修订为止。

2. 在《公约》的序言中，缔约国宣布决心"为了全人类，通过执行本《公约》的各项规定而彻底排除使用化学武器的可能性"，从而使其成为本组织的终极目标。

3. 本组织的理念仍是成为一个致力于使世界永无化学武器的国际组织，而其工作重点则在于：通过有效、高效和非歧视性地履行《公约》的所有条款来防范化学武器卷土重来。

4. 为了支持该理念，本组织的使命是作为关于化学武器事务的全球性权威以及一个基于条约的国际组织，致力于推动以下各项工作：化学武器

① 本文来源于禁止化学武器组织网站。

裁军；防范化学武器卷土重来；提供援助和化学武器防护；为《公约》的国家履行提供协助；通过核查、能力建设和各种互动和外联活动来促进化学的和平利用。

5. 为了制订本中期计划并协助本组织确定其一体化的战略方向，针对2028年的本组织在其中运行的外部环境的特定方面做出了一些假设，同时确认了若干风险。这些假设和风险包括以下内容。

（a）对所有宣布的化学武器库存经核实的销毁已于2023年7月完成。非库存化学武器（包括已回收的遗弃化学武器和老化学武器）的经核实的销毁仍将是本组织的一个重要目标，而且，对于剩余的已改装转作他用的前化学武器生产设施的核查和监测将是本组织的另一个重要目标。

（b）可能会有《公约》非缔约国作为化学武器拥有国加入本组织。

（c）随着所有已宣布化学武器库存的销毁工作完成，本组织在继续执行其裁军任务的同时，将更深入地关注如何防范化学武器卷土重来。

（d）对有毒化学品作为武器的小范围或大范围使用或威胁使用仍将构成重大关切。获取有毒化学品和关于化学武器的知识的机会正日益增多。在此方面，本组织将需要继续强化对非国家行为方（尤其是恐怖组织）以及有组织的犯罪集团和个人的各种能力。

（e）本组织将保有并发展关于化学武器的知识和核查专长，以便在收到质疑性视察、指称使用调查和其他非例行性行动的请求时随时部署其团队，并对缔约国的技术援助请求做出回应。

（f）科学技术仍将继续快速演进，而其驱动力是各种传统科学学科的相互融合、国家和国际层面的合作以及创新性筹资战略。人工智能、增材制造或生物技术等新技术的进步将应用到形形色色的行业和部门的业务活动中。与《公约》尤为相关的是这些技术被用于合成、规划、化工生产、加工和处置应用以及与核查相关的各种活动之中。

（g）全球化工行业的规模和复杂程度将不断扩大，其将日益实现数字化，同时将把新技术整合到常规用途之中。这将要求技术秘书处（以下简称“技秘处”）持续更新对范围更广的生产设备和流程以及记录保存系统的了解。本组织应对这一趋势并按需调整工业核查制度也因此更有必要。

（h）本组织将继续在核查、能力建设、互动和组织管治领域开展授权进行的活动。自愿捐款将继续发挥补充作用，从而为本组织的工作和方案做出重大贡献。

（i）禁化武组织化学和技术中心（以下简称“化技中心”）将成为本组织在研究、分析、培训和能力建设领域加强能力的重要平台。化技中心的活动将以综合协调的方式开展，而其目的将是落实《公约》以及决策机构的决定所规定的任务和义务。

（j）信息领域的情况在快速变化，其中包括人工智能的使用以及对错误和虚假信息与日俱增的担忧，这将继续对包括禁化武组织在内的多边和国际机构构成重大挑战。在此方面，更加注重信息的健全以及更加积极主动地进行外联和沟通工作将至关重要。

（k）各种费用的上涨将使本组织继续承受巨大的财政压力，而且缔约国也须面对这种压力，确保禁化武组织达到其授权业务的要求。

（l）国际安全格局的演变将会影响到本组织的工作进度。

6. 为了防范化学武器卷土重来并阻遏其进一步使用，技秘处必须保持常备状态，以在一缔约国提出请求时处理有关使用化学武器的指称，并提供技术援助。技秘处将通过以下方式增强自身在此方面的能力：使用新式和升级设备、修订培训计划（包括基于实际场景的演练）和更新业务程序。此外，还会采取以下努力以防范化学武器卷土重来：核查活动、能力建设、国家履约的改善、有效的国家防护方案、与利益攸关方互动、对负责任的化学利用的推广、对普遍性的不懈促进以及监测和适应科学技术的相关新发展。教育和外联活动将借助新工具来连接不同受众和利益攸关方，并促进他们参与到裁军相关事务中。要取得可靠的成果，将需要以连贯和系统的方式在上述每一个领域开展活动。

7. 凭借其创新性和灵活度，于 2023 年 5 月落成的化技中心是满足上述要求的一个核心要素。化技中心将确保禁化武组织跟上所有相关科学技术的发展步伐。其还提供了一个全新的综合性培训和能力建设平台，以支持高水平、多方面的国际合作和研究，从而确保禁化武组织有能力在日益全球化和复杂的世界中满足缔约国的需求。在全面投入运行后，化技中心将为跨部门合作提供新的重要机遇，借以与广泛的利益攸关方就方案的实施进行合作，从而产生协同效应和规模效应，以便提高效率。

8. 考虑到这样一种参与防范化学武器卷土重来的整体方式，取得和衡量成果将是一项更复杂的工作，而这项工作横跨本组织的所有传统方案领域。这需要做以下工作。

（a）提高应变能力和适应能力，包括采用更多的基于项目的新式工作方法和工具来提高这些能力。

（b）重新注重将基于成果的管理和文化原则纳入经改进的关键绩效指标。

（c）优化使用新的企业资源规划系统的实时管理信息。

（d）在整个组织内继续实施知识管理战略。

9. 利用这四大战略促成因素，本组织将继续在核查、能力建设、外部互动和组织管治 4 个领域取得成果。为了保持随时可以交付成果的状态，同时在今后的岁月中维持本组织的健全，技秘处将继续监测和应对有可能影响本组织实现其目标的风险。

10. 通过在上述每个领域制定中期目标，并辅以一套一直用到 2028 年的关键性目标，本文件有助于实现本组织的理念。本文件的附件对《公约》的中期履行所含的关键要素做了概述。

为维持对遵约的信心而进行的核查

中期目标 1：继续执行裁军任务并调整核查制度，以防范化学武器的卷土重来

11. 只要化学武器还存在，其销毁就仍然是本组织的根本目标。与此同时，随着 2023 年 7 月全部销毁已宣布的化学武器库存，本组织越来越重视防范化学武器卷土重来。重新平衡核查制度对于确保本组织能够应对新出现的威胁和挑战至关重要。从 2024 年起，与销毁相关的核查活动将会减少，保留与化学武器相关的知识、专长和技术。

12. 为了维持一种可行的核查制度以继续确保对遵约的信心，本组织将需要调整现行核查制度。与过去相比，这将更加要求以可靠的信息为基础来提升技秘处内部的分析能力。

13. 到 2028 年的中期目标的关键性目标如下。

（a）技秘处继续进行核查活动，以便确认已宣布的化学武器库存（包括老化学武器和遗弃化学武器以及相关设施）的销毁。

（b）维持技秘处应有的常备状态，以便应付好可能发生的新的拥有缔约国入约的情况，包括核查对化学武器的销毁。

（c）制定各种新方法，用以核查对《公约》的遵守。

（d）使用知识管理流程和信息管理工具来积极主动地解决知识保留和转让问题，其中特别强调防止化学武器相关知识的流失，例如有关化学武器的生产、安全处理、检测、分析和销毁的知识。

中期目标 2：实施核查措施，以应对《公约》目标和宗旨面临的风险

14. 作为本组织例行核查活动的一个持续的重要组成部分，将继续通过视察来评估宣布的数据和有关资料。为了防范化学武器卷土重来，本组织将提升其汇编、验证和评估有关资料的能力，以便对《公约》及这一体系的实施方式所面临的风险进行分析。

15. 本组织将继续审查工业核查制度的运行情况，且在审查时将考虑到《公约》规定和决策机构提出的要求，同时顾及化工行业的科学技术发展以及应宣布的化工设施的地理分布的变化。

16. 本组织还将处理种类更多的有毒化学品及其前体的相关性问题，包括有毒工业化学品、生物毒素和生物调节剂、用于医学或执法的化学品等。

17. 到 2028 年的中期目标的关键性目标如下。

（a）技秘处协助缔约国全面审查现行工业核查制度，以协助进行可能的调整，从而提高制度的有效性。

（b）技秘处通过广泛和量身定制的支持和资助，协助缔约国及时、完整和准确地提交宣布，包括鼓励其更多地使用禁化武组织为宣布活动提供的各种电子工具。

（c）技秘处落实缔约国即将对现行工业核查制度进行全面审查的结果，包括有关管理《公约》目标和宗旨所面临风险的最佳做法。

（d）技秘处协助缔约国提高核查活动的效力和效率，包括通过进一步优化与视察相关的实践、工具和培训来进行。

（e）利用化技中心来增强技秘处的核查能力，例如，提高执行任何类型任务和处理真实样品的能力，以支持视察员培训以及传授知识和技能，并应对和利用与新兴科学和技术相关的挑战和机遇。

中期目标 3：提高本组织开展非例行性任务的能力

18. 对于在《公约》的框架内处理违约方面的关切和应对可能的化武指称使用来说，进行协商、合作和事实调查的有效手段和工具仍将是必不可少的。为此，技秘处将需要维持并进一步开发必要的资源、技术能力、行动的常备状态和专业技能，以便为协商和合作提供便利；提供援助；进行质疑性调查、指称使用调查和其他非例行性行动；技术援助访问；与其他国际组织联合开展的任务。

19. 为了确保做好业务准备，以成功执行所有类型的任务（包括非例行性任务），必须进行投资，从而确保相关工作人员拥有必要的知识、技能、经验和设备。化技中心将为技秘处实地部署的工作人员举办培训，并提供测试和验证能力。

20. 技秘处还将增加被指定进行真实样品分析的实验室的数量，并扩大其地域范围。技秘处将发展新合作伙伴关系，以便能够维持开展非例行性行动的常备状态。

21. 到 2028 年的中期目标的关键性目标如下。

（a）技秘处维持执行不同类型的任务的常备状态，这些任务包括对化武使用指称的调查和质疑性视察，并应缔约国的请求提供技术援助。

（b）技秘处维持并发展必要的能力、工具和专长，以增强其开展非例行性行动的能力。

（c）在技秘处内保留、整合和进一步发展在非例行性任务中获得的知识、技能和专长。

中期目标 4：加强本组织跟踪并评估与缔约国履行《公约》义务有关的科学技术发展的能力

22. 技术变革将在各个方面影响核查制度的有效实施。这要求对不断进步的科学技术进行持续审查，特别是在检测、分析、对策和防护技术方面。通过禁化武组织的实验室和化技中心的技术与培训，连同指定的实验室及其他相关机构，技秘处将探索新的方法和技术，用以充实本组织在这些领域的能力。这也将包括通过与范围更广的科技界的互动来提高资源的使用效率，同时借助科学咨询委员会（以下简称“科咨委”）所提供的咨询意见。

23. 化技中心将使技秘处具备研究、更好地测试、评估和采纳与《公约》相关新技术的能力，同时，为现有的采样和分析活动维持一个强有力的科技基地。这些新能力将确保禁化武组织能够有效研究并酌情采纳新方法和技术。

24. 到 2028 年的中期目标的关键性目标如下。

（a）技秘处保有并强化一套用于审查与《公约》相关的科学技术的强健而灵活的系统。为此，技秘处继续进行以下工作：招聘与本组织工作相关的科学学科的专业工作人员；加强与有关国际组织、学术界和化工界的联系。

（b）技秘处扩充目前掌握的采样和分析方法和技术，并确保工作人员接受关于这些方法和技术的正规培训；同时，通过采纳科咨委的咨询意见并与技秘处的指定实验室进行磋商，积极发展在证据分析领域的能力，其中包括分析各种生物毒素以及生物医学样品和其他样品的能力。

（c）本组织进一步加强缔约国实验室的分析能力，并支持扩大所有区域的指定实验室。

25. 此外，本组织拥有必要的工具、程序以及既有技能又有经验的工作人员，可用以实现4个中期核查目标，特别是在数据监测、分析和解释以及独立核实获得信息的准确性和真实性方面。

有助于阻遏、预防和应对有毒化学品的恶意使用以及促进国际合作的能力建设

中期目标5：作为重点防范化学武器卷土重来的工作之一，减少与有毒化学品事件相关的风险

26. 在推动全球反恐工作以及化学安全文化更广泛培植方面，技秘处发挥着重要作用。在此方面，技秘处将通过双管齐下的战略来重点降低与化学武器相关的风险。具体而言包括以下2项工作。

（a）减少涉及有毒化学品的事件造成的伤害和影响，其方法是支持缔约国发展强健和有效的应急响应能力（通过增强紧急应对能力将产生重要的威慑效果）。

（b）阻遏有毒化学品的恶意使用，其方法是建设缔约国调查涉及有毒化学品的使用事件的能力。

27. 只要存在恶意使用有毒化学品的可能性，就需要维持和提高全体缔约国在国内应对和协助其他缔约国的能力方面的防护能力。技秘处已经在与若干区域和次区域组织进行密切合作，以提高其有效应对化学突发事件的能力。本组织将继续主动与其他区域的此类组织进行接触，从而以更有力的方式为经过区域协调的应对措施提供便利。

28. 技秘处将继续提供广泛的能力建设活动方案，这涉及从周期性区域培训到专家提供的专业人员培训课程的多个方面。此外，本组织/技秘处将与缔约国联手，通过国际合作来处理待发展的领域，以便支持缔约国制订强有力的国家防护计划。线上自我评估工具将继续是支持这项工作的

重要工具。

29. 技秘处将继续维持其常备状态，以便满足缔约国根据《公约》及决策机构通过的决定提出的任何援助请求。

30. 技秘处将加深对化学武器使用影响的了解，以确保其援助和防护计划考虑到有毒化学品可能对个人产生不同的影响。

31. 到2028年的中期目标的关键性目标如下。

（a）强化技秘处内部的专业技能，以加强预防和应对有毒化学品的恶意释放方面的能力建设活动，包括在对化学设施和交通基础设施可能发动的袭击方面。

（b）技秘处为受污染环境中化学事件的紧急应对人员提供更广泛的能力建设方案。技秘处为执法当局开发基于情景的培训模块，这些模块还重点关注采样技术和保管事宜。

（c）本组织进一步扩大与其他区域和国际组织的互动，以便预防和应对涉及恶意使用有毒化学品的重大事件。

（d）技秘处继续致力于建立可行的区域和次区域能力，以有效应对化学武器使用或有毒化学品意外泄漏事件。技秘处应保持常备状态，以便在发生使用或威胁使用化学武器事件后，对一缔约国的援助请求做出回应。

中期目标6：加强有助于国家履约与和平利用化学的国际合作的能力建设

32. 技秘处将继续加强各种能力建设方案，旨在确保缔约国长期参与，以确保化学仅用于和平且经授权的目的。本组织将确保能力建设活动以成果为导向和以对国家需求的评估为依据，并以高效、有效、可持续的方式来开展，同时为禁化武组织带来更大价值，从而继续促进化学的和平利用。

33. 国家履约措施是全面有效执行《公约》所有规定的基础，鉴于其重要性，技秘处将继续鼓励缔约国不断审查国家履约措施的有效性，以确保在各国领土和管辖范围内有效实施《公约》的规定。为此，技秘处将继续协助缔约国采取综合的方式来开展国家履约工作，除行政和立法措施外，还包括一系列广泛的国内行动。

34. 在国际合作方面，技秘处将继续查明协助缔约国发展技术能力的机会和针对性活动，并进一步鼓励缔约国之间交流化学品、设备和科学技术信息，以促进化学的和平利用。重点领域将包括：化学安全与安保管理；化学知识的推广和交流；利用指定实验室网络和禁化武组织化技中心向发展中经济体和转型中经济体的实验室提供更多支持。通过这些能力建设工作，技秘处的目标将是帮助缔约国发展技能和能力，以在民用化学设施中展现更高的安全与安保水平，同时发展其国家实验室分析与《公约》相关化学品的能力。这将被植入本组织协助缔约国创建和维护充分履行《公约》方面的监管框架中，从而为经济发展和国际交流创造更好的条件。

35. 到 2028 年的中期目标的关键性目标如下。

（a）技秘处继续为缔约国提供履约支持和资助，以使 100% 的缔约国保留其国家主管部门，并使 75% 的缔约国颁布涵盖《公约》的所有初步措施的国家立法和行政措施。

（b）技秘处提供支持，包括在每个区域最多 5 个缔约国促进制定或完善国家履约框架。

（c）技秘处支持经济处于发展中和转型中的缔约国创建有效和高效履行《公约》的科学技术能力。

（d）技秘处扩充其能力建设工具箱，并与科技界、学术界、工业界和区域或国际实体建立新的合作伙伴关系，以促进和平、安全和可持续利用化学。利用化技中心拓展与外部利益攸关方的合作伙伴关系，并使其多样化，从而帮助扩大国际合作和援助计划的规模。

（e）在外部利益攸关方的合作下，技秘处促进缔约国之间制定和交流与化学安全与安保管理相关的非约束性最佳实践和包括立法在内的指南。

中期目标 7：加强技秘处在能力建设领域的评估能力

36. 评估是一个进行观察、分析和绩效评估的综合过程，以确定某项政策或方案的效率、效力和影响。由于技秘处内的不同部门开展多种多样的能力建设活动，这将加强技秘处在这一领域中的评估能力，以逐步转向基于成果的能力建设方法。

37. 技秘处在对每项能力建设活动的结果进行各种评估的同时，还辅以对加强国家能力方面取得的成果的后续分析；同时，对这些评估进行综合处理，以形成对本组织的总体目标所做贡献的评估。这将使技秘处得以向决策机构提供关于加强在能力建设方面获得成果的可信且基于证据的建议。上述评估还将基于对缔约国需求的评估，以便为技秘处提供指导，这有助于其在能力建设方面制定更量身定制的方法。

38. 到2028年的中期目标的关键性目标如下。

（a）充实并量身定制给予缔约国的支持和资助，促进其对《公约》的主人翁意识和参与能力建设的举措，从而加大力度保留和传授通过禁化武组织能力建设活动获得的知识，并协助技秘处评估和设计新的有针对性和更加综合的方案。

（b）酌情不断改进技秘处的评估能力，包括改进评估系统；加强内部协调；对照缔约国在国家履约方面的表现，提供更多财力和人力资源用以分析已开展的能力建设活动的各种成果，并评估其影响。

开展互动，以利用其他方面的能力

中期目标8：有的放矢地开展实现普遍性的工作

39. 实现普遍加入《公约》仍是重中之重，目的是进一步巩固这一禁止化学武器的规范，并确保全面禁止此类武器及《公约》所提供防护的完整性和全面覆盖。鉴于《公约》非缔约国现已所剩无几，需要量身定制与这些国家开展有效互动，并解决其可能有关《公约》的任何关切。本组织还将继续鼓励缔约国与剩余的非缔约国进行接触，以说服其加入《公约》。为实现普遍性而开展的工作将会顾及以下情况：一个或多个目前的非缔约国可能会在拥有应宣布的化学武器库存的情况下加入《公约》。

40. 到2028年的中期目标的关键性目标如下。

（a）技秘处继续为每个非缔约国制定和实施量身定制的方法，以根据每个国家的具体情况和环境创建持续对话和深化接触的平台，从而促进或催化其入约进程。

（b）为了技秘处和缔约国利用出现的具体机会制定并实施提议，进一步鼓励非缔约国加入《公约》，包括邀请非缔约国参加缔约国的相关会议和一些强调加入《公约》的益处的活动。

（c）技秘处随时为新缔约国入约做好准备，即保留与评估初始宣布、化学品非军事化和相关入约后的能力建设活动（包括履约支持和资助）有关的知识和技能。

中期目标9：与其他国际组织开展回应式且基于成果的协作

41. 当代的全球性挑战，特别是和平与安全方面的挑战的复杂性、规模和关联性要求有协作和集体的解决方案。作为正在进行的调整工作的一部分，本组织将加强与其他有关国际和区域组织和机构的关系。这将有利于发现协同效应，并以此为合作基础。可以更广泛和更深入地开展互动的领域包括能力建设、科学技术、执行非例行性任务、全球反恐行动以及行政和机构管治问题的最佳实践比照。

42. 在此方面，本组织需要确保其体制框架在将来依然可行，并需要考虑采取新的、经过改进的互动方法。适于在其中开展此类合作的领域包括：打击化学恐怖主义构成的威胁；促进和平利用化学的能力建设；促进教育、外联和宣传；监测相关科学技术领域的发展；促进各个组织的多样性和包容性；促进化学安全与安保，包括培育一种化学安全的网络和文化。技秘处工作人员在上述方面的知识、技能和专长将使本组织得以发挥重要作用，从而为更广泛的全球努力提供支持。

43. 到2028年的中期目标的关键性目标如下。

（a）根据已确定的和不断变化的需求以及相关的基于成果的管理标准，技秘处以协调和全面的方式审查、评估和加强与其他国际组织的互动。

（b）技秘处进一步朝着理解和利用跨学科（即融汇式）科学和技术专

业知识的方向前进，而其重点是与《公约》履行相关的科学和技术。其中包括与其他相关的国际组织加强联系；在科咨委的支持下与相关的国际科学咨询机制加强联系。

（c）通过深化与伙伴的现有合作活动，本组织继续保持和加强其在打击化学恐怖主义和促进化学安全的全球努力中的重要作用，同时也审查与其他组织建立伙伴关系的潜力。

中期目标 10：加强与范围更广的利益攸关方的互动

44. 要成功履行《公约》，就要求将主人翁意识灌输给化工界、科研界、学术界、非政府组织、民间社团和公众（包括青年）中的利益攸关方，以争取其支持和积极的协作。为促成并维持来自更广范围的利益攸关方的此种支持，将要求本组织与其展开更多前后一致的战略性定期互动，以确保准确理解《公约》和禁化武组织的工作。把教育和外联咨询委员会的相关建议以及内部沟通和外联专长考虑在内将继续为这一进程提供支持。本组织将以协调和战略性的方式与各种利益攸关方进一步建立有效的网络和合作伙伴关系，以便借助其专业知识为应对新出现的履约挑战提供支持。

45. 作为知识管理、政策和外联工作的一部分，本组织将编写教育材料和学习资源，用以扩大其与职业生涯早期和中期专业人员的互动。这些资源将用于在高校、专业协会和工业界宣传《公约》，从而有助于防范化学武器的卷土重来。

46. 到 2028 年的中期目标的关键性目标如下。

（a）本组织继续利用外部合作伙伴拥有的知识、技能和专长来加强核查活动和能力建设方案和工具，以便建立协同效应，并促进信息和最佳实践的交流。

（b）促进对《公约》及其目标的广泛认知是履行《公约》的一个重要方面。本组织主动接触广泛的外部利益攸关方，包括青年、学术界和民间社会组织。

（c）已建立一种与科技界进行合作的更广泛的网络，而其正在科学界中促进负责任的科学实践和方法，并且正在加强非技术利益攸关方的科学水平，确保其更好地理解对《公约》的履行而言非常重要的科学概念和意见。

（d）本组织进一步发展与国际和区域化工行业协会的关系，同时重点开发实用工具和资料，并确定在化学安全与安保、国际合作与援助以及核查活动等共同关心的主题上的协同效应，同时应对非国家行为方构成的风险。

一个出成果的组织

中期目标 11：为使本组织继续成功运转而进行必要的结构和流程调整

47. 为了应对一系列挑战，并完成《公约》和决策机构的决定所规定的任务，本组织必须保持可持续性。组织能力必须得到一个适应未来的员工队伍支撑，同时，技秘处要继续利用具备地域多样化和性别平衡的工作人员的技能、经验和视角。技秘处将继续支持本组织在上文讨论到的 3 个成果领域的关键职能，并在必要时使其结构、资源和流程适应新的环境。技秘处将确保在组织文化中嵌入业务连续性流程，从而进一步发展其应变能力。

48. 总之，这些工作将使本组织能够展示其持续的相关性，并维护本组织作为全球关于化学武器事务和裁军的对话与合作的多边平台的声誉。

49.《公约》为通过制定政策、决策机构做出决策以及对工作和业务实践的渐进式微调而进行必要的调整提供了足够的灵活度。

50. 技秘处将继续推行人力资源战略，该战略重点关注以下几个关键方面：确保创造一个赋能而包容的工作环境，以让每个人得以发挥最大潜能；吸引和管理多元化人才；不断制定适合当前和未来需求的高效人力资源政策。

51. 除结构和资源外，技秘处还需有效的系统。为了高效完成任务，技秘处需要系统为业务提供便利，并促进有效做出决策。为此，技秘处将优先考虑以下关键信息系统的持续开发和支持。

（a）对于缩小地理距离并让利益相关方能够以虚拟方式共聚一堂，一套可靠的多语言室内混合会议系统至关重要。

（b）需要有一个不断更新的内网平台，以作为与代表团和其他外部利益相关方共享信息和资源的安全的中央平台。

（c）高效的财务管理系统对于确保透明度和问责制至关重要。禁化武组织已在上一个周期成功迁移到基于云的现代企业资源规划系统，该企业资源规划必须与更新的业务流程、工作流和数据分析需求接轨。

（d）有效的人力资源管理技术对于各组织高效地吸引和选择人才及其入职至关重要；通过学习、发展和绩效管理来协助互动和交付；利用技术来改进业务流程，以提高效率。

52. 鉴于本组织工作性质及其处理信息的敏感性，所有上述系统的开发都必须考虑到先进的网络安全实践。通过将强大的网络安全技术和实践直接嵌入上述系统，技秘处可以保护其系统和数据，从而促成中期计划的更广的目标的实现。

53. 到2028年的中期目标的关键性目标如下。

（a）技秘处解决以下需求：在组织结构和流程中，为连续性和变化找到平衡。

（b）本组织继续受益于一支多元化而且高绩效的员工队伍。

（c）本组织的管理政策应现代化，以有效和高效地满足当前和未来的需求。

（d）使达成任期政策中的灵活性的关键战略性人力资源促成因素得到落实。

（e）决策机构认可关于组织结构和流程平稳转型的建议，后续由技秘处落实这些建议。

中期目标12：加强促进缔约国的各特设小组之间的合作的能力

54. 技秘处将继续提高其能力，支持以禁化武组织为平台开展与《公约》的目标和宗旨相关问题的讨论。可从这种做法中获益的问题是多种多样的，而且横跨上文讨论的3个成果领域。

55. 到2028年的中期目标的关键性目标如下。

（a）技秘处保有以下能力：缔约国就部分缔约国感兴趣的问题召集会议，以确保就此种问题进行讨论的过程以成果为导向且顺利开展。

（b）技秘处确保其支持缔约国和利益相关方工作的流程与方法能够一如既往地提供高水平服务，且以最有效和及时的方式回应需求。

结语

56. 技秘处提交本中期计划的目的是以将其附于本组织的2024—2025年双年期方案和预算，同时也为了推进本组织的调整过程，以便使本组织能在自1997年以来《公约》及本组织的成功基础上再接再厉。本组织在已获得的知识和专业技能的基础上继续推进其转型进程，这将使本组织继续成为一种对其国际安全环境的演变做出回应的多边安全工具。各缔约国对此进程做出贡献将是成功的关键。

57. 为了实现《公约》的目标，这一调整过程将要求：进一步发展本组织的核查制度，以在保持核心专长的同时提高其监测和分析能力；通过增强其分析和满足缔约国的履约需求的能力，强化本组织在能力建设和互动方面的努力。对更加综合的组织管治结构和政策进行的上述各项改进以及化技中心等新平台将使本组织能够继续执行其裁军任务，同时更加注重防范化学武器死灰复燃。

《报告》名词索引

专有名词全称简称对照表

序号	全称	文中简称
1	《禁止化学武器公约》	《公约》
2	《禁止化学武器公约》履约工作部际联席会议	履约工作部际联席会议
3	日本遗弃在华化学武器	日遗化武
4	国家履行《禁止化学武器公约》工作办公室	国家禁化武办
5	国家履行《禁止化学武器公约》专家委员会	专家委
6	《公约》第五次审议大会	五审会
7	禁止化学武器组织	禁化武组织
8	《中华人民共和国监控化学品管理条例》	《条例》
9	《〈中华人民共和国监控化学品管理条例〉实施细则》	《细则》
10	《国务院关于深化“证照分离”改革进一步激发市场主体发展活力的通知》（国发〔2021〕7号）	《通知》
11	工业和信息化部电子第五研究所	电子五所
12	工业和信息化部国际经济技术合作中心	国合中心
13	技术秘书处	技秘处
14	执行理事会	执理会
15	缔约国大会	大会
16	“在国际安全领域促进和平利用国际合作”决议	和平利用决议或决议
17	《公约》第四次审议大会	四审会
18	遗弃化学武器	遗弃化武
19	老化学武器	老化武
20	宣布评估组	宣评组
21	调查和鉴定组	调鉴组
22	化学与技术中心	化技中心
23	不限成员名额五审会筹备工作组	五审会筹备工作组
24	不限成员名额反恐工作组	反恐工作组
25	科学咨询委员会	科咨委
26	行政和财务问题咨询机构	行财咨机构
27	教育和外联咨询委员会	教咨委

续表

序号	全称	文中简称
28	普埃布洛化学剂销毁中试车间	普埃布洛设施
29	布鲁格拉斯化学剂销毁中试车间	布鲁格拉斯设施
30	非毗邻静态引爆室	静爆室
31	叙利亚科学研究中心	叙利亚科研中心
32	“非洲地区化学紧急应对能力建设演练”	CHEMEX 非洲
33	化学武器生产设施	化武生产设施
34	化学武器储存设施	化武储存设施
35	化学武器销毁设施	化武销毁设施
36	内部监察办公室	监察办
37	《公约》的《关于执行和核查的附件》	《核查附件》

《监控化学品管理条例》和《禁止化学武器公约》专有名词对照

序号	《监控化学品管理条例》	《禁止化学武器公约》
1	监控化学品	附表化学品
2	第一类监控化学品	附表 1 化学品
3	第二类监控化学品	附表 2 化学品
4	第三类监控化学品	附表 3 化学品
5	第四类监控化学品	特定有机化学品（DOC）
6	第一类监控化学品生产设施	附表 1 化学品生产设施
7	第二类监控化学品生产设施	附表 2 化学品生产设施
8	第三类监控化学品生产设施	附表 3 化学品生产设施
9	第四类监控化学品生产设施	其他化学生产设施

后 记

中国履行《禁止化学武器公约》年度报告是反映我国履约立场和成就的主要载体，也是体现我国禁化武履约工作成绩的标志品牌，具有重要的参考意义和史料价值。

《中国履行〈禁止化学武器公约〉报告（2023）》继续坚持客观、简洁、实用的原则，还在编辑体例上做了调整，将协会篇和履约支撑篇合并为支撑篇，以方便读者全面了解支撑队伍。

报告的编制得到了多方面的关心和支持。工业和信息化部、外交部和中央军委国际军事合作办公室给予了大力支持和具体指导。中国常驻禁止化学武器组织代表团、各省级工业和信息化主管部门和监控化学品企业、相关社会团体、高校及中国电子产品可靠性与环境试验研究所参与了本报告的写作、编辑，并提出了意见、建议。此外，还有很多单位和个人为此报告编写提供了无私帮助，在此一并表示感谢！

由于编写时间仓促，书中难免有疏漏之处，敬请读者批评指正。

编者

图书在版编目（CIP）数据

中国履行《禁止化学武器公约》报告. 2023 / 国家履行《禁止化学武器公约》工作办公室 编. -- 北京 : 人民邮电出版社, 2025. -- ISBN 978-7-115-65880-7

Ⅰ. D995

中国国家版本馆 CIP 数据核字第 202528D9C6 号

内 容 提 要

本报告力求全面反映中国履行《禁止化学武器公约》的工作情况，客观展示中国的履约成就，记录履约大事件，收录履约重要文献资料，为各级履约主管部门和履约企业学习交流、研究履约经验和做法搭建了一个平台，为增进社会公众了解、关注履约工作提供了一个新的窗口，为国际相关组织和单位认识、了解、熟悉中国履行《禁止化学武器公约》工作打好基础，从而更好地树立中国作为负责任的大国良好的履约形象，进一步激发全国履约工作人员做好履约工作的责任感和使命感。本书适合中国履行《禁止化学武器公约》工作的相关从业者、监控化学品企业的管理人员阅读。

◆ 编　　　国家履行《禁止化学武器公约》工作办公室
责任编辑　赵　娟
责任印制　马振武

◆ 人民邮电出版社出版发行　北京市丰台区成寿寺路 11 号
邮编　100164　电子邮件　315@ptpress.com.cn
网址　https://www.ptpress.com.cn
三河市中晟雅豪印务有限公司印刷

◆ 开本：690×970　1/16
印张：24.75　　　2025 年 7 月第 1 版
字数：331 千字　　2025 年 7 月河北第 1 次印刷

定价：148.00 元

读者服务热线：（010）81055493　印装质量热线：（010）81055316
反盗版热线：（010）81055315